THE HEARTLAND DIARIES

By FRANK MIELE

COLUMNIST, REAL CLEAR POLITICS &
WWW.HEARTLANDDIARYUSA.COM

PREVIOUS

FORTHCOMING

Collected from the author's 18 years as managing editor
of the Daily Inter Lake in Kalispell, Montana.

HEARTLAND DIARY VOLUME 5

HOW WE GOT HERE

The Left's Assault on the Constitution

BY FRANK MIELE

HEARTLAND PRESS

KALISPELL MONTANA 2020

How We Got Here:
The Left's Assault on the Constitution

Back cover photo: Meredith Miele

ISBN: 978-1-7329633-4-4
First Edition

Library of Congress Control Number: 2020912390

Heartland Press
Kalispell, Montana

DEDICATED TO
MY SON HUZHAO,
WHO SHARES MY PASSION
FOR MAKING AMERICA GREAT AGAIN

ACKNOWLEDGEMENTS

Thanks to my readers at HeartlandDiaryUSA.com for your continued support. It has been my honor to work with all of you to make America great again.

I also have to acknowledge my debt to the publishers of the Daily Inter Lake for giving me the opportunity to write the collected columns in the "Heartland Diaries" over the course of 14 years and to Hagadone Montana Publishing Company for giving me permission to reprint them in this form.

Of course, as any author will understand, I owe a deep debt of gratitude to my wife, Yuzhao, for her continued patience with what surely seems like self-absorption to anyone who has not lived with a writer. She rightly qualifies for sainthood, and I would be remiss if I did not mention so.

—FDM, May 2020

Introduction

HOW DEWEY, FDR, AYERS, ALINSKY AND OBAMA TRIED TO SUBVERT THE CONSTITUTION, AND WHY THEY MUST NEVER SUCCEED

BY FRANK DANIEL MIELE

The book you are about to read represents the very best work I have ever done, or expect to do, in defense of liberty. As I assembled the enclosed essays, many of which I have not read since they were written, I was struck by the recurring themes that had occupied my writing since 2004 — the Constitution, American exceptionalism, the importance of a shared history and identity, and the continuing assault on the Constitution waged by the left for more than 100 years.

You will read some of the my own story in here, how I grew up in the 1960s at the end of an era of patriotism and the beginning of an era of radicalism, but much more important is the story of a nation at war with itself. How had the vision of the Founding Fathers of a self-righting republic been turned on its head? How had so many of our citizens failed to embrace the gift they had been given through birth or grace? How had the truths we used to hold to be self-evident become so cryptic that we could no longer even agree on the right to life? Time after time, I came up with the same explanation — that too few Americans were consulting the operating instructions — the Constitution — and that we were therefore on the verge of running off the rails.

What became clear to me in my research was that the devaluation of the Constitution was not accidental — it was a strategy adopted by a group of people who went by many names — progressives, socialists, communists, Democrats — but who had one single solitary purpose — to acquire power for the purpose of meting out what they called social justice.

Social justice, it turned out, was roughly the equivalent of what Satan was after when he advised Eve that God was holding out on her and Adam. It was the promise of a better life inevitably followed by the exile from paradise, except no one ever tells you about the down side of trying to live on other people's money. There's the loss of self-esteem, the lack of incentive, the inevitable realization that someone else still has more than you do, and the absolute certainty that you can never get back the inheritance you sold for a mess of potage.

I've arranged the essays in this book in chronological order as they were written so that you can follow along with me as the nation went down the rabbit hole of socialism with President Obama, and then fought its way back to an attempt to restore normalcy under President Trump. You will also be able to follow along with me as I learned about the methods and manipulations of the far left to subvert our culture and our Constitution. The oldest essay in the book dates to 2004, just two months after I started writing my "Editor's 2 Cents" column for the Daily Inter Lake. "More and more," I wrote, "courts and the government as a whole seem intent on using the documents of liberty to dismantle liberty from within." I didn't yet have any idea how to counter the leftist agenda, but I saw the problem pretty clearly, and I had set in my own mind a challenge — how to save the country from itself?

By the end of the next year, I had settled on restoring the plain language of the Constitution as the key. In November 2005, I wrote, "Our Constitution is no longer the law of the land; it is instead a magic mirror that tells its owner whatever it wants to hear." The next week I concluded that "the right of self-government, is primary, and it is this which we have lost by allowing the Constitution to be hijacked by the judiciary." I had thus begun my quest to educate the public about natural law and natural rights and to restore the Constitution to its original purpose. By 2013, I had even developed what I called "The Restoration Amendment" to provide a clear path to taking pack the Constitution as originally written:

For a long time, I have thought that the only hope for our country to continue as a bastion of freedom is to return to the original principles of the Constitution. But how exactly could you do so? An amendment demanding that the Constitution be interpreted according to the plain language in which it was written seemed too vague, just another lost cause like the 10th Amendment. An amendment throwing out case law as it applied to the Constitution and declaring a clean slate seemed hopelessly academic.

What was needed was an amendment which both stated plainly its intended goal — to strip the federal government of the power it has grabbed without authority over more than 200 years — and at the same time provided a clear mechanism for restoring America to the principles envisioned by the founders.

Article I of my proposed amendment established that "If a power is not expressly granted to the combined federal government of these United States by this Constitution, then that power cannot be exercised, acquired, or enumerated without specific amendment to this document. Therefore, all laws and interpretations of laws which have resulted in the federal government imposing its will on the states or the people without specific authorization from this Constitution or its amendments shall be declared null and void."

A grand vision, if an unrealistic one!

The reason it is unrealistic, of course, is that the power of the people as the sovereign authority has been under constant attack for more than 150 years. That assault is the second theme that runs as a constant through these pages.

Starting with two essays in April 2006 about the threat of nationalized health care, I had gone to great lengths to explain the dangers of socialism. I never believed when I wrote "Will Karl Marx have the last laugh?" that we were just four years away from Obamacare. How could that happen when we had fought against socialism for more than 80 years? I answered that question in December 2013 in an essay called "Progressives & patience," where I looked at the decades-long campaign for socialized medicine that had been waged alongside our Cold War against communism. The quote attributed to socialist Norman Thomas says it all: "The American people would never vote for socialism, but under the name of liberalism the American people will adopt every fragment of the socialist program."

It was around 2010 that my research into the roots of our national crisis reached fever pitch. The Nov. 14 column that serves as the prologue to this volume asked the question, "How did we get here?" and I spent much of the next two years looking for answers. Taken together, these essays are a mini-course in American history. In the six essays starting with the one dated Dec. 10, 2010, for instance, I explore Franklin Roosevelt's New Deal and noted wryly that "Many did dare call it socialism." Staring on April 10, 2011, I explored how the Greek goddess Athena was a perfect symbol for the Tea Party, and then wrote about "women warriors" who have fought to better our country such as Ayn Rand, Sarah Palin, Dorothy Thompson and Jean Walterskirchen, 1958 candidate for Congress from Montana.

Starting in June of 2011, I switched gears and took a look at how the education system had been used by radicals to corrupt American youth and indoctrinate them in anti-American leftist ideology. Here, I took an in-depth look at pedagogical philosopher John Dewey — the godfather of generations of self-absorbed students who were taught that their half-formed thoughts were of equal value with the foundational principles of Western civilization. The moral relativism of Dewey made a perfect foil to the natural law cherished by our Founders and provided the underpinnings for the social revolution that infected America from the 1950s forward. As I described it in one of those essays, "Progressive education was a necessary predecessor for America's plunge into willing acquiescence to progressive economics — also known as socialism. Thus, we are close to a solution to our initial question: 'How did we get here?' We have exposed the lever of progressive education as the mechanism by which Americans were primed to surrender the blessings of liberty in exchange for the bonds of socialism." It remained to discover the fulcrum that had provided the wedge that broke American society in half. I found that fulcrum in the counterculture revolution of the 1960s, which had mistakenly been written off as a failure, but in fact was a masterpiece of social engineering.

Bill Ayers, who generally has been dismissed as a two-bit terrorist, was in fact the architect of a grand strategy to overthrow the American order. Remarkably, it looks like he is close to achieving that goal. In a series of essays starting on July 24, 2011, you will read about how Ayers relatively quickly realized that violent revolution was unlikely to persuade Americans to give up the benefits of their "capitalistic decadence," and that revolution instead should be waged through education rather than bomb-throwing. Yes, Ayers and the Weather Underground took advantage of the unpopular Vietnam War to spread their revolutionary message on the streets, but after spending a decade in hiding, Ayers emerged with a new strategy learned from community organizer Saul Alinsky. In 1971, Alinsky had written his seminal book "Rules for Radicals" in which he tutored radicals that in order to achieve their revolutionary goals they needed to "work inside the system" and act more like neighbors than activists. This was the turning point. It took Ayers and his wife Bernardine Dohrn another decade to recognize that Alinsky was right and they were wrong, but eventually, in 1980, they emerged from the underground ready to resume the revolution.

With Dewey as his inspiration, Ayers empowered youth as his ambassadors of change, and worked with others to co-opt systems of social welfare, criminal justice and education to work within the system to topple the system. A couple of sociologists named Cloward & Piven provided a blueprint for overwhelming the U.S. treasury by creating a demand for welfare and other benefit programs that could not possible be afforded by society. That — combined with growing distrust of government, disdain for religion and disrespect for our traditions — gave Ayers the formula he needed to weaken our 200-year-old republic. It was an apt coincidence that just as I finished writing about Ayers' revolution, his political acolytes were trying to crash the economy with their Occupy Wall Street campaign in 2011.

The fact that many of these essays were written in the shadow of the Obama presidency is no coincidence at all. President Obama was the spiritual godchild of Bill Ayers and Saul Alinsky, and with his disarming manner he was a perfect Trojan horse to introduce socialism into mainstream America. For the past four years, Donald Trump has worked to restore the original vision of America as a place of endless opportunity, but with the courts, Democrats and the Deep State against him, his plan to Make America Great Again may be doomed. As we enter the election of 2020, we stand at the crossroads. After you read this book, you will know how we got here, but if Trump loses his re-election bid, it is unlikely anyone will ever again be able to get us out of here.

And remember, if you enjoy the essays in this collection, please visit me at www.HeartlandDiaryUSA.com or follow me on Facebook @HeartlandDiaryUSA, or on Twitter or Parler @HeartlandDiary.

Kalispell, Montana
June 2020
frank@HeartlandDiaryUSA.com

PROLOGUE

HOW DID WE GET HERE?
A STARTING POINT

November 14, 2010

"How did we get here?"

That is a question I have asked myself a thousand times. When I look at the America we live in today and compare it to the America I grew up in 50 years ago, I am heartsick. And I am not alone.

Were there problems 50 years ago? Yes, of course. In particular, there were issues of racism that continued to plague the nation as a result of the scourge of slavery even though it had been abolished 100 years before. Other forms of discrimination also existed and were the subject of continuing reform efforts.

But in almost every other major aspect of life, we were better off then than we are today. Our economy was better. Our families were stronger. Our morals were firm. Our military was respected both at home and abroad. Our education was the best in the world.

Today, everything has been turned on its head — and what's worse, plenty of people are glad of that. Our weaker economy has been a boon to the Third World and those who promote "social justice" at the expense of the American worker. Our weakened families have been a boon to government control of our personal decisions. Our weakened morals have allowed liberty to be mistaken for license, resulting in an ever more narcissistic culture that panders to appetites instead of aspiring to greatness. Our weakened military gives strength to those who would leave us at the mercy of their misguided conception of the goodness of human nature. Our weakened education system has compounded all of this by failing to teach our citizens the truth, leaving them untethered from their own heritage and adrift in a sea of moral relativism.

So — "How did we get here?"

That question can never be answered definitively, but it does seem to have its roots sometime in the last century when the globe was divided into the free world and the totalitarian world. Leading the former was the United States with assistance from Great Britain, France, Canada, Australia and other Western democracies. Leading the latter were the Soviet Union, Nazi Germany and Communist China, in alignment with numerous small dictatorships throughout Africa, South America, Eastern Europe and the Middle East.

Such a division of nations cannot be doubted by anyone who has studied history. The global geopolitics of the 20th century was a chess game in which many nations were pawns that moved back and forth between the two camps. But the 20th century itself can be divided in two as well, and the strategic position of the United States shifted dramatically sometime in the middle of the century from a defensive posture against anti-American ideologies to a position of smug assurance that America had nothing to fear from its enemies.

Exactly when or how that happened would take a book-length exposition to make clear, but let's draw an imaginary dividing line sometime around 1950 and see what we find.

Before World War II, the United States was plainly opposed to tyranny and considered it a threat not just to the world, but to its own republic. Thus, we had committees in Congress whose sole purpose was to root out enemies of the American way of life. The famous House Committee on Un-American Activities, which in one form or another dated back to 1934, was dedicated to exposing subversives in our homeland whose intent was to attack "the form of government guaranteed by our Constitution."

Now, of course, the idea of a Committee on Un-American Activities would itself be considered by many to be un-American, not to mention unconstitutional. That in and of itself should be evidence that some kind of a sea change happened in the mid-20th century. Whether this change was a result of intention or simply inertia is again a topic too large to be settled in a short weekly column; however, it is possible to establish the world view that made the change acceptable.

Prior to 1945, the safety of the West from foreign enemies was in doubt. Thus, despite the isolationist forces that remained strong in our country, the United States went to war both in World War I and World War II to oppose empire building that could eventually affect our own position in the world.

Between those two wars, as Marxism developed into Bolshevism and finally Stalinism, it became apparent to many American leaders that the communist ideology was not only dangerous when espoused by our enemies abroad, but was also contrary to our constitutional republic's ideals and thus a potential danger from within as well. The emergence of Hitler's National Socialism (aka Nazism) created a new threat that also had its domestic component intent on subverting the Constitution.

Americans who cherished their system of government — and the liberties and rights which it protected — took seriously the oath of office which they had sworn — to "support and defend the Constitution of the United States against all enemies, foreign *and domestic*" and to "bear true faith and allegiance to the same [emphasis added]."

This oath explicitly acknowledged that the Constitution — and the government which it established — could have enemies who lived AMONG US, and who presumably could well be citizens. The Constitution therefore assumes that federal officials are empowered IN FACT to take action to DEFEND the Constitution against its enemies, even if they are citizens and regardless of their race, religion or any other defining characteristic.

Yet today we are confronted with a federal bureaucracy and Congress that are not only sluggish to defend the Constitution against its enemies, but go so far as to offer them protections so that they may enjoy virtual immunity as they seek to destroy our way of life. Thus, freedom of speech has been perverted into a shield for sedition, and protections intended only for citizens have even been granted to enemy combatants.

Indeed, today it is part of mainstream thought to believe that anyone should be welcomed in America whether they are enemies of the Constitution or not. This is presumed to show just how marvelously open-minded we are, as opposed to those countries and cultures which zealously protect themselves against destruction.

Perhaps that point is instructive. No sentient being could possibly prefer open-mindedness over self-destruction. Therefore we have to assume that Americans, as a whole, at some point lost the ability to conceive of their country's destruction. Without that consequence to consider, open-mindedness is of course preferable to narrow-mindedness. But with destruction in the mix, open-mindedness loses its allure quite rapidly.

So why is it that in the midst of the Korean War, the Vietnam War, and with the memory of World War II still fresh in the national consciousness, that Americans no longer feared any threat to their way of life or their Constitution. Why did the American public presume that our country, our system and our way of life were inviolate — that they could not be corrupted by the influence of socialists, communists or other totalitarian ideologies?

My best guess is that the American military primacy established by World War II, and confirmed by our devastating nuclear arsenal, resulted in just such a feeling of invulnerability. Sure we had real problems in a land war in Southeast Asia, but our homeland never came under attack, and we knew that if worse came to worst, we could always drop The Bomb and be done with it. That lulled most of us into a false sense of security that allowed the nation to drift into a Rip Van Winkle slumber that lasted for half a century or more.

So, to answer my own question — "How did we get here?" — I guess the honest answer is that we sleep-walked into the 21st century. Now the question is, "When will we wake up?"

How We Got Here

ENOUGH IS ENOUGH

December 5, 2004

At some point when the snake begins to swallow its own tail, it should get indigestion.

That, at least, is the effect one hopes for if one loves the snake and wants to see it survive its suicidal mischief.

But it seems like today's America is almost to the point of swallowing its founding principles, and hardly a burp has been uttered about it.

More and more, courts and the government as a whole seem intent on using the documents of liberty to dismantle liberty from within. The latest example comes from California, where a school teacher has been forbidden by his principal from handing out the Declaration of Independence to his students because it contains references to God.

Whoa! Hold on there!

Isn't that why our forebears left England and those other merry states of Europe in the 17th and 18th centuries in the first place? To rid themselves of the tyranny that would not let them acknowledge a God who was greater than the tyrant?

Could anyone truly make the case that the Declaration of Independence is inappropriate for fifth graders? The same fifth-graders who are assaulted with (or is that "insulted" with?) Brittany Spears, gangsta rap, "Grand Theft Auto" and, of course, Janet Jackson's breast?

These words from the Declaration should never be inappropriate:

"We hold these truths to be self-evident, that all men are created equal, that they are endowed by their Creator with certain unalienable Rights, that among these are Life, Liberty and the pursuit of Happiness."

The principles embedded in the Declaration go far beyond the list of complaints against King George III that provoked them to be enunciated in this form. Nor are these principles a mere matter of religiosity. They are the foundation stone of our republic.

So how do we get to a place in history where Steven Williams, that fifth-grade teacher in Cupertino, Calif., has to sue his principal in order to bring those sacred principles to the attention of his students?

What makes the snake start to swallow its own tail?

I don't have any brilliant ideas on the topic, but I do remember saying prayers in school before the Supreme Court said I couldn't do so anymore, I do remember pledging allegiance to the republic that we knew was "one nation under God," and I do remember a time when we cherished our heritage enough to teach about it proudly.

I do know the difference between not allowing "an establishment of religion" and "prohibiting the free exercise thereof," two of the pillars of the First Amendment. Sometimes, it seems the first pillar has been distorted out of recognition, and the second all but forgotten.

And if push comes to shove, then I have to align myself with those Founding Fathers who took up their pens at great risk to themselves and signed on to the great American experiment by saying:

"...for the support of this Declaration, with a firm reliance on the protection of Divine Providence, we mutually pledge to each other our Lives, our Fortunes and our sacred Honor."

Without that "firm reliance," perhaps there is nothing to stop us from giving up on not just the Declaration, but also the Constitution and even those "self-evident" truths they embody.

To paraphrase a patriot, "Give me Divine Providence or give me death."

TIME TO RETHINK ABORTION POLITICS

July 24, 2005

How about a new idea about abortion?

Maybe it's time we tried one, after a half century of bitter fighting about the issue.

Everyone seems to think that President Bush's nominee for the Supreme Court ought to be judged not on his intelligence, temperament and experience, but on whether he will support or vote to overturn Roe vs. Wade, the case law that established a woman's constitutional right to have an abortion.

Indeed, both sides are so emotionally invested in this issue that many are afraid to talk about it at all. It's almost as though "abortion rights" and "pro-life" have become so important as fund-raising slogans that any kind of middle ground is considered a kind of "no man's land" where you will be shot by both sides.

There are a couple of things that everyone should remember if we are going to have a serious discussion about abortion and the law. First of all, people must understand that if Roe vs. Wade were overturned, it would not automatically make abortion illegal. It would simply return the right to regulate this medical procedure to the states, where it had always been handled before 1973.

The second thing to remember is that before 1973 there was no constitutional right to have an abortion. That right was "discovered" by the Supreme Court in 1973 as part of a "penumbra of privacy" that had been "divined" in the Constitution a few years earlier, even though it had evaded discovery for the previous 175 years.

The third thing to remember is that a vast majority of Americans, in every nationwide poll, supports the right of a woman to have an abortion. This, of course, is not based on a love of abortion, but on a recognition that the alternative may be even worse in individual cases. Those of us who are old enough to remember when abortion was illegal in most states can attest to the fact that many women died horrible deaths at the hands of "back-alley butchers" in an effort to rid themselves of a pregnancy that was either shameful, painful or maybe just "one too many."

So it's a complicated issue, with well-intentioned people on both sides.

But isn't it just possible that Roe vs. Wade is not of fundamental importance to the future of our Union? Are we even allowed to take time to think what would happen if the precedent were overturned? Or are we just supposed to move along in lockstep to marching orders from one side or the other?

The world we live in resembles 1973 to about the extent that the iPod resembles the Hi-Fi. (Younger readers may want to Google "Hi-Fi" in order to see what we are talking about.) The fact of the matter is that in 1973 we were still living in a society that bore some similarity to the world of 1788, when our Constitution was ratified. Today, everything is different. Families, values, technology — it's all flipped on its head.

So — if Roe vs. Wade were overturned, does anyone really think that the clock would automatically roll back 32 years? Does anyone think those polls in favor of abortion rights would suddenly switch 180 degrees? Does anyone think women are going to quietly step aside and let men once again tell them what is "best" for them?

Not at all. What would happen is that many states, perhaps representing a majority of the population of the country, would quickly pass "abortion rights" legislation of their own. It goes without saying that New York, New Jersey, California and Massachusetts would be among those states.

It also is likely that much of the Deep South, along with Utah, would automatically pass laws making abortion a crime of some sort.

The rest of the states would split the difference. Some would join one side or the other. Some others would pass carefully crafted compromises to ensure abortions were available in certain circumstances but not in others.

Most women who come from families that support abortion would be able to have one — either in their own state or by traveling to another state by car, bus or plane. In 1973, air travel was still something of a novelty. Probably more than half the population had never taken a flight anywhere. Today, air travel is taken for granted.

If people can afford air travel to visit Disney World or Aunt Nancy in Indiana, then they could probably find the money to travel to complete what they considered a crucial medical procedure that would change their lives forever.

It is unlikely we would ever return to an era of "back-alley butchers." Too much has changed.

But we would also live in a new America where we would no longer need to have a tug-of-war for the Constitution.

That would make me feel better.

I'd like to think that the Constitution will survive and thrive for another 215 years, but I wonder if that could happen if we continue to use the Constitution like a Ouija board to "talk" to the ghosts of the founders and get messages about the secret meaning of words like "secure," "due process" and "liberty."

The Constitution is the bedrock of our republic. It is written in plain language. If we can't agree about what it says in some fundamental way, then we are doomed to be the losers of Ben Franklin's sardonic challenge when asked what kind of government the constitutional convention had given to the new nation: "A republic, madam — If you can keep it."

My thinking is that we had better be more committed to keeping the republic than to keeping Roe vs. Wade if we expect our nation to last into the unforeseeable future. Face it, Roe — along with numerous other decisions of the court in the past few decades — has led to increasing conflict, skepticism, selfishness and cynicism about our government and our way of life.

That doesn't mean there couldn't be a constitutional protection for abortion rights either. We have a way to change the Constitution that doesn't involve judges using a microscope to discern previously unnoticed rights. It's called the amendment process.

Since abortion rights advocates say they represent the vast majority of Americans, why don't they just put before the

American people a constitutional amendment that would explicitly guarantee the right to have an abortion?

If passed and ratified, it would put an end, once and for all, to the uncertainty inherent in basing our rights on reversible Supreme Court rulings. Fundamental rights should be fundamentally clear; they should not be discovered in "penumbras, formed by emanations," as Justice Douglas laughably wrote when he located "the right to privacy" in the Bill of Rights.

For the good of all, let's change the debate and stick with the Constitution.

TH-TH-THAT'S ALL, FOLKS

November 20, 2005

In the Sixties, they had a saying: "If it feels good, do it."

If you think that makes sense, then you don't have to spend any more time thinking why the previous president of the United States got caught with his pants down a few years ago. It's because of you, and people who think like you.

In fact, you can pretty much attribute all the problems in our society today to that slogan and its corollary — "If it doesn't feel good, why bother?"

We have become — for lack of a better word — a hedonistic society, one that bases its success or failure on how happy it is — or more accurately how happy its individual members are. This has led us by and large to abandon the traditional set of Judeo-Christian ethics which made Western civilization possible by encouraging a certain amount of self-sacrifice in order to promote the greater good.

Now, what is interesting is that our country is based in part on the very principle that may eventually become our undoing. It is no accident surely that a society that values individual freedom as much as ours would have among its founding truisms that all men are endowed by their Creator with a right to "the pursuit of happiness."

What exactly that means, and why it could contain the seed of our ultimate destruction, should be worthy of consideration in an era when the pursuit of happiness has been expanded far beyond anything imagined by our forebears. It might be instructive therefore to list a few of the things now considered normal and appropriate that would have been considered evil and abhorrent in 1776, when the Declaration of Independence was penned by Mr. Jefferson and company.

Let's start with abortion. It is the most obvious starting point in any discussion of the changing moral landscape in our country, and though it is typically argued from a constitutional perspective, it can also be looked at from the point of view of the Declaration's guarantees of the right to "liberty" and "the pursuit of happiness." Women today say they can't be free (enjoy the fruits of liberty) without the ability to control their own bodies and determine how their bodies are used. Thus, in pursuit of their individual happiness, women have successfully argued that they are free to engage in any sexual activity of their choosing without needing to worry about any consequences that might impede the enjoyment of their way of life. Society's interests in protecting its progeny must thus give way to the individual's pursuit of happiness.

The same, of course, has now been determined to be true regarding sexual behavior. Take pornography, for instance. Yes, pornography, in one form or another, has probably always been around, and it will always have its fans, but does that mean society needs to accede to it? And yes, it will always be a subjective determination whether one piece of art or writing is pornographic or not, but does that mean society should not have the right to make that determination?

There is no doubt that when our country was founded, and right through the 1950s, pornography was considered an inappropriate endeavor that did enough harm to the general welfare that it could be banned by states or municipalities. Today, on the other hand, the general welfare has subsided to the point where it is almost invisible, and the individual "right" to "pursue happiness" by looking at dirty pictures or selling them or taking them (except when children are involved) has become pretty much a constitutional right.

Which brings us to the U.S. Constitution, where these matters must rightly be settled in any case.

We have heard a lot about the Constitution in recent months as we have gone through three different Supreme Court nominations, and listened to various arguments about how these nominees might threaten or protect constitutional rights, especially the so-called right to abortion.

What would be instructive at this point would be if everyone could take out their copy of the Constitution of the United States and read it. One thing you will not find is any reference to abortion whatsoever. Plain and simple, the constitutional right to abortion does not exist; what does exist in this country is a right granted by the judiciary to have an abortion as a result of "the right to privacy," which was also granted or invented by the judiciary.

These shadow rights are based in large measure on the Supreme Court's interpretation of the 14th Amendment, where it says "... nor shall any State deprive any person of life, liberty, or property, without due process of law." Yes, that's right, the whole wrangle over abortion is based on a constitutional provision that protects us from being thrown into jail or having our property seized without a fair trial or other administrative action known as "due process."

It seems that in the Supreme Court's collective mind, "due process" is not accomplished when a state Legislature does what it is legally constituted to do — make law. According to this theory, the greater right to "liberty" can only be denied by the state upon show of some extraordinary cause rather than because the state Legislature has expressed the will of its people. But if that is the case, then no law that restricts or narrows the liberty of an individual can hold sway any longer either. Laws that control such matters as public drunkenness, public nudity, and drug use must also come under the same fig-leaf of privacy that the Supreme Court uses to cover its naked re-write of the Constitution.

Folks, there is no "right of privacy" in the Constitution. To say that there is would be to stretch logic and language with Clintonian perversity to the point that we would have to say "it depends what the meaning of 'in' is."

The trouble is not with the Constitution; the trouble is with ourselves. Thanks to our hedonistic tendencies, we have now come to the point where we unwittingly accept as true the following precept:

"If it feels good, it must be constitutional."

This — in plain language — is the root of the problem. Our Constitution is no longer the law of the land; it is instead a magic mirror that tells its owner whatever it wants to hear.

But the problem is, not all good ideas are constitutional. It may indeed be a good idea to allow abortion under certain circumstances; that does not mean it is a constitutional right. It may be a good idea to allow gay marriage; that does not mean it is a constitutional right. It may be a good idea to instruct all children in the importance of religion, but that does not mean it is a constitutional right.

Unfortunately, it is probably too late to make such distinctions.

Otherwise we would not only have to jettison decades worth of legal precedent, we would also have to throw out most of the laws passed by Congress, since they plainly don't emanate from the powers granted to Congress in the Constitution under Article 1, Section 8, or anywhere else.

We are living in a constitutional republic to the same degree that Porky Pig is living in the real world. Uh, bibba-dibba-dibba, uh, th-th-th-that's all folks!

THE NAKED EMPEROR AND THE NAKED TRUTH

November 27, 2005

I wrote about the Constitution last week, and a few readers took offense at my suggestion that the Constitution might not actually contain some of the rights and guarantees in it which they cherish.

The argument of these people seems to be that we are better off living in a country that has such rights and guarantees, so keep quiet about it, you fool.

I suspect the little boy who told the emperor he was butt naked got the same reaction from the imperial guard.

What no one who wrote to me bothered to do was take up my implicit challenge of demonstrating where the Constitution guarantees a right to privacy and, by extension, a right to have an abortion. That's because there is no such guarantee in the document itself.

If there were, I can assure you it would not have taken 200 years to have found it (or 100 years if you think the right can be found in the 14th Amendment.)

What was discovered after that long period of time was that society had changed, not that the Constitution had changed. It had become a consensus opinion that people generally did not want the government "in the bedroom," regulating sexual behavior, and therefore courts — swayed by the ethos of their time — cobbled together tortuous constructs (based not on the simple language of the Constitution, but on the torturous language of judges and lawyers) in order to provide what "right thinking" had determined to be appropriate anyway.

As I said last week, if it feels good, it must be constitutional, right?

But what exactly is the point of having a written constitution if the words contained in it are treated as if they were handed over to the country with a wink and a nod.

Lawyers may think that words can be stretched in any direction at any time, but I for one don't like the idea of the Constitution as a magician's balloon that can be twisted into the shape of a dog one day and a fish the next. There is a way to change the shape of the Constitution — it is called the amendment process. But that apparently takes too long, and requires participation of the people, so we have instead gotten this new thing called the Supreme Court shortcut, which allows judges to make laws for the "good" of us all.

Well, maybe these learned judges really do know what is best for us. But that is not the point. What matters is not whether we agree with the result of the judges' decisions, but whether they have any business making law in the first place.

And this is not a personal complaint; it is a philosophical one, and a practical one. I have no personal interest in the legality of abortion one way or the other. If the state of Montana permitted legal abortion either through legislative action or because of our explicit constitutional guarantee of the right to privacy, I would not have any problem with that. My concern is entirely with whether the American public has been able to keep the republic whose birth Ben Franklin pronounced as he walked out of the constitutional convention in 1787.

It would seem that turning our sovereignty over to judges and courts which "find" rights because it is convenient to do is one good sign that the republic is in peril of being lost.

Again, show me the plain language in the Constitution that gives the federal government any jurisdiction in the matter of abortion, and I will shut up about it. Or tell me what right guaranteed under the Constitution is being violated when a state Legislature makes a law restricting abortion?

The general answer is "the right to privacy," but such a right is not found in either the original Constitution, the Bill of Rights, or any other amendment. And if such a "right to privacy" did exist, would it not by necessity and fairness have to apply to any number of other activities and behaviors which the state chooses to regulate?

Would it not, for instance, permit unlimited drug use? Perhaps so — and maybe it will next week. Court is in session after all.

There are those who find sanctuary for "inventing" new rights in the vagueness of the Ninth Amendment, which holds that "The enumeration in the Constitution of certain rights shall not be construed to deny or disparage others retained by the people."

But, in fact, the Ninth Amendment is no friend of Roe vs. Wade, which was an imposition of a federal decree upon the states and their people. By judicial fiat, the people have been denied the right of self-determination.

The Ninth Amendment should actually protect the right of the people, in the form of their state legislatures, to regulate their own lives in ways they find appropriate. This right, the right of self-government, is primary, and it is this which we have lost by allowing the Constitution to be hijacked by the judiciary.

WILL KARL MARX HAVE THE LAST LAUGH?

April 9, 2006

Karl Marx lost the battle, but he may be winning the war.

We all thought back in the late 1980s when communist governments were collapsing under the weight of their own excesses in Eastern Europe, that the discredited ideas of communism's founder would disappear, too.

But old Karl Marx may have the last laugh.

From each according to their ability; to each according to their need.

That is the simplest statement of Marxist philosophy that exists, and if it doesn't set off alarm bells when you hear it, then you haven't been paying attention to the political debate in our country recently. More and more, it looks like our country and our people are supposed to feel guilty for being successful, and we are supposed to make up for it by throwing money at people who haven't earned it. In the old days, they called that begging; now they call it "entitlement."

The United States has jobs, and Mexicans need them, so therefore Mexicans are entitled to those jobs.

Hospitals have health services, and poor people need them, so therefore poor people are entitled to those health services.

Bill Gates has billions of dollars, and the government needs billions, so therefore he should fork over as much as the government wants — no questions asked.

(Oh yes, and because he has so much money, the government is going to want more of his than yours. Heck, they're entitled to it, right? From each according to their ability; to each according to their need.)

While we're on the topic, the government has billions of dollars it already got from Bill Gates and other taxpayers, and people with less initiative, intelligence and good fortune than Bill Gates need it, so therefore they are entitled to it in the form of tax credits. It doesn't matter if they paid taxes or not. They "need" the money — so they get it. You can call it an earned-income tax credit or you can call it communism. Either way, it's the same story:

From each according to their ability; to each according to their need.

If you are a hard worker, it ought to make you mad. There you are, putting in extra time and effort to accomplish the best for yourself and your family, but the next guy over is less driven ("I like to enjoy the good things of life!) so he ends up taking it easy. You provide health insurance for your family; he provides nothing. When your family gets sick, you bring them to the hospital, pay the deductible, follow the rules, borrow if necessary, set up a payment plan, but you do the right thing. When his family gets sick, he brings them to the hospital, demands the best care, then complains when he gets the bill. "Why is my family not entitled to the best health care," he whines. "Are we not people?" So instead of trying to pay the bill, he lets the rest of us pay in the form of higher bills, higher insurance payments and higher taxes.

From each according to their ability; to each according to their need.

Now, before anyone accuses me of locking the hospital doors and letting people die on the street, let me explain myself. I do believe in charity. I do not believe in entitlements. Charity helps to bring us closer together; entitlements drive us further apart.

It is a good thing for the government or a church or an individual to help someone in need, but it is a bad thing to let people expect that every time they get in trouble, there is going to be someone there to bail them out. That is not called charity; it is called enabling.

When you enable an alcoholic to continue drinking by helping him to avoid the consequences of his disease, you are not doing him any favors — you are just speeding him on the way to his death — and you will encourage resentment at the same time.

Likewise, when you enable the chronically unsuccessful to avoid the consequences of their lack of education, resourcefulness or toil, you are just speeding them on the way to a life of dependency and despair, and if you don't think people on welfare resent the hand that feeds them, visit the inner city in a major urban area for a day. You will not discover an attitude of gratitude.

Maybe Karl Marx should have said it this way: "From everyone else because they've got it; to me, because I damn well want it."

HEALTH CARE OVER EASY, WITH FRIES ON THE SIDE

April 16, 2006

People sure are funny.

Take the response to last week's column on how Karl Marx's philosophy is slowly but surely taking over the United States. A number of readers wrote to let me know they appreciated my willingness to challenge the "entitlement mentality" that has pervaded our country, but a few others wrote to call me names.

I enjoy nothing more than a well-reasoned argument, but being called an "egotistical, arrogant jerk" has its charms, too.

Almost everyone who wrote to complain about my column focused on the paragraph that talked about health care. I compared the example of two hypothetical families, one which tries to pay its own way and one which feels that "health care" is a right and thus should be available to everyone, with or without the ability to pay.

Put aside the notable lack of reference to "health care" in the Constitution of the United States. Forget about the fact that the Declaration of Independence does not mention the right of the people to commandeer medical services whenever necessary. The Declaration does say that people have an unalienable right to life, and apparently some people think that includes the extended service warranty with full checkups until death and unlimited repairs at no cost.

Except, of course, there is a cost.

When someone gets free medical service, it means someone else paid for it — the doctor, the hospital, the insuror, the taxpayer. Someone, somewhere is shelling out the dollars. You can take that to the bank.

In the old days, before the New Deal, most of the largesse that helped the less fortunate pay their medical bills came in the form of what is now quaintly called "charity." It was the idea of individuals helping each other, or in a grander sense, the idea of institutions such as the Catholic Church helping those in need. Thus, it was common in many communities to have a Charity Hospital, where the poor and indigent could count on service thanks to the kindness of their fellow man.

Somewhere along the way charity got twisted into "welfare" — the difference being extreme. Charity is an act of giving. Welfare is an act of taking — namely the forced taking of money from one set of citizens for the betterment of another.

This is not to condemn people on welfare. They have no choice in the matter. This is the only option society has given them, and that should be the point which you take away from a study of entitlements. Once you create them, it is inevitable that people will take advantage of them. Poor people are no different than rich people when it comes to opportunism. If you create a loophole in the tax code, then rich people are going to take advantage of it. Why shouldn't they?

By the same token, poor people are going to take advantage of anything given to them for free. Why shouldn't they?

So we should not be surprised by the fact that as soon as private charity became institutionalized as public welfare, it also inevitably mutated into an entitlement. Instead of receiving help with gratitude, people with an "entitlement mentality" receive it with certainty that they deserved it all along. And to be honest, once an entitlement is granted in a democracy, it is virtually indestructible. That's because entitlements eventually translate into voting blocs — also known as special interests — and politicians for obvious reasons are beholden to the voters who vote for the politicians who granted the voters the entitlement in the first place. It's called a vicious cycle.

Of course, the issue of public health care is a complicated one, which cannot be reduced simply to a discussion of entitlements. One underlying cause of almost any problem in our society today is the lack of an extended family such as existed for millennia before technology allowed us all to become mobile. When you lived in a small town with your mother and father and five to 10 brothers and sisters and your rich Uncle Allan and your great-grandmother Rose and you all knew each other and got together for holidays, then if you got sick, it wasn't going to be the problem of Uncle Sam; it was going to be the problem of Uncle Allan and whoever else in the family had some money to help.

Today, it is much more likely that you live in a town where you have no relatives other than the immediate nuclear family. That means there is no private support structure — which is why more and more people turn to the government for more and more help.

Then, of course, you have to factor in the wonderful achievements of modern medicine. The average life expectancy increased by 50 percent during the 20th century. Over the course of about 160 years, life expectancy has increased by as much as 40 years. That is quite remarkable, and it means that health care costs for society as a whole have increased exponentially. You also have to kick in the value of all those high-tech gadgets and gizmos that diagnose us and cure us. Or if you want cheaper health care, you can just go to a hospital that doesn't use MRIs, miracle drugs, computer-assisted surgery — you know, the kind of hospital they had 100 years ago.

But that isn't going to happen, is it? Because everyone wants the very best medical care they can get — for obvious reasons. And because we are a caring people, American society tries to give it to them, but let's be realistic about what that means — not just to the individual but also to the society.

It is nice that we live in a society where individual well-being is highly valued, but before we declare "quality" health care a human right, let's remember that every time we "declare" a new right, it costs society money. The way that rights have been piling up lately, we may well be on our way to a bankrupt society. Perhaps that will come when we declare that everyone has a right to free food. After all, you need it to live, so why should you have to pay for it. Just back your truck up to the grocery store and take what you want.

Then we will have to change the old slogan to "There ain't no such thing as a free lunch, but I'll take mine with mustard on it."

SELF-MUTILATION, AMERICAN STYLE

April 23, 2006

Maybe it is time for a civics lesson.

We had them in school when I was a kid, and probably anyone over the age of 50 or so remembers them. If you are younger than that, maybe not so much.

It seems that about the time our country was debating whether or not the war in Vietnam was a good thing, we also started questioning whether or not the United States of America was a good thing.

It became unfashionable to be overtly patriotic and became politically incorrect to say we lived in the best country in the world. It's all relative, after all. You have to walk a mile in the other guy's chains to see how well they fit.

Eventually, it became fashionable to insult our leaders, to question our foreign policies and to doubt our values. As a nation, we have become the equivalent of the young women who scar themselves with razor blades. Why do they do it? No one knows, but it certainly has something to do with low self-esteem. The ironic thing is that "cutting" just has the effect of increasing self-hatred rather than doing anything to make the person feel better.

That's kind of where we are as a nation today. With our political leaders, our comedians, even the people who write letters to the editor, we see a tendency to gleefully announce yet another failure of American might, or yet another mistake by the ruling party. And before the wound has a chance to heal, someone picks the scab off in order to start it bleeding again.

Occasionally, a leader has the capacity to withstand the steady drumbeat of attacks through the force of his own personality. Such was the case with Ronald Reagan, and also with Bill Clinton, different as those two men were from a political point of view.

But despite occasional upturns in American self-esteem, we have been on a steadily downward trend for the past 40 years — and if we continue to doubt ourselves, our values and our leadership, it is inevitable that our nation will plummet just as dramatically as our self-esteem. Think Roman empire, and you get the picture. Outward signs of decline such as increasing vulgarity, vandalism and violence are accompanied by inward decay such as a slow collapse of the education system, inability of the bureaucracy to service the needs of the people, and general disrespect for institutions of government and religion.

It's not a pretty picture, but hey, why should we worry about it? After all, we have our iPods and MTV. We have McDonald's and Applebee's. We have the NFL and Nascar.

Oh wait a minute, those are the bread and circuses, aren't they? And we have plenty of those, don't we? Distractions that feed our appetites and deflect our gaze from the growing chaos around us.

And as each succeeding generation has less connection to its heritage, there is less chance of turning back the darkness.

I'm sure there were Roman senators who shook their head in wonder that their empire was past the point of no return. But what could they do? The inertia of history plows under many good men. Besides, if you shout too loudly against the darkness you are considered a madman. So most good people keep quiet and go about their business in the dying light. Others just pull tight their shutters and shiver in the light of the last embers while listening for the barbarians at the door.

But still a few do rage against the dying of the light, and maybe they offer a small amount of hope that all is not yet lost. The Minutemen, for instance, sounded the alarm on our borders, and they may have acted quickly enough to stem the invasion of illegal aliens into our midst. But that battle is still being fought, and the outcome is by no means certain.

More importantly, as a nation, we have exhibited no inclination to admit that we have a problem, nor shown any understanding of the importance of being united in national identity.

Which brings us back to civics.

The purpose of civics is to educate citizens about the rights and responsibilities of citizenship and to give young people an understanding of the fundamental values and principles which underlie our great republic.

But in our politically correct age, such education is called "indoctrination" and is thus frowned upon. We are not free to pass on to our progeny that which makes us proudly American; instead we are to cower in shame and run the razor blade through our national identity until we draw blood. One cut for racism, one cut for greed, one cut for imperialism. Cut, cut, cut.

And not a word about freedom, liberty, or democracy. Not a word about fighting to ensure that the world is safe for freedom. Not a word about hard work and ingenuity. Not a word about caring and compassion. Hang your head in shame and take a cut for slavery, for the death penalty, for Abu Ghraib. Thomas Jefferson was a slave owner — hang your head in shame. FDR locked up the Japanese — hang your head in shame. President Bush didn't find weapons of mass destruction in Iraq — hang your head in shame. Halliburton made another billion — hang your head in shame.

It's inevitable that with such a burden of shame and so little understanding of our inherent greatness, the United States of America cannot long stand. And it does not do enough just to say you love your country. Love of country is irrelevant. As President Reagan said in his farewell address, "This national feeling [of new patriotism] is good, but it won't count for much, and it won't last, unless it's grounded in thoughtfulness and knowledge."

Which is where civics fits in.

President Reagan, in his warning to the nation, asked, "Are we doing a good enough job teaching our children what America is and what she represents in the long history of the world?" Do our children today have any chance to absorb, in Reagan's words, "a love of country and an appreciation of its institutions"?

If they do, they probably have their parents to thank for it. They certainly won't get it from the popular culture of television, movies or music. They won't get it from schools without a large dose of skepticism and ambivalence. Unbelievably, they won't even get it from their own government, where many of our leaders use their public forum to decry American greatness.

Ronald Reagan left office just 17 years ago, but in that short time his hope of an "informed patriotism" has been dashed. Instead of a love of country, today we are more likely to experience the "erosion of the American spirit" that Reagan predicted would be the result if we did not cherish the proud memory of what it means to be an American.

And once that spirit is extinguished, this world will never be the same again. Ask any Roman.

'CULTURE OF CORRUPTION'?
OR JUST PLAIN DUMB?

May 28, 2006

A few months ago I made a case for heeding the plain language of the U.S. Constitution instead of allowing courts and special interests to insert their wish list of rights, duties, obligations and cotton candy into the document.

That's because I have a very high regard for the Constitution — and the framers who gave it to us — and a very low regard for the average politician's ability to avoid the siren call of self-interest.

Last week, we got a stunning reminder of just how easy it is to hijack the Constitution for political purposes, and we have been granted once more an opportunity to demand that the government obey the simple language of the Constitution instead of stretching it like silly putty to meet the needs of expediency. The Constitution is flexible, but it should not be elastic.

But don't tell that to the leaders of Congress.

When the FBI raided the congressional offices of William Jefferson, a Louisiana Democrat who is under investigation for allegedly accepting bribes, it was as if the Romans were once again entering the Holy of Holies at King Solomon's Temple in Jerusalem. The outraged men of the Capitol stood aghast as their "privileges" were trampled by the executive branch.

Former House speaker Newt Gingrich called the raid "the most blatant violation of the constitutional separation of powers in my lifetime."

The current speaker, Dennis Hastert, R-Ill., said, "Insofar as I am aware, since the founding of our republic 219 years ago, the Justice Department has never found it necessary to do what it did Saturday night, crossing this separation of powers line, in order to successfully prosecute corruption by members of Congress."

That all sounds good. Anybody with a fifth-grade education knows that separation of powers is a fundamental cornerstone of our form of government.

But based on the statements made so far, you have to wonder whether our leaders of Congress, past and present, ever got past fifth grade at all.

First of all, to keep it simple enough for even congresspeople to understand, separation of powers works like this: The legislative branch makes the laws, the judicial branch interprets them, the executive branch enforces them.

But as of last week, it got changed to this: The legislative branch makes the laws, interprets them, and tells the executive branch not to enforce them if a member of Congress got his hand caught in the cookie jar.

Montesquieu, no doubt, is turning over in his moldy grave. It was that French political philosopher who developed the modern theory of separation of powers, and the accompanying theory of checks and balances.

The idea wasn't to create a Congress with the powers of a monarchy, but rather to create a government where each branch could limit the powers of the other two branches. Thus, Congress must submit to the legitimate powers of the executive branch and the judiciary — not hold itself above the law.

The separation of powers, after all, is not a shield for wrong-doing. In fact, it is the very opposite. It is a guarantee of the ability to hold wrong-doers accountable.

President Nixon learned to his chagrin that just being president did not mean he could avoid the subpoena power of the courts. His aides and deputies learned that being part of the executive branch did not mean they could stay out of jail. President Clinton learned that he could not lie to a court and then tell the Congress it was none of their business.

In these cases, senators and representatives have powerfully orated on the sanctity of our system, where no man is above the law. They have warned presidents to behave or be chastised.

But now these same senators, in defense of a scoundrel, have rewritten the Constitution to protect one of their own.

Instead of standing with the American people in favor of integrity and decency, the leaders of Congress have tried to mislead the public into granting them rights which they have never had before, and never should have.

Don't take my word for it. Read the Constitution for yourself. Print out a copy from the Internet (www.usconstitution.net/const.txt is one of many sites where it may be downloaded) and take it with you wherever you go. Read it every minute from now until the day you die, and you will never find one word that exempts members of Congress from the principle that no man is above the law.

Here's what you will actually find — the plain language of Article 1, Section 6:

"The senators and representatives ... shall in all cases, except treason, felony and breach of the peace, be privileged from arrest during their attendance at the session of their respective houses, and in going to and returning from the same; and for any speech or debate in either house, they shall not be questioned in any other place."

That, in sum, is the entire privilege granted to members of Congress in protection against an overzealous executive branch.

Please note that there is no wholesale exclusion of searches and seizures of documents in congressional offices. Please note also that it is entirely permissible for the FBI to enter the Capitol and actually arrest a senator on the floor of the Senate if he is charged with a felony. Please note also that bribery is a felony.

So Rep. William Jefferson can be arrested by the executive branch on the floor of the Senate for bribery, but — according to Hastert and Gingrich — his offices cannot be searched with a duly sworn and executed search warrant, even when he refused to honor a prior grand jury subpoena for the same documents.

Huh? How so?

The shaky underpinnings of the argument hinge on that "speech and debate" clause of the Constitution. It seems that those who are trying to make Congress safe for bribery think that documents prepared in the line of duty by a congressman or his staff must be protected from prying eyes, even if the eyes have a warrant.

But the plain language of the Constitution doesn't say that. It says that a congressman may say anything he wants in official speech and debate and shall not be charged with any crime as a result, nor even be questioned about it. That is a fundamental doctrine of fair and open debate and guarantees that Congress shall not be intimidated by the executive with the threat of arrest for simply arguing against a presidential policy. The framers were brilliant to include that passage, and did so because of their experience with a crown that did not respect open legislative debate.

It is the invisible asterisk in Article 1, Section 6, which concerns me. Because it must be in the emanations of the invisible writing next to that invisible asterisk where the congressional leaders have found their penumbral protection from legal investigation of criminal wrongdoing.

Since the ink is invisible, we will have to ask Hastert and Gingrich whether members of Congress may hide evidence of all crimes in their offices or just crimes done on the job. Does the protection extend to evidence against members of their family? What about their friends? Is it possible that congressmen can start making a little extra money on the side legally by advertising their services as hiders of evidence? After all, if the FBI is forbidden to search on Capitol Hill no matter what crime is committed, then why not turn that to advantage. Heck, it may ultimately make bribery old-fashioned and irrelevant. Skilling and Lay probably would have paid big-time to get all the Enron corporate records safely shoved into congressional offices.

Thanks to a little invisible ink in the Constitution and the ever-increasing gullibility of the American public, this could actually be the best scam since diplomatic immunity!

FORGING THE CHAINS OF LIBERTY —
AND FORGETTING THEM

July 23, 2006

When I was growing up in Stony Point, N.Y., I was surrounded by reminders of the birth of our nation, and the sacrifices that were made to wrest our liberty from the yoke of a tyrant.

You can look up the Battle of Stony Point on the Internet and get some feel for the drama of the Revolutionary War that surged throughout the Hudson River Valley in those years. Gen. Anthony Wayne earned his sobriquet of "Mad" Anthony Wayne partly for this battle when he sent his forces against the British in the dark of night with unloaded rifles and bayonets to gain the element of surprise. Gen. Washington himself supposedly came up with the strategy, which gave the Continental Army its last crucial victory in New York before the war moved south.

Not far away from my old home town is West Point, where the U.S. Military Academy is found today, but which in 1778 was the site of one of the grandest statements of American ingenuity ever. At that time the Royal Navy hoped to use the Hudson River to divide the New England colonies from those to the west and south, and since they were a far superior naval force compared to anything the colonies could muster, they had the upper hand.

But Gen. Washington was not to be deterred. He ordered a great chain to be forged that would be stretched across the entire river, which at that point is nearly a third of a mile wide. More than 800 wrought iron links that were each two-feet long were used in the chain, which was intended to halt naval traffic dead in the water so that artillery could bombard British ships from either shore.

West Point, Stony Point, George Washington, Anthony Wayne — those were the places and faces of my boyhood. Perhaps that is why I am inclined to be a bit romantic about the Revolution, and about the American nation it engendered. I saw the surviving links of that great chain at West Point when I was a boy, and everywhere you would go in that region there were small blue and white signs along the roadways that told what momentous event had taken place nearby.

I don't suppose many people growing up amidst those signs today spend much time thinking about our common forefathers. I doubt there is even a Fourth of July parade down Filors Lane anymore where I grew up and watched the Doughboys of World War I and the heroes of World War II (still young then in the early 1960s) march past my door and alongside a stone wall that had stood those 200 years.

But what is it that the philosopher taught us? Those who cannot remember the past are condemned to repeat it? Ah yes, and there is so much to remember. It is an arduous task indeed to forge those links of memory that must stretch from 1776 to 2006, but if we don't pull that chain of liberty taut, then we are defenseless against the superior forces of lethargy, sloth and selfishness which always try to divide us from our own best interests.

Yet many are daunted by the challenge, or fail to see the danger. In 1778, no doubt there were naysayers, too, those who laughed at Washington and his plan to dissect a great river. It was indeed a grandiose statement, one nearly mythic in proportion, but yet it served a practical purpose. The British gave up their dominion over the river and never tested the chain at West Point.

But do we face any kind of challenge today comparable to the British army and navy? Is there any reason to harp on the battles of yesteryear?

To ask such a question in today's politically correct climate is almost to invite calumny. After all, we are at peace, aren't we? Oh wait, no, we are at war. But yet there is no immediate danger to our sovereignty, is there? Oh wait, there is an entire worldwide culture which would destroy us. But surely that is to overstate the immediate danger, isn't it? We are not in danger of being overrun by Islam as Spain was overrun in the 8th century, are we?

Perhaps not, but Islam is not the only danger we face either. What about the immediate danger of 10 million to 25 million foreign nationals crossing our border and imposing their culture on us? Spain was forced to learn Arabic when it was overrun by the armies of the Caliph al-Walid in 711 A.D. Today we are in the process of being overrun by a horde of people flooding our southern border and ironically we are being forced to learn Spanish.

To add to the irony, those Mexicans who press into our nation call their movement the Reconquista, because they say they are reconquering the lands which hundreds of years ago belonged to Mexico, and before that to Spain. But friends of the illegal immigrants here in the United States just smile and put up a welcome sign. "It's a big country," they say. "Immigration is what made us great. Let's welcome these foreigners and build our country together.

Thank goodness, the Spanish took a different view when they were invaded from the south. It was not an easy battle for them when the Islamic armies came ashore at Gibralter. Thousands upon thousands died. Hundreds of thousands were forced to convert to Islam, until only one small bastion of authentic Spanish culture remained. It was from the Kingdom of Asturias in northwest Spain where the European resistance to Islam began in 718. That battle was not completed until 1492, more than 750 years later, when the Moors were finally pushed back across the sea.

Whether we Americans have the heart for such a battle has not yet been decided. But do not think that we are untouched by the forces of history. In this coming century, we face not one challenge to our sovereignty, but two. Internally, we are already weakened by a movement that would change our way of life through intimidation and sheer numbers. Externally, we are in the midst of a worldwide battle against Islamic fascism that has not changed much from that July day nearly 1,300 years ago when the Islamic army crossed the Guadalete River in Spain, captured the Emperor Rodrigo, and sawed off his head to be displayed on a pole.

Interestingly, the forced conversion of Spain to Islam also has a direct connection to my youthful days in New York and to New York history. Just across the Hudson River from where I lived was the hometown of Washington Irving, most famous for his headless horseman of Spooky Hollow and the narcoleptic Rip Van Winkle. Irving was named after Gen. George Washington and later wrote a famous biography of that worthy. But Irving also spent many years in Spain and wrote an account of the battles that ended Muslim power in Spain in his "Chronicle of the Conquest of Grenada."

Clearly there is much to learn from even a casual perusal of history. Perhaps, as I suggested earlier, it is too much. We Americans do not have much of an attention span these days. Between our trips to the movie theater, the baseball diamond, the shopping mall and to cyberspace, it's hard to squeeze in an understanding of where we came from or to think about the possibility that someone might want to take away what we have.

But there are enemies of our way of life among us. There always have been. I think of one more blue-and-white sign that you could see on a quiet little street near Filors Lane in Stony Point, N.Y. That street was called Major Andre Lane and was named after the British officer who had assisted Gen. Benedict Arnold in plotting to surrender the fort at West Point to the British in exchange for 20,000 pounds. Major Andre, the sign informed me when I stopped to read it on my bike, had been captured on that hill in 1780 and arrested. He was later hanged as a spy while Benedict Arnold fled to live out his years in disgrace in England. One last history lesson.

One last lesson that is easy to ignore as we tempt fate and see if we are really doomed to repeat the mistakes of the past or not. I for one wish we could learn from history, but I have my doubts. There is just too much stubborn insistence on how wonderful we are, or how lucky.

We can't count on our luck to save us, but only our vigilance, and we have precious little of that.

Perhaps it is time to consider a corollary to Santayana's famous aphorism about history. My proposal? Those who close their eyes to the dangers of the present are condemned to die in the dark.

10 YEARS THAT CHANGED EVERYTHING

November 26, 2006

I'm sure I'm not the only person in America who has grown increasingly pessimistic watching history unfold in the last half century, but I thought it might be instructive to look at how my own political thinking — and perhaps our nation's destiny — was shaped by three crucial presidencies in the mid-20th century.

I am confident that the decade between 1963 and 1972 will turn out to be the most significant pivot point in American history other than the Civil War, when Abraham Lincoln declared that the United States of America was not just a civil union but a holy matrimony that no man should put asunder.

In a sense, the years between Kennedy's assassination and Nixon's resignation were themselves something like a civil war, although one with few shots fired. But whereas the first civil war strengthened our nation, and taught us to remember our unity, the second civil war weakened us and left us uncertain of our loyalties. Moreover, the succession of presidencies from Kennedy to Johnson to Nixon left us increasingly cynical and sowed the seeds of a political disunity that perhaps even Lincoln could not have overcome.

I have no particular recollection of the election of 1960. I was just 5 years old then, but suffice it to say that John F. Kennedy was elected president, and I went about life in kindergarten with the same exuberant confidence I would have felt if Richard Nixon were president.

Soon thereafter, however, I began my political education in earnest. Unlike this contemporary era — in which our children are insulated from the real world by Cartoon Network, iPods and Play Stations 1 through 3 — children and their parents in those days shared the same cultural milieu and there was a much greater continuity of thought between the older and younger generations.

Thus, while I was playing with Erector Set robots and rocket ships on the living room floor, I was absorbing the same

TV and radio reports that my parents heard. The Bay of Pigs incident probably did not make much of an impact on me, but the Berlin Wall crisis did, and like every other child of the era I very well remember practicing how to "duck and cover" to avoid the impact of a thermonuclear blast. When the Cuban Missile Crisis played out in October of 1962, I started to develop a real awareness of the presidency, and in particular of this president — the one with the funny accent and the perfect hair.

It became clear to me that my future was in President Kennedy's hands, and with or without my mother crying about the likelihood that we were going to be blown up, I had probably begun my inevitable conversion to dread realism. Then, one year later, something happened which changed my life and this country forever.

I was 8 years old when President Kennedy was assassinated. To sum up the impact of that event is impossible. Lack of certainty about what happened on Nov. 22, 1963 — or why — clearly set the nation on a path of self-doubt and puzzlement from which it has never wholly recovered. Every attempt to find a simple explanation for the death of the president seemed to lead to additional questions and additional doubts about the veracity of our government.

Meanwhile, despite the trauma of the assassination, politics continued as usual. In 1964, Kennedy's vice president, Lyndon Johnson, was re-elected president in a landslide. Although I was just 9 years old, I remember feeling comfortable with the idea that Kennedy's Democratic legacy would live on. Little did I or anyone else know then that there was a dark side to that legacy, but part of that dark legacy would surface soon in the form of the Vietnam War.

Perhaps Kennedy would have handled Vietnam differently; perhaps not. Questions like those can never be answered, but it is clear that Lyndon Johnson did not know how to handle it and squandered much of the good will that Kennedy had left behind. Despite overseeing implementation of much-needed civil rights reforms and trying to address issues of poverty, health care and education as he sought to use presidential power to shape a "Great Society," Johnson lost his way in

Southeast Asia. By 1968, all that most people could see was the increasing quagmire of Vietnam, and the body bags returning home with our boys inside.

We were a different country then, still an optimistic country because of our successes in both war and peace, and the prospect of losing a war was just unfathomable. But Johnson did not seem to know what to do. He looked tired, overwhelmed — as he told us in an address to the nation, he had a "heavy heart." Eventually, with the humiliating campaign challenge of Sen. Eugene McCarthy developing steam, Johnson dropped out of the presidential race.

I had learned a valuable lesson. Just being a Democrat did not mean you had all the answers. And yet there was no reasonable Republican alternative to the Johnson policy either. By the time of the election in 1968, it seemed as though the Republicans were even more set on what was apparently a disastrous war policy than the Democrats.

Thus in 1968, I and many other Americans supported Bobby Kennedy for president. He seemed like a genuinely caring and compassionate man, more bookish and pensive than his brother John, with a greater sense of irony perhaps, but forced to action by his conscience. When he spoke after the murder of Martin Luther King Jr., he soothed an entire nation's troubled heart. It appeared to many of us that Bobby was the best hope for restoring a sense of order to a nation that was increasingly divided and chaotic. But Bobby, of course, did not live to see the election he might very well have won. Another assassination, another lost cause.

Ultimately, for many of us, the election of 1968 was an irrelevant afterthought — the age of Camelot had ended, and whatever came next had to be a disappointment. I supported Vice President Hubert Humphrey somewhat half-heartedly as he campaigned against Richard Nixon, but instead Nixon won and the nation would have a chance to see what a Republican presidency could bring.

It reminds me of the excitement Democrats feel today about regaining control of Congress, and their anticipation of winning the White House in 2008. No doubt Nixon thought he would change this country for the better, and that he would wield power wisely. But sometimes power wields the man, not the other way around. And despite his agenda for doing good, Nixon wound up creating a legacy of distrust and disdain for government that has tainted everything which has happened since then. His example should be studied attentively by anyone who expects to change things for the better, including Nancy Pelosi.

The problem of course is that new leaders don't get to begin their leadership with a clean slate. Everything that has come before them must be factored into the equation. Pelosi and company cannot just posture about the war in Iraq any longer; they must develop a policy that will get us out of Iraq without leaving behind a powderkeg and a book of matches. Nixon likewise, who said he had a secret plan for getting us out of Vietnam, learned that reality cannot be fashioned to fit a political slogan.

Nixon had to deal with the Vietnam War for the next four years as president. And despite his complaints about Johnson's policies, he could do no better, so everything else Nixon did is seen today through the blood-red prism of the war. Many young people, myself included, were eager to get Nixon out of office, partly because we were terrified of being sent to Vietnam when we graduated from high school and partly just because we did not trust him.

That meant I took an active interest in the campaign to find a Democratic candidate who could unseat Nixon. At first I was for Sen. Edmund Muskie, but in one of the earliest instances of Big Media destroying a political career, Muskie was filmed crying (or appearing so) while defending his wife from an editorial that said she liked to drink and tell dirty jokes. I never understood why defending your wife was a bad thing, so I stuck by Muskie, but the rest of the nation didn't, so we were left with George McGovern, a South Dakota senator who had made his political reputation by opposing the war and by — well, um — by opposing the war. Proving to be a dismal campaigner and a bumbling oaf when it came to policy matters, McGovern went down in flames.

Before we leave the Nixon White House, it is interesting to note that Nixon — though a Republican — was the last great liberal president this country has had. It was Nixon who gave us the Environmental Protection Agency, the Clean Water Act, the Clean Air Act, the Occupational Safety and Health Administration, federal affirmative action, detente with Russia, and a renewed relationship with Communist China. He also started the space shuttle program and ended the gold standard. So even though Nixon is despised by liberals for Watergate and Vietnam, he is also despised by conservatives for his big-government agenda.

Meanwhile, even though I despised Nixon, too, I also had a begrudging admiration for him. He was a self-made man who had used will power and brain power to become the most powerful man in the world, and despite his paranoid tendencies which resulted in Watergate and his ultimate downfall, he did indeed attempt to use his power to make the world a better place.

In a sense, Presidents Kennedy, Johnson and Nixon were all modern Shakesperean tragic heroes. Each had the capacity for greatness, each did some good, yet each possessed a flaw that not only brought him down, but also marred his legacy for all time.

Kennedy has attained the martyr's exemption from too close of a look at his flaws, but there is no doubt that his hubris led him to take unnecessary risks both in his personal life and also with the nation's security. Even though we know of these lapses now, we have forgiven Kennedy. It is not so with Nixon and Johnson. Familiarity in those cases has bred contempt.

Yet already by the early 1970s, I was aware that both Nixon and Johnson had been players in a drama that was much larger than themselves. Although they were despised by many of my generation, including by me, I recognized in them a greatness that is little evident in today's leaders. In fact, if anything defines my brand of politics, it is that I recognize the enormous difficulty of successfully taking the helm of state, and have learned to accept that failure should not necessarily earn opprobrium. I also learned from the examples of Johnson and

Nixon that failures happen without regard to partisan affiliation, and I learned that the mob will turn on anyone, even its heroes.

So despite the turmoil of the 1960s and '70s, and partly because of it — because I came to recognize the inevitability of failure under certain circumstances — I admire both Lyndon Johnson and Richard Nixon. Even when Johnson died of a heart attack in 1973, I broke down in tears and sobbingly told my mother that "He tried, Mom. He really tried."

I was sure that if not for Vietnam, Johnson would be remembered as a great president, but instead he had been hobbled and hated. Eighteen months later, when Richard Nixon resigned in disgrace, I cried again, and for the same reason. For all of the complicated flaws of Richard Nixon as a human being, "He tried."

I learned in that decade from the death of President Kennedy to the resignation of President Nixon that power has its limits, that ambition can be thwarted, that success is often tempered, that greatness may mask insincerity, and that a nation must not expect too much from its leaders.

Yet it seems as if these lessons — repeated over and over again in our recent history — have not been absorbed by the body politic. Thus, we have the spectacle of "the loyal opposition" turning into the gang of senatorial thugs who surrounded Caesar and punched daggers into his body 23 times. "We can do better," they shout as they slay him, but of course they cannot.

This has nothing to do with partisan politics. It was just as true when Republicans did everything in their power to destroy the presidency of Bill Clinton, as it is today when President George W. Bush is mocked and belittled for his inability to be perfect. Ultimately, we must decide if we think it is better to destroy our imperfect presidents, or to lift them up in our expectations so that we may inspire them to be better.

I am sure of one thing only — if we continue to destroy our presidents, we will destroy our country as well.

'BACK TO THE FUTURE': IRAQ AND VIETNAM

December 10, 2006

Recently it has become fashionable to compare the Iraq War to the Vietnam War, and such a comparison is certainly instructive.

Both are wars which the United States entered as part of a greater global conflict of ideologies. Both are wars which began or escalated as the result of incorrect information supplied to Congress and the American public (WMDs in Iraq, the Gulf of Tonkin incident in Vietnam). Both were continued in the name of bolstering a fledgling democracy. Both were fought on our side as limited engagements rather than as all-out wars, and both were fought against enemies who would stop at nothing to win.

You would think it would be fairly easy, therefore, to make an analogy between Vietnam and Iraq and come away with good information about how to proceed as we enter the fourth year of the Iraq conflict.

But nothing is easy in either the world of ideas or the world of nations, and an easy analogy is oftentimes just a misleading one. Comparisons are odious, as the poet said.

Nonetheless, despite their limitations, historical comparisons can be valuable. Any analysis of history is to be lauded as we try to understand our present-day challenges and quandaries. But what I have noticed in the current discussion about Vietnam is that too often our past is seen as a template for failure rather than for success.

By this, I mean that we greedily digest our history — so it seems — only for the purpose of nourishing our fears, rather than to strengthen us to tackle the future.

I suppose this skewed view of history is best summarized in George Santayana's dictum: "Those who cannot learn from history are doomed to repeat it."

I myself have frequently quoted Santayana, including in this column, but now I wonder whether or not Santayana's sentiment is not a kind of recipe for disaster. It contains a hidden assumption that history itself is inherently bad, that what happened in the past must be avoided in the future, and that the alternative is a kind of "doom."

But of course most history is the story of man's progress from barbarism to civilization, from oppression to freedom and from ignorance to knowledge.

So Santayana really should have been more specific, and offered a bifurcated prescription: "Those who cannot learn from the mistakes of history are doomed to repeat them; those who cannot learn from the successes of history are unlikely to duplicate them."

Even that prescription is skewed toward failure, however. It is all about people who can not learn. To be more fair, and more accurate, it would need to be worded thus:

"Those who cannot learn from the mistakes of history are doomed to repeat them; those who can learn from the mistakes of history have a chance to avoid them. Those who cannot learn from the successes of history are unlikely to duplicate them; those who can learn from the successes of history are mankind's best hope for a better future."

It's not as catchy as Santayana's famous line, but it seems more accurate. History is not a plague to be avoided, after all, but a resource which we may either take advantage of, or not.

In the case of the Vietnam War, most people seem to prefer to forget about it altogether, but among those who study it, there is a tendency to look at it only as an abject failure. Thus, the fact that there are similarities between the Vietnam War and the Iraq War is seen to warrant an automatic conclusion that the Iraq War must itself be an abject failure and the United States must quit the war and come home, no matter what the consequences.

This appears to be the virtual conclusion of the Iraq Study Group, which essentially said, "There's a big problem over there in Iraq, we don't know how to fix it, we better get out." That of course is not a new approach to the war, and is shared by a majority of Americans. It also appears to be an accurate assessment — based on the current leadership in the White House and the will of the American people.

I would like to propose, however, that the Vietnam War was not an abject failure, although it clearly was a military one.

The purpose of the Vietnam War, from the point of view of the American presidents who fought it, was after all to prevent the spread of communism, first in Southeast Asia and ultimately elsewhere. This vision of one country after another falling under the sway of communism was known as the domino theory.

In general this theory is considered to be disproven because communism was unable to supplant all the existing governments in Southeast Asia. Many dominoes, in essence, are still standing to this day, and opponents of the domino theory take that to mean the theory was incorrect from the start.

But consider this: North Vietnam did conquer South Vietnam and turn it into a united communist government. The governments of Cambodia and Laos — the countries closest to Vietnam — did fall into the hands of communists, with particularly disastrous results in the case of Cambodia, where as many as 3 million people died in genocidal relocations.

Moreover, despite our ultimate military defeat in Vietnam, the United States did wage war there for 10 long years. The question which must be answered is whether that presence — that sacrifice of blood and treasure — had any impact in the politics of the world and the region for the good.

Here, we cannot rely on historians to make conclusive judgments, because they can only see the results of what was actually done. It is left to our imagination how things might have been different under other circumstances. Call it the "Back to the Future" version of history, as we ponder the "what ifs" and "what might have beens."

But whatever you call it, please try to keep an open mind when you try to imagine a world where the United States had not taken an interest in the well-being of people forced to live under totalitarian regimes in the post-WWII era. Does it not seem reasonable to conclude that the United States spending billions of dollars to wage war in Vietnam meant that the Soviet Union was also forced to keep its attention focused there instead of financing insurrections elsewhere?

And if Vietnam had turned communist in 1965 instead of 1975, is it not possible that they would have quickly shared their joyous victory with their brothers in Laos and Cambodia? If all three of those countries had become communist states before the end of the 1960s, is it not possible that Thailand and Burma would have followed? If there had been no anti-communist push by the United States, what would have prevented Indonesia from going down that path?

Perhaps when we look at the history of the Vietnam War, we should not look at it only as an example of the difficulty of fighting a guerrilla war against an indigenous people, but as an example of how even a failed war can be a successful political strategy to change the world for the better.

Does anyone honestly think the world would be a better place today if Southeast Asia were a solid bloc of communist countries? If the Soviet Union had not bankrupted itself trying to keep up with the American military, and were still today maintaining its grip on Eastern Europe?

We will never know for sure what the world would look like if the United States had not fought the war in Vietnam along with a few of its allies such as Australia and New Zealand. But it is certainly easy to imagine that an isolationist policy by the United States after World War II would have plunged the world into chaos and chains.

Now, the question arises, thanks in part to the Iraq Study Group, what the world will look like if the United States withdraws from Iraq and lets matters there unfold without us. You don't need to read tea leaves to get a sense of foreboding in this regard.

There will be bloodshed. There will be sectarian violence. There will be regional battles that will likely divide up Iraq between the Turks, the Iranians, the Syrians and the Saudis. The Kurds will continue their war of independence. The Sunnis and Shiites will continue their centuries-long battle for dominance, and the only winners will be the Islamic fascists, as their brand of absolute submission will take hold with Taliban-like rigidity in one country after another in the Middle East.

Gen. Colin Powell accurately said, prior to the invasion, "If you break it, you bought it." This was an insightful acknowledgment by the general that the United States, in waging war against Saddam, would need to assume responsibility for the country in the event that things did not go as well as anticipated.

If we forget this, it is at our own peril. The impending crisis in the Middle East will make the dangers of Southeast Asia seem like a thrill ride at Disney World. Whether you initially approved of going into Iraq or not, you need to recognize that our fear of staying there any longer will only embolden Iran and Syria as they seek to widen their spheres of influence. And a nuclear-powered Iran will be quite bold indeed.

Perhaps, our new slogan should be, "If you break it, run like hell."

Dominoes, anyone?

TO DO – OR NOT TO DO – WHATEVER WE WANT TO DO

February 25, 2007

Shame is nothing new.

In the Bible, it is present in man from the beginning, from Genesis, from the time when Adam and Eve discover their nakedness in the Garden of Eden and are ashamed and cover themselves.

We need not debate the veracity of the Bible to understand the psychological legitimacy of this story, which illustrates how self-consciousness has a built-in censor which guides our conduct and shapes our behavior.

It is that internal, essentially human, self-consciousness which is the seed of what the philosophers call "natural law," and thus we can say that individual self-consciousness has an elemental role in mankind's continuing urge to legislate and to regulate human behavior. In a very real sense, the legal system is society's way of imposing shame on those who lack an adequate amount of it on their own.

To the libertarian, of course, this is a challenge.

There are always people who believe they should be free to engage in any behavior they choose, as long as it does no harm to anyone else. For Adam and Eve, they see no shame in being naked, and for the rest of us, they see no shame in living as though there were no natural law. Libertarians have made the case, at one time or another, for freedom to use recreational drugs, engage in public nudity, drive without a license, and enjoy their sexuality in any form it takes. These days, of course, they also wish to safeguard their ability to be as vulgar as they want.

One of the tactics which such libertarians employ to advance their agenda is to appropriate shame as their badge of honor. Instead of leading to humility or repentance, such expectation of shame instead leads to defiance and recklessness. You only need to read the latest "Britney Spears enters/exits rehab" story to understand this.

This also illustrates the fundamental danger of libertarianism. It believes that the behavior of the individual has no effect on the collective known as society. But that is patently false. Instead, every time society allows vulgar, selfish behavior to go unpunished — unshamed if you will — then it sends a message to everyone that such behavior is acceptable. Yes, we all have the freedom to switch the channel if something we don't like is on TV, but switching the channel as an individual will not save the society we all inhabit together.

The American Civil Liberties Union exemplifies this libertarian instinct more than any other institution in our country. It routinely defends behavior which society finds offensive, and condemns the traditional values which nurtured our freedom in the first place. Thus, it opposes traditional marriage, supports pornography, opposes religion in the town square, supports terrorists, opposes the Boy Scouts, supports the North American Man-Boy Love Association, and so on.

An average American who studied the legal briefs filed by the ACLU would be shocked and appalled, yet this radical group has slowly but surely chipped away at our ability to define ourselves as people "endowed by their Creator with certain unalienable rights," and we seem unable to do anything to stop them. Indeed, so far as the ACLU is concerned, the Creator doesn't exist — and mustn't exist — within the United States. I am confident that if the Declaration of Independence were written today as an official government document, the ACLU would be in court before the end of the week to demand an injunction against it.

This is so absurd that it is scary, but it is the plain truth.

The First Amendment has been so twisted by legal interpretation and misinterpretation that it now barely resembles the intent of the Founding Fathers. When they wrote that "Congress shall make no law respecting an establishment of religion, or prohibiting the free exercise thereof," the Founding Fathers had something specific in mind. First of all, note that the law specifically addresses only what Congress shall do. But the courts quickly broadened this to include the entire federal government, and eventually the state governments, and now to include pretty much any municipality or township as well.

Secondly, note that the amendment prohibits Congress from establishing a religion, and also prevents Congress from prohibiting the people from exercising their own religious beliefs. Anyone who knows anything about American history knows that this was not meant to prohibit government from acknowledging God and not meant to prohibit the Christian tradition which cradled our democracy from being honored. But that is what the courts, largely at the goading of the ACLU, have concluded. Indeed, these days, the First Amendment ought to more accurately read that "Congress shall make no law prohibiting the free exercise of religion, but the Supreme Court shall do so on a regular basis."

But it is not just the "establishment clause" which the ACLU has used to do battle with America's traditional Christian heritage; it is also in the clause of the First Amendment which prohibits Congress from "abridging the freedom of speech, or of the press." These words in the First Amendment were intended as guarantors of our political liberty, and were meant to ensure our rights to speak out against the government, not as cudgels to force the nation to submit to vile and vulgar discourse as the lingua franca of the realm.

It is quite apparent that the First Amendment was never intended as an unqualified permit for any and all speech, and as early as 1798 Congress adopted the Alien and Sedition Acts, which expressly forbade the publication of "false, scandalous, and malicious writings against the government of the United States... with intent to defame ... or to bring them ... into contempt or disrepute." Several of those members of Congress who voted for this act had also voted to ratify the First Amendment, so they clearly did not see them to be in conflict.

Moreover, there is absolutely no one who supports freedom of the press who can claim that at the time the First Amendment was adopted, it was intended to protect vulgar or indecent speech since there were numerous laws in our early history which prohibited such behavior. Even today, the First Amendment's freedom of the press clause, which appears to be an absolute protection, does not in fact apply to such things as child pornography, commercial speech such as advertising, campaign finance, hate speech or slander. But in the 215 years since the First Amendment came into effect, the urge of the court (largely at the urging of the ACLU) has been to increase protection for vulgarity and decrease protection for society's traditional values and standards.

In essence, the court has taken away the right of society to consider certain kinds of behavior and speech to be shameful, and by removing such restrictions, it has left us vulnerable to the acidic corrupting influences of teen-centered popular culture, Internet pornography and filthy lucre.

Meanwhile, a huge swath of our society celebrates this decline as a healthy enjoyment of liberty, but in the long run the apotheosis of the individual and the vilification of society will have two unavoidable consequences which only a fool could anticipate gladly — moral decay and social collapse.

Now that would be a shame.

COME TO THE AID OF YOUR COUNTRY

May 20, 2007

I used to think we needed to leave the Constitution alone.

That was before the Senate decided to extend citizenship to as many as 20 million lawbreakers whose sole purpose in breaking the law was to gain U.S. citizenship. Talk about making the punishment fit the crime! This punishment fits the crime exactly — they are identical!

Forget about the billions of dollars it will cost the taxpayers of this country to give amnesty to illegal immigrants. Forget about the fact that it will forever change the nature of our country. Forget about the fact that if 9/11 terrorist Mohammed Atta had not blown himself up in the World Trade Center, he would have been eligible for a Z visa under the Senate's plan so that he could enjoy the fruits of American citizenship before he attacked us.

Forget about all that. Even forget the fact that this immigration bill was hammered out in the dark of night by senators who think they can make better law without interference from everyday Americans. Forget the fact that there is every indication that this bill is being bought and paid for by multinational corporations who want a source of cheap labor, and don't care about the future of the United States of America.

Just forget all that, and focus on the fact that for a few more short months, you still have a chance to make a difference. Think about how unresponsive your government is, and how you have no confidence that your senators or even your congressman will do what is best for this country, and then ask yourself who is going to fix it if you don't.

Yeah you. Because I am pretty sure you scare the bejeezus out of Mr. Congressman and Mr. Senator.

If you are waiting for them to fix the problems in this country you will wait for a long time. The Senate and the House do not speak for you. They speak for the campaign contributors who financed them into office. It is time that the real rulers speak up, and that is "We the People."

It is time for "We the People" to run our own country for a change, and not assume that someone else is doing it for us. We can do that, if we do it quickly, by seizing control of the Constitution and stopping the Congress from giving away our country to the foreigners who have invaded it.

All it would take is a simple amendment to establish that citizenship shall not be granted to anyone who entered the country illegally. It should also establish that citizenship is not granted automatically to anyone born in the United States while their parents are here illegally. And finally such an amendment should spell out that it is the duty of the commander in chief to act to secure the borders of the country against foreign intrusions of any kind. The amendment could also establish the authority of the Congress to regulate legal immigration but rule out blanket amnesty of any kind for illegal residents of this country.

The problem, of course, is that such an amendment could never pass in Congress. Congress has no interest in securing our borders, and certainly the president has proven time and again that he has absolutely no desire to protect the rights of American citizens against the costly invasion from Mexico and elsewhere.

So that means we are doomed, right?

Not quite.

Listen to what the Constitution says about the amendment process:

"The Congress, whenever two thirds of both Houses shall deem it necessary, shall propose Amendments to this Constitution, or, on the Application of the Legislatures of two thirds of the several States, shall call a Convention for proposing Amendments, which, in either Case, shall be valid to all Intents and Purposes, as part of this Constitution, when ratified by the Legislatures of three fourths of the several States, or by Conventions in three fourths thereof, as the one or the other Mode of Ratification may be proposed by the Congress..."

As a matter of historical record, all of the 27 amendments ratified and joined to the Constitution thus far have originated with the Congress. But it may be time for the Legislatures of the several states to act, and act swiftly, to demand a constitutional convention to establish once and for all the will of "We the People." It would not by any means be easy to get 34 states to call such a convention, but this is do or die.

Every special interest group in the country would be terrified of what such a convention might do, but that is the point. It is time for the special interests to stop running this country, and for "We the People" to take it back. Thomas Jefferson would have thought we were long overdue. In a letter to James Madison in 1789, he said that "no society can make a perpetual constitution or even a perpetual law. The earth belongs always to the living generation." In the same letter he warned that the people's "power of repeal" was not of great value because it depended on representation in the legislature which was "unequal and vicious," and warned that the people's representatives were tainted by factionalism, corruption and personal interest. Today, we would call it party politics, campaign finance, and ambition, but the message is the same — don't trust the Congress to represent your interests. They have their own agenda.

Today, in this so-called immigration reform bill we have the best example we will ever need. This bill is not immigration reform; it is national reform — a fundamental change in the rules of citizenship — and it must not be allowed to stand.

WHY 'WE THE PEOPLE' MATTER ...

May 27, 2007

In the France of Louis XIV, the king could say without a shred of irony, "L'etat, c'est moi! The state, it is I."

In the years following the adoption of the U.S. Constitution, Americans could proudly say, "The state, it is we the people."

But in this day and age, who exactly is invested with sovereignty in the United States of America? Is it "we the people"? And if so, why do we feel so disenfranchised, so alienated, so used?

Or is it the president? Could it be? Then why does he look so drawn and haggard, so diminished and so beaten?

Or perhaps sovereignty today belongs to the Congress of the United States? Could our elected representatives have seized power from us, right under our noses, and left us none the wiser?

It sure feels that way to many of us who watched the Quentin Tarantino-choreographed pantomime in the Senate the past two weeks as all 326 pages of the "comprehensive immigration reform" bill were shoved down America's throat to the tune of "La Cucaracha."

The senators claim that America wants — no, demands — "comprehensive immigration reform," so the senators all have cleaned their hands just like jesting Pilate when he freed Barabbas and sent Jesus to his death. Only doing what America wants, they say. But America doesn't want reform that throws up its hands in surrender; it wants reform that enforces the law and enforces the border. It doesn't want immigration reform; it wants immigration control. It doesn't want a government that washes its hands; it wants a government that does its job.

Which is why last week I proposed that the people of the United States, through their state legislatures, ought to take back the reins of power and ask for — no, demand! — a convention to propose amendments to the U.S. Constitution — in particular, an amendment that requires border enforcement and denies citizenship to anyone in this country illegally, including those who were born here because their parents were here illegally.

If you think it is going to happen any other way, you are mistaken. And if you think the Constitution should not be handled by "we the people" because it is too fragile and too delicate, then you missed the point of having a Constitution. We are a self-governing people. It is not "we the dead people" who have the power in this country; it is "we the living."

But yet I have heard from many people who are afraid that a constitutional convention would give power to the wrong people — presumably the left wing of the Democratic Party or the right wing of the Republican Party — who would strip away all the liberties enshrined in the Constitution.

Such a fear is absurd for two reasons. First of all, it would never happen. The "convention to propose amendments" to the Constitution would do just that — propose. Any amendment proposed by the convention would still have to be ratified by three-quarters of the several states, which currently means 38 state legislatures would need to approve any changes. It is safe to assume that wholesale changes to our fundamental liberties would not survive such a process.

Second, it is absurd because such changes could only be accomplished if they represented the will of "we the people" — and to deny the will of "we the people" is to deny the whole principle, basis and intent of the Constitution in the first place.

God forbid that anyone tamper willy-nilly with that divinely inspired document, but also God forbid that anyone deny "we the people" the authority of self-government. Our forefathers did not write the Constitution to enslave us, but rather to empower us — and to protect us from either tyranny or mob rule.

In fact, you can think of the Constitution as the chariot which tamed the power of a pair of dangerous, belligerent snorting horses named Majority and Minority.

Those two stallions, not quite thoroughbreds, always want to go in opposite directions, and without the constitutional chariot of a republic to harness them, they would always be trying to overthrow each other. Majority is the bigger, meatier horse and has the natural advantage to dominate and destroy the much smaller Minority, but that does not mean the matter can be so simply decided. It turns out that even the tiny Minority can use terror and fear like a set of pincer teeth to keep Majority at bay, and in some ways that is an even more frightening picture.

So the strictures of the Constitution, which keep both the rough and tumble Majority and lean and hungry Minority in check, were clearly a brilliant feat of social engineering. You certainly would not want to tamper with it.

But on the other hand you probably would not want to leave it alone either, anymore than you would leave your 1967 Rolls Royce alone. You would not let just anyone mess with it, but you would surely expect a certified mechanic to do the necessary work to keep it running in smooth order.

That finally is what I realized about the Constitution, too. For a long time I mistakenly thought that if we had a constitutional convention, it would be like throwing dynamite into the chariot. But then I realized that a constitutional convention was not about tampering with the Constitution, but rather about bringing in an expert mechanic to look at it and figure out why it is chugging and clicking instead of whirring and purring.

Because the expert about the Constitution is not a blue-blood senator, and it is not the president, nor even the good men and women of the Supreme Court. The expert about the Constitution, and the one mechanic you would want to call in if things started to go wrong is "We the People."

Which is why a great many people who give lip service to the ideals of democracy quiver at the thought of actually trying it. Such people, and I'm not at all sure if they are mostly liberals or mostly conservatives, will tell you that the Constitution is too valuable and rarefied to be messed with by common folk.

But one thing our Founding Fathers were is ingenious. They seemed to anticipate many of the conflicts that would inevitably ensue in a constitutional republic, and provided safety valves in the somewhat ambiguously worded document so that if at all possible the Constitution would be self-correcting as the decades and then centuries passed.

Most obviously they provided for amendments to the Constitution to be made when experience and reason taught us that something was amiss. That amendment process has been used sparingly — just 27 times in the past 220 years — which is testament to the enduring quality of the workmanship in the original Constitutional Convention.

But we should not assume that a lack of change is automatically a good thing. It took, for instance, 78 years, from the ratification of the original Constitution to the admission in the 13th Amendment that slavery ought to be abolished. Other changes came more quickly, such as changing the way presidents and vice presidents were elected in 1804 or repealing the prohibition on liquor just 14 years after it was first passed in 1919.

Change is built into the Constitution, but for the most part the changes made have been relatively minor, relatively technical. Those which are most significant such as the addition of the income tax or giving women the right to vote show how powerful a document the Constitution is, and how much it shapes our society as a whole.

But up until now, all change to the Constitution has been in the hands of Congress. The amendments proposed have all originated there, and been approved by two-thirds of the members of the House and Senate, then ratified by three-quarters of the states. Considering that challenging process, it is surprising that any amendments have ever been approved, let alone the important ones.

That slow and deliberate quality has served us well, and protects us from mistakes which could harm or even imperil our great republic. But such mistakes, have, of course, been with us from the beginning, perhaps most recognizably in slavery and denial of full citizenship to women. Whether we act quickly or slow, we are subject to the same human foibles as all other people, and fool ourselves to think otherwise.

But we also possess the same human majesty which was celebrated and exemplified by our Founding Fathers, and by such token we should not be afraid to seize the power granted to us by our forbears and by God in order to revivify the words of Thomas Jefferson in the Declaration of Independence that "Governments are instituted among Men, deriving their just Powers from the consent of the governed" and "That whenever any Form of Government becomes destructive of these ends, it is the Right of the People to alter or to abolish it, and to institute new Government..."

It may be scary to think about changing the Constitution, but living in fear of consequences is a guarantee of paralysis, and paralysis is a guarantee of atrophy and ultimately dissolution. Jefferson was our foremost political philosopher at the start of our republic, and he argued forcefully for change in the Constitution that would keep it current and honest. Indeed, he promoted the idea of a constant freshening of government by the forced entry of We the People into the halls of power in every generation.

Thus, taking my cue from Jefferson, I am calling for a constitutional convention to quickly and once and for all establish the duty and necessity of the commander in chief acting to secure the borders of the country against foreign intrusions of any kind and establishing the authority of the Congress to regulate legal immigration but never to provide blanket amnesty of any kind for illegal residents of this country.

Such drastic action is necessary because it now becomes apparent that the people of the United States can no longer depend on the Congress of the United States to do our business. A constitutional convention may well be the only way to deprive the Senate of its plan to legitimize as many as 20 million illegal immigrants and change the face of America for all time.

The Senate's smug, secret plan was introduced two weeks ago with great fanfare, as if the people might not notice that our sovereignty was being sold for a mess of pottage. But even if that "comprehensive plan" goes away in defeat, the problem will remain. There is no enforcement of border security or of immigration control. We certainly cannot depend on the Senate to fix the problem.

Perhaps, the senators are so out of touch with reality that they are truly convinced that what they are doing is supported by the great mass of the American people. Or perhaps the Senate is convinced it can get away with anything it wants regardless of the people. I'm not sure which of those delusions is more accurate, but it leads me to decide that the time has come for Jefferson's ideal to be implemented.

Let's take back our Constitution, and take back our country.

A WARNING ABOUT PEACE WITHOUT VICTORY — IN 1942

October 7, 2007

A little knowledge is said to be a dangerous thing, but perhaps even a little history is better than none. It at least provides the possibility of perspective as we try to navigate the reefs of modernity.

Case in point comes from a World War II era newspaper which arrived at my desk almost arbitrarily two weeks ago, and which shed extraordinary light on our own contemporary wartime crisis with a seven-inch story that appeared on Page Two.

The newspaper was the Coos Bay Times of Oregon, and the date was June 4, 1942. Get that date through your head — June 4, 1942 — less than six months after the attack on Pearl Harbor by the Japanese air force that left nearly 3,000 people dead and the U.S. Navy crippled.

The headline was somewhat suggestive, but unclear to a 21st-century reader: "Thurman Arnold Warns Against New Peace Moves by International Units."

The lede provided a little more explanation: "Thurman W. Arnold, special assistant U.S. attorney general, warned last night in an address to the Illinois Bar Association against the influences for a negotiated peace which 'would leave our enemies still strong enough to prepare for another war.'"

That phrasing piqued my interest for what parallels might exist between the peace movement of World War II and the peace movement of 2007. To be honest, I did not know there was a peace movement in June of 1942, so shortly after we had been attacked by an enemy that brazenly provoked us into battle.

But the cautionary note sounded by Mr. Arnold (also unknown to me before this time) was remarkably evocative of the risk that I and others perceive in the Democratic demand for withdrawal from Iraq.

Certainly it is easy to argue about how or why we got into the war in Iraq in the first place. Democrats love to do so. It is also easy to complain about the manner in which the war has been waged. I do so vociferously.

But to fail to realize that we have an enemy in Iraq is sheer folly. To fail to recognize that we have enemies throughout the Mideast is insanity. And to strengthen or embolden those enemies by allowing them to watch us retreat impotently back to our homeland is frightening at best. Indeed, as Mr. Arnold said about the Germans and Japanese, a negotiated peace (or timed withdrawal) "would leave our enemies still strong enough to prepare for another war."

The next paragraph of the United Press report from 1942 is perhaps the most instructive:

"Arnold cautioned against the possibility of a 'second Munich' through the secret influence of an international cartel thrown in favor of peace without victory when the first opportunity arises."

Peace without victory... what a pungent phrase! That is clearly what Sens. Barack Obama, Harry Reid, John Kerry, Dick Durbin, Chuck Schumer and Hillary Clinton are after. They don't deny it. This is not name-calling. It is a simple fact check.

Winston Churchill beseeched the British people to seek victory at any cost in World War II. "You ask, what is our aim? I can answer in one word: Victory — victory at all costs, victory in spite of all terror, victory, however long and hard the road may be; for without victory there is no survival."

But such an entreaty must be based on a firm belief in the strength of one's enemy. No doubt the Democrats I have named above, and others, do not consider the Islamic fundamentalists who spawn terrorism to be a serious enemy, one that can — as Churchill recognized about fascism — threaten the very survival of our way of life.

So instead of seeking victory, these Democrats seek peace. In their own minds, it is a reasonable and wise end, for it will save the lives of hundreds and perhaps thousands of our brave soldiers. Peace is naturally to be preferred over a state of war by all reasonable people, and so it is easy to convince the American people to seek peace — peace at any cost — because only peace will allow us to enjoy the quality of life we have worked so hard to achieve.

Unfortunately, peace is not a permanent condition. As soon as it is declared, it begins to dissipate. Like the universe we live in, which is constantly in a state of transition from order to disorder (known as entropy to physicists) the human condition is constantly in a state of transition from order to disorder (known as human cussedness to front-porch philosophers).

Both kinds of disorder can be kept in check, but only by an expenditure of considerable energy. In the case of the universe, life itself is the most notable exception to the tendency of all things to decay, but even the engine that burns inside all of us also eventually burns out. Chaos eventually prevails.

The disorder of the human condition is kept in check, too, by a variety of external forces such as police, religion, government, mores, and — yes — armies. But so far, there has always been a limit to how long a society can maintain itself against the forces of disorder that constantly seek to tear it apart. "The glory that was Greece, the grandeur that was Rome" are no more, except in the poet's words and the historian's pen. Ditto the empires of Assyria, Egypt, Czarist Russia, and Her Royal Majesty. As William Butler Yeats accurately noted, "Things fall apart."

Perhaps, given all that, it would be better to just surrender to the inevitable, declare the era of American influence to be over, retreat to our shores, and await the conquering army that eventually will visit our shore (or the silent invasion that could nibble us to death from within).

As Neville Chamberlain declared when he returned to England from Munich with that piece of paper signed by him and the devil Hitler, "Peace for our time," so too it might be worth a listen to the folks who think we can appease our Islamic foes with a timed withdrawal from Iraq. The only problem is that with the sad history of the Munich Agreement behind us, we would no longer be able to declare "Peace for our time," but rather "Peace FOR a time." A brief time. In the case of Chamberlain's appeasement, he bought a total of six months of peace before Hitler drove his Nazi armies through the rest of Czechoslovakia while laughing at the British prime minister whom he called "an impertinent busybody."

Thurman Arnold knew all of this, not from history books, but from living through it. That's why his complaint about a "second Munich" is so potent.

It is interesting, finally, to note that the "international units" that Arnold feared would get us OUT of war were what he called "the international cartels which permeate the structure of American industry."

Today, Democrats fear that such international cartels (or the multinational corporations we more commonly speak of today) are getting us INTO wars and keeping us in Iraq. Such a possibility always exists and must be vigilantly guarded against. Modern warfare should never be waged for personal aggrandizement or corporate or national enrichment. If I really thought the war in Iraq were being fought to increase oil profits for Exxon or Halliburton, I would be against it, too — or else I would be much more pragmatic in my support of it.

But the history of the world is a history of kings, crowns, emperors and tycoons making money in both war and peace. There is no reason to believe ExxonMobil won't make money after U.S. forces leave Iraq; nor is there any reason to hope they don't make money while the war continues. What happens to ExxonMobil is frankly irrelevant, or should be, to our foreign policy.

Just as Assistant Attorney General Arnold warned against shaping foreign policy during World War II on the interests of "the small group of American businessmen who are parties to these international rings," it behooves us also not to shape foreign policy based on the interests of Halliburton.

Let us instead focus on the effect on the nation and world of "peace without victory." Let us ask what kind of peace we will buy if we leave Iraq to its own devices, and for how long we will have that peace. The notion of an Iraq carved up by an emboldened Iran, a strengthened Saudi Arabia, a genocidal Turkey, and a suicidal Syria does not give me any hope of "peace for our time."

Let each of us make our decision and then live with our conscience as we vote for our leaders and the future they will bring us. Peace is one possible outcome. Survival is another. The question of whether both are possible at the same time has yet to be decided, but certainly the forces of peace are strong.

It was the same in 1938. While still the crowds were cheering Chamberlain for his Munich "peace agreement," Churchill lamented in the House of Commons what he called "a total and unmitigated defeat... a disaster of the first magnitude... a defeat without war... an awful milestone in our history..." Perhaps he looked like a grumpy old man, a greedy neo-con, or a lackey for some clansman of George W. Bush, but he made a stand, and he stuck by it.

As he said then, perhaps we will say soon: "[T]he terrible words have for the time being been pronounced against the Western democracies: 'Thou art weighed in the balance and found wanting.' And do not suppose that this is the end. This is only the beginning of the reckoning. This is only the first sip, the first foretaste of a bitter cup which will be proffered to us year by year unless by a supreme recovery of moral health and martial vigour, we arise again and take our stand for freedom as in the olden time."

Or perhaps, as empires always do, we will just fade away.

A HEALTHY DEBATE ABOUT HEALTH CARE — OR: JUST SAY NO TO FREE STUFF YOU CAN'T AFFORD

October 28, 2007

The last time I looked, insurance was a business, not a social service.

But maybe I had better look more closely because after listening to Hillary Clinton, Arnold Schwarzenegger and numerous other politicians who are eager for votes, I am starting to think maybe health insurance is not a business at all, and not even just a social service, but actually an entitlement.

Here's how health insurance works, or at least how it had always worked until the government got involved:

It's really not that complicated. You pay money today as a gamble that you are going to get sick in the future. Insurance companies take your bet because they have statistics which show the likelihood you are going to get sick. The higher the likelihood, the higher your premiums (the money you put at risk).

If you don't get sick, then the insurance company has won the bet. You are out the cost of the premiums, and they don't have to pay you anything. Of course, you still have your good health and you didn't have to suffer any anxiety over how you would pay your medical bills if you did get sick.

If you actually got sick, on the other hand, then you would still be out the cost of the premiums, but the insurance company would have to pick up a large percentage of the cost of your actual medical care. In that case, the insurance company loses the bet.

That's good for you, but of course if the insurers lose too many bets they go out of business. That's why they base rates on actuarial tables to clearly delineate how much everyone should pay for their insurance to make it a profitable business. That's also why some people are uninsurable. If someone already has cancer, his or her premiums would basically have to equal or surpass the expected cost of the medical care or it would make no sense for the insurer to take the risk.

I don't know why I have to explain this. It should be pretty obvious to everyone. Insurance is not a new concept. But since Congress discovered they have way too much money on hand, politicians have been trying to think of new ways to spend all the extra dough. And because everyone gets sick some time, apparently some folks in government decided a good way to spend the billions of dollars of extra money would be to help the insurance companies pay for health care for people who don't have enough money to gamble on their own.

Notice: There are two fallacies in this proposal.

The first fallacy should be obvious to anyone. The government does not have any extra money! In fact, our government owes $9 trillion, give or take a few billion. That is what we call the national debt, but really, it is not owed by the government; it is owed by you and me. Every time some politician gets another bright idea to give away a million dollars here or $250,000 there, it comes out of your pocket. Don't just believe me; ask your pocket.

The second fallacy may be more subtle. What is being called "health insurance" by the politicians is nothing of the sort. As we have already established, insurance is a financial gamble where you put money at risk on the chance that you will reap a reward later. Notice the word "risk." But the only one assuming any risk in the "feel-good" version of insurance being proposed by Clinton, Obama, Edwards and the gang is the American taxpayer. What they are talking about is "free health care," not insurance. But it is only free for the sick person; instead of them paying for their own care, you and I pay for it.

That's a nice, pleasant sentiment, and I wholly support the government establishing an independent agency like the Postal Service which can accept charitable contributions to be used to pay for health care. Everyone who thinks they have extra money that they don't need for their own families can send a check to the Charitable Health Service, and people who are sick can apply for money to be given out on the basis of need. A voluntary system of this sort, which clearly would have the backing of the entire Democratic Party, should be able to ensure that everyone can get health care, even illegal immigrants.

Which brings us to the unstated third fallacy of the health-care debate, the one which is pivotal and sadly which is accepted as truth by the vast majority of people. It is this: If there is something that is good for me, I am entitled to it, whether I can afford it or not.

Is there a medicine available that might extend my life by a month or two? I want it, even if it costs $200,000 per month. Is there a treatment which might, just possibly, give me a better chance to survive the lung cancer I got because I chose to smoke for 30 years? I want it, even if it costs $2 million. And I don't want to pay for it, so let's call it "health insurance." That way I can have it and not feel guilty for taking the free ride. Am I too sick to be insurable? Tough. I still want it. Am I not human?

But the fact of the matter is we cannot have everything we want just because it is good for us or just because we are human. Modern science has already doubled the average life expectancy in just over a century — without free health insurance! But if we expect every person to have the right to take advantage of every form of medical care ever invented, then we may as well just send ourselves to debtor's prison today, because we can't afford it. Or maybe we should just send ourselves to the asylum — because we are clearly insane. (At least there will be no cost for our care!)

Of course, pointing out that not everyone in the world can afford the same level of health care makes me a horrible person. I am well aware of that, so please let's get beyond the name-calling and into the facts of the argument. The fact is, there are many things in this world which would be good for us, but we accept that we cannot afford them, and move on with our lives.

For instance, it would have been good for me to be able to attend an Ivy League college, but my family couldn't pay the bill. It would be good for me (and my circulation) if I could afford to fly first-class, but I can't, so I ride in economy and stand up every half hour or so to stretch my legs. It would be good for me to eat steak every night (all right, maybe not good for me, but very tasty), yet I eat ramen about three nights a week and steak maybe once a month because it suits my budget better. I even think it would be good for me to be riding in a 2008 BMW instead of a 1996 Saturn, but my checkbook says otherwise.

This used to be called living within one's means. Today, it is called being a chump. I don't care what they call it. The fact of the matter is there ain't no such thing as a free lunch. All of that "free" health care is costing somebody plenty. If you want that somebody to be you, then call your senators and congressman and tell them to vote for national health insurance and send the bill to your house.

But opt me out. I can't afford it.

WHAT WOULD TEDDY DO?

December 2, 2007

More and more these days, as the world turns topsy-turvy, I find myself asking, "WWTRD?" — What would Teddy Roosevelt do?

How would Teddy Roosevelt handle it if an American citizen were locked up in the Sudan for teaching a classroom of 7-year-olds who had named a stuffed bear Muhammad? Even forgetting about Roosevelt's interest in making sure that all such bears should be named Teddy, we can assume he would see the absurdity of the situation, which actually exists today for a British woman. Would TR let the woman suffer 40 lashes of the whip as originally intended by the "court"? Would he even allow her to remain in jail for the 15-day sentence while mobs roamed the streets outside with swords demanding her head?

And what would Roosevelt do about Osama bin Laden? How would he react to the death and destruction at the Twin Towers, just a few short miles from his birthplace in the Gramercy neighborhood of Manhattan? Would he be more concerned about offending Muslim sensibilities or more concerned about getting the killers no matter how hard it was or how long it took?

You don't even have to ask what TR would think about illegal immigration. He as much as told us in a letter to the American Defense Society in 1919:

In the first place we should insist that the immigrant who comes here in good faith becomes an American and assimilates himself to us. He shall be treated on an exact equity with everyone else, for it is an outrage to discriminate against any such man because of creed, or birthplace or origin.

"But this is predicated upon the man's becoming an American and nothing but an American. There can be no divided allegiance here. Any man who says he is an American but something else also, isn't an American at all.

"We have room for but one flag, the American flag, and this excludes the red flag which symbolizes all wars against liberty and civilization, just as much as it excludes any flag of a nation to which we are hostile.

"We have room for but one language here, and that is the English language... and we have room for but one sole loyalty and that is a loyalty to the American people."

It is not too hard to imagine that Roosevelt would also expect immigrants to our country to follow the rules and regulations set up for them, thus not tolerate illegal immigration. Why exactly, after all, should we tolerate illegality in anything?

Of course, that is mere idle speculation, because Teddy Roosevelt could not exist today. His outspoken, some would say politically incorrect, manner; his racial Darwinism; his belief in the supremacy of civilization over barbarism; his willingness to use force to accomplish his goals — all of these would have disqualified him from a life of public service.

Even his time as a war hero would have worked against him. If it had occurred in this decade, the Spanish-American War would have been known as Bush's Blunder, and Roosevelt's participation would have been subject to endless congressional hearings to find out why he had not respected the enemy sufficiently. The Rough Riders unit he headed up would be considered roughly the equivalent of the so-called Blackwater mercenaries of the Iraq war, except they didn't get paid so well; they just liked to shoot and carry on.

But Roosevelt, nonetheless, remains an icon of the untamed American spirit — a man born of Eastern wealth, he had gone West after the tragedy of losing his mother and wife to disease on the same day in 1884. In a few short years in the Badlands of North Dakota, a stone's throw from Montana, young Roosevelt sponged up all the energy and excitement of the Wild West that he could. He was a rancher, a deputy sheriff, a raconteur and a big-game hunter.

Then he took that experience, went back east after a disastrous winter wiped out his herd of cattle, and wrote an influential four-volume history called "The Winning of the

West." A few years later, he began his career of public service in earnest. He worked on the U.S. Civil Service Commission, was president of the board of the New York City Police Commissioners (where he played a key role as the reformer of a corrupt system) and then became assistant secretary of the Navy, where he prepared the Navy for the Spanish-American War. It was during this time that he made one of the many statements which would disqualify him for public office today: "I should welcome almost any war, for I think this country needs one." Under modern rules of etiquette, a country cannot need a war unless it is in the throes of a fascist dictatorship (also known as the Bush presidency in certain circles).

It was the Spanish-American War which cemented Roosevelt's reputation for being a man of action, as well as a man of ideas. It also catapulted him to a successful campaign for governor of New York in 1898 on the Republican ticket. His penchant for reform and rooting out corruption apparently made him unpopular with the Republican machine in New York and thus, to get him out of the way, he was named as President McKinley's running mate in 1900. McKinley won in a landslide against William Jennings Bryan, but was assassinated late in 1901, elevating Roosevelt to the presidency.

_It was there that he exercised his greatest influence on our nation and the world, accomplishing much through the sheer power of his will and according to the virtues of his own moral code. Indeed, it is impossible to imagine a modern president accomplishing anywhere near as much as Roosevelt did.

Quite soon, he developed a reputation as a "trust-buster," taking on corporate tycoons who had amassed wealth and power through the establishment of monopolies that prevented competition. He also pushed Congress to establish a system to regulate food and drugs which essentially is still in place today. It was, of course, also Roosevelt who promoted the establishment of the U.S. Forest Service and set aside 194 million acres for national parks and nature preserves. Such treasures as Glacier National Park owe their legacy of preservation to Roosevelt's foresight and love of nature.

It was perhaps in foreign affairs, however, that Roosevelt made his greatest impact of all. Certainly changing the world forever was the construction of the Panama Canal, a project made possible by willpower, money and a little bit of leverage to get Panama to declare its independence from Columbia. Of course, today we would be told that such a project is impossible, just as a border fence is impossible, but Roosevelt did not let impossibility stop him.

That stubbornness may also be how he won the Nobel Peace Prize, thanks to his bully negotiations to end the Russo-Japanese War in 1905. This conflict and a later conflict between France and Germany, which Roosevelt also helped to defuse, could easily have escalated into a world war.

It is well known that Roosevelt's motto was to "talk softly but carry a big stick." In such a manner, he was willing to use American force to project our power on the world without necessarily have to fight to do it. Most notably he greatly increased the size of the Navy and sent a fleet around the world to be gawked at by our friends and foes. He also established that the threat of force was sometimes enough, as in his standoff with the Moroccan renegade Ahmed ben Mohammed el Raisuli, which was popularized in the film "The Wind and the Lion."

Likewise Teddy declared that American power could be used to intervene in Latin American countries, but he was wise enough to not bite off more than he could chew. When elements in the Dominican Republic were seeking annexation in 1904, he said, in typically colorful fashion, "I have about the same desire to annex it as a gorged boa constrictor might have to swallow a porcupine."

The fact of the matter is that Teddy Roosevelt could not exist anymore, and neither could Teddy Roosevelt's America. We are neither smart enough, strong enough, or daring enough to do what is right no matter the cost. So although we may ponder, "What would Teddy Roosevelt do?" — we are stuck with the same old question as always, "What are we going to do?" and the same sad answer, "Vote for the lesser of two evils and hope for the best."

IT'S THE JUDGES WHO NEED
A LEGAL GUARDIAN

October 5, 2008

Rule of law in this country has been replaced by rule of judges.

In case after case, citizens have watched as judges assumed sovereignty and ruled, like Humpty Dumpty, that the law is "just what they choose it to mean — neither more nor less."

The latest case of such legal hubris comes from Missoula, Montana, where a judge has ruled that a parent is whoever he decides is a parent, regardless of what the law says.

Here, in summary, is the case:

Barbara Maniaci adopted two children, a son in 2004 and a daughter in 2006, while she was engaged in a live-in partnership with another woman, Michelle Kulstad. The two women had lived together in the Missoula area for about 10 years before breaking up in 2006, but Maniaci had adopted the children on her own as a single parent. Maniaci later married a man and expected to raise her two children with her husband as she saw fit, but Kulstad had other ideas. She went to court and sought joint custody of the children, arguing that she had been like a mother to the boy and girl. On Monday, Sept. 29, District Judge Ed McLean ruled in favor of Kulstad.

Using language that clearly was intended to shame Maniaci and the rest of us who believe in common sense, McLean wrote, "To discriminate further against Ms. Kulstad because of her sexual preference in this day and age is no different than telling a person to go to the back of the bus because of their skin color."

Huh? Say what?

This wasn't a case about sexual preference; it was a case about adoption law — about what the law permits and what it doesn't permit. And the judge clearly overstepped his bounds.

What should have been at play was the fact that Maniaci of her own free will adopted two small children. She went through the appropriate legal process to do so, and with Ms. Kulstad's full understanding that only Maniaci was the legal parent. In everyone's mind except Judge McLean's, it is quite clear that saying you are a parent does not make you one. And shacking up with someone, whether of the same sex or not, should not be seen as a way to bypass adoption law in order to sneak into a parental relationship with someone else's children.

Maniaci's lawyers wasted no time in appealing the case to the Montana Supreme Court, and now we can only hope wisdom will prevail over McLean's brief but harrowing reign as a judicial despot.

The fact of the matter is the whole of the matter should have been resolved quite simply. There is plainly no statute that makes cohabitation a means to gain parental rights. Yes, hopefully, people who move into a household will be caring and nurturing of children who live with them, but in this age of liquid relationships, it makes no sense to confuse children with the possibility of serial parenthood as each new live-in boyfriend becomes the latest to gain custody rights.

And remember, what is supposed to prevail is the best interests of the child, not the best interest of former boyfriends and girlfriends.

No one is saying this is a case where Kulstad doesn't have an emotional connection with the children, and perhaps she could convince the children's legal mother, Barbara Maniaci, to allow her to visit occasionally as a courtesy. But that is a far cry from the court telling Maniaci, who followed the legal and proper procedure for adoption, that she must share custody with someone who avoided a legal connection with the children until she decided it was convenient to have one.

Perhaps there is no simple solution in matters of family law. That is understandable. You are dealing with real people, not corporate entities. But there are clues in the law that suggest McLean was wrongheaded in his judicial reasoning. Take Title 40, Section 4, Part 228 of the Montana Code Annotated, for instance. Therein, it is plainly established that when a nonparent seeks to establish a parental interest in a child, they must first prove by "clear and convincing evidence" that "the natural parent has engaged in conduct that is contrary to the child-parent relationship."

Although adoptive parents are not "natural parents," they are given by law the same rights and responsibilities, and thus the court should have held Kulstad to the standard of proving that Maniaci had proven herself unfit to be a mother. Lacking that, Kulstad should have been told that the court did not have authority to substitute its judgment for the agency which had found Maniaci to be a suitable parent in herself and on her own.

In the trial, Kulstad reportedly told the court that she was not listed on the children's adoption records "because it is illegal in Montana for same-sex couples to adopt." That might give her argument a little more weight, and might even make the judge's over-the-top language seem appropriate, but the fact of the matter is Kulstad's claim is not accurate.

According to Rose Saxe, an ACLU attorney from New York, (as quoted in an Associated Press article) "Montana law does not specifically address adoption by same-sex partners but does allow a step-parent or someone who functions as a step-parent to adopt."

If Kulstad chose voluntarily not to be part of the adoption proceedings in the first place, then she should forfeit the later right to claim to qualify for parental rights as a step-parent. Again, there is no reason why there should be a backdoor parental privilege granted in this case.

And most importantly, no one wants judges sticking their noses into family business. Unless the children's health and well-being were at stake, the judge should have let their mother decide what was in their best interest. As it stands now, it looks like the judge was more concerned about promoting a liberal social agenda than two happy, healthy children.

OBAMA AND MARX: A CRASH COURSE

October 19, 2008

"A spectre is haunting Europe — the spectre of Communism."

With those words, Karl Marx launched a revolution with "The Communist Manifesto." Interestingly, the opening of his essay, cowritten with Friedrich Engels, begins with the assertion that the European powers are using the "branding reproach of Communism" to label their opponents. Marx then says, "It is high time the communists should openly, in the face of the whole world, publish their views, their aims, their tendencies, and meet this nursery tale of the spectre of Communism with a Manifesto of the party itself."

If Marx were alive today and living in San Francisco, perhaps he would have instead written this: "A spectre is haunting Democratic politics — the spectre of socialism." Certainly, the "branding reproach of socialism" is now publicly acknowledged to have been used against the Democratic Party, and against its standard bearer, Barack Obama. It is high time for Obama and his allies to publicly assert their political and economic philosophy. If it is socialism, say so. If it is not, please explain why.

This, of course, is made immediately relevant by Obama's famous comment to Joe the Plumber that, "I think when you spread the wealth around, it's good for everybody." In particular he was talking about his tax plan, which is a plan for redistribution of wealth from top to bottom.

This is a matter of fact. When Obama tells you that his tax plan will benefit 95 percent of taxpayers, he is misstating the truth. The fact is that 30 to 40 percent of Americans, the poorest among us, already don't pay any taxes. But what Obama's plan will do is allow them to sign up for a variety of tax credits, so the government will send them a check for a couple thousand dollars or more every year. Where does the money come from to make those payments? From Americans who do pay taxes. It literally is redistribution of wealth. Instead of using taxes to pay for the necessities of infrastructure and defense that they were intended for, the government as envisioned by Obama will be "spreading the wealth around."

The question is whether Americans care. And if they don't, why not?

Ask yourself, why did we spend 50 years after World War II fighting a Cold War to eliminate communism if we actually believe in it? Is this nation actually prepared to admit we were wrong, and Karl Marx was right? Marx's credo, "From each according to his ability; to each according to his need," has a nice ring. It can easily be seen as an institutionalized form of Christian charity — providing for the less able, or the less advantaged. But look at the results of communism and socialism in Europe, and you will quickly conclude that any philosophical niceties are vastly outweighed by the political realities.

When you look at Marx's list of goals for communism in chapter two of "The Communist Manifesto" (www.marxists.org/archive/marx/works/1848/communist-manifesto/ch02.htm), you can see that socialism has already made great advances in the United States. But in particular pay attention to No. 2 — "A heavy progressive or graduated income tax."

In this regard, Obama has outdone Marx himself. A progressive tax just puts a greater share of the burden on the rich. We already have long since had such a tax. But now Obama wants to find a way to hand out money to the poor. Is it any wonder that he is ahead in the polls?

As Ben Franklin reputedly said, "When the people find they can vote themselves money, that will herald the end of the republic."

LIVING WITH OUR POLITICAL LOSSES

November 16, 2008

One of the curious attributes of democracy is that the minority is always "wrong." Not morally wrong, mind you. Just on the wrong side of a political divide that can be as big as a mountain or as small as a single vote.

It's frustrating, to say the least — especially if you are convinced that you are morally right and yet politically powerless.

Nonetheless, moral absolutes can't be undone by elections, and political decisions can't be overturned by moral polemic.

That's just a fact of life. Morality and politics, after all, are two separate spheres which only on rare occasion are in perfect alignment.

As a result, those of us who live under a system that employs the trappings of democracy have to agree to abide by outcomes that may disappoint us, distress us, or even injure us. The pro-life forces who want to see abortion made illegal are a classic case of that. They have fought, ever since Roe vs. Wade was declared the law of the land in 1973, to overturn legal protections for abortion, yet they have been by and large unsuccessful. Although these folks believe murder is being done in their name, they have thus had to accept the result with prayer and protest.

More recently, gay-rights advocates suffered a loss in California when voters there, in a much-publicized vote on Proposition 8, amended the state Constitution to say that "only marriage between a man and a woman is valid or recognized in California."

California voters had already declared their support for heterosexual marriage and opposition to homosexual marriage in the year 2000. Proposition 22, which passed then with a 61-37 percent majority, revised state law to say that "only marriage between a man and a woman is valid or recognized in California." That law had remained on the books until earlier this year when the California Supreme Court declared it to be unconstitutional.

Such court intervention can be quite frustrating (there's that word again) for people who don't think courts should be in the business of making law. But nonetheless, that is in fact what courts often do — whether they admit it or not. And whether or not you agree with the morality of gay marriage, the argument that a law is unconstitutional cannot easily be trumped once the high court has spoken. Indeed, as opponents of abortion have found out on the national scene, it is almost impossible to get the court to reverse itself once it has ruled on a constitutional issue.

On the other hand, there is no bar against the people of a jurisdiction following the prescribed procedure and changing their constitution to make clear what is and what is not allowed under that ruling document. That's what the citizens of California did when a court ruled that gay marriage was indeed legal. In a few brief months, they were able to get a constitutional amendment on the ballot that would let voters say once and for all whether the state should recognize gay marriage. The voters decided on Nov. 4 that gay marriage should NOT be legal in California, and yet that strangely enough is not the end of the story.

Almost immediately, opponents of Proposition 8 announced that they would go to court again to get the constitutional amendment declared unconstitutional. For a number of reasons, they are considered to have a good chance of succeeding.

In the meantime, gay-rights advocates are protesting throughout California and nationwide over what they believe to be a denial of their civil rights by California — not to mention by the other 42 states that have constitutional bans or laws against same-sex marriage.

That kind of protest is certainly well within reason, as long as it is done peacefully and without violating other laws. But the question of overturning the will of the people through court intervention is not so reasonable. Here's why:

Elections are the cornerstone of our system of government, whether it is the democratic republic that elects representatives to make laws on our behalf or whether it is the direct democracy inherent in California's system of allowing the people to amend their own Constitution through a simple majority vote.

If elections are going to have credibility and integrity, they also need to have consequences. It is up to all of us to honor the results of our elections, even when we find them to be abhorrent. This is true whether we are talking about the election of a president or the will of the people being expressed on a constitutional issue.

As an example, there are a number of people who made the argument before the recent election that Barack Obama was not a natural born citizen, and thus would be ineligible to be president of the United States. This argument was made publicly and forcefully, and yet the citizenry elected Obama by a fairly wide margin. Were these arguments to succeed in court now, after the election, and somehow forced the removal of Obama from office, it would have the effect of nullifying the clear choice of the people and might very well trigger riots as well. Almost no one would countenance such an outcome, especially if it were accomplished by a court instead of through the impeachment process established by the Constitution.

By the same token, it behooves the gay community to persevere in their cause without short-circuiting elections. They have every right to seek to change the law through legislative or constitutional changes, but they ought not to circumvent the plainly spoken will of the people by crying to the courts. Let's remember: Everything in our system, from the executive branch to the courts to the legislature itself, comes from the power of "we the people."

Government operates on a mandate from us, not the other way around. And if the system is used to thwart the people's will, then all hell will break loose — and that is something hopefully none of us wants to see.

DIVIDED LOYALTIES ... OR JUST CONFUSED?

March 15, 2009

The hydra-headed monster we call our federal government is not going to be tamed by any one of us – certainly not by me, nor by Rush Limbaugh, nor even by someone as powerful as President Obama.

There are too many levels of deception, too much corruption and way too little respect for the Constitution in the halls of power for any individual citizen to be able to make a difference.

It is written that Benjamin Franklin said of the Founding Fathers, "We must all hang together, or assuredly we shall all hang separately." Something similar could be said in these perilous times about the good citizens of the United States: "We must all work together to cut the head off this beast of a government that we have created or it will surely cut off ours."

Everyone can no doubt cite dozens of examples of the government exercising rogue authority over the people, or simply ignoring the popular will, in order to amass greater power to itself. And there is certainly some degree of confusion about just what government should be doing for us when we have become habituated to being fed tender morsels of pork from the public trough. Education, home-loan assistance, health care – just what aren't we entitled to these days?

But that question is easily answered by reading the Constitution and applying a constitutional test to each act of Congress and the president. Unfortunately, it seems as though very few guardians of liberty work for the government, which leaves the job in the hands of "we the people."

The problem is that our public officials seem to have divided loyalties – they are loyal to the voters from the time they announce their intention to run for office until they are elected, and then they are loyal to their political party for as long as practical until their re-election is put in jeopardy. Loyalty to the Constitution seems not to be a factor in the equation.

Consider earmarks. President Obama campaigned on a pledge to reform the earmarks process, but last week he signed an omnibus spending bill that included 8,000 of them.

Of course, he's not alone in finding that earmarks are hard to resist. Sen. Jon Tester of Montana campaigned against earmarks when he was elected in 2006, saying, "I don't support earmarks, period. If a project's a good project ... [it] could withstand scrutiny in front of the entire Congress. I'm not for earmarks because they don't pass public scrutiny with the transparency that our government and our forefathers set up."

Then, of course, Sen. Tester voted to support the omnibus spending bill with its 8,000 earmarks. Like I said, principles seem to change before and after an election.

Or maybe principles don't really exist at all among politicians. As an example, let's look at the recent vote on the District of Columbia House Voting Rights Act. This bill would grant one vote in the House of Representatives to the District of Columbia.

That's certainly a nice, well-intentioned gift to the citizens of D.C. But what it isn't, and never can be, is legal. The Constitution only allows representation in Congress to the several states, and the district is by direct constitutional provision NOT a state. Even the Congressional Research Service advised Congress in 2007 that "it would appear likely that the Congress does not have authority to grant voting representation in the House of Representatives to the District of Columbia."

But that did not stop 61 senators on Feb. 26 from explicitly voting to violate the Constitution. Yes, Senate Bill 160 passed 61-37, and now the only thing standing between you and tyranny is the House of Representatives. If you know a better name than tyranny, kindly send it to me — as the wanton disregard of the rule of law by the legislative body itself would appear to me to meet the test of tyranny.

For the record, Montana's Sen. Max Baucus voted against this abomination. He should be thanked for that. Sen. Tester, on the other hand, voted in favor of bypassing the Constitution for the expedient effect of picking up one more Democrat vote in the House of Representatives. We can be generous and assume he did not understand the vote, so I encourage everyone to write to the senator, and explain that the Congress cannot amend the Constitution without the consent of the states.

These are two small examples of how politicians in Washington do whatever they want or whatever their political parties want — not what is right or what is constitutional or even what they said they would do. If you need more examples, just read this newspaper every day and you will find them. An informed citizenry, as was noted by Thomas Jefferson, is "the only sure reliance for the preservation of our liberty."

PROTECTING PARENTHOOD

April 19, 2009

The Montana Supreme Court has a chance to set right a monumental injustice, and this time what hangs in the balance is not the fate of a death-row inmate, but something just as important — the future of the American family.

Barbara Maniaci is asking the high court to come down from the mountain with the legal equivalent of the Ten Commandments, or more particularly the traditional Fifth Commandment: "Honor thy father and mother."

What she hopes for from the distinguished justices is no less than a promise that the state of Montana will, must and should "honor the mothers and fathers" of all legally recognized families, and shall not take away inalienable parental rights or bestow them upon others because of a political agenda that would allow gay rights to trump family law

Yet Dr. Maniaci must have precious slim hope indeed, based on what has happened to her so far in district court, where politics, not law, was the basis for a ruling that forced her to share her adopted children with a woman who for all intents and purposes was a legal stranger to them.

Maniaci and Michelle Kulstad had lived together as a couple for 10 years, starting in 1995 or 1996. Late in that time period, Maniaci legally adopted two children, a son in 2004 and a daughter in 2006. Kulstad and Maniaci were never legally married, nor did Kulstad adopt the children herself. Yet when the relationship between the couple ended in 2006, Kulstad sought joint custody of the children, one of whom she barely knew.

Maniaci, meanwhile, had later married a man and expected to raise her two children with her husband as she saw fit, but Kulstad's court action instead turned this family upside down just as District Judge Ed McLean's decision of Sept. 29, 2008, turned logic upside down. McLean awarded Kulstad a parental interest in the children, with joint decision-making authority and regular visitation, despite the clear fact that she was never married to Maniaci, was never a legal guardian of the children, and had no more standing than any ex-girlfriend.

As I have written before, there is no statute that makes cohabitation a means to gain parental rights. Yes, hopefully, people who move into a household will be caring and nurturing of children who live with them, but in this age of transient relationships, it makes no sense to confuse children with the possibility of serial parenthood as each new live-in boyfriend becomes the latest to gain permanent custody rights.

How exactly can the court be representing the best interests of the children if it treats them as property to be divided up between any number of former boyfriends and girlfriends of legal parents? Plainly the court cannot do so unless we view the law as Silly Putty to be stretched into any shape necessary to advance a political agenda. One parent cannot and must not be able to confer parental rights to another person without following the prescribed legal process.

Title 40, Section 4, Part 228 of the Montana Code Annotated states that when a nonparent seeks to establish a parental interest in a child, they must first prove by "clear and convincing evidence" that "the natural parent has engaged in conduct that is contrary to the child-parent relationship." There is no evidence of any such conduct on the part of Maniaci. Indeed, the only evidence that could be mustered is that Maniaci broke off her lesbian relationship with Kulstad and thus deprived her children of a continuing relationship with a woman who had formerly assisted in their upbringing.

But do we really want courts putting their stamp of approval on whether we may or may not break up with live-in lovers? Is their any remotely reasonable explanation in law for how the once inalienable rights of parents to raise their children as they see fit became instead dispensable rights? Do the Constitution's guarantees against an intrusive, invasive government now mean nothing?

Some might want to phrase this as a battle between traditional families and untraditional families, between heterosexual marriage and gay marriage, but that is an inappropriate distinction to make in this case. Here, we are only interested in the difference between a legally recognized adoption and an effort to hijack parental rights through cohabitation.

Mind you, there has been considerable talk about Kulstad's supposed "rights" as a lesbian, but that talk is again nothing but an effort to force the legal facts into a politically correct framework where it can be claimed that Kulstad is a "victim" because she is gay.

Judge McLean went so far as to write in his decision that, "To discriminate further against Ms. Kulstad because of her sexual preference in this day and age is no different than telling a person to go to the back of the bus because of her skin color."

Sorry, Judge McLean, but that is not germane to the case. And for the judge to even talk about sexual preference is clear evidence that McLean made his ruling outside the basis of law, because this case was never about discrimination; it was about whether or not Kulstad could prove a parental right to these children.

It is certainly no accident, however, that Kulstad's attorneys from the American Civil Liberties Union have turned her case into a "cause celebre" for gay rights. Indeed, this is just one of several cases being argued across the country that challenge society's traditional definition of marriage and question the state's ability to limit parenthood to either single men and women or to married heterosexual couples.

In a Florida case with striking similarities to Maniaci v. Kulstad, a woman wants to be recognized as a second parent of the biological child of her former same-sex partner. A lower court refused to recognize a same-sex adoption from another state because Florida law does not permit same-sex adoption, yet the case is being made that Florida doesn't have the right to set its own standards in this matter, but rather must follow the moral precepts of Washington state instead.

In another case, a California court granted parental rights to a woman who had been in a same-sex relationship with a woman who became a mother prior to breaking off the lesbian affair. After the mother and child moved to Alabama, that state's Court of Appeals held that California parental law must be recognized by Alabama even though Alabama's marriage policy clearly affirms that marriage is between one man and one woman.

Similar cases are being heard in courts throughout the country. And in all of them, the common thread is that social activists want to change state policy not through legislation but by convincing a handful of judges to impose their will on society.

Let's hope the Supreme Court of Montana, which heard the case on Friday, will put an end to such efforts here. If Montana wants to recognize same-sex marriage or grant adoption rights to gay men and women, it can do so — through the law-making powers of the Legislature. In the meantime, everyone should be following the same rules. That means judges should apply the law as it is written, not as they envision it, and for that reason alone, Maniaci must prevail.

RECLAIM THE CONSTITUTION OR ELSE IT'S ADIOS TO THE REPUBLIC

May 10, 2009

It's gotten to the point where the federal government can do whatever it wants, and that is just plain scary.

Last week, you could turn west to California, east to Washington, D.C., or stop in the middle at Detroit to find numerous examples of federal power gone so far out-of-whack that it can no longer rightly be called government but should be recognized for what it is — assisted suicide.

In Detroit, it came to light that the White House had threatened to harm creditors of Chrysler if they did not buckle under and accept a pennies-on-the-dollar settlement from the troubled automaker. Columnist Michael Barone called this the "first episode of Gangster Government," and pointed out that the shakedown worked. One of the bondholder firms, Perella Weinberg, did buckle under. They wound up accepting 33 cents on the dollar for their secured debts, while the Obama administration guaranteed 50 cents on the dollar to the United Auto Workers union for their unsecured debts.

That's just the beginning. Tim Hubbard, the president of the Montana Auto Dealers Association, wrote an impassioned plea for small-town American to rise up and stop the president's order that General Motors and Chrysler should rapidly reduce their dealer networks throughout the country.

"The President's Auto Task Force is effectively mandating the largest Main Street layoff in the history of America — almost 190,000 Americans will lose their jobs and most of these will be on Main Streets all across the country," wrote Hubbard. "The current policy of the Auto Task Force will increase unemployment, increase the ranks of the uninsured, and create more potentially toxic assets for the financial sector."

No problem, right? The federal government can do whatever it wants. That's the way it's always been.

Umm, not exactly. Listen to James Madison, fourth president of the United States, in the Federalist Papers, from Jan. 26, 1788, prior even to the adoption of the Constitution:

"The powers delegated by the proposed Constitution to the Federal Government, are few and defined. Those which are to remain in the State Governments are numerous and indefinite. The former will be exercised principally on external objects, as war, peace, negotiation, and foreign commerce; with which last the power of taxation will for the most part be connected. The powers reserved to the several States will extend to all the objects, which, in the ordinary course of affairs, concern the lives, liberties and properties of the people; and the internal order, improvement, and prosperity of the State."

There are indeed only 20 powers granted to Congress in Article I, Section 8, of the U.S. Constitution, and monkeying around with car dealerships in Montana is not one of them. Madison notes that "the regulation of commerce," as enumerated by the Constitution, "is a new power," but then with an unfortunate lack of foresight, dismisses concerns about it because "that seems to be an addition which few oppose, and from which no apprehensions are entertained."

Well, apprehensions are being entertained now, and plenty of them.

The "commerce clause" in the Constitution — which grants Congress the power "to regulate commerce with foreign nations, and among the several states, and with the Indian tribes" — has been used to justify all manner of federal interference in people's day-to-day lives. Rest assured, originally it was intended only to provide oversight of the individual states imposing legislative restrictions on each other concerning commerce. It was not meant to give Congress, let alone the president, the power to take over car manufacturers or banks.

Speaking of banks, it would be useful if all Americans — in particular the president, senators, congressmen and judges — were to revisit the wisdom of Thomas Jefferson, third president of the United States, who declared flatly that Congress ought not be in the business of owning a bank. But yet today, the U.S. government finds itself in the peculiar position of being a major shareholder in not just one, but numerous financial institutions.

For what purpose? Can this be considered regulation of commerce?

Hardly, for as Jefferson notes, "to erect a bank, and to regulate commerce, are very different acts." Likewise, although the current case is not about the establishment of a national bank, the same concern arises that Jefferson expressed in 1791, namely that the government's action would produce a "considerable advantage to trade" and thus tilt the level playing field that merchants and the public ought to expect.

Again, it's all about the Constitution.

As Jefferson wrote, "I consider the foundation of the Constitution as laid on this ground that 'all powers not delegated to the U.S. by the Constitution, not prohibited by it to the states, are reserved to the states or to the people' [a paraphrase of the 10th Amendment]. To take a single step beyond the boundaries thus specially drawn around the powers of Congress, is to take possession of a boundless field of power, no longer susceptible of any definition."

Perhaps, that "boundless field of power" can best be seen today in the bank bailout, but it also has implications in the stimulus bill, whereby the federal government spent billions of dollars it doesn't have in an apparent quest to: A) end the recession, B) increase the power it already holds over all aspects of life in America; C) increase the dependency of the people on their government; or D) enrich certain sectors of the public at the expense of others.

Most recently, the Obama administration (not to be confused with the equally power-crazed but fortunately feckless Bush administration) has threatened to bankrupt the state of California by withholding stimulus dollars that had previously been promised unless the state gives in to union demands for higher wages. California, in case you didn't know, has a deficit of more than $40 billion and tried to save a skimpy $74 million by imposing wage cuts on unionized home health-care workers.

The lesson here from Washington is the same as the one in Detroit: Don't mess with unions!

And don't even begin to think that the "sovereign state" of California has any real sovereignty. That vanished a long-time ago. We live in a feudal system now where the states must swear their fealty to the lords of the Congress, who must in turn pay homage to the king of the White House. As for the rest of us, we are but lowly vassals or serfs. Do as you are bidden, and all will go well for you. Buck the system, and you could wind up under the bus.

Heck, look at the many banks that got conned into taking bailout money from the federal government. For the past several months, they have been trying to give it back so they can avoid intrusive, dictatorial regulation by the White House, but most of them have been stymied. Is this because the government intends to hold on to their newfound assets? Or just their awful power?

And just how dangerous is it when banks and government get together? Again, we turn to the wisdom of Thomas Jefferson for perspective. He was worried about the national bank that was established by Congress, but it is obvious he had a larger, principled concern as well:

"I sincerely believe... that banking establishments are more dangerous than standing armies; and that the principle of spending money to be paid by posterity in the name of funding, is but swindling futurity on a large scale."

"Spending money to be paid by posterity in the name of funding" — does that sound familiar? Call it a "stimulus" or a "bailout" if you wish, but a swindle by any other name still promises to hurt our "futurity on a large scale."

There is almost certainly only one solution — reclaiming the Constitution as it was originally written. But short of that impossible dream, we can lament the national suicide first supposedly foretold by Ben Franklin: "When the people find they can vote themselves money, that will herald the end of the republic."

ARE FEDERAL 'EVILS' STILL 'SUFFERABLE'?

May 17, 2009

Last week I tried to make the case for the American public "reclaiming the Constitution" as it was originally written.

One person wrote back to me and said, "OK. How?"

That, of course, is the tricky part.

I personally have in the past encouraged a constitutional convention to add safeguards en masse to the original document. This would allow us to revoke a number of dangerous court-imposed interpretations on the Constitution which over the years have amassed on the hull of the ship of state like so many barnacles on a sailing vessel. Of course, each individual barnacle is just a nuisance, and even taken together, they remain conveniently submerged and thus out of view so they are easy to ignore. But if you have a ship, you also have to scrape off barnacles. They are a fouling organism that can destroy your vessel from below.

We have the same problem with all the interpretations and doctrines which have encrusted our beautiful Constitution. Whether it is the absurdity of corporate personhood or the obscenity of the Commerce Clause, the penumbra of privacy or the elastic definition of citizenship — year after year of "precedent-setting" court rulings have made the original document almost irrelevant in huge swatches of public policy.

A constitutional convention would allow us to address these grievances wholesale. Nonetheless, most advocates of the original Constitution are afraid to see the country enter into a new convention for fear of what mischief might occur. The thinking is that we would end up with even less liberty after a constitutional convention rather than more.

Perhaps so, but that was also an argument to dissuade people from taking up arms against the crown in 1776. Many thought that George III was a tyrant, but few had the courage to stand up to him, thinking that they would surely end up in prison, or worse, dead.

Nonetheless, the colonists took a chance, and history has thanked them for it.

Consider the words of the Declaration of Independence: "We hold these truths to be self-evident, that all men ... are endowed by their Creator with certain unalienable rights... That to secure these rights, governments are instituted among men, deriving their just powers from the consent of the governed. That whenever any form of government becomes destructive to these ends, it is the right of the people to alter or to abolish it, and to institute new government..."

Thomas Jefferson, the author of most of the Declaration, thus challenges us from the grave "to alter or abolish" the government if we find it to be oppressive. God forbid we need another revolution to effect such change, especially when the hope is to restore our governing document to its original intentions. We should be able to bring about such change through reason, should we not?

Jefferson has a warning for those who would tamper with history in the following lines, but he concludes with a new challenge:

"Prudence... will dictate that governments long established should not be changed for light and transient causes; and accordingly all experience hath shown that mankind are more disposed to suffer, while evils are sufferable, than to right themselves by abolishing the forms to which they are accustomed. But when a long train of abuses and usurpations, pursuing invariably the same object evinces a design to reduce them under absolute despotism, it is their right, it is their duty, to throw off such government, and to provide new guards for their future security."

If you think the evils of the federal government are still "sufferable," then by all means continue to suffer. But if you are tired of the "evils" of government excess, if you think that "we the people" have suffered from "a long train of abuses and usurpations," then perhaps you will agree with Jefferson and the other signatories of the Declaration of Independence that it is our "duty" to "provide new guards for [our] future security."

Perhaps the citizens of this country would muck it up and leave us with even less liberty than before as a result of a constitutional convention. That is certainly a valid fear. But, on the other hand, if we believe in constitutional government, can we really be afraid to let the people write their own constitution? Seems a bit hypocritical to me.

Nonetheless, because I am a realist, I don't really expect to see Americans "reclaiming the Constitution" via the route of a constitutional convention. Yet, perhaps there are some small measures that can be taken that will help to educate the government that it is "we the people" who are in charge, not those we elect to serve us.

Of particular symbolic value would be the "Enumerated Powers Act" sponsored by Rep. John Shadegg of Arizona. This bill would force Congress to cite the specific constitutional provision that authorizes each law passed.

Sounds easy, right, but it could be the perfect way to ensure that the public sees just how far the Constitution has been stretched to accommodate the amassed powers of both Congress and the presidency.

After all, the Constitution only authorizes 20 federal functions for congressional oversight, and the 10th Amendment specifically limits the federal government to no more than those 20 "enumerated" powers. As a simple example of what wouldn't fly under the "Enumerated Powers Act" is the Department of

Education. There is, plainly, no constitutional authority for Congress or the federal government to regulate education. This used to be understood to be a local function, although states may well have their own right to regulate education processes through their particular state constitutions.

What would ultimately happen if the "Enumerated Powers Act" were to become law is that Congress would either have to admit that it has grossly over-reached and has no legal authority for most of what it does, or it would have to pile 90 percent of federal law under the umbrellas of the generic "Commerce Clause" and "General Welfare Clause."

They might be able to get away with it for a while, but sooner or later it would be so embarrassing that even Congress might be shamed into following the law of the land. Or maybe not.

PROPAGANDA, FREE SPEECH
AND THE SLIME ATTACK

May 24, 2009

History is either a gentle teacher or a mocking scold.

Before the fact, history is a warning not to repeat the mistakes of the past, but after the fact, history cries out with harsh reproach: How could you have been so stupid as to let this happen — AGAIN!

I am reminded of that dichotomy by a story in the newspaper in which "the former president asserted that in the past 15 years 'every dictator who has ascended to power has climbed on the ladder of free speech and free press' and then 'suppressed all free speech except his own.'"

He could be talking about Hugo Chavez of Venezuela certainly, or Mahmoud Ahmadinejad of Iran. If it weren't for the time frame, you could throw in Saddam Hussein, Robert Mugabe, and numerous others.

Only the ex-president who was being quoted wasn't President George W. Bush, as you might assume, or even any other living president; it was Herbert Hoover, and the story

appeared in the Daily Inter Lake on Nov. 8, 1937, at a time
when the world was coping with Hitler, Mussolini and the rest
of the rat pack.

Hoover noted, in a speech at Colby College in Maine, that
free speech, free press and free debate are the "very life stream
of advancing liberalism," which reminds us healthily that
"liberalism" was not always a dirty word to Republicans.
Technically, liberalism is a branch of political philosophy that
esteems individual liberty and equality as the most important of
political goals, and limited government as a close third. By such
reckoning, it should be a universal American philosophy, but
instead the word has been hijacked by the far left and stripped
of its association with liberty. Indeed, it has been
transmogrified into almost its opposite by being merged with
the vague notion of social justice, so that government is now
seen by modern liberals as the main tool with which individuals
can be cudgeled into action or inaction for "the greater good."

Moreover, as a recent column of mine lamented, liberals
have a tendency these days to promote free speech only when it
toes the party line. Straying away from groupthink can have the
regrettable fallout of being ostracized as a socially inept
Neanderthal, as we saw in the case of Miss California not too
many weeks ago.

The efforts of political parties and social movements to gain
sway over the national media in general is lumped under the
rubric of propaganda. Hoover takes dead aim at what a
headline writer called "the poison of propaganda" and said "we
must incessantly expose intellectual dishonesty and the purpose
that lies behind it."

Describing propaganda as "a sinister word meaning half-
truth or any other distortion of the truth," Hoover said it works
by "tainting of news, by making synthetic news and opinions
and canards. It promotes the emotions of hate, fear and
dissension."

It's almost like the president was peering into a crystal ball
and pulling in a cable feed from MSNBC. Anyone who has ever
witnessed one of Keith Olbermann's "special comments" on
that channel can precisely identify that synthesis of "news and

opinion and canards" that worried Hoover. And if you don't see enough "hate, fear and dissension coming from Olbermann, you can throw in his frequent guest Janeane Garofalo for good measure.

The sometime actress had the audacity to say that the Tea Party" movement wasn't about honest protest against public policy, but was "about hating a black man in the White House." She said the national Tea Party movement was "racism straight up." Remarkably, we have even had local residents who should know better who have repeated this canard.

It is too easy to "blame the Internet" for the decline in civil discourse in American society, so it is worth paying attention to Hoover's history lesson on propaganda in the political field.

The ex-president notes that in the years since World War I, "refinements" had been applied to the art of propaganda as it applied to politics. "The great quality of this improved poison," he notes, "seems to be that it must be artistically done."

I suppose that may be what Garofolo's interest is in propaganda — the artistic element. It probably is a challenge to try to make it appear that you are being fair-minded and liberal when you are actually slandering a whole class of people. The technique, however, is nothing new. Hoover nailed it:

"If you don't like an argument on currency or the budget or labor relations or what not, you put out slimy and if possible anonymous propaganda reflecting upon your opponent's grandmother or the fact that his cousin is employed in Wall Street or is a Communist or a reactionary."

That fits perfectly the attacks on Tea Party protesters, who — let's remember — were actually arguing against the stimulus bill and the president's budget bill, not against a particular skin color.

As Hoover concluded, "You switch the premise and set up straw men and then attack them with fierce courage."

And even the "slimy" attack as described by Hoover was employed in the mainstream media in discussions of the Tea Party protesters, who were incessantly referred to as "teabaggers" by the "artistically" inclined slimers such as Anderson Cooper on CNN. Although most folks would have no idea what "teabagging" was, Cooper and others in the "liberal" media did, and used this obscene reference gleefully to smear American citizens exercising their right of free speech.

The only thing remaining to bring history full circle is for the attack on Hoover to get under way in reader comments about this column. One thing is safe to predict; most of the comments will not be about Hoover's words (or even mine) in this column, but about the "straw men" that are conveniently available to deflect attention from a serious argument. They may not have the audacity to call Hoover a "teabagger," but at the very least you can expect to be reminded that he single-handedly gave us the Great Depression. That line worked for Roosevelt, and there's no reason to let go of a "tried and true" smear formula. Set up the straw men and let 'em fly.

'ATLAS SHRUGGED': AYN RAND LAUGHS; THE REST OF US WEEP

June 7, 2009

"I will stop the motor of the world."

With those words, a charismatic hero was born. John Galt, the mysterious character at the heart of Ayn Rand's "Atlas Shrugged," decided that he could not stand idly by as the nation put on chains and fetters as if they were party favors.

Today, more than 50 years after the novel was written, Galt is offering hope to many Americans who see the country on a slow but steady slide toward socialism. As we talk about the government takeover of General Motors, it is educational to remember that the fictional Galt rose up out of the ashes of another car company, the Twentieth Century Motor Company, which like GM, ended up in bankruptcy.

The allegoric lesson of Twentieth Century Motors is much more instructive for the country as a whole, however, than for another automaker, because it is about how "hope" and "change" can motivate people to make choices that lead inevitably to "despair" and "stagnation."

A former worker at the plant, now a lonely tramp, tells the story years later of how the workers let themselves be inspired by the company's new owners to work for the common good. "They told us that this plan would achieve a noble ideal."

Yes, a noble ideal, a way to help each other, something no one could possibly oppose. But there were few details on the table when the company's workers were asked to vote on their future, just these vague promises and a few catchphrases on which to pin their hopes.

"None of us knew just how the plan would work, but every one of us thought that the next fellow knew it. And if anybody had doubts, he ... kept his mouth shut — because they made it sound like anyone who'd oppose the plan was a child-killer at heart and less than a human being."

And so the workers voted overwhelmingly to follow the new plan, which would mean that no worker would fall through the cracks — everyone would take care of everyone else. "We thought it was good," the tramp says wearily. "No, that's not true, either. We thought that we were supposed to think it was good."

And so begins this experiment in "modified" capitalism. As the worker explains it, "The plan was that everybody in the factory would work according to his ability, but would be paid according to his need." Of course, in the long run, "modified capitalism" turns out to be socialism or worse, and as Rand points out with brutal logic, it leads inevitably to a system that encourages laziness and lying and punishes success.

The tale of Twentieth Century Motors is one small sliver of "Atlas Shrugged," but on virtually every page of the gargantuan novel, there is some bit of wit or wisdom that presages the mess of the current era.

The "shrug" of the title tells it all. It is a symbol of indifference, but also a symbol of frustration, and a telling representation of the tremendous power wielded by the talented individual such as John Galt. Atlas, the great being on whose shoulders rests the world, finally gets tired of being taken for granted, and up-ends literally everything with the slightest of gestures.

Likewise, "Atlas Shrugged" tells the tale of a handful of innovators who struggle to survive in an era of big government and corporate greed, and seem doomed to fail, until one man — Galt — dares to change everything. Rand said the idea came to her during a phone conversation when she asked a friend, "What if all the creative minds of the world went on strike?"

Few prophetic novels get everything right, and "Atlas Shrugged" gets plenty wrong, but Rand's image of recession-weary America as a nation sputtering toward collectivism and running out of intellectual steam is so familiar to observers of the current scene that her excesses and errors are easily forgiven.

In particular, her ability to lampoon government intervention in business is deadly accurate. Time after time, Congress passes laws in the novel that are trumpeted as necessary for the common good, but which ultimately weaken society in unexpected ways and enrich only a few (those whom Rand characterizes as "looters"). It is almost scary how much of the villainous agenda of Rand's novel would fit perfectly well into the world as envisioned by readers of the Huffington Post.

The "Anti-Dog-Eat-Dog Rule" passed by the railroad industry gives the National Alliance of Railroads the authority to protect established railroads from new competition. The theory seems to be that the established company has only limited resources and shouldn't have to stretch itself thin by defending itself against fresh and innovative competition. This is great if you care about protecting established companies, but not if you care about providing the consumer with the best service and prices.

It has to remind you a little bit of the government's takeover of GM. Pity poor Ford Motor Co. which was the only one of the Big Three automakers in the United States that was healthy enough to pass up government bailout money last November. Now, instead of owing money to the government, they actually have to compete AGAINST the government (the new owner of GM) selling cars.

Supporters of government intervention, of course, say they are doing what is necessary to clean up after the horrid capitalists who mismanaged their companies into bankruptcy, but that fails to acknowledge the fact that the American economy is far from capitalism. It is instead what Rand called with unfeigned disgust a "mixed economy" — namely, a mix between freedom and regulation — and it is the government's own policies which lead inevitably to economic failure.

The latest real-life government intrusion being plotted by the "looters" in Congress is to force the health insurance industry to jettison the basic principles under which it operates in order to once again serve the "common good," or as Rand put it, "a noble ideal." This suggests a basic misunderstanding of the principles of liberty and equality. "Equality of opportunity" is the God-given right that our Constitution is supposed to protect, but instead our government has decided to ensure "equality of results" and is willing to bankrupt us all to do so. In its wrong-headedness, at least, it is reminiscent of the "Equalization of Opportunity Bill" from "Atlas Shrugged," which forbids any one person or corporation from owning more than one type of business concern.

One disastrous result of that bill in the novel is that companies which had planned on expanding must instead shut down their older, still viable, operations in order to be able to expand into much more prosperous new ventures. Thus, when companies, following the logic of the Equalization of Opportunity Bill, start closing their factories on the East Coast in order to move to the West (Colorado is the symbol of American resilience and energy), Congress is suddenly enlisted to try to correct yet another unintended consequence. This time, there is demand for a Public Stability Law that would forbid companies from abandoning their current territory for a new one. The argument is that people have a right to expect jobs that existed yesterday to continue to exist tomorrow. But no explanation how Colorado is going to get the equipment, factories and jobs it needs while the government is propping up foundering industrial dinosaurs elsewhere.

Rand's vision of the economic madness of government "do-good-ism" culminates in Directive 10-289, which mandates that everything must stop where it is. The order doesn't just freeze wages and prices; it also forbids workers from changing jobs without permission from a federal board. It halts new product development (too confusing) and makes the U.S. government the keeper of all intellectual property as a means of ensuring that no one takes advantage of anyone else. Needless to say, with the government in charge of everything, chaos ensues.

These are just a few of the touchstones of "Atlas Shrugged" which resonate as pure prophecy to an audience that has lived through the American Recovery and Reinvestment Act of 2009. Perhaps that's why the book is more popular than ever, and why "Going Galt" has become a symbol for our time of resistance to over-regulation.

Critics were merciless in mocking Rand's magnus opus when it appeared in 1957, but 50 years later, as her worst fears are realized, it appears to be a bet certain that Ayn Rand will get the last laugh.

HUXLEY'S 'ENEMIES OF FREEDOM' — REVISITED

June 14, 2009

It seems we really are going "back to the future," to quote the title of a popular movie. As a matter of fact, you could make a pretty good case that the future is an open book that was read (or written) in the last century.

I'm talking about the uncanny ability of literary writers in the middle of the 20th century to foretell the downward spiral of the current era. That includes George Orwell's "1984" and Ayn Rand's "Atlas Shrugged" — both of which this column has recently examined, as well as "Brave New World" by Aldous Huxley.

Huxley's dystopian novel is arguably the most relevant of the novels that predict the downfall of Western civilization because it is based for the most part on an understanding of the human temperament and its weaknesses, rather than on an understanding of a particular political principle, as you might say of "1984," for example.

That is not to say that "Brave New World" is an accurate summation of where we have arrived in 2009, but it is certainly frightening in its portrayal of mankind as so easily malleable with diversions, feel-good slogans, sex, drugs and what Huxley would later call "man's almost infinite appetite for distractions."

Nonetheless, being itself a form of literary diversion, "Brave New World" may not be the best conduit for Huxley's ideas to make themselves heard through the din of self-indulgence that surrounds us today. Instead, a less well-known follow-up work, "Brave New World Revisited," which is a collection of brief essays, is much more accessible and unavoidable in its analysis of the threats to freedom.

In fact, the book was first written under the title of "Enemies of Freedom." Mike Wallace, later famous for his role on "60 Minutes," interviewed Huxley about this book in 1958, and from that interview it is easy to be scared to death about where we have gone in the last 50 years.

Huxley had the advantage of speaking about his fears in the future tense, so he did not have to worry about being called a fear-monger. You can say whatever you want about the future, but Huxley knew that once the future arrived it would be too late to prevent it.

"That's why I feel it so extremely important, here and now, to start thinking about these problems. Not to let ourselves be taken by surprise by the ... new advances in technology," Huxley told Wallace.

So what were the "problems" that worried Huxley about the future of America and the world?

1) Overpopulation. Now this may not concern you in itself. America, after all, has plenty of land to go around, but Huxley points out that it is the effect of overpopulation that is to be feared, not the overpopulation itself.

Using one example, he says, "The people have less to eat and less goods per capita than they had 50 years ago; and as the position ... the economic position becomes more and more precarious, obviously the central government has to take over more and more responsibility for keeping the ship-of-state on an even keel, and then of course you are likely to get social unrest under such conditions, with again an intervention of the central government.... One sees here a pattern which seems to be pushing very strongly toward a totalitarian regime."

This very neatly sums up the increasing pressure on the federal government to take care of all our daily needs — whether they be for day care, health care, jobs or TV converter boxes. Orwell worried about Big Brother; Huxley worried about Aunt Matilda. Can anyone say "nanny state"?

2) Propaganda. "Hitler used terror... brute force on the one hand, but he also used a very efficient form of propaganda... He didn't have TV, but he had the radio which he used to the fullest extent, and was able to impose his will on an immense mass of people. I mean, the Germans were a highly educated people."

Which is Huxley's way of saying that propaganda doesn't just work on poor bumpkins and rubes. It works on city folk, too. It works on the college educated and on the highly paid. As a matter of fact, it works better than ever on people who think they don't have to worry about it because they are too sophisticated and educated.

Mike Wallace was skeptical that "it could happen here." He asks Huxley whether there could possibly be any parallel between Hitler's Germany and the United States in the use of propaganda, and Huxley does not falter in his response:

"Needless to say it is not being used this way now, but ... the point is ... there are methods at present available, methods superior in some respects to Hitler's methods, which could be used... I mean, what I feel very strongly is that we mustn't be caught by surprise by our own advancing technology. This has happened again and again in history with technology's advance... Suddenly people have found themselves in a situation which they didn't foresee and doing all sorts of things they really didn't want to do."

It comes as no surprise to anyone, I hope, that television is a hugely powerful influence in our society. The question which must be answered is whether it is a force for good or a force for evil. Huxley said in 1958 that television was being used "quite harmlessly" to "distract everybody all the time." But could he still say the same thing today? Is distracting everybody all the time really harmless?

As for the true dangers, Huxley posits a time when "television ... is always saying the same things the whole time; it's always driving along. It's not creating a wide front of distraction. It's creating a one-pointed 'drumming in' of a single idea all the time." He calls this an "immensely powerful" tool of propaganda.

But what we have today is even more powerful, because it takes the worst of both of Huxley's proposals and puts them together — television, newspapers and what is collectively called "the mainstream media" working in sync to both "distract" everybody all the time and to "drum in" a single idea all the time. The single idea does change — from "Bush is bad" to "Obama is good," for instance — but the mechanism to persuade through use of repetition, shame and sincerity does not. Now that is powerful propaganda. If Hitler had that at his disposal, he might not have ever been stopped.

3) Dictatorship. "I think this ... dictatorship of the future ... will be very unlike the dictatorships which we've been familiar with in the immediate past," Huxley warned Mike Wallace.

"I think what is going to happen in the future is that dictators will find, as the old saying goes, that you can do everything with bayonets except sit on them. That if you want to preserve your power indefinitely, you have to get the consent of the ruled."

Huxley imagined this would be done partly by drugs and partly by propaganda. He was partly right and partly wrong. Yes, drugs are responsible for a certain amount of deadening of the American consciousness, but nowhere near as significantly as video games, the Internet and the entertainment industry in general. These sources of distraction along with the steady blare of propaganda have turned modern man into as willing a slave as ever existed.

Huxley said the modern dictatorship would gain power "by bypassing the ...rational side of man and appealing to his subconscious and his deeper emotions and his physiology even, and so making him actually love his slavery. This is the danger: That actually people may be... happy under the new regime, but... they will be happy in situations where they oughtn't to be happy."

Not to put too fine a point on it, but can anyone say "$11 trillion national debt"?

In "Brave New World Revisited," Huxley went so far as to suggest that the American public could easily be duped into voting against their own self-interest:

"All that is needed ... is money and a candidate who can be coached to look 'sincere.' Under the new dispensation, political principles and plans for specific action have come to lose most of their importance. The personality of the candidate and the way he is projected by the advertising experts are the things that really matter. In one way or another, as vigorous he-man or kindly father, the candidate must be glamorous. He must also be an entertainer who never bores his audience. "

The remarkable thing about these words is that they were written before John F. Kennedy was even a candidate for president. The scary thing is that they fit our current president so well.

But don't make the mistake of thinking this is a partisan issue. If Huxley is right, if the kind of "centralized government" dictatorship he fears could come to pass, then it has to be with the "consent of the governed." Essentially, what he is talking about is a serial dictatorship, a series of supreme rulers "elected" under the trappings of whatever political party is convenient in order to continue the "happy slavery" of the masses.

George W. Bush? Barack Hussein Obama? Are they really doing what you want? Or what they are "coached" to do? Dictatorship may not come to America with jackboots on, but if it has the "consent of the governed," it doesn't need to.

Everyone who cares about freedom owes it to him or herself to read Aldous Huxley's "Brave New World Revisited." The entire book is posted online at www.huxley.net/bnw-revisited/index.html, and Wallace's 1958 interview with Huxley is available online as well.

PALIN'S WAR WITH MEDIA
MAY NOT BE HER 'LAST STAND'

August 2, 2009

President Harry Truman, known as "Give 'em hell Harry," famously said, "I never give them hell. I just tell the truth and they think it's hell."

That could aptly describe the relationship between Sarah Palin and the national media these days. Palin, the now former governor of Alaska, has a knack for stirring up the hornets' nest of the national press corps with her unambiguous, unvarnished, undying love for this country. Every time she talks, it seems like she's got a swarm of angry wasps on her tail.

Palin's formula for avoiding the stings and arrows of outrageous mischaracterization is something like this: "Tell the truth and then run like hell — 'cause the hornets are sure to come after you."

When she announced on July 3 that she would resign as governor, there were loud hoops and hollers in newsrooms across the country. "Ding dong, the witch is dead!" screamed the liberal pundits. They thought they had bagged another political scalp for their trophy room. They called her a quitter. They said her political career was dead.

But obviously they weren't listening to Palin, who specifically said she wasn't a quitter. She said that in her mind it would be the "quitter's way out" to just "plod along and appease those who demand: 'Sit down and shut up!'" She said she had a higher calling and was taking a stand to "actually make a difference."

But the press didn't get it. They must not have been listening when she said this:

"Productive, fulfilled people determine where to put their efforts, choosing to wisely utilize precious time — to BUILD UP. And there is such a need to build up and fight for our state and our country. I choose to FIGHT for it! And I'll work hard for others who still believe in free enterprise and smaller government; strong national security for our country and support for our troops; energy independence; and for those who will protect freedom and equality and life... I'll work for and campaign for those PROUD to be American, and those who are INSPIRED by our ideals and won't deride them."

Wow! That doesn't sound like a quitter to me.

She said she thinks she can do "what is best for Alaska" by resigning as governor and taking her fight to a larger stage. That's because our 50 states increasingly operate at the mercy of the federal government, and Gov. Palin knew that if she remained frozen in Alaska for the next two years she would not be able to effect change in Washington where it is so badly needed.

I understand that liberals hope and pray Palin will be the nominee of the Republican Party because they consider her foolish and small-minded and pathetically provincial, but the worst mistake to make in politics is to underestimate your opponent. Palin may not be able to save a party as dismally ineffective as the Republicans have proven to be, but she is almost certainly the best chance they have to remain the voice of conservatives rather than a mirror of liberal Democratic values.

So last week, Palin completed her announced plan to resign as governor, with a little over a year left in her term before the next election. She spoke quickly, forcefully and passionately, and then got out of the way. The media swarm was not far behind, but this time Palin took them on directly.

"... first, some straight talk for some, just some, in the media, because another right protected for all is freedom of the press, and you all have such important jobs reporting facts and informing the electorate, and exerting power to influence. You represent what could and should be a respected honest profession that could and should be the cornerstone of our democracy. Democracy depends on you...

"And that is why, that's why our troops are willing to die for you. So... how 'bout in honor of the American soldier, ya quit making things up! And don't underestimate the wisdom of the people... and one other thing for the media, our new governor has a very nice family too, so leave his kids alone!"

To the liberal press, that meant Sarah was thin-skinned and not tough enough to play the game of national politics. But to many Americans across this great country, those who believe in our exemplary success as a nation, it meant someone is finally speaking for them, for their values, for their traditions.

Toward the beginning of her farewell address, Palin reminded her fellow Alaskans that "what the rest of America gets to see along with us is [that] in this last frontier there is hope and opportunity and there is country pride." She compared that to the message from the left where some seem to "just be hell bent ... on tearing down our nation, perpetuating pessimism, and ... suggesting perhaps that our best days were yesterdays."

Toward the end of her speech, Palin again spoke directly to Alaskans, and said, "There is much good in store further down the road, but to reach it we must value and live the optimistic pioneering spirit that made this state proud and free, and we can resist enslavement to big central government that crushes hope and opportunity. Be wary of accepting government largess. It doesn't come free, and often, accepting it takes away everything that is free."

Did I say she was speaking to Alaskans? No, she was speaking to Americans everywhere, to patriots who love this country, and realize our founding principals were about individual liberty and not about bending to the will of a tyrant government.

But for some reason, the national media didn't quite get the message: They think they won't have Sarah Palin to kick around anymore. In fact, the general conclusion after she announced her resignation was that Sarah had quit politics because she just wasn't tough enough to stand the heat (to borrow another Harry Truman metaphor).

Well, Palin may wish she could be a stay-at-home mom instead of a national political figure, but somehow I don't think she will be staying in her kitchen in Wasilla, Alaska, for the next few years. Indeed, I'd be willing to bet right now that Palin is on the verge of launching a national campaign that may or may not end at the White House, but which will certainly prove that she is no shrinking violet.

In her July 3 speech, she didn't talk about going on the sidelines; indeed she spoke like a take-charge quarterback. "My choice is to take a stand and effect change — not hit our heads against the wall and watch valuable state time and money, millions of your dollars go down the drain... Rather we know we can effect positive change outside government at this moment in time, on another scale, and actually make a difference in our priorities — and so we will, for Alaskans and for Americans."

We are often told that those who cannot remember the past are condemned to repeat it. Less often, it seems, do we realize the inverse is also true: "Those who learn from the past have the opportunity to successfully repeat it."

The past, you see, is not all bad. In fact, for the right kind of mind it is loaded with possibility, even more so perhaps than the blank slate of the future.

Indeed, when one considers the many accomplishments of the past, of human history, of individual leadership, it is humbling indeed to trudge the road of our common destiny and imagine the possibility of an even brighter future. For many of us, that bright future only seems possible if we hang on to the traditions and heritage that gave us the glory that was Greece, the grandeur that was Rome, and the miracle that is America.

So good luck, Sarah. You may be tilting at windmills, but that is a good place to start.

CHARITY AND THE GOOD OL' CONSTITUTION

September 6, 2009

"Where do you find in the Constitution any authority to give away the public money in charity?"

It might be a question out of today's headlines, but it isn't.

No doubt, it could rightly be asked in the health-care debate, but it goes well beyond that. In every disaster, in every disturbance, the federal government today is ready with a checkbook at hand to help those in need. Hurricane Katrina?

California fires? Montana snowstorms? They've all been declared disasters in order to justify federal spending to help out the victims and to speed recovery. The average number of disaster declarations reached as high as 130 during the George W. Bush administration, an increase of almost 50 percent over the Clinton era.

Of course, no one could be against helping the innocent victims of natural or manmade disasters, could they? Well, no. Not anyone in their right mind, at least. Charity is one of the highest impulses of mankind, and our desire to help and protect each other is a noble heritage that we all cherish.

But that does not answer the original question:

"Where do you find in the Constitution any authority to give away the public money in charity?"

That question was asked not of President Obama nor of Sen. Max Baucus or Rep. Nancy Pelosi, but of the less well-known Tennessee congressman, David Crockett.

It was a question that Rep. Crockett was not well-prepared to answer, but his constituent wanted to know why he had voted to spend federal funds for the relief of families that had been left homeless as the result of a ravaging fire in Georgetown. Crockett had actually seen the fire and gone to help rescue women and children and to fight the flames, so he was more than happy a bill came before Congress to aid those victims further. As he himself said, "We put aside all other business, and rushed it through as soon as it could be done."

Again, sort of reminiscent of the "rush" to pass health-care "reform" in the current Congress, but whereas we are talking about spending a trillion dollars or more for health-care reform, the fire relief was the relatively paltry sum of $20,000.

That's because this was back in the 1820s, and Rep. Crockett was none other than the American folk hero, Davy Crockett, "king of the wild frontier." Crockett served three terms in Congress altogether before being killed defending the Alamo in Texas.

But back to our story, which comes from an 1884 biography, "The Life of Colonel David Crockett" by Edward S. Ellis, it is instructive to note the puzzlement of Rep. Crockett when he was challenged by his constituent Horatio Bunce while out stumping for votes. Bunce told Crockett in no uncertain terms that he could not vote for him again.

"You gave a vote last winter which shows that either you have not capacity to understand the Constitution, or that you are wanting in the honesty and firmness to be guided by it. In either case you are not the man to represent me," Bunce said in the story, as allegedly recounted by Crockett.

By today's mainstream-media standards, Bunce would clearly be known as a right-wing extremist, and if he expressed his concerns at a town-hall meeting this summer he would have been labeled "un-American."

Even Crockett, before finding out what was on Bunce's mind, said, "I had been making up my mind that he was one of those churlish fellows who care for nobody but themselves, and take bluntness for independence."

But that was before the Tennessee farmer had asked his devastating question, which Crockett described colorfully as a "sockdologer!" which roughly translated means a comment that could set a person to thinking.

And think, Crockett did, trying in vain to find some justification for his vote in favor of the $20,000 in charity.

"When I began to think about it, I could not remember a thing in the Constitution that authorized it. I found I must take another tack, so I said: 'Well, my friend; I may as well own up. You have got me there. But certainly nobody will complain that a great and rich country like ours should give the insignificant sum of $20,000 to relieve its suffering women and children, particularly with a full and overflowing Treasury, and I am sure, if you had been there, you would have done just as I did.'"

But Horatio Bunce, a one-man "Tea Party" of his day, was having none of it. Rather than be hornswoggled by Crockett's attempt to deflect the argument away from the Constitution, he circled right back to it:

"In the first place," he said, the Government ought to have in the Treasury no more than enough for its legitimate purposes. But that has nothing to do with the question. The power of collecting and disbursing money at pleasure is the most dangerous power that can be entrusted to man... [W]hile you are contributing to relieve one, you are drawing it from thousands who are even worse off than he. If you had the right to give anything, the amount was simply a matter of discretion with you, and you had as much right to give $20,000,000 as $20,000. If you have the right to give to one, you have the right to give to all; and, as the Constitution neither defines charity nor stipulates the amount, you are at liberty to give to any and everything which you may believe, or profess to believe, is a charity, and to any amount you may think proper. You will very easily perceive, what a wide door this would open for fraud and corruption and favoritism, on the one hand, and for robbing the people on the other. No, Colonel, Congress has no right to give charity. Individual members may give as much of their own money as they please, but they have no right to touch a dollar of the public money for that purpose."

Now, how this applies to health care is quite simple. There's no difference between giving money to individual citizens because they have lost their house in a fire or giving money to citizens because they have fallen ill. It is, to use Horatio Bunce's word, "charity." It is, thus, not surprising that the recipients of this government-funded charity, who would number in the millions, have taken to acting as if they are entitled to health-care assistance, whatever you wish to call it.

Likewise, the victims of the fire who were the beneficiaries of Congress' generosity with other people's money were happy to have it, and so were the average and well-to-do citizens who might otherwise have been asked to contribute to a fire-relief fund. Bunce lectured Crockett accordingly:

"The people about Washington, no doubt, applauded you for relieving them from the necessity of giving by giving what was not yours to give. The people have delegated to Congress, by the Constitution, the power to do certain things. To do these, it is authorized to collect and pay moneys, and for nothing else. Everything beyond this is usurpation, and a violation of the Constitution."

The well-spoken farmer concluded his presentation thusly: "It is a precedent fraught with danger to the country, for when

Congress once begins to stretch its power beyond the limits of the Constitution, there is no limit to it, and no security for the people."

That, ladies and gentleman, is a powerful statement, which has been amply demonstrated to be true in the subsequent 180 years. Those folks who today meretriciously dismiss the constitutional argument as an irrelevancy in the health-care debate show just how far off course we have gotten.

The only hope we have now is that our congressional representatives and senators have a smidgen of the integrity of Davy Crockett, who having been instructed in the truth was man enough to accept it.

"Well, my friend, you hit the nail upon the head when you said I had not sense enough to understand the Constitution," he told his accuser. "I intended to be guided by it, and thought I had studied it fully. I have heard many speeches in Congress about the powers of Congress, but what you have said here at your plow has got more hard, sound sense in it, than all the fine speeches I ever heard. If I had ever taken the view of it that you have, I would have put my head into the fire before I would have given that vote, and if you will forgive me and vote for me again, if I ever vote for another unconstitutional law I wish I may be shot."

Bunce wryly shot back at Crockett: "Yes, Colonel, you have sworn to that once before," referring to his sacred vow to uphold the Constitution, a vow that not only he but all congressmen and elected representatives take, whether they have read the Constitution or not.

In this day and age, the only congressman I know of who follows Crockett's example as a born-again constitutionalist is Ron Paul, who never votes for a bill without first confirming in his own mind that Congress is authorized by the Constitution to pass such a law. Most of the rest of them just ask themselves how popular the bill will be, and whether it will help or hurt their efforts to be re-elected.

Yes, the Constitution is a relatively old document, but it is not moldy, and if we think of it as quaint and irrelevant, we do so at the ultimate cost of our liberty. That would be unconscionable.

Let's hope that this story of Rep. David Crockett and a plain old U.S. citizen who held him accountable helps to remind each and every one of us that America's exceptional quality is partly based on the fact that we are ruled from the bottom up. It is "we the people," not "we the governed."

It is important also to remember that solutions to most American problems are to be found in American lore and history — if one could but be bothered to look. Although times change, human nature doesn't, nor does the nature of our republic, as long as it stands fast and hews to the line of the Constitution.

JUST WHO DO THEY 'REPRESENT'?

September 13, 2009

Virtually every day when Congress is in session, I get a press release or two from each of Montana's representatives explaining how they are looking out for our state.

Usually, those press releases are proud announcements of how the senator or representative wants credit for the U.S. government agreeing to spend millions more of taxpayer money in Montana. For some reason, these announcements never seem to reference the national debt that they are expanding.

Occasionally, there are also press releases from our senators taking credit for confirmation votes such as when the Senate approved the nomination of Sonia Sotomayor as the nation's first Hispanic woman on the Supreme Court.

I've been checking my e-mail frequently today waiting for that kind of note from Sens. Max Baucus and Jon Tester proudly proclaiming that they have just voted to confirm the nomination of Cass Sunstein as the nation's regulatory czar.

So far I have been disappointed. Not a word has arrived from Max and Jon, as they like to be known in our "small-town" state.

Maybe that's because, in order to be honest, the press release would have to read something like this one which I just made up:

"Sen. Max Baucus announced today that he voted to approve President Obama's nomination of Cass Sunstein to head the Office of Information and Regulatory Affairs, despite Sunstein's apparent antipathy to many beliefs held dear by Montanans.

"Baucus said he was joined in this "rally round the president" partisan vote by his fellow Montana Democrat Jon Tester. Sunstein was approved on a 57-40 vote.

Sunstein, who is a prolific author and law professor, holds many views that are the opposite of common thinking in Montana, most notably on animal rights and gun rights.

"Sunstein is widely noted for his animal-rights philosophy and for his belief that animals should be able to bring lawsuits against humans to protect their rights. An attorney for Americans for Limited Government said that, if confirmed, Sunstein 'could plunge the livestock industry into a litigation abyss from which it may never emerge.'

"Sunstein is also on record as favoring an end to hunting as a recreational sport, which — let's face it — the less said about that the better.

"In addition to his radical views on animal rights, Sunstein holds questionable beliefs about the Second Amendment rights which most Montanans cherish. In 2007, he said, 'The individual right to bear arms reflects the success of an extremely aggressive and resourceful social movement and has much less to do with good standard legal arguments that [it] appears.'

"Although Jon and I recognize that we were elected by Montanans to protect their traditional values, we thought we could vote for Sunstein and his extreme left-wing views without anyone noticing because the Mainstream Media has not paid any attention to this nomination and because neither of us is up for re-election for at least three more years anyway."

Please remember, that this is a FICTIONAL press release. But it reflects accurately the beliefs of Mr. Sunstein, and frames the question I think Montanans ought to be asking themselves:

Just who do Max Baucus and Jon Tester think they are? And this goes for Rep. Denny Rehberg and anyone else you voted for. Don't let their votes go unquestioned — or unpunished! — if they appear to be voting against your interest.

We call them our elected "representatives" — after all, they vote on our behalf in Congress and state legislatures — but more and more you have to wonder, just who do they represent?

Is it you the voter? Or is it the political party whose initial (usually R or D) hangs off their last name like a brand on a beast of burden?

The blatant disregard of Baucus and Tester for the concerns of Montana in their vote to approve Cass Sunstein to head the Office of Information and Regulatory Affairs is a good place to start for Montanans who wonder if they just got sucker-punched.

You can bet one thing. Baucus and Tester know exactly what they did. Sunstein is not exactly a shrinking violet. He is a constitutional scholar, a University of Chicago and Harvard law school professor, a prolific author, and moreover a frequent witness before congressional committees. He also happens to be a close personal friend of President Barack Obama, and that apparently was all that mattered to most Democratic senators, even the ones who represent states where Sunstein could not be elected dog-catcher (Oops! sorry, but that human-centric position will be banned if Sunstein has his way!)

You might well ask, "What is the Office of Information and Regulatory Affairs" anyway? Created in 1980 by the Paperwork Reduction Act, the federal office carries out economic analysis, sets policy on information technology, and generally oversees implementation and reform of federal regulations — all those administrative rules which the bureaucracy develops in order to carry out the laws passed by Congress and the wishes of the president.

Thus the "regulatory czar" might or might not be an important office, depending on how it is used, but it should be noted that the Wall Street Journal reported that "although obscure, the post wields outsize power."

The Journal's Jan. 8 story also noted that, "Obama aides have said the job will be crucial as the new administration overhauls financial-services regulations, attempts to pass universal health care and tries to forge a new approach to controlling emissions of greenhouse gases."

Sounds important to me, but you can decide for yourself.

The question persists, however, just what kind of person do you want to oversee this office, or for that matter serve the public interest in any kind of office? The Senate has the responsibility of offering its advice and providing its consent to all presidential appointees unless the Congress exempts them from such scrutiny (Article II, Section 2 of the Constitution). And that means senators are the gatekeepers of government, the ones who can protect "we the people" from the whims of presidents and the personal agendas of presidential nominees.

Sunstein has an agenda as long as ACORN's rap sheet. You can look it up for yourself on the Internet, but our poor overworked senators have lots of people to do that for them. I'm sure they discovered, for instance, that Sunstein's nomination was opposed by the U.S. Sportsmen's Alliance, the National Shooting Sports Foundation, the National Wild Turkey Federation and numerous other outdoor groups who generally share common ground with our Montana values and, supposedly, our Montana senators.

Indeed, both Baucus and Tester are members of the Congressional Sportsmen's Caucus. They use this affiliation to show their constituents that they are "on their side" — pro-hunting, pro-gun rights and generally pro-outdoors. Or is that just a political ploy?

Hmmmm... I guess I will just have to keep checking my e-mail for that explanation from Max and Jon. But so far, the silence is deafening.

WHO SAYS THEY'RE YOUR KIDS? NOT IN MONTANA

October 11, 2009

The Montana Supreme Court just made it a whole lot harder to be a parent, and a whole lot easier to become one.

Let's review the travesty of Maniaci v. Kulstad, decided on a 6-1 vote in an opinion released on Oct. 6 (hereinafter known as Black Tuesday).

The court affirmed a Missoula District Court ruling by Judge Ed McLean that Michelle Kulstad had earned the right to be known as a parent to two children because she had "shacked up" with the children's adoptive mother during the time when they were adopted.

That's a crude way of saying they were living together, but don't be misled by any grandiloquent claims of "civil rights" that attach to this case because Kulstad and Barbara Maniaci were engaged in a homosexual partnership prior to their 2006 breakup. There is nothing "civil" about what the Supreme Court did, and nothing "right" about it either.

All parties agreed that the matter of sexual preference was not an issue in the case, so it should not be seen as a victory for gay couples. In fact, it is as detrimental to gay parents as to anyone because what it establishes is that a rightful parent can lose custody or be forced to share custody with anyone who shares household obligations and acts in a kindly manner to children in the house. As Barbara Maniaci has learned, this can cruelly rip apart her family that began while she was in a gay relationship as easily as it can destroy the family of a heterosexual who lets her children form a relationship with her live-in lover.

Let's be plain. The "family" relationship between Kulstad and Maniaci was the kind of "family relationship" which is endemic in our society — one based on convenience and need — rather than one based on commitment and law. The two women were not married, legally could not be married, and could not adopt a child together without taking extraordinary measures that they did not choose to pursue. In the case of both adoptions, Barbara Maniaci adopted the children on her own, assumed responsibility for them, and asked Michelle Kulstad for help in fulfilling those responsibilities.

The same situation takes place in thousands of families in Montana, and millions of homes across the United States. Only a tiny percentage of those families involve a homosexual relationship, however. This is about parental rights; not gay rights. If you have a complaint about Montana's marriage laws or adoption laws, change them, but don't give homosexuals "special privileges" in custody cases because you think they are victims elsewhere.

Everyone involved in the adoption process knew that Maniaci was homosexual at the time (she has since married a man), but everyone also knew that there was no attempt to include Kulstad as a legal parent in either adoption.

Yes, Maniaci informed the social workers who did household visits prior to the adoption that Kulstad would be present in the house and would help to raise the children. It would be fraudulent for her to pretend otherwise considering the circumstances. By the same token, a single woman adopting children on her own (or involved in a custody battle) might well inform any official household visitors that her live-in boyfriend would be available to help pay the bills, take the kids to school and generally provide assistance.

Such information might be taken into account, but it obviously should not be given too much weight because live-in relationships, by their very nature, are fluid, non-committed, and subject to change without notice. And it certainly does not mean the mother wants her boyfriend to get joint custody of her children.

When the state awards custody of a child, a precious human life, to a mother or father, it obviously is expecting a lifetime relationship to develop between the child and his or her new parent. No such expectation attaches to the "live in" boyfriend or girlfriend.

At least, not until now.

The Montana Supreme Court has thrown all that on its head. Because by awarding parental rights to Michelle Kulstad, they have in essence changed the playing field for all parents. From now on, it is not the state alone which will have the power to determine custody, but each and every parent. Every time a parent invites another adult into the home as a partner (even should no sexual relationship at all exist) there is a chance that the "partner" may eventually sue for custody of the children in the house.

There is certainly nothing stopping them from doing so because the Montana Supreme Court has ruled inexplicably that parental rights may be abridged or abrogated even with no finding of unfitness on the nominal parent's part. This completely reverses the constitutional principle which had prevailed in all previous Montana case law that "a natural parent cannot be denied custody of his or her child absent termination of that person's parental rights for abuse or neglect."

The one bright spot in the ruling came not from the benighted majority, but from the lone dissenter, Justice Jim Rice, who spoke eloquently for parents and for sanity.

"The Court's decision," Rice noted, "will open a Pandora's Box of potential attacks upon the right of fit and capable parents to raise their own children."

After establishing that the Montana Supreme Court has previously held fast to the rule that "a finding of abuse, neglect or dependency is the jurisdictional prerequisite for any court-ordered transfer of custody from a natural parent to a third party," Rice demonstrates conclusively that his fellow justices in this ruling have ruled in favor of Kulstad "for the apparent purpose of diminishing the reach of the constitutional rights previously declared for parents."

And they did so, remarkably, without openly acknowledging what they were doing. Rice notes that the court mistakenly offers that the "pre-1999 statutes made termination of parental rights, based upon dependency, abuse or neglect, the only option available to the Court before it could award a non-parent a custodial interest."

That is the language used by Justice Brian Morris in his majority opinion, and it is clearly intended to convey the impression that statutory changes in 1999 had the effect of giving third parties new parental rights that did not exist previously.

However, this interpretation is inaccurate, flawed and deceptive, as Rice points out: "Contrary to the Court's analysis, it was not the pre-1999 statutes that limited the claims of third parties, but the Montana Constitution." Therefore statutory changes would still have to meet the constitutional test, and they plainly don't.

I invite everyone to read Rice's dissent for themselves to see how many holes he pokes in the majority's "politically correct," but legally errant, opinion. In essence he notes that the court has failed its statutory responsibility to interpret the Constitution and has "permitted the Legislature to legislate Maniaci's constitutional rights out of existence."

In a broad rebuke of his colleagues, Rice declares, "the Court offers no rationale explaining how a third party's relationship with a child can overcome, constitutionally, a fit and capable parent's right to raise the child. It offers no analysis about how the Legislature's elimination of the fitness requirement can withstand strict scrutiny. The Court simply declares that the Legislature's will trumps this Court's declaration of constitutional rights."

Ultimately, Rice proves beyond a shadow of doubt that the majority opinion is simply a case of legislating from the bench. In order to prevail in her lawsuit, Kulstad needed to establish that Maniaci had "engaged in conduct that is contrary to the child-parent relationship." Such proof was not possible, because from all accounts Maniaci was a good mother. Therefore, in its ruling, the District Court changed the statutory requirement and said that Maniaci had engaged in conduct contrary to "an exclusive child-parent relationship," by allowing the children to have a relationship with Kulstad in the first place.

This is so bizarre as to be unfathomable, but for legal purposes all that matters is that such a finding is based on some notion of "social justice" and not on law. As Justice Rice notes, the very first section of the Montana Code Annotated instructs the judiciary how to interpret statutes contained therein:

"In the construction of a statute, the office of the judge is simply to ascertain and declare what is in terms or in substance contained therein, not to insert what has been omitted or to omit what has been inserted."

Yet by adding the word "exclusive" to the statutory requirement, the District Court did just what it is forbidden to do. As Justice Rice says, "It inserted new language into the statute," and the Supreme Court simply "affirmed the error."

Unless this ruling is overturned on appeal to the Supreme Court of the United States, Montana parents will never again be sure that the state won't be able to take their children from them. After all, according to the statute (MCA 40-4-228), "It is not necessary for the court to find a natural parent unfit before awarding a parental interest to a third party..."

If the court wasn't smart enough to throw out that usurpation of a fundamental right guaranteed not just by the Constitution but by the natural order, then it must be time to throw out the court. Remember, in Montana, Supreme Court justices are elected. For the record, the justices who voted against parents in this case were Brian Morris, Mike McGrath, James Nelson, John Warner, W. William Leaphart, and Patricia Cotter.

TAKE A MEMO: WATCH YOUR BACK IF YOU ARE A CONSERVATIVE

November 2, 2009

Everyone knows that the administration doesn't like being criticized. No administration does.

But the problem may be even more serious than anyone guessed. The opposition movement faces a significant challenge to its very existence. Whether you call it the tea-party movement, the anti-socialism movement, the anti-communism movement, or anything else, the fact is there are plenty of people in power who want it shut down, and that includes both Republicans and Democrats.

Face it, those are the parties of entrenched government power, and any power that returns to the people must of necessity reduce the power of those who wield it currently. So men and women on both sides of the political aisle have ranted about the growing power of the "radical" element on the right, never admitting that what they are really worried about is losing their own grip on power. But steps are being taken, and have been under way for quite some time, to shut down opponents of the liberal movement in America.

Indeed, one well-known political theorist has written a memorandum to the attorney general in which he encourages the administration to focus its attention on "policies and programs to combat the radical right."

That's not entirely unexpected.

The author of this memo notes that "the radical right or extreme right-wing, or however it may be designated, includes an unknown number of millions of Americans" and asserts that "these radical right groups are probably stronger and are certainly better organized than at any time in recent history." More importantly, "they are growing in strength and there is no reason to expect a turning of the tide in this regard."

The author of the memo acknowledges that some pundits believe the radical right is a "Republican problem" because it drains strength from mainstream Republican candidates:

"The growing strength of the radical right may indeed be an inconvenience to the Republican Party, but it is far worse than that for the Nation and the Democratic Party — for it threatens the President's programs at home and abroad. By the use of the twin propaganda weapons of fear and slander, the radical right moves the national political spectrum away from the Administration's proposed liberal programs at home and abroad."

So just who are these groups and individuals who comprise the "radical right"? Of course it could be the usual right-wing suspects such as the John Birch Society or the Minutemen. Or who knows? It might be you and me. The memo says that "All of these radical right organizations have the same general line: The danger to America is domestic Communism."

Well, come to think of it, I have said publicly that I consider communism to be a threat to our way of life, and that I see signs of creeping communism (and galloping socialism) everywhere in our federal government. So I guess I AM covered by the memo. The next part of the memo also sounds familiar from some of the criticism leveled against me by the occasional reader:

"They [the radical right] traffic in fear. Treason in high places is their slogan and slander is their weapon. They undermine loyal American confidence in each other and in their government.... Americans feel they are 'losing' for the first time in history. Since Americans intuitively tend not to believe they ever lose fairly, the radical right's charges that we are 'losing' ... because of treason in high places falls on fertile soil."

In other words, don't say anything bad about the president, or try to educate the public about the dangers of his policies, because that is "fear-mongering." You could well find yourself on an "enemies list" the way that Glenn Beck and Fox News have found themselves on the "enemies list" of the Obama White House.

But this is not a column about President Obama; it is a column about how the "radical right" is perceived as a danger to the United States because of its dedicated opposition to socialism and communism.

I guess we all have to ask ourselves if we support socialism or not. If you do, then, by God, get out there and fight for it. And please realize that what you will get is definitely a fight. Because there are, as the memo said, millions of us who will not surrender easily to a way of life that threatens our cherished freedoms, our Bill of Rights, and our very liberty.

And if you oppose socialism, as I do, then don't just remain on the sidelines while your government swings closer to Karl Marx and further away from Thomas Jefferson.

Don't let the author of that memo get his way. He encouraged the attorney general that, "What are needed are deliberate Administration policies and programs to contain the radical right from further expansion and in the long run to reduce it to its historic role of the impotent lunatic fringe."

In fact, it is safe to assume that if the left wing has made a concerted effort to reduce someone of Sarah Palin's stature to the "impotent lunatic fringe" simply because she is a passionate advocate of conservative principles, they will try to do the same to you.

But this is nothing new. Indeed, as the memo's author noted, "the struggle against the radical right is a long-term affair." So long, in fact, that it has stretched 48 years since the memo was written in December 1961.

That's right. The so-called "Reuther Memorandum" was written by Victor Reuther at the request of Attorney General Robert Kennedy in the first year of President Kennedy's administration. If it seems strangely familiar, that is because the battle under way today for the heart and soul of America is not a new one.

Indeed, Reuther represents a link between today's stealth socialists and the more up-front ones of 100 years ago. Reuther was the brother of Walter Reuther, the powerful president of the United Auto Workers union. Their father was a supporter of Eugene V. Debs, the famous socialist who ran for president in 1904, 1908, 1912 and 1920.

Victor and Walter Reuther apparently shared their father's love of socialism, and they lived for a while in the Soviet Union, where they were apparently even too liberal for the communist regime. The brothers were expelled for leading a strike demanding safer working conditions at the automobile factory where they worked.

A letter that the Reuther brothers wrote to friends back home in 1934 from the Soviet Union later famously surfaced in testimony before Congress. Here is the letter's conclusion:

"We are witnessing and experiencing great things here in the U.S.S.R. ... We are daily watching Socialism being taken down from the books on the shelves and put into actual application. Who would not be inspired by such events? ... Carry on the fight for a Soviet America."

It almost reminds you of some of the members of the current administration such as Anita Dunn, who shared with graduating high school seniors last May that Chinese Communist dictator Mao Zedong is one of her "favorite political philosophers." Depends, I suppose, whether or not you like to get your political philosophy from homicidal despots.

And it also helps put into perspective the Obama Administration's push-back against Fox News for their role in "outing" the socialist allegiance of many in the White House.

As Reuther wrote prophetically in 1961, "The radical right cannot be wished away or ignored [and] its demise is not something that can be readily accomplished."

But with the right combination of "Administration programs and policies" and assistance from "the press, television, church, labor, civic, political and other groups," he insisted, the radical right can be reduced to "its historic role of the impotent lunatic fringe."

At least, that is what White Houses have been hoping for the past 50 years.

FIRST THINGS FIRST: PROTECT YOUR FREEDOM

November 15, 2009

Free speech is not free. Like all of our freedoms, it was earned with the blood of patriotic Americans who put their principles ahead of their personal safety. It has been defended by generation after generation, but it should not be taken for granted.

As Ronald Reagan said, "Freedom is never more than one generation away from extinction. We didn't pass it to our children in the bloodstream. It must be fought for, protected, and handed on for them to do the same, or one day we will spend our sunset years telling our children and our children's children what it was once like in the United States where men were free."

Unfortunately, there seems to be little understanding of that today, which is why for the last several weeks I have been sounding the alarm about threats to the First Amendment that have been broached in recent years. There are unfortunately too many examples to include them all in a short weekly column such as this one, but I will at least try to touch the surface.

The Fairness Doctrine is the most well-known attempt by the federal government to control access to the media. When instituted in 1949 by the Federal Communications Commission, it was intended to "afford reasonable opportunity for the discussion of conflicting views of public importance." Maybe that was "fair" back in 1949 when radio and television were relatively young and stations were relatively few.

But that was then, and this is now. The problem today isn't getting enough information; it is getting too much. It isn't getting too few points of view; it is getting too many. Our culture has fractured into a million pieces. Diversity is not our goal; it is our curse.

Mind you, I am not suggesting a new government regulation to restrict access to the media, but it would make just as much sense as bringing back the "Fairness Doctrine," which died in the mid-1980s. Face it, we already have virtually endless channels with myriad points of view available on cable and satellite TV and on the Internet. On the one hand, if you want balance, all you have to do is change the channel. On the other hand, if you feel overwhelmed by information overload, all you have to do is turn the darned thing off.

But what we don't want to do is use government regulation to tell broadcasters or other parts of the media how to do their jobs. That is the first step toward censorship. Yet Democrats regularly promote just that.

Sen. John Kerry, the former presidential candidate, said in 2007, "I think the Fairness Doctrine ought to be there, and I also think equal time doctrine ought to come back."

Last year, Speaker Pelosi told a forum hosted by the Christian Science Monitor that she supports bringing back the Fairness Doctrine, and Assistant Majority Leader Dick Durbin has said the same.

Sen. Debbie Stabenow has been one of the most outspoken advocates for a return of the Fairness Doctrine, and her words are instructional about what liberals are really after.

In February of this year, Stabenow told radio host Bill Press, "Whether it's called the "Fairness" standard, whether it's called something else, I absolutely think it's time to be bringing accountability to the airwaves. I mean, our new president has talked rightly about accountability and transparency. You know, that we all have to step up and be responsible. And I think in this case there needs to be some accountability and standards put in place."

Accountability? To whom? Wait a minute, did a U.S. senator really say she thinks that the media needs to report to the government, and give an account of itself for government approval? Unless you can finagle some other interpretation of her words, it sure looks like she did.

And if CBS, ABC and NBC have to report to the government, what really makes our freedom in this country any different than the freedom enjoyed in Hugo Chavez's Venezuela, or for that matter, Stalin's Russia?

And don't think the threat to free speech stops with broadcasters. Yes, the FCC can dictate to TV and radio stations by invoking the principle that broadcast licenses are a commodity that is granted by the government and therefore subject to government oversight. But what we have learned more and more of late is that government doesn't need any reason, justification or constitutional provision to infringe on our freedoms. The Constitution is largely irrelevant to our lawmakers, who seem to think that mustering a slim majority of votes in Congress is sufficient cause to do anything they want.

That's why people who crow about the inviolability of the "free press" make me laugh. They explain pedantically that the print media is safe from government "accountability" or pressure, thanks to the First Amendment, but they forget that smart socialists are hard at work in law schools formulating new rules, regulations and policies that will make the world safe for "progressive" causes.

Controlling and intimidating the media is clearly part of that agenda. And if you can't "abridge the freedom" of the print media because of the First Amendment, that doesn't mean you can't intimidate them — or buy them.

That's right, buy them.

After all, there is no "separation of press and state" written into the Constitution, is there? What we have is an informal agreement that the country works best if the government doesn't own the media, but in our post-Obama efforts to "transform" the country, who knows what cherished traditions will be jettisoned as "old-fashioned" or "anti-progressive"?

Groups like Free Press are encouraging the government to subsidize newspapers as non-profit entities, which will thus inevitably be subject to review and extortion. Robert McChesney, the avowed socialist who is cofounder of Free Press, has called for direct federal subsidies to newspapers as well as Americorps "volunteers" staffing newsrooms. He also blithely denies that this would result in state-run media. Reminds me of the rhetoric after President Obama took over General Motors but denied he was in the car business.

By the way, Free Press worked with Obama to develop his communications policies prior to the 2008 election and has been to the White House several times since then. That doesn't mean the president is a socialist, but if guilt by association were evidence in a court of law, then President Obama would stand convicted of having bad judgment in his choice of friends at least.

Here's some of what McChesney has had to say for himself in the past year:

— "Any serious effort to reform the media system would have to necessarily be part of a revolutionary program to overthrow the capitalist system itself." —From his Sept. 2008 Monthly Review article on "The U.S. Media Reform Movement."

— "There is no real answer [to the U.S. economic crisis] but to remove brick by brick the capitalist system itself, rebuilding the entire society on socialist principles." From his Dec. 2008 Monthly Review essay, "A New New Deal under Obama?"

— "Only government can implement policies and subsidies to provide an institutional framework for quality journalism... The democratic state, the government, must create the conditions for sustaining the journalism that can provide the people with the information they need to be their own governors." From his article, "The Death and Life of Great American Newspapers," in the April 6, 2009, edition of The Nation magazine.

If those quotes don't scare you, then you have your head so far up your Marxist philosophy that the sunlight of freedom doesn't shine any more.

McChesney is in the same socialist bandwagon as several other past and present players on the Obama team. That includes the soon-to-be-ex-White House Communications Director Anita Dunn, the FCC Diversity Czar Mark Lloyd, and former Green Jobs Czar Van Jones.

Dunn famously took on Fox News as "a wing of the Republican Party" and then was outed for her own role as a proponent of the "Mao wing" of the Communist Party. Lloyd has gone on record as promoting "fairness" in the media through "structural" changes, and Van Jones is the guy responsible for the catchy slogan, "You cannot have an opposition movement without opposition media." (Did I mention that Jones was a board member of Free Press until 2008? Did I say Free Press? Oh yeah, I meant Controlled Media.)

The bottom line is that President Obama has surrounded himself with partisans who are so far to the left that they are a danger not just to the "radical right" but to freedom as we know it.

Hard to believe? Partisan caterwauling? Maybe. Or maybe we are just so complacent we don't know a threat when we see it. It has been just 20 years since Ronald Reagan left office, and it appears this generation may be the one he warned us against, the one that would let freedom slip away.

And if you don't want to listen to Ronald Reagan because he was a (shudder) Republican, then perhaps you will listen to John Adams because he was a Founding Father of our country.

"Posterity," he wrote, "you will never know how much it has cost my generation to preserve your freedom. I hope you will make good use of it."

'HATE GROUP' MASQUERADING AS ADVOCATE OF HUMAN RIGHTS?

March 7, 2010

A funny thing happened on the way to this week's column — I got "targeted," "frozen," "personalized" and "polarized."

In other words, I got lumped in with the majority of Americans as the "radical right" — you know, the scary people who believe in God, the Constitution, family values, and an honest day's work for an honest day's pay.

"Targeting" the opposition is the tactic made famous by left-wing political theorist Saul Alinsky, who wrote in "Rules for Radicals," that one key route to power is to "Pick the target, freeze it, personalize it, and polarize it." This goes along with another of Alinsky's rules: "Ridicule is man's most potent weapon. It is almost impossible to counterattack ridicule."

That's the methodology employed by the Southern Poverty Law Center, a so-called human-rights group, in a new report called "Rage on the Right," which seeks to convince Americans that "the anger seething across the American political landscape" as represented by the Tea Party movement is "shot through with rich veins of radical ideas, conspiracy theories and racism."

As an example of how "targeting" works, you have to realize that this SPLC report is allegedly a review of "The Year in Hate and Extremism," but there is not one mention of Islamic extremism included — nothing about the alleged murder of 13 people at Fort Hood by Maj. Nidal Malik Hasan; nothing about the Muslim convert who apparently killed a soldier at a recruiting center in Little Rock, Ark.; nothing about the father who allegedly killed his daughter by ramming her with a car for being "too Westernized"; nothing about the founder of a

Muslim TV station in Buffalo, N.Y., who was charged with beheading his wife for seeking a divorce; nothing about the murder of a college professor in New York state by his Muslim student, allegedly in revenge for "persecuted" Muslims.

Just plain nothing.

Because the Southern Poverty Law Center is not legitimately concerned about hate and extremism, but rather about marginalizing conservatives such as myself as "the radical right." Can't accomplish that by talking about actual murders carried out by Islamic extremists. Besides, what's more dangerous: A Muslim unloading a semi-automatic weapon at a military base while shouting "God is great" in Arabic? Or American citizens "raging against the machinery of the federal bureaucracy and liberal government programs and policies"?

Of course, that's a rhetorical question. We all know that Americans are dangerous, especially when seeking to guarantee their constitutional rights. Among the "signs of growing radicalization" that SPLC spokesman Mark Potok notes in his "Rage on the Right" report is "Politicians pandering to the antigovernment right in 37 states [that] have introduced 'Tenth Amendment resolutions,' based on the constitutional provision keeping all power not explicitly given the the federal government with the states."

Apparently, supporting the Constitution is now considered radical.

So too is quoting the Founding Fathers. As one sign of the growing "radicalization" that threatens America, we are told by Potok that armed men have attended speeches by President Obama "bearing signs suggesting that the 'tree of liberty' needs to be 'watered' with the 'blood of tyrants.' " What Potok fails to mention is that the source of the quotation is Thomas Jefferson — yeah, THAT Thomas Jefferson, author of the Declaration of Independence, third president of the United States, HIM.

What Jefferson said in full was, "The tree of liberty must be refreshed from time to time with the blood of patriots & tyrants." It is hard to argue with the sentiment unless you are a defender of tyrants, but taken out of context, it is easy to use as a means of "personalizing" Tea Party protesters as dangerous right-wing kooks.

This kind of "scare tactic" would be more alarming if it came from a source other than the Southern Poverty Law Center, but that group's credibility has already long since vanished. Even a writer for the left-wing Huffington Post wrote a scathing rebuke of the SPLC for its lack of interest in the Obama administration's decision to drop charges against members of the New Black Panther Party who had tried to intimidate voters in Philadelphia in 2008.

Carol M. Swain wrote last year that, "The SPLC has been mum on the issue, despite the fact that in 2000, it included the New Black Panther Party among its annual list of hate groups."

She concluded, "...what is most shocking is that the SPLC has spent far more resources hounding conservative organizations, such as the Center for Immigration Studies, and prominent citizens like CNN's award-winning anchor Lou Dobbs, than it has protecting the civil rights of American voters, which includes white people as well as black. The unrelenting attacks on Mr. Dobbs and others are shameless. The once venerable organization wages war against conservative individuals, principles, and organizations. How unfortunate for America. How unfortunate for the organization's founders."

Nor is Swain a voice on the right who can be marginalized as yet another neo-Nazi racist by the Southern Poverty Law Center. She is a black woman who is a professor of political science and law at Vanderbilt University, and has written a book entitled "The New White Nationalism in America: Its Challenge to Integration."

Yet from her vantage point as an expert on race relations, she has no trouble seeing through the polarizing tactics of the Southern Poverty Law Center. Her summation is the best final word:

"Rather than monitoring hate groups, the Southern Poverty Law Center has become one."

CONGRESS AND THE INCREDIBLE SHRINKING CONSTITUTION

March 21, 2010

Con-sti-tu-tion-al — *adj. (3) of, in, authorized by, subject to, dependent on, or in accordance with the constitution of a nation, state, or society.*
Cri-sis — *n. (2) a turning point in the course of anything; decisive or crucial time, stage or event (3) a time of great danger or trouble, whose outcome decides whether possible bad consequences will follow. —SYN. see EMERGENCY.*

•••

You don't need Webster's Dictionary to know a constitutional crisis when you see one, but it helps to have a starting point we can all agree on.

As I write this column on Thursday, it appears that the Democrats in Congress intend to force a vote on some variation of the health-care bill by Sunday. By the time you read this, the deed may already be done.

But the constitutional crisis is just beginning. What we face in this vote on "health-care reform" is indeed "a time of great danger or trouble" whose outcome will decide "whether possible bad consequences will follow."

The problem is multi-faceted — too much to catalog thoroughly in a brief column such as this — but it starts with the fact that regulating health care is not a federal power authorized by the Constitution. The only tiny hook the Democrats can hang their 2,400-page monstrosity of a bill on is the "Commerce Clause," which allows Congress to regulate interstate commerce.

This clause was essentially intended by our Founding Fathers to make sure that states all treated each other equally, and did not form trading blocs amongst themselves that would jeopardize the union as a whole. Over the years, however, it has been jiggered and twisted until now it allows the federal government to regulate anything it wants.

But even if Congress has the authority to regulate insurance companies which operate in more than one state, that should not grant it the power to force you, an individual private citizen, to buy insurance or any other good or service. That, however, is just what the Democratic Congress and President Obama want to do with health insurance.

You might not be able to do anything to stop them either, but it is possible the courts will. Idaho and Virginia have already passed laws requiring their attorney generals to sue Congress if it passes a bill that requires residents to buy insurance. And at least 35 other states are considering similar legislation, which could ultimately result in the nation's greatest constitutional crisis since the Civil War.

This fight thus goes well beyond abuse of the Commerce Clause and is ultimately an existential threat to the very "Blessings of Liberty" which the Constitution was originally written to enshrine.

One of the most keen of those blessings of liberty is freedom of choice - the opportunity to decide for myself how I shall live my life, with full understanding that I accept the consequences for my own actions.

Of course, there are restrictions on any behavior that detrimentally affects other people or society as a whole, and those restrictions are implemented through laws that "we the people" impose on ourselves. The supreme law of the land is the U.S. Constitution, and it firmly establishes the LIMITED role of the federal government in our lives. The individual states are permitted a much broader role in regulating our lives, but in no case can states or the federal government deprive us of our liberty without due process.

Part of the problem with the Democrats' frantic "anything goes" approach to passing the health-care legislation is that they don't think "process" matters. They say that they can vote on the health-care bill by voting on another bill. This process called "deem and pass" is intended to allow the members of Congress to say they did one thing while they were actually doing another. But process does matter, and when process violates the Constitution then it most certainly should matter.

Take this, for instance: The House of Representatives is currently voting on the SENATE health-care bill, which is illegal. The Constitution mandates that "all Bills for raising Revenue shall originate in the House of Representatives, but the Senate may propose or concur with Amendments as on other Bills." What happened in this case is that the Senate took an unrelated bill that originated in the House, amended it by completely removing the previous provisions and then substituting 2,400 pages of bureaucracy-creating, money-stealing, rights-restricting health-care reform. This is a blatant end run around the Constitution, and means that Congress can do anything it wants.

How could they, you ask? Because we the people let them get away with it.

This is, sadly, tantamount to saying that the Constitution itself doesn't matter, which unfortunately many modern American citizens do say. Their thinking, and the thinking of Congress, is that if they have a goal which they consider noble, they can rightly use any means to achieve that goal. That makes nobility the supreme law of the land rather than the Constitution, and that makes our freedom look as vulnerable as that granted to the king's subjects by noblesse oblige.

The danger of having a Congress of nobles that feels obligated to shower the public with benefits should be obvious to anyone - especially anyone who has noted that the United States government is at least $14.5 trillion in debt.

The Congress of the United States today is as isolated from the people as Marie Antoinette was before the French Revolution. In the story about her callousness when told that the public had no bread to eat, Antoinette is famously (but inaccurately) supposed to have replied, "Let them eat cake." When informed that the national treasury has been stripped bare by profligate spending and that "we the people" are broke, Nancy Pelosi might have advised, "Let them have health care."

Antoinette faced the guillotine for being out of touch with the mood of the people. Such a fate is no longer contemplated for arrogant rulers, for which Pelosi should consider herself lucky. Nonetheless, she and her fellow Democrats can and must face the wrath of the people — at the ballot box if nowhere else.

WHO OWNS YOU?
THE RISK OF 'UNLIMITED SUBMISSION'

March 28, 2010

Hear ye, hear ye:

"Resolved, that the several States composing the United States of America, are not united on the principles of unlimited submission to their General Government; ... that whensoever the General Government assumes undelegated powers, its acts are unauthoritative, void, and of no force..."

Do you agree?

Or do you think it is crazy for states and individuals to reject unlimited submission to the federal government?

Certainly, in the wake of a new law that orders American citizens to surrender their right to make their own decisions about the most personal of matters — their health and well-being — it is no surprise that many states have indeed risen up to protest against what appears to be an unconstitutional seizure of power by Congress.

But the words quoted above are not the latest resolution to come out of some "right-wing wacko" tea party convention, as MSNBC would put it. They are instead the words of the Founding Father who wrote the Declaration of Independence, Thomas Jefferson.

In the Kentucky Resolutions, Jefferson gave voice to the notion that the several states — as the creators of the federal union — must retain some level of judgment over whether that "General Government" had overstepped its bounds as originally agreed to by the states in the compact known as the United States Constitution.

Jefferson, our third president, maintained that the sovereign states had the right to reject (or "nullify") any law which the federal government passed without constitutional authority. He further maintained that "without this right, they [the states] would be under the dominion, absolute and unlimited, of whosoever might exercise this right of judgment for them..."

Jefferson ultimately lost that argument, but his long-ago words serve as inspiration today for, yes, those very tea-party patriots who still read and honor the Constitution and are vilified on the left as ugly Americans precisely because they DO read and honor the Constitution.

That, of course, is the situation which we have reached now.

Thanks to the "judgment" of Congress that it can "create" new rights "ex nihili" (out of nothing) — namely the peculiar right to be forced to buy health insurance — the states, and the individual citizens therein, have fallen under the "dominion, absolute and unlimited," of the federal government.

You will not find anything like this power of Congress in the Constitution, which is why more than a dozen state attorneys general have already filed suits to block the health-care bill from taking effect.

The argument is simple — that without any constitutional authority, the Congress of the United States has arrogated to itself the power to tell American citizens how they must spend their money. In doing so, it thumbed its nose at "we the people," and at the Constitution. We have been ordered to buy health insurance whether we want it or not. So much for freedom.

Mind you, this is not a tax, although there are most certainly taxes and fines levied in the Patient Protection and Affordable Care Act signed into law by President Obama Tuesday. But what Congress did was establish an individual mandate that every citizen must buy health insurance as a condition of citizenship. This is an unprecedented abuse of power in the 221-year history of our precious Constitution.

Nor, for that matter, can Congress claim that it is using its power to regulate interstate commerce to justify this new law. Commerce is the buying and selling of goods and services. But what this strange law does is claim that anyone who chooses NOT to buy a good or service (namely, health insurance) is breaking the law. This is not regulation of interstate commerce, but dictatorship.

As I have pointed out previously, even the Congressional Budget Office recognized the unfairness of mandatory insurance as long ago as 1994 when they wrote the following about Hillary Clinton's proposal for national health care:

"A mandate requiring all individuals to purchase health insurance would be an unprecedented form of federal action. The government has never required people to buy any good or service as a condition of lawful residence in the United States."

Moreover, the 10th Amendment plainly prohibits the federal government from adding new powers that are not plainly delegated to it by the Constitution. That is the strong foundation many states are basing their lawsuit on.

But don't think President Obama and his Democratic allies will give up easily. The president's adviser David Axelrod has said he is confident that the health-care bill will survive all constitutional challenges, and so apparently is the mainstream media.

Legal experts quoted by newspapers and TV stations say the lawsuits have little chance of succeeding because, under the Constitution, federal law trumps state law. Here are a couple of examples:

— Richard Pildes, New York University: "If there's anything that's settled in American constitutional law, it's that when the federal government acts within the scope of its constitutional powers, federal law prevails over any conflicting state law."

— Michael McConnell, Stanford University: "If the federal bill is constitutional, then the state laws will be of no legal effect. If the federal bill is unconstitutional, then the state measures will be unnecessary."

This is nonsense, of course. The first scholar begins with the assumption that the federal government IS acting "within the scope of its constitutional powers." To use the common phrase taught in law school, this "assumes facts not in evidence." The attorneys general of the various states maintain that the Congress is claiming an undelegated power by forcing citizens to purchase a good or service against their will. Were the states not to sue, the issue could never be resolved and Congress would have gotten away with a brazen expansion of its powers.

The second scholar makes a valid point with his first statement. If the federal bill IS constitutional, then the state laws rejecting it clearly will have no legal effect. That really goes without saying. But his second statement is mere chicanery. The ONLY way the federal bill COULD be found to be unconstitutional is IF the states (or some individual lucky enough to be granted legal standing) were to challenge it. Thus the state measures that challenge the federal law are not only necessary, but indispensable.

On the other hand, it is hard to be optimistic that the Supreme Court will ultimately rule in favor of the people over the government. Too often in the past, the court has merely rubber-stamped power grabs by the federal government. If it does so again in this case, then the federal government does not merely run the country. It owns you.

On Liberty and Legal Plunder ...

April 4, 2010

It's not socialism. It's just an "income shift" from the rich to the poor.

At least, that's what Montana's Sen. Max Baucus called it on the Senate floor — adding that the health-care bill passed by Congress "will have the effect of addressing [the] mal-distribution of income in America."

Fellow Democrats are probably worried about Baucus letting the cat out of the bag, but they needn't worry. America already bought the "pig in the poke" known as health-care reform, and it doesn't seem as though even now very many people are paying attention to the con game that has been played on them.

Who cares if Baucus accidentally told the truth? The deed is done, and the loot is being divided up. It's time to celebrate the "fundamental transformation" of America that is under way.

And Sen. Baucus isn't the only Democrat suffering from "foot-in-mouth disease" anyway. Former Gov. Howard Dean seems to have the same malady.

On CNBC'S "Squawk Box," Dean said, "When [wealth distribution] gets out of whack as it did in the '20s and it has now, you need to do some redistribution. This [health-care reform] is a form of redistribution."

But much more serious than the "foot-in-mouth" problem of Baucus and Dean is the affliction of Barack Obama and his gang of Chicago ward heelers known as a White House staff. Call it "hand-in-pocket disease." Or call it socialism, if you dare.

Nineteenth-century French philosopher and economist Frederic Bastiat had another name for it — "legal plunder" — and if you want a real education, you are invited to read Bastiat's essay on "The Law" in its entirety on the Internet (http://bastiat.org/en/the_law.html).

The book first appeared in 1850, two brief years after Karl Marx published "The Communist Manifesto," and though Bastiat never mentions Marx by name, "The Law" totally discredits his socialist philosophy.

The concept of the book is that "the law" is intended as a way for people to band together to collectively protect their individual rights. When law is applied fairly, it acts "to protect persons, liberties, and properties; to maintain the right of each, and to cause justice to reign over us all." However, Bastiat recognized that two forces conspire to pervert the law: "stupid greed and false philanthropy." Both, of course, are at work in health-care "reform" legislation.

Bastiat fashions stupid greed as "a fatal tendency" among people that "when they can, they wish to live and prosper at the expense of others."

He distinguishes therefore between property and plunder as the two forms of wealth acquisition, noting that property is acquired through man's "ceaseless labor" (mental or physical) and that plunder is acquired "by seizing and consuming the products of the labor of others."

Just as water tends to run downhill, so too does mankind follow the path of least resistance, and so — to avoid the pain of labor — "it follows that men will resort to plunder whenever plunder is easier than work."

"It is evident, then," he concludes, "that the proper purpose of law is to use the power of its collective force to stop this fatal tendency to plunder instead of to work. All the measures of the law should protect property and punish plunder."

Despite Bastiat's clear warning, however, modern government has turned aside from the proper role of protecting property from plunder and has instead become an instrument of plunder itself. Thus, Barack Obama could say on the campaign trail in 2008, "I think when you spread the wealth around, it's good for everybody" — and still be elected president.

Bastiat, however, was dead on when he said that plunder is a "fatal tendency" of mankind, and at some point turning the U.S. government into a mechanism for plundering wealth from one group of Americans to be consumed by another group of Americans will destroy the republic.

Most people, of course, would not be a party to theft, so it is vitally important that those who benefit from plunder do not ever let it be discovered for what it is. That's where Bastiat's second force comes in — false philanthropy, or what he calls "the seductive lure of socialism."

He might as well be speaking of the United States of Obama. Are homes being foreclosed on because of bad financial decisions? Scold the banks and forgive the loans! Are banks and insurance companies going down the drain because of greed and selfishness? Bail out the banks and reward their selfishness! Are jobs being lost because the country has removed all incentives for creativity and productivity? Spend billions on road projects to put people to work for a month or two! Call it a "stimulus" program, and no one will realize that it's a lost cause.

Finally, that brings us to the one-two punch that President Obama used against the nation last month. First, nationalize health care in ways that people don't even begin to understand. Claim that you can spend billions of dollars for millions of new patients with unlimited access to health care and that by doing so you will lower the deficit. Then, while people are trying to figure out just how much money you lifted out of their wallet, move quickly and nationalize the student loan program so that billions of dollars will be available to cover up the huge hole you have just created in the economy.

Of course, it's socialism. Just don't say it too loud.

None of this manipulation and lying would have come as a surprise to Bastiat, who was much more prescient than Nostradamus ever dreamed of being. In fact, when Bastiat speaks of "the most popular fallacy of our times," you are almost sure he is talking about 2010, not 1850.

"It is not considered sufficient that the law should be just," he said. "It must be philanthropic. Nor is it sufficient that the law should guarantee to every citizen the free and inoffensive use of his faculties for physical, intellectual, and moral self-improvement. Instead, it is demanded that the law should directly extend welfare, education, and morality throughout the nation. This is the seductive lure of socialism. And I repeat again: These two uses of the law are in direct contradiction to each other. We must choose between them. A citizen cannot at the same time be free and not free."

Did you hear that?

Repeating for those who have ears but do not hear: "A citizen cannot at the same time be free and not free."

Yet... Yet... Millions among us stubbornly insist that they can surrender decisions over their very own life and well-being to the government and yet maintain their freedom. Well, you are free — free to do whatever the government lets you do. Free to be indoctrinated. Free to march in lockstep. Free to receive the welfare, education and morality that the government feels you should have.

And everyone who thinks he knows what is best for you, every socialist in the Senate or the White House, will tell you it is for your own good, and for the good of society.

The dirty little secret of socialism, however, is that it is not about a better society; it is about bigger government. It might as well be called "governmentalism," but for the fact that no one would tolerate such a movement. After all, if you call a mosquito a butterfly, you are much more likely to find willing victims for it than if you call it a bloodsucking leech.

But no matter what you call it, government that steals from you to reward someone else is your enemy. Do not be fooled by your own "stupid greed" or someone else's claims of "false philanthropy" and give in to the temptation of legal plunder. Seize back your liberty.

TEA: VACCINE AGAINST THE PARTISAN VIRUS

April 18, 2010

Democrats cannot save this country. Neither can Republicans.

If you are counting on a political party to rescue us from the downward spiral we are on, then you have not been paying attention. The political parties are the problem, not the solution. They are the ones that created the country's downward spiral, which like the spiral of DNA is a double helix — in this case, one part elephant and one part donkey.

Think of it as a virus that has invaded the body politic.

For years, the Partisan Virus had remained fairly harmless, sort of like the common cold — a nuisance, but not generally life-threatening. At some point, however, it mutated and became deadly. Exactly how or when this happened no one can say, but the current state of the nation should prove to any rational mind that the Partisan Virus is now so dangerous that the body politic must be wheeled into intensive care or perish from lack of treatment.

Anyone who doubts this needs merely to look at the housing bubble under President Bush, the disastrous recovery program that began in 2008, and the rapid expansion of the deficit under President Obama. Neither Republicans nor Democrats have been telling you the truth. And if John McCain had been elected president instead of Barack Obama, the country would have been in much the same mess, with a multi-trillion dollar debt and no visible means of (life) support.

Symptoms of the Partisan Virus are well-known — deafness (to the pleadings of the people); an uncontrollable urge to spend (other people's money), and hypnotic suggestibility (to do whatever party leaders tell you to do). The most virulent cases are drawn incontrollably toward Washington, D.C, where they band together in a manner similar to the vampires of popular mythology. This perhaps has something to do with the common characterization of the worst-hit victims of the Partisan Virus as "bloodsuckers." The virus unfortunately strikes young and old alike, and usually remains present until treated.

The treatment, fortunately, is also readily known. Like many vaccinations or antiviral drugs, it employs a non-toxic variation of the harmful element present in the virus itself to protect against infection or actually to bring about a cure.

Thus, we can say simply that the cure for those who have been exposed to the harmful effects of either the Democratic Party or the Republican Party is to enjoy the reviving medicine of the Tea Party, which looks almost like the other parties but has had the toxins of corruption and self-aggrandizement removed.

This patriotic brew can only be taken voluntarily, and though it creates a violent reaction in some people who already have the Partisan Virus, there appears to be no alternative treatment available that can bring the patient back to health.

Unlike the Republican and Democratic parties, the Tea Party has no leadership. Therefore its proponents cannot fall victim to the usual propaganda that is the bread and butter of political parties. Likewise, because the Tea Party IS "we the people," there is no chance that it can be steered against the popular will. Finally because the Tea Party consists of Tax Payers, the urge to spend has been nullified by the fact that it's not "other people's money" that is being spent, but our very own children's future and inheritance.

The words of Patrick Henry at the First Continental Congress of 1774 are instructive: "The distinctions between

Virginians, Pennsylvanians, New Yorkers, and New Englanders are no more. I am not a Virginian, but an American!"

This statement came shortly after the original Boston Tea Party that helped inspire American patriots to seize their liberty, and by the same token, those who drink the hearty brew of patriotism today should consider making the following declaration: "I am not a Republican. I am not a Democrat. I am an American."

Indeed, it is healthy to remember that partisan politics is not part of the corporate structure of the American body politic — there is no place for the Republican Party or the Democratic Party in the Constitution. They evolved as a matter of convenience to those who were eager to gain or hold power.

The Tea Party, on the other hand, is an evocation of our deepest founding principles, which Samuel Adams warned us are "worth defending at all hazards." Just as the original Tea Party was a rebellion against entrenched power, so too the modern Tea Party is a small but potent force to protect the liberties and Constitution that were "purchased ... for us with toil and danger and expense of treasure and blood."

Let Adams, who knew as much about tea parties (and patriotism) as anyone, have the last word:

"If ever a time should come, when vain and aspiring men shall possess the highest seats in Government, our country will stand in need of its experienced patriots to prevent its ruin." ... "It does not require a majority to prevail, but rather an irate, tireless minority keen to set brush fires in people's minds."

JUST WHO DO THEY THINK THEY OWN?

April 25, 2010

I have for some time been looking for a model to describe the relationship that currently exists between the people and the federal government. At different times, I have labeled it as feudalism, serfdom or slavery.

None of them is quite right, and yet they all hint at the problem — the American people, who ostensibly still pride themselves on freedom have long since been co-opted as nothing more than a labor force by their masters in Washington.

"We the people" have become "we the workers."

This is a fact known to one and all, but for some reason, of late it has been treated like a crazy uncle — the less said about it the better. But that was not always true. President Reagan often warned against letting the government control too much of your life. In his farewell address to the nation in 1989, he said this:

"I hope we once again have reminded people that man is not free unless government is limited. There's a clear cause and effect here that is as neat and predictable as a law of physics: As government expands, liberty contracts."

That's either a true or false proposition. If anyone wants to defend a larger role for government in our lives, they are welcome to do so ... but I sure wish they would demonstrate how more government can exist without taking away more of my freedom. I don't think they can do so.

And we are living in the time of the greatest expansion of government in the history of our country. Every day, the Congress and the president propose or implement some new restriction, some new regulation, some new entitlement that further extends the control of government into our personal lives. And to add insult to injury, they make us pay for it. Thus, it is clear that while we work at the local grocery store, or in a hospital or a law office or in any other kind of business, our real boss is Uncle Sam.

Or maybe "boss" is not the right word either. I am starting to think the real model for our relationship with the federal government is the sharecropper's relationship with his landlord. We do the work; they get a share of the money. There's no fieldwork or farming in this kind of sharecropping, but basically isn't the federal government putting us to work in our various "fields" of endeavor and then grabbing a percentage of our profit.

Where this model falls down is that at least the landlord really did own the land and had a contract with the sharecropper, but what stake does the government have in us? Just our citizenship? Are we actually the property that the government is harvesting its share from? Do they own us?

Which, I guess, brings us back to the slavery model after all.

Think of the debts that have been incurred by the federal government in our name. We are on the hook for $17.5 trillion for Social Security; more than $75 trillion for Parts A, B and D of Medicare; and unknown trillions for the new health-care reform.

Since the federal government doesn't have any money of its own, every time it creates a new entitlement or guarantees a new service it has to get more money from you the taxpayer or else borrow more money from them the Chinese (metaphorically speaking, of course; it could actually be the Saudis, the British or the Russians, for beggars are equal opportunity borrowers).

But if the government borrows money it can't pay back, that's just another way of putting you on the hook, and trust me, there is no way the government can pay back what it owes. Plus, interest rates are expected to go up substantially when our foreign creditors realize we have no visible means of support — and every percentage increase in the interest rate will mean more trillions in unfunded liabilities.

Now, some have said that the federal government has incurred this massive debt without the approval of the taxpayers, that in essence the Congress has usurped the authority of the public, and thus created a kind of taxation without representation.

While poetically apt, this description throws on its head the whole notion of "representative government." Clearly, it is our representatives who are spending themselves silly. We cannot argue that we did not elect them.

But we can still argue against their reckless spending because they are stealing from our progeny, who just as clearly do not have representation.

As Jefferson wrote: "The generations of men may be considered as bodies or corporations. Each generation has the [use and enjoyment] of the earth during the period of its continuance. When it ceases to exist, the [use and enjoyment] passes on to the succeeding generation, free and unencumbered... We may consider each generation as a distinct nation, with a right, by the will of its majority, to bind themselves, but none to bind the succeeding generation, more than the inhabitants of another country."

As Americans, we have passed on a heritage of freedom and prosperity to our children "free and unencumbered," for generation after generation. Until now. And the generation that follows us will be so encumbered that it will not be able to lift itself up off the ground. It shall have small chance of freedom and no hope of prosperity, unless the chains of tyranny are thrown off now.

It seems as though more and more we have to return to the words of the Founding Fathers if we hope to return to the nation they created. In one quote, Jefferson even anticipated the role of the government as a tyrannical landlord, and warned us against it:

In his autobiography, he wrote, "I am for a government rigorously frugal and simple. Were we directed from Washington when to sow, when to reap, we should soon want bread."

Everyone knows this is true. It is just a matter of how hungry we are willing to become before we demand back our individuality, our liberty and our right to use and enjoy the free republic that our forefathers handed down to us.

LAY CLAIM TO CONSTITUTION — OR LOSE IT

May 16, 2010

One of the most worrisome social trends today is that many Americans no longer claim ownership of the Constitution.

Every time I write about some constitutional issue, I inevitably hear from some smug liberal scoffing at how "Frank the Constitutional Scholar" knows more than the judges and congressmen who reign in Washington. Apparently we are supposed to be comfortable with the idea of letting President Obama, Harry Reid and the judges they appoint and confirm tell us what the Constitution means.

This is a scary thought. First, it is the judges, congressmen and presidents in Washington which the Constitution is supposed to protect us from. It codifies the LIMITS of their power over "we the people." Second, why should anyone in America be made to feel ashamed for holding up the Constitution as their shield of liberty? Should it not be as familiar to us, and as vital, as the air we breathe?

If "we the people" surrender interpretation of the Constitution to those in power, then we have abrogated our responsibility as sovereign citizens. Each and every person in this country should know and understand the Constitution. Otherwise our country is the moral equivalent of the church in the Middle Ages when only the priests knew what was in the Bible, kept hidden in the mysterious code language of Latin, and doled out to the flock in dribs and drabs as the priesthood deemed appropriate.

The arrival of the printing press and the ensuing Reformation and Enlightenment gave back to the people the ability to make their own decisions about religion. It is about time "we the people" take back the Constitution as well. Indeed, the fact that people in this country don't understand their responsibilities as the guardians of the Constitution is a damning indictment of our educational system. Can we really be so naive that we are willing to accept the pronouncement from "on high" about what the ruling law of the land proclaims instead of studying it for ourselves and making our own decisions?

As much as anything, the Tea Party Movement is a reaction to just that haughtiness of Washington, D.C. The ruling elites have used the Constitution as their equivalent of a get-rich scheme for too many years, and the people are sick of it. Now, finally, we are seeing signs that "we the people" will not go down without a fight.

And a terrific fight it promises to be.

Indeed, we are probably in the midst of the country's most serious constitutional crisis since the 1800s. As many as 33 states are in some stage of suing the federal government over the federal health-care "reform" law, which adds billions of dollars in burdens to state treasuries and also forces citizens to buy health insurance, whether they want it or not.

On another front, Arizona is the first of what will probably be several states to pass statutes to essentially demand that the federal government fulfill its duty to uphold the laws on immigration.

And here at home, Montana was the first state to pass the Firearms Freedom Act, which argues that if a gun does not cross the state line, then the federal government has no regulatory power over it.

And in both the Arizona and Montana cases, the federal government is contemplating lawsuits against the states for claiming the rights guaranteed to them under the 10th Amendment.

Yep, we have a constitutional crisis all right. Either that or we don't really have a Constitution anymore anyway. Because despite what some people believe, the federal government does not have unlimited powers; it only has the powers granted to it by the states when they signed the Constitution.

Thus, the federal government DOES have a delegated power to regulate "interstate commerce," but they DO NOT have the authority to regulate intrastate commerce — trade that takes place entirely within the borders of a state. That's why "What's MADE in Montana and STAYS in Montana" is none of the federal government's business — including guns. Of course, the court can just "deem" that intrastate commerce IS interstate commerce, but that would only worsen the constitutional crisis, not end it.

Nonetheless, that's just the kind of ruling we can expect from the Supreme Court — because it's what we have gotten in the past. And it makes clear why the further we get from the plain written words of the U.S. Constitution, the more trouble we've got. If judges can "deem" and "discover" new powers for the federal government, then we might as well rip up the Constitution.

Indeed, some politicians seem to find the Constitution a bit inconvenient, whether it was George W. Bush with the Patriot Act or Barack Obama with the Health-Insurance Mandate. There is an oft-repeated story that President Bush dismissed the Constitution as a troublesome "piece of paper." That may be apocryphal, but there is ample evidence that his successor did call the Constitution "an imperfect document and ... a document that reflects some deep flaws in American culture."

Perhaps that view of the Constitution is why President Obama once famously pledged that if elected that he would be "fundamentally transforming" the United States of America.

After all, it would not be possible to "fundamentally" transform America without altering or doing away with the Constitution. "Fundamental" change means change which affects the "foundation," and the foundation of our country is the Constitution given to us by our FOUNDING Fathers. There is really no other interpretation possible.

The fact that the states and the people of the United States are resisting this "transformation" is not just a bit of political theater; it is rather a manifestation of the core beliefs that stream through our body politic. The Tea Party movement is aptly named because it is steeped in the foundational principles of this nation.

Consider, for instance, these words from the Declaration of Independence:

"Prudence... will dictate that governments long established should not be changed for light and transient causes; and accordingly all experience hath shown that mankind are more disposed to suffer, while evils are sufferable, than to right themselves by abolishing the forms to which they are accustomed. But when a long train of abuses and usurpations, pursuing invariably the same object evinces a design to reduce them under absolute despotism, it is their right, it is their duty, to throw off such government, and to provide new guards for their future security."

This paragraph is doubly important. First, it assures us that "governments long established" should not be lightly changed. Yet how else can we describe the presumptuousness of a president who deigns to "fundamentally transform" the republic that for two centuries has been the standard bearer of freedom for the entire human race?

Secondly, it assures us that "usurpation" — the wrongful seizure or exercise of power — is grounds for the people to rise up and "provide new guards for their future security." Note that it is not just the "right" of the people to throw off such an abusive government, "it is their duty."

Each of us can decide for ourselves whether we think such abuses are under way now, but if "usurpation" means bypassing the established order, then we should at least be worried when we hear that a president's avowed goal is to "fundamentally transform" the country.

There is indeed another eerie echo in the Declaration of Independence which reverberates mightily in response to that foul chord. It comes in the list of excesses of King George III which the colonists submitted to the world as evidence of tyranny, and notes that the king had given "his assent to ... acts of pretended legislation" that had the effect of "taking away our charters, abolishing our most valuable laws, and altering fundamentally the forms of our governments" [emphasis added].

Whether a president or king should not matter. Neither has the authority to either "alter fundamentally" or "fundamentally transform" the nation we live in. Anyone who reads the Constitution and the Declaration already knows that. Maybe that's why some people don't want us to read them, or to understand them.

WHAT THE WORLD NEEDS NOW IS MORE REAL LIBERALS

May 23, 2010

Liberals — God bless them!

No, seriously. Don't let my conservative credentials sway you into thinking I am being facetious. I am not.

But consider which liberals I am praising, and then stop and ask yourself if the people who use that title today are fit for the honor.

Taking the definition from a good "liberal" source — Wikipedia — to make sure it is not some accident of warped conservative thinking, let's consider the following:

"Liberals in the 19th century wanted to develop a world free from government intervention, or at least free from too much government intervention. They championed the ideal of negative liberty, which constitutes the absence of coercion and the absence of external constraints. They believed governments were cumbersome burdens and they wanted governments to stay out of the lives of individuals."

Like I said before, God bless liberals. I just wish we could find one worthy of the name today.

There were many who came before us, including John Stuart Mill, the British philosopher whose "conception of liberty justified the freedom of the individual in opposition to unlimited state control." (For convenience' sake, I am again quoting Wikipedia.) That's my kind of liberal, and why — for the first 45 years of my life — through the Kennedy era, in opposition to the Nixon era, and even into the Clinton years ("The era of big government is over!") I considered myself a liberal.

But what we still call liberals today are an altogether different animal. The era of big government is now "in your face." Government bailouts, forced participation in health insurance, nanny-state bureaucracy — it's all about what government can do to make itself indispensable, which of course leads to "unlimited state control."

Mill had occasion to write that, "Now, as ever, the great problem in government is to prevent the strongest from becoming the only power; and repress the natural tendency of the instincts and passions of the ruling body to sweep away all barriers which are capable of resisting, even for a moment, their own tendencies."

It is not entirely surprising that Mill's warning about the "great problem in government" comes from his famous appraisal of Volume II of "Democracy in America," the brilliant analysis of the American political and social revolution that was still erupting in 1840 when the book was published.

"Democracy in America" was the brainchild of another classical liberal, Frenchman Alexis de Tocqueville, who came to America to make a study of its prisons and instead found himself enthralled with the freedom he found everywhere. The two-volume study he published of his observations of the nascent democracy in America remains fundamental to our understanding of the responsibilities of liberty and the dangers of freedom.

It is indeed clear that Tocqueville recognized that America's roiling republic contained the seeds of its own destruction, and that he recognized that despite our Constitution, and perhaps because of it, we were not immune to dictatorship, or, as he called it, despotism. Yet he realized that tyranny in the United States would never come in the usual form — that it would not choke us with an iron fist but rather with a velvet glove.

As he said, "...It would seem that if despotism were to be established among the democratic nations of our days, it might assume a different character; it would be more extensive and more mild; it would degrade men without tormenting them."

In other words, it would seduce free men to act like slaves by taking care of their every need, watching over them like parents do their infants, and thus securing their total dependence.

Here is how Tocqueville described his vision of the greatest threat to democracy once those in power decided to use government as a giant teat to placate the public:

"Above this race of men stands an immense and tutelary power, which takes upon itself alone to secure their gratifications and to watch over their fate. That power is absolute, minute, regular, provident, and mild. It would be like the authority of a parent if, like that authority, its object was to prepare men for manhood; but it seeks, on the contrary, to keep them in perpetual childhood: it is well content that the people should rejoice, provided they think of nothing but rejoicing. For their happiness such a government willingly labors, but it chooses to be the sole agent and the only arbiter of that happiness; it provides for their security, foresees and supplies their necessities, facilitates their pleasures, manages their principal concerns, directs their industry, regulates the descent of property, and subdivides their inheritances: what remains, but to spare them all the care of thinking and all the trouble of living?"

Have we really reached that stage? Has America gone in scarce over 150 years from a nascent democracy to a doddering idiot? You decide:

"After having thus successively taken each member of the community in its powerful grasp and fashioned him at will, the supreme power ... covers the surface of society with a network of small complicated rules, minute and uniform, through which the most original minds and the most energetic characters cannot penetrate... The will of man is not shattered, but softened, bent, and guided; men are seldom forced by it to act, but they are constantly restrained from acting. Such a power does not destroy, but it prevents existence; it does not tyrannize, but it compresses, enervates, extinguishes, and stupefies a people, till each nation is reduced to nothing better than a flock of timid and industrious animals, of which the government is the shepherd."

Wow! Imagine that! A government that encourages dependence and timidity — can anyone say "sheeple"?

Tocqueville's description of "a network of small complicated rules, minute and uniform, through which the most original minds and the most energetic characters cannot penetrate" suggests immediately the federal tax code, with all its minutiae and loopholes. But let's not stop there. How about 2,000-page health-care bills that are too complicated even for senators to read? How about 1,000-page cap-and-trade bills that could eventually regulate whether or not you are allowed to hold a barbecue?

"Subjection in minor affairs breaks out every day and is felt by the whole community indiscriminately. It does not drive men to resistance, but it crosses them at every turn, till they are led to surrender the exercise of their own will."

But what about elections? This is a democracy, right? The people make the ultimate choices about their government as a result of our constitutional guarantees.

Umm, sorry, not so quick. Tocqueville has already anticipated that argument, and answered it:

"It is in vain to summon a people who have been rendered so dependent on the central power to choose from time to time the representatives of that power; this rare and brief exercise of their free choice, however important it may be, will not prevent them from gradually losing the faculties of thinking, feeling, and acting for themselves, and thus gradually falling below the level of humanity."

Of course, there has been a growing resistance to the nanny state over the past year or two, most notably in the Tea Party Movement, but there has been considerable resistance to the Tea Party Movement as well. And let's face it, there is no empirical evidence that Republicans, if returned to power, would do any better job of dismantling the nanny state than Democrats. We are truly in a bind.

Of course, a true liberal would prefer to be left alone, rather than be told what to do, what to think, or what to buy. Yet because of the increasing role of government in our lives, we have reached a stage of despotism that Tocqueville warned us against — a stage in which the "collective" good is considered more important than the individual:

"...it happens that, at the same period and among the same nations in which men conceive a natural contempt for the rights of private persons, the rights of society at large are naturally extended and consolidated... It is therefore most especially in the present democratic times, that the true friends of the liberty and the greatness of man ought constantly to be on the alert to prevent the power of government from lightly sacrificing the private rights of individuals to the general execution of its designs."

Yet how else can we describe the tyranny of the health-care law passed by Congress? Have not our private rights been diminished and the powers of government been extended? And of course, we are told that the government is just doing what is "best for us." Many good folks, liberals and conservatives both, cannot help themselves from trying to make America a better place, but ultimately they run the risk of destroying what made America great in the first place, as Tocqueville warned us back in 1840:

"It would seem as if the rulers of our time sought only to use men in order to make things great; I wish that they would try a little more to make great men; that they would set less value on the work and more upon the workman; that they would never forget that a nation cannot long remain strong when every man belonging to it is individually weak; and that no form or combination of social polity has yet been devised to make an energetic people out of a community of pusillanimous and enfeebled citizens."

If we truly want more freedom and less government, then there may be no better prescription for economic and social health than this: "Buy Alexis de Tocqueville's 'Democracy in America'; read liberally."

BUYING THE LIE: 'SOMETHING FOR NOTHING'

June 6, 2010

I suppose it was just plain greed that got us to this point.

Isn't that one of the Seven Deadly Sins? So maybe we should not be surprised to see the country brought to its knees by avarice.

But it's not the "greedy" bankers and industrialists whom we have to blame. Remember, it's the bankers and industrialists who create the jobs that give the rest of us an opportunity to make something of ourselves in the first place. Sure, some of them will earn their place in hell, but those few people could not bring down the whole country.

For that, we must blame ourselves.

Because it was our own greed that made us think we could get something for nothing. We fell for a fairy tale — that it was possible for everyone everywhere to have everything they need to be happy — and that the government is the fairy godmother who will make it all happen.

This guaranteed two results — it legitimized stupid greed as a way of life, and it made the government all-powerful as the arbiter of every transaction between two people.

It also put us on an inexorable path of destruction as the government bought happiness for everyone by spending someone else's money. At first it was called a progressive income tax; then it was called borrowing; soon it will be called bankruptcy. Today it is called Greece; tomorrow it will be California.

Somewhere along the line, most people became afraid to call it what it really is — redistribution of wealth.

Of course, that sounds harmless enough, doesn't it? Barack Obama even got elected president on a platform of "spreading the wealth around." After all, which man wants to deny his brother if he does not have enough? So, yes, sure, take a little of mine to make the life of my brother easier.

But that is the camel's nose under the big suffocating tent of socialism.

Everyone wants a home; therefore everyone is entitled to a house. Everyone wants an education; therefore, college should be made as close to free as humanly possible. Everyone wants to live forever; therefore, health care should be a right, not a commodity.

But if we no longer use the market system to determine the value of what we all want, then how exactly do we pay for anything? If the government pays for everything we want, then where is the government getting the money to square the account? Not from you or me! After all, why should we be the ones working for a living when our neighbor is living on the dole. What's good for my neighbor is good for me. If he gets a handout, then I want one too, only bigger.

Mind you, no one wishes to be greedy.

No. Heaven forbid. I just want what I have coming to me, not a nickel more or less. But the problem is that what you have coming to you may not be the same as what your neighbor has coming to him. Through a variety of reasons — luck, skill, genius, hard work — each of us gains a different amount of the benefits that life offers.

In fact, you don't really have ANYTHING material coming to you — not as a simple result of being alive anyway. You just get the right to life, liberty and the PURSUIT of happiness, as some wise men once put it. How you use your life and liberty was once the key to how successful you were in pursuing happiness, but not anymore.

Today, the government tells you what you can and can't do, and they don't want you to get too far ahead of your neighbor. Even the illegal neighbors from Mexico or elsewhere, we are told, have a legitimate claim to "keeping up with the Joneses." It doesn't matter if they earned it or not — they want it. After all, why should they look over the fence — or the border — and see things they don't have? Why should Americans get all the breaks? Isn't everyone entitled to a "fair share"?

There's another name for that, of course, and it's been around for thousands of years. When we complain about what our neighbor has — when we try to get our "fair share" that we haven't really earned and have no right to — we have begun down the road to war, the road to pillage and the road to barbarianism. Isn't that why the Bible warns us explicitly, "Thou shalt not covet."

Of course, try telling that to the modern man or woman who not only thinks that the Bible is an out-dated rule book, but doesn't even have a mind big enough to conceive of a God in the first place.

But when man makes himself God, that's when you get systems like communism and socialism and Nazi-ism. Those are all instances of man making the rules, determining what is fair, meting out justice — and they are all examples of pure evil.

Ayn Rand, the philosopher and author who lived under the strictures of communism in her early years, somehow managed to predict the decline of America into the thralldom of socialism even when we were at the height of our economic power as an engine of capitalism.

Her descriptions of the faltering, dying gasps of American enterprise in the 1957 novel "Atlas Shrugged" are so accurate that it should bring a tear to your eye. We have really made a mess of things, as we bought into the notion that work was no longer a suitable gauge of value. The words of a former worker who is now an unemployed tramp, in the latter part of "Atlas Shrugged," sum up the horror of creeping socialism brilliantly:

"At first, I kept wondering how it could be possible that the educated, the cultured, the famous men of the world could make a mistake of this size and preach, as righteousness, this sort of abomination — when five minutes of thought should have told them what would happen if somebody tried to practice what they preached. Now I know that they didn't do it by any kind of mistake. Mistakes of this size are never made innocently. If men fall for some vicious piece of insanity, when they have no way to make it work and no possible reason to explain their choice — it's because they have a reason that they do not wish to tell. ..."

The reason, of course is stupid greed. Not the Horatio Alger greed of someone wanting to work hard in order to provide a better life for himself and his family, but the lazy greed of wanting to do nothing — or as little as possible — and still being given a good life by someone else's hard work. That greed is impossible, unworkable, unsustainable — as corrupt as a Ponzi scheme, as delusional as a perpetual motion machine. But there is a sucker born every minute, as Rand explained:

"There wasn't a man rich and smart enough but that he didn't think that somebody was richer and smarter, and this [socialistic] plan would give him a share of his better's wealth and brain. But while he was thinking that he'd get unearned benefits from the men above, he forgot about the men below who'd get unearned benefits, too. He forgot about all his inferiors who'd rush to drain him just as he hoped to drain his superiors. The worker who liked the idea that his need entitled him to a limousine like his boss's, forgot that every bum and beggar on earth would come howling that their need entitled them to an icebox like his own. That was our real motive... but we didn't like to think it, so the less we liked it, the louder we yelled about our love for the common good."

Oh yes, the "common good." That is the oldest trick in the con man's repertoire — appeal to pity, appeal to humanity — dig deep into your pocket in order to help some poor starving schlep in far-away Africa or Asia, forgetting that you are only one meal away from hunger yourself. But the rhetoric falls apart when you analyze it. The common good can't be served effectively if one man has to be impoverished in order to enrich another. Giving what is mine is called charity; taking what is mine is called theft.

Maybe that's why millions of Americans are finally fed up. They've caught on to the Ponzi scheme at long last. The unfunded pensions. The shrinking Social Security fund. The endless bailouts. The billions of dollars going to Greece to ensure that Greeks can maintain their unsustainable mendicant lifestyle. The looters in government grabbing every penny that isn't nailed down. And if you challenge them, it's you who are the problem! It's you who are chastised as selfish and dangerous!

"Do you care to imagine what it would be like, if you had to live and to work, when you're tied to all the disasters and all the malingering of the globe?" asked Rand's jobless philosopher-tramp in "Atlas Shrugged."

"To work — and whenever any men failed anywhere, it's you who would have to make up for it. To work — with no chance to rise, with your meals and your clothes and your home and your pleasure depending on any swindle, any famine, any pestilence anywhere on earth. To work — with no chance for an extra ration, till the Cambodians have been fed and the

Patagonians have been sent through college. To work — on a blank check held by every creature born, by men whom you'll never see, whose needs you'll never know, whose ability or laziness or sloppiness or fraud you have no way to learn and no right to question — just to work and work and work — and leave it up to [those in power] to decide whose stomach will consume the effort, the dreams and the days of your life. And this is the moral law to accept? This — a moral ideal?"

Count me out.

It's time for Americans to return to the principles of thrift and industry that made us great and turn our backs on the socialism, Marxism and communism that pretend to offer easy solutions to every problem. Greed in the service of hard work is one thing; greed in the service of theft is quite another.

WHEN POLITICAL WORLDS COLLIDE ...

June 27, 2010

Did you feel the ground shake?

America is undergoing the political equivalent of continental drift right now, with two powerful forces battling it out like giant tectonic plates crashing against each other in slow motion.

On the one hand are radical leftists pushing an agenda of false hope and dangerous change — ripping at the very foundations of the country, substituting man for God, and preying on the weak and ignorant with promises of social justice and endless charity.

On the other hand are the Tea Party conservatives — defenders of the Constitution, advocates of the Founding Fathers and proponents of unchanging morality, hard work and natural law.

If you are offended by those descriptions, we can guess which side you are on. But you don't have to be offended. You can rewrite the adjectives so that I am the dangerous defender of a failed and corrupt social order which was invented to protect wealth against the demands of the masses. It doesn't matter what you call me, or what I call you. What matters is that the political landscape is shaking. The Jacobins and the royalists cannot both stand. The White Russians and Red Russians cannot compromise and remain true to themselves. The Pacific Plate and the North American Plate cannot crash into each other without unleashing a terrible fury. Nor can the Constitution and the Communist Manifesto peacefully co-exist in the same body politic. Something must give.

Which force will be submerged and which will thrust upwards like the Rocky Mountains to dominate the landscape of the next political era we simply cannot know at this time. But we most assuredly will live with the consequences.

That is why, week after week for the past four years, I have been writing about the cultural war that threatens to pulverize the principles of equal justice, resistance to tyranny, and primacy of the individual — the principles on which our nation was founded.

I am not the first to notice that the concept of equal rights has been transformed in the past 100 years from the right to enjoy one's own possessions and accomplishments without interference to the right to possess as much as my neighbor does without the need to accomplish anything at all.

Such a fundamental transformation has left our nation virtually unrecognizable from the one I was born into 55 years ago. And it has inspired the resistance of the Tea Party Movement, which offers a chance to restore equal justice to its original intent — a challenge to excel, not a surrender to mediocrity.

Am I confident of victory? No, but I am sure of the battle. It is as certain as the San Andreas Fault, and as necessary as the Declaration of Independence. Let each of us fight for what he or she believes in, and not try to avoid taking sides. There is no neutral ground.

Remember, if you stand in the middle of an earthquake, you will be swallowed up first.

WELCOME TO WONDERLAND

July 11, 2010

In Tim Burton's recent film version of "Alice in Wonderland," the adventuresome heroine finds her world turned literally upside down.

Seems that when she first comes to her feet after falling down the rabbit hole, she is actually standing on the ceiling in Wonderland. Then, after taking her bearings for a few seconds, she falls to the ground and begins to try to make sense of the mixed-up world of the bulbous-headed Red Queen. Her adjustment occurs quickly, but it is worth reminding ourselves that no matter how normal everything looks from that point on in the film, Alice's world has been fundamentally transformed — down is up, and up is down.

That's kind of the same position a lot of us were in after going through the rabbit hole of the 2008 elections and finding ourselves in the equally mixed-up world of the pointy-headed Black President.

Can I call Barack Obama a black president? Not without offending someone, even though it is just a play on the "Red Queen." This is indeed a measure of just how mixed up our political world is. By actually noticing the color of his skin, I run the risk of being declared presumptively to be a racist.

But wasn't it Eric Holder, Obama's attorney general, who said we were "a nation of cowards" for shying away from a direct discussion of race?

"If we are to make progress in this area," he said last year, "we must feel comfortable enough with one another and tolerant enough of each other to have frank conversations about the racial matters that continue to divide us."

In that spirit, how about if we talk about the mess that Eric Holder's Justice Department made of the voter intimidation case that had been filed against members of the New Black Panther Party?

If you ever saw the videotape of the three thugs who were standing outside a polling place in Philadelphia in November

2008, there was never any question that they were trying to scare white people (known as "crackers" to the Black Panthers) into not voting.

The Justice Department official who was pursuing charges against the three black men, however, was told to drop the case. In fact, the official, J. Christian Adams, said he was ordered by the Justice Department to ignore all cases involving black defendants and white victims.

Curiouser and curiouser.

It is almost as though words have taken on a new meaning. Justice now apparently means racism. As Adams said in his testimony before the U.S. Commission on Civil Rights last week, "We abetted wrongdoing and abandoned law-abiding citizens." The reason? Just because of who is white and who is black. It reminds me of one of those Logic 101 problems that are used to teach students how easy it is to be fooled by false syllogisms:

Some victims are black.

Some oppressors are white.

Therefore all blacks are victims.

Of course, it's not correct, but that doesn't matter. In the court of the pointy-headed king — er, I mean president — as in the court of the Red Queen, the trick is to believe what you are told, whether it is true or not. It's not correct, but it is politically correct.

Alice was stubbornly insistent that she could only believe in things that were real, not things she was told to believe because they were convenient. "There's no use trying,"Alice said. "One can't believe impossible things."

But some people can, unfortunately.

As the Red Queen proclaimed, "I daresay you haven't had much practice... When I was your age, I always did it for half-an-hour a day. Why sometimes I believed as many as six impossible things before breakfast!"

The past two years, we have been getting a lot of practice in believing impossible things. "Debt is wealth. Weakness is strength. Aliens are citizens." You may not like it, but that doesn't matter. Your world has been fundamentally transformed. Welcome to Wonderland.

IT'S OUR DUTY TO PRESERVE THE 'BLESSINGS OF LIBERTY'

August 15, 2010

Liberals love to call the U.S. Constitution a "living document" — in other words, one that changes through time in order to keep up with the times.

And at one level, they are certainly right. Because the Constitution can be amended at any time through a difficult but manageable process, it can reflect the changing needs of our people.

Unfortunately, what liberals mean by "change" is that an activist judge can force the rest of us to do whatever he or she wants by dint of judicial fiat. If a judge (or ultimately the Supreme Court) says the Constitution allows the government to force you to buy health insurance, then it's a done deal, regardless of whether the Constitution says so or not.

Under such a scenario, the Constitution thus becomes a tool for social engineering rather than a protection against government excess, as it was originally intended.

What is missing from this liberal formula of constitutional re-interpretation is an acknowledgment that the Constitution is an "immortal document" as well as a "living" one — and that it enshrines principles that are true not just for one time but for all times.

Its core values cannot be changed without turning it into just a mere "piece of paper" — as at least one recent president is alleged to have called it. But for millions of us, it is plain that politicians have no regard for the Constitution or see it as a way to control the people, rather than a way for the people to control the government.

Do we really need to remind ourselves that the Constitution begins with "We the people" and not "We the overseers"? It is "we the people" who wrote and "ordained" the Constitution, and it is we who should hold the power to change it — through the prescribed amendment process, not through subterfuge and politically correct judicial appointments. Nor should we forget the stated purpose of the Constitution — to "secure the Blessings of Liberty to ourselves and our Posterity."

Notice that it was not just the founders of this country, but all of us — their national posterity — who are guaranteed under the Constitution the "Blessings of Liberty." This is a clause of the Constitution which is too little spoken of — perhaps because the people's liberty is a significant inconvenience to the government's authority.

As the ruling class has more and more isolated to themselves the power to dictate what is and is not an appropriate use of the blessings of liberty, we have seen a corresponding decrease in the actual liberty we enjoy. This is true whether the power is exercised by the Legislature, the Executive or the Judiciary.

In the past two years, under the increasingly arrogant one-party rule of the Democrats, we have seen the Congress and president not only ignore the Constitution, but do so enthusiastically. Many examples exist of congressmen and senators who have laughed at the Constitution. Most recently Rep. Pete Stark of California intoned at a town-hall meeting that "there are very few constitutional limits that would prevent the federal government from rules that could affect your private life.... The federal government, yes, can do most anything in this country."

It is just such a matter-of-factly despotic view of government that terrifies millions of Americans today, as without the protection of the Constitution we are no longer citizens but rather subjects, and we may have reached a point where the Constitution offers just about as much protection to "we the people" as an umbrella in a hurricane.

But if the Congress and president have overstepped the bounds of their authority, the only hope for securing the Blessings of Liberty for our own posterity is the judiciary holding back the other two branches of government with a proper restraint.

Unfortunately, it now appears all but certain that the judiciary is poised to join Congress and the president in a ruling troika that will crush not just the Constitution, but the

underlying liberty and self-evident truths on which it was
based.

An activist judiciary that tells the people what they can and
cannot do as sovereign citizens is the enemy of liberty, no
matter how much it pretends to uphold it in the name of
political correctness.

In the past two months, we have seen the people of two
formerly sovereign states — Arizona and California — told that
they do not possess self-rule. In both cases, the judges used the
U.S. Constitution as a bludgeon to crush the people's expression
of their own liberty, rather than a guard against government
encroachment as it was intended.

In the first case, a judge in Arizona ruled that the people of
Arizona have no right to protect themselves against an invasion
of illegal immigrants because the "overseers" in Washington,
D.C., have chosen not to address the problem. The judge
ignored the plain facts of the case and indeed misstated the
facts in order to craft a ruling that protected illegal immigrants
and reduced the citizens of Arizona to a form of federal chattel.

Now, in a stunning reversal of hundreds of years of
jurisprudence, a judge in California has ruled that the people of
the state of California have no right to determine for themselves
what rules they shall approve for the consecration of the
institution of marriage. With Proposition 8, the people of
California amended their state Constitution to succinctly say
that marriage shall be between one man and one woman, just as
it has been for thousands of years.

What is most annoying about this ruling is that Judge
Vaughn Walker based it on the U.S. Constitution, claiming that
it was "unconstitutional under both the due process and equal
protection clauses." This would no doubt have come as a
surprise to the millions of Americans who have lived and died
since those clauses were written. It is a plain and simple fact
that those clauses were not intended to force Americans to
adopt a new morality to please a California judge.

Equal protection means that once the legislature has
pronounced the will of the people, that edict shall be applied
fairly and evenly to all people. In other words, if the state of

California says that marriage is between one man and one woman, then every man and every woman shall have the free opportunity to enjoy that relationship. The equal protection clause means that a gay man cannot be prohibited from marrying a woman just because he is gay. He would have as much right to marry a woman as anyone else. Discrimination shall be prohibited in the application of the law. Period.

But the law itself shall be decided by "we the people" and our legislatures, not by a runaway judge who thinks he knows better than everyone else.

Sooner or later, the people will rise up and demand "the blessings of liberty" promised to them by the Constitution. That does not mean that we are all free to do whatever we want, but rather that together we have the right to control our common destiny.

Thomas Jefferson, who in many ways was a libertarian, understood this truth well. Thus, he wrote in the Declaration of Independence that "Governments are instituted among Men, deriving their just powers from the consent of the governed."

If the President, Congress and Judiciary continue to impose their will on the country, rather than taking their marching orders from us, then it is only a matter of time before the "consent of the governed" is withdrawn.

When that happens, heaven help us.

THE CONSTITUTION: IS IT FOR US, OR AGAINST US?

August 22, 2010

It is amazing how easily the American people have let the hood be pulled over their eyes as they are led on their way to political slaughter.

No, I'm not talking about the elections of 2008, 2010 or 2012, but rather the "fundamental transformation" of our U.S. Constitution from a document that protected "we the people" from the government into a tool the government can use to control us.

Year after year, the people have had fewer rights and the government has had more control. Don't just blame Barack Obama. This transformation has been engineered over many years by many presidents, both Republican and Democrat, and ratified by courts that have been packed with progressives. Congress has been complicit in the transformation by its very pronounced silence.

We may or may not still live in a republic, but if we do, it is by the grace of God, not the efforts of our politicians. And the way our Constitution has been manipulated, it is unlikely we will have a republic long, as God is not prone to help people who refuse to help themselves.

Until we shake the death hood off and see for ourselves that we are standing on the edge of the gallows, there is no chance to avoid our imminent fate. And since the noose around our necks is the very Constitution we love, it is going to be nigh on impossible to wake people up before it is too late.

It used to be said that the Constitution is not a "suicide pact." Of course, the same thing also might have been said about the Bible before Jonestown. Now, we know better. Ruthless people can always turn our hopes and dreams against us — use our innocence to manipulate us into violating our own best interests, and indeed our own survival.

It was Supreme Court Justice Arthur Goldberg who, in a 1963 ruling, wrote that "while the Constitution protects against invasions of individual rights, it is not a suicide pact." This concept, however, goes back much further than 1963 — to the very founding of our nation, in fact, and we might more appropriately refer to the words of Thomas Jefferson, who wrote:

"A strict observance of the written law is doubtless one of the high duties of a good citizen, but it is not the highest. The laws of necessity, of self-preservation, of saving our country when in danger, are of higher obligation. To lose our country by a scrupulous adherence to the written law, would be to lose the law itself, with life, liberty, property and all those who are enjoying them with us; thus absurdly sacrificing the ends to the means."

Nor was Jefferson the only president to recognize the importance of preserving the country AND the Constitution by occasionally putting a higher value on the first than the second. Lincoln suspended habeas corpus illegally during the Civil War. FDR rounded up thousands of Japanese-Americans during World War II at least partly from a legitimate fear that some of them still had allegiance to the Japanese emperor.

No one likes such exercises of brute power, but the necessity of "preserving the union" should be a foregone conclusion to most Americans. Practically speaking, without the actual country of the United States of America to enshrine it, the Constitution is nothing more than a piece of paper. Kill the country, and you have turned the cherished rights of the Constitution into mere nostalgia.

Today, it appears to many of us that the Constitution itself is being used against us. This complicates greatly the effort to preserve the country, because now in order to save the Constitution, we must first do significant surgery on it. Before you scream about the "crazy right-wing assault" on the Constitution, do yourself a favor. Ask your Uncle Allen whether or not he is glad a bunch of surgeons cut him open and sliced the cancer out of his belly to save his life, or whether he wishes he could have died then and there just to say he was whole.

Our Constitution is just like Uncle Allen; it's got cancer, and it's not going to be cured just by good intentions. Without action, the outcome is predictable, certain and fatal, so we need to get over our fear of blood, take out the knife and start cutting.

Where to start is a good question. There are many places where the Constitution has been co-opted by vested interests who do not share the common interests of "we the people." I will address some of those points of concern in a future column, but for now it is enough that we begin to agree that something needs to be done.

Unfortunately, many people who love the country have been fooled into thinking that changing the Constitution is the equivalent of rewriting the Bible. It isn't. The Constitution isn't God's law, but man's law, our American law, and we Americans

— "we the people" — have the right to change it, using the amendment process that is prescribed for just such a purpose.

Yet more and more, liberals have been screaming about Republicans trying to change the Constitution as if they are committing treason. The Democratic talk-show host Bill Press wrote a column recently entitled "The Constitution Works, Don't Change It." In it, he says, "Republicans are coming up with another phony crusade to amend the Constitution."

He's talking about the effort to revise the 14th Amendment, but it doesn't matter what he is talking about. When he talks about a "another phony crusade," he has made his point. In his mind, no effort shall be made to amend the Constitution by conservatives without it being phony. No doubt, he has forgotten that it was Republicans who led the crusades to end slavery with the 13th Amendment and to ensure that former slaves were guaranteed full citizenship in the 14th Amendment. I presume he doesn't think those were "phony" crusades.

And what makes an issue phony? Clearly, to pass an amendment to the U.S. Constitution, you need to garner huge support in both Congress and among the several states. The bar is set incredibly high for a compelling reason — to ensure that changes made DO reflect the will of "we the people."

But that should not restrict the right of all Americans to seek to amend the Constitution in any way they see fit. There is nothing phony about participating in the civic dialogue and engaging in a constitutionally prescribed process to shape the law of the land through persuading public opinion.

One can bet that Bill Press and his colleagues on the left do not ever use the term "phony crusade" to describe the amendments that gave women the right to vote or that set the voting age at 18. These were good liberal causes that improved our nation through recognizing limitations in the original Constitution that ought to have been corrected.

The same privilege to work to improve our nation should extend to all citizens. Do not let the Constitution be used against you, and do not let politicians or anyone else shame you into thinking you have no power as an American citizen to influence your government. It is time that we get creative about using our power as citizens to restore the republic that was handed to us in 1787 by our Founding Fathers. If we do not think ourselves worthy to amend the Constitution, then we are not worthy of the Constitution — period.

TAKING BACK THE CONSTITUTION PIECE BY PIECE

August 29, 2010

It is an immutable fact that the Constitution is the law of the land, but the law of the land should not be presumed to be immutable.

It isn't.

No artifact of the human mind can be maintained intact like a formalin-preserved insect on a pin. No matter how much comfort it would give us to have predictability and certainty in our law, the elements of human curiosity and cussedness would always give rise to unpredictability and chaos.

This introduces the possibility of improvement, whether through design or through accident, but it also raises the spectre of decline, whether through stupidity or sabotage.

Improvements have come in the form of amendments that accomplished the abolition of slavery and giving women the right to vote. Those were both long overdue by the time they passed.

But there have also been mistakes made in the amendment process, including the prohibition of alcohol and the decision to turn senators into panderers by making them directly electable by the people instead of through the choice of each state's legislature.

With more than a hundred years of monkey-wrenching the prime law of the land through "progressive" court decisions, there is also lots of damage to undo that is based on "precedent" rather than the plain language of the Constitution.

You could start with the Commerce Clause, which has been shaped into a choke collar to restrict the freedom of the people to engage in trade and seek prosperity. You could start by re-instituting real limits on the powers of Congress or the president, as enumerated in Articles I and II. You could force the nation to honor the Ninth and 10th Amendments, which are included in the Bill of Rights but might as well have been written in invisible ink since they are treated as if they were nonexistent by the Supreme Court, Congress and many presidents.

But let us instead begin with an easy one — the 14th Amendment. This amendment, ratified in 1868, followed close on the heels of the 13th Amendment, which abolished slavery after the successful prosecution of the Civil War by President Lincoln. The purpose of the first article of the 14th Amendment is plain for everyone to see who has eyes to see. It established that the freed slaves were citizens in order to prevent individual Southern states from denying basic rights to black people. The rest of the 14th Amendment is mostly of limited importance today, but the first article has been used to do considerable damage, whereas its plain language should be a tool for good.

In total, it reads:

"All persons born or naturalized in the United States, and subject to the jurisdiction thereof, are citizens of the United States and of the State wherein they reside. No State shall make or enforce any law which shall abridge the privileges or immunities of citizens of the United States; nor shall any State deprive any person of life, liberty, or property, without due process of law; nor deny to any person within its jurisdiction the equal protection of the laws."

The first sentence of the first article is what concerns us today. It establishes that freed slaves who were born in the United States are citizens. Obviously no one today could object to that, but the provision has been twisted into an unrecognizable mess over the past 140 years. This is where the doctrine of "birthright citizenship" supposedly originates — except it doesn't. You've had the wool pulled over your eyes.

History is plain. So are the words in the 14th Amendment. But both are now being ignored thanks to a feckless adherence to judicial precedent no matter how wrong-headed the decision.

We are told that every child born in the United States has the right to claim citizenship in our country based on the wording of this amendment, but for goodness' sake, before we sell our birthright for a mess of pottage, shouldn't someone actually read the amendment?

It PLAINLY says that there are TWO elements which are BOTH necessary to qualify for citizenship. One is that you must be "born or naturalized in the United States." The meaning of that is more or less self-evident. The meaning of the second element — that a potential citizen must be "subject to the jurisdiction" of the United States — has been conveniently forgotten or obfuscated. More invisible ink?

Anyone who bothers to spend half an hour researching the history of this amendment will find ample proof that the phrase is intended to exclude the children of foreign nationals from acquiring citizenship just due to the accident of being born in the United States. To claim otherwise requires a willful ignorance so profound as to be frightening.

Of course, the natural inclination of supporters of "birthright citizenship" is to just claim that children born in our country ARE "subject to the jurisdiction" of the U.S. government because, after all, they are citizens. That, however, is a tautology which adds nothing to our understanding.

Plainly, there are some people born in the United States who are NOT "subject to the jurisdiction thereof" — otherwise the phrase would not have been necessary at all. Therefore, children born in the United States MAY or MAY NOT be citizens depending on whether they are subject to our jurisdiction.

If you read the history of the amendment, you can see for yourself that children NOT subject to the jurisdiction of the United States specifically refers, among others, to those children who are born to alien residents, legal or otherwise — those, in other words, who owe their allegiance to another nation.

Sen. Jacob M. Howard, the very author of the citizenship clause in the 14th Amendment, said the citizenship provisions, "will not, of course, include persons born in the United States who are foreigners, aliens, who belong to the family of ambassadors, or foreign ministers accredited to the Government of the United States, but will include every other class of persons."

But even if you don't acknowledge the history, you must acknowledge the language of the amendment itself. Clearly, anyone who has entered our country illegally, whether from Mexico or China, is NOT subject to our jurisdiction. We cannot, for instance, conscript them into the military, or otherwise obligate them to any kind of service or allegiance. Nor can we charge them with treason because they don't owe allegiance to the United States.

Unfortunately this distinction has withered away, leaving us only with the politically correct formulation that all babies lucky enough to be born here are citizens by reason of geography.

This is one of many instances where the two choices left to concerned citizens are to either accept the blatant violation of the intent of the Constitution or to rework the Constitution so that its original intent is explicitly restored.

It would not take much. Just a simple amendment that says the following:

"The first article of the 14th Amendment shall not be construed to mean that birth in the United States automatically confers citizenship. The children of temporary or illegal residents of the United States, because they are not subject to the jurisdiction thereof, shall not be considered citizens of the United States unless and until they fulfill the requirements of naturalization."

Despite the left-wing agenda of attempting to extend citizenship to everyone we feel sorry for, it is probable that this new amendment could be ratified by "three-fourths of the several states," as mandated in Article V of the Constitution. On the other hand, it is not at all likely that Congress would be able to muster two-thirds of its members to vote for the good of the country and against the good of their political parties; therefore we are unable to ever see such a simple clarification instituted.

Which is why, of course, so many citizens are frustrated with the members of Congress to the point of "unarmed rebellion." It's not their country; it's our country. It's not their Constitution; it's our Constitution.

And if we don't stand up for our country and our Constitution, and do it soon, then shame on us. Vote as if your future depended on it — because it does.

Tea Party is Expression of 'General Will' of the People

September 26, 2010

It's not politics that drives the Tea Party movement; it's patriotism — and not just flag-waving patriotism, but the underlying stream of the American consciousness that fueled our revolution and built our country.

Unless and until the mainstream media gets that message, there is not much hope for reporting that doesn't try to smear, twist or trash the Tea Party.

For now though, most reporters assume that the Tea Party is a Republican invention, and thus worthy of the disdain typically shown by the left-leaning press for Ronald Reagan, George W. Bush, Sarah Palin and numerous other Republicans.

Indeed, the only Republicans who seem to escape the smear treatment are the ones who sound like Democrats. Thus, there was the brief flirtation between the media and John McCain in 2000, and the near-beatification of David Brooks, the ersatz conservative columnist who scribbles for the New York Times, and has proven himself to be a truly "independent" conservative by constantly attacking conservative ideals. Call it the "adoration of the magpie."

But the Tea Party is not Republican, it is conservative — which is why neither McCain nor Brooks qualify for admission short of a "Road to Damascus" conversion. And it is not just conservative in the sense of believing in conservative issues such as fiscal responsibility or traditional marriage, but rather in the fundamental sense of "conserving" that which our Founding Fathers built.

To get it right, you would actually have to say that the Tea Party is made up of conservators, rather than conservatives, which is why the Tea Party movement fundamentally rejects the effort to shoehorn it into the Republican Party. Republicans are as guilty as anyone of spitting on the Constitution, and when they do, heaven help them.

It's true that the Tea Party doesn't like big-spending, Marxist-oriented liberal Democrats like Barack Obama (surprise!) but it also doesn't like hypocritical, pandering Republicans who see their job as compromising their espoused principles for the sake of helping Democrats advance their social agenda in the name of "bipartisanship."

In fact, some of the Tea Party's greatest rancor is reserved for two-faced Republicans — witness the spanking of Pennsylvania's Sen. Arlen Spector, Utah's Sen. Bob Bennett, Alaska's Sen. Lisa Murkowski, Florida Gov. Charlie Crist, and most recently Delaware's longtime congressman Mike Castle, who got whacked by part-time witch and full-time Tea Party loyalist Christine O'Donnell in the GOP primary for an open U.S. Senate seat.

Most of these losing Republicans, or erstwhile Republicans, owe their defeats to the Tea Party movement. Most of them earned that animus due to their slavish devotion to big government, their disrespect for their constituents, and their susceptibility to the swooning effects of Potomac Fever — an illness peculiar to politicians whose main symptom is an uncontrollable desire to spend other people's money in an earnest effort to secure re-election.

Such Republicans are of no use to the country. To paraphrase Benjamin Franklin, those who are willing to trade their constituents' trust for a little political security deserve neither. Or as American folk wisdom would have it — "Vote the bums out!"

That sentiment explains why pundits and the establishment press have been shocked by one election result after another this year. The victors had exactly one thing in common — no matter how bad they were as candidates, no matter how flawed they were as individuals, they were expressing the communal outrage of "we the people" at the disastrous arrogance of those we had elected to represent us.

Nor should it be considered an accident that the best-known victims of Tea Party anger are senators or candidates for the U.S. Senate. One thing that has become clear in the past several decades is that senators no longer reliably represent the people of their state, but rather their own self-interest.

This phenomenon is one of the unintended consequences of the 17th Amendment — which shifted the election of senators from the individual state legislatures to the people of each state. This was supposed to be a good idea because it gave "power to the people." It was thus an easy sell. But it tampered with a crucial component of the architecture of the American republic that was devised by the genius of our Founding Fathers to withstand the rigors of time, temperament and outright treason.

The initial structure of the Congress brilliantly divided power between the mercuric mass of "the people," who would elect their own representatives from among themselves to go to the House, and the sluggish, resistant "establishment," which would choose a guardian of the individual state's abiding interests to send to the Senate. This ensured a fundamental check on the growth of federal power by guaranteeing the separate states a voice through their senators. If a senator strayed from representing the interests of the state from whence he came, he would be replaced at the end of his term by the overseeing legislature.

With popular election of senators, however, came the inevitable shift of power away from the states to the individual senator and ultimately to their political parties. Rather than representing a state's interests, a senator's only concern from this point forward was representing himself TO the people as their friend and guardian — no matter who he was really beholden to.

So, it is indisputable that the 17th Amendment, which was supposed to give power TO the people, ironically took it away instead. It also moved power away from the individual states to the gargantuan federal monster.

The effect of the 17th Amendment in shifting the balance of power was not immediately apparent, however, because during the first part of the 20th century, America remained true to its foundational roots. As DeTocqueville noted in 1835, the American democracy could not exist without a moral people. The governor of our behavior throughout the 19th century was not our government, but our morality.

By the time of the early 20th century, that was starting to change. Government, especially the federal government, was growing, and morality was on the decline. The social contract between the people and their government was shredded. More and more, our elected officials were our "rulers," not our "representatives." And because morality no longer was recognized as a universal absolute truth, but rather as a relativistic matter of convenience, our rulers could talk themselves into doing literally anything for the so-called good of the people.

No doubt when the 17th amendment was ratified in 1913, most Americans congratulated themselves on putting their trust in "the people," but really they had put their trust in the good will of politicians. For a while — when patriotism and morality were still held in high regard — it looked like it might even work. Popularly elected senators still strove to represent the sovereign citizens of their states; they did so out of a sense of loyalty, decency and dignity. By the end of the 20th century, however, most citizens would have come to doubt that such qualities still existed in their elected representatives, especially in their senators — and senators seemed to doubt that their loyalty should be placed in anyone other than the political party that told them how to vote.

Thus, we witnessed the decline of politics from the art of statesmanship to the craft of gamesmanship. This change solidified when the people lost confidence in their government, and the government lost touch with the people. Although not often voiced explicitly, a tacit realization of this change is what finally inspired the Tea Party movement.

As Jean Jacques Rousseau, one of the inspirations of the American Revolution, wrote in "The Social Contract" in 1762:

"Finally, when the State, on the eve of ruin, maintains only a vain, illusory and formal existence, when in every heart the social bond is broken, and the meanest interest brazenly lays hold of the sacred name of 'public good,' the general will becomes mute: all men, guided by secret motives, no more give their views as citizens than if the State had never been; and iniquitous decrees directed solely to private interest get passed under the name of laws."

A better description of the state of current American politics has never been written. Whether the country can be saved from ruin at this late juncture is not yet known, but the Tea Party movement is proof that the the "general will" is no longer mute. And this party is just getting started.

JEFFERSON AND THE ROOTS OF THE 'LIBERTY MOVEMENT'

October 10, 2010

If Democrats and Republicans were ever truly interested in finding common ground, a good place to start might be with Thomas Jefferson, who was the co-founder of the fortuitously named Democratic-Republican Party.

Today's Democrats traditionally hold themselves to be the lineal descendants of Jefferson's party, which was seen as the common man's advocate as opposed to the Federalists, who favored consolidated power and a national bank.

Today's Republicans, on the other hand, find themselves sympathetic to Jefferson's defense of individual and states' rights, even though it was their "founder" Lincoln who created the modern system of a centralized government where more and more power has been federalized.

It may be the Tea Party movement which encapsulates Jefferson's philosophy best in the modern era. Like the Democrats, it sees itself as the advocate of the everyday

American. Like the Republicans, it promotes individual rights above all. And unlike both of them, the Tea Party movement stands with Jefferson in opposition to big government and centralized control over individual decisions.

As Jefferson wrote in his autobiography, "I am for a government rigorously frugal and simple. Were we directed from Washington when to sow, when to reap, we should soon want bread."

Alas, the time may be short to renew Jefferson's philosophy before our entire system of bloated government collapses. Washington, D.C., has indeed taken over control of more and more of our decision-making, down to the most intimate details of our health care. The common people don't like it, but the people in power DO.

So "We the People" stand in need again of a clear declaration of principles that will hold us firm against the encroachments of a tyrannical government. The Declaration of Independence, penned by Jefferson, is one such document, but another — considerably less well-known — is President Jefferson's second inaugural address.

I researched that speech for my recent column on a prayer that had been commonly (and apparently falsely) attributed to Jefferson, and came to realize that many of the concerns of the Tea Party today were already worrying Jefferson in 1805. Moreover, the political environment in which Jefferson struggled to lead was as fractious, foul and fierce as what we bemoan today.

It is particularly Jefferson's assessment of the relationship between the people, the government and the press that is eerily familiar — if not actually prophetic — of the complaints being lodged today by Tea Party supporters such as Sharron Angle in Nevada and Joe Miller in Alaska.

If we could get both Democrats and Republicans to read the words of Jefferson today, far from the current turmoil over "Obama this" and "Palin that," we might be able to generally acknowledge that the Tea Party movement transcends any one ideology and instead encapsulates the "liberty movement" that Jefferson was part of in 1776.

In his 1805 speech, Jefferson acknowledges his re-election and begins his list of accomplishments at home by bragging that his administration's "suppression of unnecessary offices [and] of useless establishments and expenses" had allowed him to eliminate the nation's internal federal taxes.

Imagine that! Cutting existing government programs, cutting government spending, and cutting taxes! Those are the fundamental principles of the Tea Party movement, being espoused just a few years after the BOSTON Tea Party.

But, of course, those who vilify the modern Tea Party movement argue that shrinking the government is cruel and malicious. The mainstream media caricaturizes those who raise constitutional concerns as kooks and crackpots, and riles up opposition with emotional distortions. How can we NOT have a Department of Education? Or Social Security? Or a prescription drug benefit? Or mandatory government-ordered health insurance? What will the poor people do?

Well, Jefferson didn't think that it was the role of the federal government to control people's lives, but rather to stay out of the way. That's why, within 15 years of the country's founding, Jefferson was already bragging about ELIMINATING government programs that he said forced We the People to "open our doors to their intrusions."

He noted that this "process of domiciliary vexation ... once entered in [was] scarcely to be restrained from reaching successively every article of property and produce."

Amen to that. Both taxation and regulation have proceeded apace in the succeeding 205 years since Jefferson spoke, to the point where the federal government is far and away the largest vexation not just in our houses, but in our businesses and our schools. No doubt, our churches will be next.

And if the Tea Party movement really stands for Taxed Enough Already, as some people say, then Jefferson certainly ought to be acknowledged as the party's patron saint. He bragged about whittling away everything except a tax on "consumption of foreign articles," and noted that, "it may be the pleasure and pride of an American to ask, What farmer, what mechanic, what laborer ever sees a taxgatherer of the United States?"

It need not be emphasized that such a question would be impossible to ask today. Jefferson obviously lost his battle to put the people and states first, and the federal government second. But we really owe it to ourselves and our children to study what kind of government the Founding Fathers tried to bless us with, and what we got stuck with instead.

Jefferson noted that there was a REASON why so few taxes were needed by the federal government — because its expenses were limited to only a few specific areas enumerated by the Constitution. He envisioned a time when even the federal tax on imported items would not be needed by the U.S. government and could instead be passed on to the individual states so that it could be applied by them to "rivers, canals, roads, arts, manufactures, education and other great objects within each State."

This is important. Notice that it is the individual states which are responsible for their own roads and their own educational needs. Yet today we have a federal Department of Transportation which spends billions of dollars on interstate highways. We have a Department of Education that spends billions of dollars on who-knows-what. We even have a National Endowment for the Arts, which spends millions of dollars on subsidizing art that most of us would never spend a dime on.

So to follow up on question raised earlier — "How can we NOT have a Department of Education?" — the answer is simple: Return the country to what it was intended to be by Jefferson, James Madison and George Washington — a collection of states protected BY and FROM a federal government that was seen as a necessary evil, not a welcome addition.

There is much more in Jefferson's second inaugural address that sounds like it comes directly out of the Tea Party playbook. Here is a sampling:

• On the national debt: The limited taxes levied "may meet within the year all the expenses of the year without encroaching on the rights of future generations by burdening them with the debts of the past." Protecting our children's heritage has been one of the main themes of the Tea Party movement, whereas those in favor of a massive federal government like Paul Krugman want to create even MORE debt.

• On keeping the federal government out of our churches: "On matters of religion I have considered that its free exercise is placed by the Constitution independent of the powers of the General Government. I have therefore undertaken on no occasion to prescribe the religious exercises suited to it, but have left them, as the Constitution found them, under the direction and discipline of the church or state authorities acknowledged by the several religious societies."

Notice that Jefferson distinguishes here between what it is right and proper for the federal government to do and what is acceptable for a state government to do. Many of our early states were set up under a religious charter, and both Jefferson and the Constitution understood that. It was the purpose of the First Amendment to keep the federal government out of religion, not to keep religious people from influencing government. The role of religion in our lives and beliefs should not be restricted by federal policies, period.

• On the national media distorting the truth for its own political purposes: "The artillery of the press has been leveled against us, charged with whatsover its licentiousness could devise or dare. These abuses of an institution so important to freedom and science are deeply to be regretted." As if he were taking note of the slanderous coverage of the Tea Party movement itself, Jefferson laments the wide divide between the "inestimable liberty of the press and its demoralizing licentiousness."

However, Jefferson remained an optimist, despite the attacks which he had withstood for the previous four years. His confidence in the American people outweighed his disdain for the press, which sought to destroy him as enthusiastically as much of the press today persecutes the Tea Party. Despite the falsehoods that he said had been told about him, he saw "harmony and happiness" on the horizon and predicted that truth and reason would "at length prevail."

Let us hope that we can indeed rally around the words of Jefferson once again. Let us remember that it is government of, for and BY the people, or as Jefferson said in his FIRST inaugural address:

"A wise and frugal Government, which shall restrain men from injuring one another, shall leave them otherwise free to regulate their own pursuits of industry and improvement, and shall not take from the mouth of labor the bread it has earned. This is the sum of good government..."

CONGRESS TO US: DAMN THE CONSTITUTION, FULL SPENDING AHEAD ...

October 17, 2010

Hardly a day goes by when I don't get a press release dropped in my in-box from someone announcing that the federal government is kindly spending another $50,000, $100,000, $1 million, or $10 million in Montana.

Gee, thanks. I'm sure we appreciate it, Uncle Sam.

But don't you think maybe, what with the $1 trillion deficit and the $14 trillion national debt, you should stop showing off and buying stuff with money you don't actually have?

Isn't there a name for that?

Actually, there are many names for it. Take your pick.

Fraud. Pork. Spending like a drunken sailor. Vote-buying. Business as usual.

But, dear citizen, you don't have to worry about it.

In fact, if you do, you are a spoilsport, a party pooper, a Grinch. How dare you raise the possibility of dismantling a federal program — any federal program — that funds something that someone somewhere likes, needs or just plain wants.

Expect the government to operate Social Security in a financially sound manner? Cut off grants for green energy? Turn off the spigot of agricultural funding? Less money for colleges?

Not bloody likely!

Remember, people in Washington are spending your hard-earned money for the best of reasons — they like the way it makes them feel.

And, face it, the people who get the money like the way it makes them feel, too.

And with all those happy feelings beaming from happy faces, it's hard for regular folks like me and you to peep up with little old questions about the Constitution or fiduciary responsibility.

Still, someone has to do it.

So here goes.

The United States Constitution — written in 1787, ratified in 1788, and taking effect in 1789 — is indisputably the supreme law of the land. All powers of the national government must emanate from it, or else be fraudulent and tyrannical. No act of the president or the Congress should be allowed to stand unless it is directly authorized by the Constitution. That is plainly spelled out in the 10th Amendment, which says, in its entirety, "The powers not delegated to the United States by the Constitution, nor prohibited by it to the States, are reserved to the States respectively, or to the people."

Got that? If the Constitution doesn't say the Congress or President can do it, then they can't! Unfortunately for us — for We the People — this amendment is utterly ignored by the government it is supposed to restrain.

So, dear citizen, please take a look at Section 8 of Article I of the U.S. Constitution. It's not hard to do so. The section runs to less than a page of printed material. You can look for it online under the heading of "Powers of Congress," and when you find it, be prepared to have your world rocked — because Congress has almost no power to spend money. You, ladies and gentlemen, have been taken for a ride.

In a nutshell, you will find that Congress can do the following: Collect taxes, pay debts, borrow money, regulate commerce with foreign nations and between states, establish rules of naturalization, establish bankruptcy laws, coin money and regulate its value, establish laws regarding counterfeiting, establish post offices and roads to ensure that the mail can be delivered, regulate copyright; establish lesser courts; "define and punish" crimes committed on the high seas and "offenses against the Law of Nations"; declare war; grant letters of marque and reprisal; raise and support armies; provide and maintain a navy; make rules to govern the military; provide for "calling forth the militia" and for "organizing, arming, and disciplining the militia"; exercise legislative control over the District of Columbia and over military forts and facilities; and make such laws as are needed to carry out these duties.

There you have it — just a long paragraph's worth of "powers," and nary a word in there about health care, education, farm subsidies, or a national endowment for the arts. Don't take my word for it. Look for yourself. Try in vain to prove me wrong. Or admit the truth, no matter how much it hurts.

Because it is time to say it plainly — the American people have been swindled. This isn't government of the people, by the people and for the people. It is government of the looters, by the looters and for the looters.

How did they — how DO they — get away with it?

Two simple words — "general welfare." At the beginning of section 8 of Article I of the Constitution, the looters found this phrase, which was the "open sesame" for trillions of dollars of treasure — "Congress shall have Power to ... provide for the common Defence and general Welfare of the United States."

Through the portal of the "general welfare" — and with the acquiescence of the judiciary — Congress has been able to loot the wealth of this great nation for any purpose it deemed worthy, thus neutering the Constitution and leaving Americans without a fig leaf to their name.

If there ever were an independent judiciary, this sham would be exposed in a minute. It doesn't take long to figure out that the "general welfare of the United States" is something quite different than the individual welfare of one farmer, one student, one university, one automobile manufacturer — yet most of the largess handed out by the federal government is done so on an individual basis.

Besides, if "general welfare" allows the Congress to spend money on anything it wants, the Founding Fathers could have saved a lot of time by writing Section 8, Powers of Congress, as this: "Congress can do whatever it thinks is in the best interest of the United States."

Moreover, even the use of the phrase United States in the Constitution means something quite different than what we imagine it does. Before the Civil War, it was well understood that our country was indeed a federation of individual and sovereign States. Thus, when contemplating the "general" welfare of the "united" States, we were specifically talking about what was good for ALL the states as a UNIT, not what might please one state, and certainly not the kind of targeted spending that has become famous in congressional earmarks. A half-million dollars to fund a Teapot Museum is probably good for the welfare of the people who run the museum, and maybe for teapot collectors, but it doesn't have anything to do with the welfare of the 50 united States.

And it's a lot more than a half-million dollars.

Consider the evidence of my in-box. In the week of Oct. 3-9, I kept track of the goodies coming to Montana by way of Uncle Sam's charitable contributions. Lots of it doesn't have a specific dollar amount for Montana, as it is part of a bigger handout, but let's just concentrate on the ones with a pricetag attached,and which ultimately trace back to federal dollars.

Oct. 4: "The Montana Department of Agriculture this week mailed award letters to seven successful applicants for specialty crop block grants [funded by the U.S. Department of Agriculture] totaling $292, 955."

Oct. 4 "U.S. Transportation Secretary Ray LaHood today announced a combined $776 million for urban and rural transit providers in 45 states and the District of Columbia to help bring buses, bus facilities and related equipment into a state of good repair." The Missoula Urban Transportation District project to renovate the downtown transfer center received $590,400.

Oct. 5: "Montana Senators Max Baucus and Jon Tester are applauding the Community Oriented Policing Services (COPS) Hiring Program for the Flathead County Sheriff's Department... The Flathead County Sheriff's Department will receive $209,304."

Oct. 7: "Montana Public Radio receives $500,000 in grants [from the U.S. Department of Commerce] to expand coverage."

Oct. 8: "Montana's senior U.S. Senator Max Baucus announced today Montana is one of three states selected for a new initiative to improve health care for veterans in rural areas, particularly when they're in need of emergency care. Today's news means Baucus' legislation has come full circle, now that Montana was awarded nearly $300,000 to enhance health care services offered to veterans in rural Montana under the new authority created by his legislation."

So let's add it up. That comes to $1,892,659 for one week of handouts. Some of that is just for Flathead County or Northwest Montana and similar grants may have been made across the state, but let's just assume that is everything done for the entire state for one week.

Then multiply that $1.9 million by 52 weeks. You can see that the kitty for federal payouts to Montana is then $98,418,268 for one year. What the heck, let's call it $100 million.

Now let's figure that Montana has about 1 million people (we actually have less, but round numbers are cool). Let's figure moreover that the United States population is 310 million (you can probably see where I am going by now).

That means we can multiply Montana's total amount of federal largess for one year by 310 to get the total amount being doled out by our good-hearted senators and representatives in Washington.

Do the math. That comes to $31 billion in goodies for our senators and representatives to feel good about.

Yeah, but a lot of that money is spent on worthy causes, our liberal friends will argue. It may or may not be worthy. That isn't the issue. Most of it, however, is constitutionally suspect, at best, and criminal at worst.

Mind you, the $1.9 million in grants I know about are just the goodies that they bothered to send me, and mostly are focused on Northwest Montana. It would probably still be a conservative estimate to say that during the same week, all of

Montana received at least $5 million in federal grants and awards.

If that's true, then using the same multiplier formula, we would get $260 million spent on the state in one year, and $80 billion spent on the 50 states in the form of feel-good spending.

We can look at that number — $80 billion — and say one of two things: "So what?" or "What an outrage!"

If you said, "So what?" then I say to you, "What an outrage!"

YOUR CHOICE, YOUR COUNTRY, OUR PROBLEM

October 24, 2010

Election Day is fast approaching, and there is a tendency among some pundits to think that it can solve everything.

It can't. Voting is a short-term solution to a long-term problem.

Or, rather, to many long-term problems — declining education, increasing deficits, disappearing industry, expanding government, border invasion, terrorism — will those do for a start?

One of the worst of the long-term problems, however, is the long term of U.S. senators — six years — which almost guarantees that senators immediately after being elected develop a strong "independent streak" that means they are more likely to do what their party asks them to do than what their state voters expect them to do.

I'm not proposing changing the term of senators, but it is one more example of why the citizenry is restless, why "we the people" don't trust "they the politicians," and why nothing ever seems to get done to fix the real challenges facing this country.

Yep, there may be a Republican-led House of Representatives as a result of the elections on Nov. 2. There may even be a Republican-majority Senate, though that possibility is more remote. But let it never be said that a

Republican Congress is a magic formula for "hope and change," any more than a Democratic president was.

Even when there was a Republican House and a Republican-led Senate during most of the first six years of the George W. Bush administration, there was no hope and very little change for the better. It was politics as usual.

Of course, hope springs eternal in the human breast, so Republicans and some independents are actually being seduced into thinking that simple solutions to fundamental problems are going to be found in the next few years.

Would that it were so.

But anyone who thinks that a GOP majority in Congress is going to "fundamentally transform" America from the dysfunctional mess it is today is likely to be as disappointed in 2012 as the 2008 Obama voters are in 2010. Think of it this way: If our representatives don't feel obligated to represent us, then what exactly do we as a people base our hopes for change on?

That's why the Tea Party movement is so adamant on not being co-opted by either political party. At this point, the movement has pinned its hopes on Republicans, but Republicans who ignore the people will be just as unpopular as Democrats.

That point is met with skepticism by Democrats, of course, who continue to view the Tea Party movement as "the enemy." It is often asked by Democrats or their surrogates in the media why Tea Party activists, if they are truly non-partisan, did not protest against George W. Bush's spending policies. The answer is simple and two-fold: First, the terrorism of Sept. 11 and two ensuing wars diverted our attention from domestic problems to a large extent. Second, the American public (like the political establishment) had largely bought into the notion that effective governance must be rooted in compromise.

Say what you will about him, President Obama did everyone a favor by teaching us that you could govern quite effectively without ever compromising your principles. He pushed through health-care reform over the objection of the American people and with virtually no support from

Republicans. He did what he thought was right, and he did what he told the American people he would do when they elected him.

Now he will reap the consequences.

At least we think he will. It all depends on how long the memory of voters is. In Montana, Sen. Jon Tester might be in trouble this year because of his votes for health-care reform, Cass Sunstein and energy. But he isn't running for re-election until 2012 so it's entirely possible that voters may forget those votes. In the meantime, Tester — who got elected on a platform of "making Washington, D.C., more like Montana" — has been spending his "safe year" raising money for very liberal Democratic senators like Russ Feingold of Wisconsin and Barbara Boxer of California.

Sorry, Jon, but if you really wanted to make Washington more like Montana, you would be campaigning against Boxer and Feingold, not for them.

But that's not the way politics works, is it? It's all about getting elected — which brings us back to the short-term solution we started with: Election Day.

Do your duty; make your choice. But do yourself a favor. Don't vote based on what candidates tell you — vote based on their record. If they don't have a record, vote based on their party's record because it is a certainty that they are going to vote with their party most of the time, no matter how "independent" they promise you they are.

It would be best for all of us if every politician were willing to state their principles boldly when standing for election, then stick to them when voting on legislation. Don't say one thing in October, and another thing after the voting is over in November. I believe that is what all voters want to see.

But so far it hasn't happened.

I think, as much as anything, that is why the Tea Party movement has arisen. It has become the institutional memory of "we the people" to hold accountable our elected representatives. That may be the only hope we have that we can restore honor or sanity in our country.

If you want to solve the long-term problems, don't keep electing the people that caused the problems. That goes for George Bush-era Republicans as well as Obama-era Democrats.

Don't let them off the hook just because six years has passed. If you don't elect true patriots to the Senate and other offices, people who put their country first and their party a distant second, then we are six years closer to collapse.

Remember, the only real cure for our country's long-term problems is a long memory — voters need to sniff out the phony politicians who can't be trusted to do what they say, and replace them with statesmen who will lead the people BEFORE the election and follow through AFTERWARDS.

A WORD TO THE WISE: THE FIGHT IS NOT OVER

November 7, 2010

Now that the conservative movement has prevailed at the ballot box, it's worth taking note of the movement's goals and aspirations, which seem so reasonable to some and so wild-eyed to others.

I found one account that seemed to put succinctly what many have been fighting for nationwide the past several years. Because it conveys the Tea Party's agenda as well as anything I have seen, I am using the Tea Party as the generic name of the conservative movement represented here in discussion of the battle fought on Election Day.

"[The Tea Party] does not claim sole credit for these successes. However, the statements of many candidates indicate that the help of the [Tea Party movement] was effective, and in many cases accounted for the victory" and will help to achieve "significant restraints on government profligacy..."

"The visionary policies of the socialist-liberals have enmeshed our nation in an assortment of national crises unprecedented in our history. These destructive policies fall into the following categories:

"1. Abdication of national sovereignty and neglect of our national defense...

"2. Neglect by government of its primary duty to protect the lives, limbs, liberties and property of its citizens against internal and external aggression in favor of policies of indulgence and permissiveness which promote anarchy and favorable treatment for criminals at the expense of their victims.

"3. Pursuit of fiscal and monetary practices which debauch our currency and endanger our economy. Included among these are profligate government spending, imbalanced budgets [and] excessive taxation ...

"4. Denial of the fundamental concept of our American way of life, an economically independent citizenry, supporting and controlling a government that is the servant of the people, not their master. This has led to legislation by judicial decree, usurpation of states' rights and local authority, socialized medicine, and government controls and competition with private industry.

"All of these ruinous policies and practices can be corrected by bold action by a properly motivated Congress. For this reason, [the Tea Party] has adhered to its original goal of electing constitutional conservatives to the Congress. We are convinced that most of our people believe in the ideals of our Founding Fathers. They have been misled by false prophets. Once they are given the truth, they will rally to discharge their duties to God and Country to the end that our free Republic will be saved."

Sound familiar?

Of course it does, if you've been paying attention to what Tea Party conservatives like Sarah Palin, Marco Rubio and Rand Paul have been saying since the 2008 election. People are fed up with a federal government that has turned its back on the Constitution.

But there is another reason why the list of complaints about liberals should sound familiar — because we have fought this battle before. In fact, the words cited above are not a follow-up to Tuesday's elections and were not written about the Tea Party. They were part of a column written in 1968 by Adm. Ben

Moreell to describe another group's ongoing fight against the slide toward socialism.

According to Moreell, Americans for Constitutional Action was founded "by a small group of concerned men" in 1958 "to arrest the movement of our nation toward a Socialist State, which they believed would end in destruction of our Republic and loss of individual freedom."

Moreell was a significant figure in American military history, being credited as the founder of the legendary Seabees, the Construction Battalions that helped build the infrastructure of America's naval victories in World War II. After his retirement from the Navy in 1946, Moreell became an industrialist and was CEO of Jones and Laughlin Steel Company.

None of these accomplishments meant anything to the liberal elite, however, when in 1958 Moreell spearheaded the creation of Americans for Constitutional Action as a counterpoint to the growing influence of Americans for Democratic Action. At that point, Moreell became as laughable to the media as Sarah Palin is today. He was dismissed as a member of the "radical right" — one of the kooks (or as we say today "wingnuts") who wanted to stop the encroachment of socialism in American government and society.

So what exactly was the "radical" agenda of Adm. Moreell? Listen again to his own words, from that same 1968 column, when he described the founders of Americans for Constitutional Action:

"They called themselves 'constitutional conservatives.' They used this term to designate persons who work to conserve the spirit and principles of the Declaration of Independence and our Constitution, which embody the ideals of liberty, justice and opportunity for all, on which we can build, moving neither to the right nor to the left, but upward, toward higher levels of awareness of our duties to God and to our neighbor."

Wow, scary stuff. It does remind me of the Tea Party, and like the Tea Party movement today, it was smeared and vilified by the left-wing media, who painted Moreell and his associates as paranoid conspiracy theorists and, no doubt, racists.

But let's just hold on and consider the facts.

America was at its zenith in 1958 — universally recognized to be at the height of its power, the peak of its creativity, and the most affluent it would ever become. You might well think, as many did at the time, that America was safe from any threat, foreign or domestic. It seemed like a perfect time to "spread the wealth around," and over the next decade that's just what happened. The invention of the Welfare State didn't begin with LBJ's "Great Society," but it certainly became an inseparable element of public policy at that time, first with Medicare and then with more and more taxpayer-funded entitlement programs.

Americans for Democratic Action was already — and still is today — an influential organization that helped to shape the modern American state. You can call it liberal or you can call it progressive, but you can't disguise its long-range goals: To move America from its founding principles of republican democracy to the failed policies of socialism.

That, of course, is the same "fundamental transformation" of America that Barack Obama promised before he became president — and it is no accident.

As the ADA website itself proclaims, the goal of ADA was "To keep the New Deal dream — its vision and its values of an America that works fairly for all — alive for generations to come. With the election of Barack Obama, the moment to realize so many elements of that long-deferred dream has come."

The 100-year-old dream of socialists to replace America's Constitution with foreign principles of "social justice" is what is really scary. And that's what motivates Sarah Palin and millions of Main Street Americans to fight back to preserve and protect our cherished way of life.

No, the fight didn't start in February 2009 when Rick Santelli urged Americans to meet up at Lake Michigan for a Chicago Tea Party. It didn't start in 2010 when Americans turned out at the polls to say "no more." It didn't even start back in 1968 when Adm. Moreell wrote his column about the "ruinous policies and practices" of a left-leaning Congress.

It is both comforting and scary to know just how long this fight has been continuing. Think of how much wealth has been drained out of our country in the 42 years since 1968 — think of how much sovereignty "we the people" have surrendered. Yet Americans have not given up.

I suppose it is encouraging that the Tea Party movement has the upper hand for the time being, but just as most of you have never heard of Americans for Constitutional Action, it is entirely possible that the Tea Party will be relegated to the trash heap of history by the considerable forces marshaled against it.

This fight must be seen in perspective — not as Republican against Democrat, but as the proponents of liberty against the forces of slavery. Modern supporters of the Constitution must never underestimate the will power of those who think they are smarter than Thomas Jefferson, James Madison, George Washington, and Samuel Adams.

But we must also never give up the fight.

As Adm. Moreell wrote 42 years ago, "It is increasingly evident that socialist-liberals who have been in control for 35 years cannot make good on their extravagant promises of achieving a 'Heaven on Earth' and they are losing public confidence. But in spite of these conservative gains, the battle is far from over."

Just as true today as it was then, so don't declare victory just because Republicans elected a few more senators and gained control of the House of Representatives on Tuesday. It's not about victory for Republicans; it's about preserving the Republic — and those are two very different things.

FREEDOM OF CHOICE: JUST ANOTHER THING WE'VE LOST?

November 21, 2010

I've been musing on some historical trends for the past few weeks in an effort to explain how America went from a country that fought communism to one that embraced socialism in the course of about 50 years.

Communism and socialism are not exactly the same thing, of course, but they are both based on governmental control of individual choices. At the macro scale, that means government ownership of industries, so that competition is restricted and private use of capital is subject to the discretion of the government rather than the free market. At the micro scale, it means that the government can tell each of us individually what kind of health insurance we can buy and ultimately what kind of hamburger we can eat.

For those of us who believe that choice is the essence of liberty, it is dismaying to watch our fellow Americans voluntarily — if unwittingly — cede power to the government over matters large and small.

I suppose it is not surprising, however. As Thomas Jefferson, the father of American liberty, wrote to Edward Carrington, in 1788, before the new Constitution had even been ratified: "The natural progress of things is for liberty to yield, & government to gain ground."

Thus, today we have a Constitution that is seen as securing the national government's power over all, whereas in Jefferson's day the Constitution was seen as guaranteeing the people's and states' sovereignty over — and establishing just and proper restraints on — the national government.

It is with this in mind that the Tea Party has begun to speak of the tyranny of the federal government. It is also no coincidence that within the last two years, many Americans have noted and condemned the socialist tendencies that have beset our government at every level.

Remember, the American tradition of liberty enshrines the rights of the individual; the European tradition of socialism enshrines the rights of the state. The two traditions are thus mutually exclusive. The idea of democratic socialism is poppycock. It is doublespeak of the most pernicious kind for its goal is to enslave us under the banner of freedom. Democratic socialism is nothing more than free slavery — but do slaves who serve willingly have more OR LESS dignity that those who serve under duress?

Perhaps we have reached the point where everyday Americans have had enough, and are ready to take back control from the bureaucrats and entrenched officeholders who have used their power to restrict our freedom instead of protect it. I suspect more Americans have read the Constitution in the last two years that did so in the previous two decades. Thus we may have reached the point predicted by Jefferson when he wrote in 1789:

"Whenever the people are well-informed, they can be trusted with their own government; whenever things get so far wrong as to attract their notice, they may be relied upon to set them to rights."

Let's hope so. But, as for now, I am still not sure that Jefferson was right. After all, things have gone wrong for a long time, and it always seems as though the American people resist the truth, perhaps because they have a misguided faith in the institutions of justice rather than in the source of justice.

But there is also a long line of truth-tellers who have encouraged Americans to remain faithful to the traditions and ideals that made America great. They are often belittled and besmirched like Barry Goldwater in his day or Glenn Beck in ours. They are sometimes nearly anonymous, known only by their signatures on letters to the editor in papers like the Daily Inter Lake. Sometimes they just make their point by asking a question.

That was the case with Inter Lake reader Dennis Gollsneider, who commissioned me to answer the question, "Why did the Magazine Publishers Association launch a nationwide Freedom of Choice campaign in 1968? What were they afraid of? What were the policies that they feared would be enacted?"

These simple questions, along with a couple of photocopied ads from Sports Afield in 1968, led me on a quest that challenged me to ultimately ask whether or not the policies that the Magazine Publishers were afraid of in 1968 had actually come to pass by 2010. It almost seemed as though the ads were a message in a time capsule that mysteriously predicted the mess that we face in America 42 years later.

One of the ads was addressed to automobile drivers. It said:

"Someone wants to change your world. He's one of the new breed of social critics on the scene today. Intelligent, well-intentioned, he wants to do a little tinkering with the economy. Oh, he admits our free choice economy has produced a lot for us. In fact that's his problem. He thinks maybe it's produced too much. He thinks there are too many brands competing in the marketplace. He thinks Mrs. Smith is confused by too much free choice. His solution? Make both free competition and free choice a little less free. Let the government restrict the number of brands on the market — brands of just about anything presumably, from cars to cigarets to mouthwashes. And standardize their design and contents with grade labels. You know it's too bad somebody didn't think of that about 40 years ago. Then we'd all still be driving Model A's. And that was a fun car."

Wow, I thought when I read it. That sounds uncomfortably familiar.

Perhaps you don't think so. After all, there are still plenty of brands of mouthwash, cigarettes and cars to choose from. Right? But let's think about it.

Starting about 1968, the federal government started imposing new guidelines on manufacturers of cigarettes to tell them what they could and could not sell. The justification was obvious — to save people's lives — but the effect was to reduce choices for consumers.

Same thing with cars. You can no longer buy a car without seatbelts. You can no longer buy a car without a catalytic converter. To a large extent, you can no longer buy a car that is cheap. That is because, the American auto industry is regulated to the point where to it is impossible to even include automobiles when talking about the "free market." Virtually every aspect of the production and design of passenger cars is regulated by the federal government, leading to increased costs and in some cases increased death (for instance, lightweight cars meet federally imposed fuel-economy standards, but are demonstrably less safe).

Once you start to think about all the ways that the federal government has imposed itself into our lives since 1968, it becomes obvious that the Magazine Publishers Association lamentably failed in their campaign to rouse the public.

In fact, social critics, environmentalists and know-it-alls of every variety have done just what the Magazine Publishers warned us would happen, and not just at the federal level. This month, you even had the San Francisco City Council voting to ban McDonald's Happy Meals in their not-so-fair city.

Why? Because the free toys might entice little Jimmy and Joanie to order a meal with too much sugar and calories. McDonald's could still sell the meals, and they could still give away the toys, but not together. Talk about the Nanny State!

As a spokeswoman for McDonald's said, "Parents tell us it's their right and responsibility, not the government's, ... to choose what's right for their children."

Well, maybe before 1968... but not anymore. In fact, the government's job now seems to be entirely based on telling us what to do and how to do it. Want a mortgage? Check with the federal government to see what they have ordered banks to do in that industry. Want a credit card? Check with the federal government to see what you are allowed to have. Want health insurance? Better check with Uncle Sam.

In fact, the Freedom of Choice may soon be considered as outdated as the Ford Model A that the Magazine Publishers wrote about in 1968. But if we don't have Freedom of Choice anymore, then what will happen to us in the future?

Perhaps we should refer to the second of the two ads that Dennis Gollsneider brought to my office last month. In it, Benjamin Franklin is quoted in his guise as Poor Richard, to the effect that laws written by the government to protect us from our own lavishness might actually spur us to laziness. The few choices we have, the less incentive we have to think for ourselves and to strive to make the right choice.

We are left at the mercy of government, which is not an institution known for either mercy or wisdom, which is an ingredient necessary to apply mercy justly.

Let the Magazine Publishers have the last word. After pointing out that Freedom of Choice had given us "the most dynamic economy in man's history," they warned, "Shouldn't we be worried about how we tinker with the forces that have created all of this? The simple, troubling truth is, nobody knows for sure how far you can regulate our economy without damaging it."

Well, now we know. The free market cannot exist under the enslavement of endless regulation. Something will eventually break. As Lincoln said of another form of slavery more than 150 years ago, "this government cannot endure, permanently half slave and half free."

But, unfortunately, whether Americans will shake off their economic yokes and return to the free state of their forefathers or simply adjust to slavery is not yet known.

THE MODERN-DAY BATTLE FOR INDEPENDENCE

November 28, 2010

In my research for the past three columns, I accrued quite a wealth of information on the American battle for independence. No, not the battle against England at the end of the 18th century, but the battle against Washington, D.C., at the end of the 20th.

Time after time in my research from the late 1960s, I found evidence that plenty of people tried to sound the warning against the "big brotherism" if not outright socialism that they saw threatening our fundamental freedoms in America.

But then as now, these warnings largely fell on deaf ears. As long as people had enough for themselves and their families, it didn't seem as though they cared whether it came in the name of socialism or hard work.

Newsweek magazine famously ran a cover last year that proclaimed, "We Are All Socialists Now." The magazine argued that the conversion of the United States to a European-style socialist state was virtually a done deal, and that "The sooner we understand where we truly stand, the sooner we can think more clearly about how to use government in today's world."

Scarier words have never been spoken, except perhaps these — from a famed newspaper columnist of yesteryear, Sidney J. Harris, who wrote in 1967:

"If social security is called 'socialism,' as it was 30 years ago, and if Medicare is called 'socialism,' as it was last year, then the public will say, 'If this is socialism, then we are for it' — and if thorough-going socialism is ever proposed by the government, it will find a ready audience."

What is most scary about these words is not their deadly accuracy — because it has all come to pass just as he said — but that Harris was a liberal columnist who was urging conservatives to keep quiet about the socialist intrusion, the same way that liberals want to silence conservative critics like myself today.

Apparently, the idea is just take the money from the federal government and shut up about it.

But some people in the 1960s, just as the Tea Party now, were smart enough to realize that taking money from the federal government is really taking money from your neighbors — or yourself.

Many of you have no doubt heard this dictum attributed to Alexander Fraser Tytler, the 18th century Scottish historian:

"A democracy cannot exist as a permanent form of government. It can only exist until the voters discover that they can vote themselves largess out of the public treasury."

I found it reprinted in a 1968 column by Don Oakley of the Newspaper Enterprise Association in which he held up the British welfare state as the latest example of the inevitable truth of Tytler's words. It seems the people of Britain had just learned that they would have to pay for their free health care after all.

"Britons are learning that the good life for all is not something that can be decreed by government. Government can only dispense that which it first takes from the people."

This is a hard lesson to learn, and perhaps Sydney Harris was right that Americans, like Britons, cannot resist the lure of "something for nothing," however much they know in their hearts that it is just a Ponzi scheme. Bernie Madoff got rich by following the formula perfected long ago by Uncle Sam: Take from the many, give to the few — and hope like hell that no one wakes up and smells the poverty.

But it would appear that from time to time, some people do get a glimmering of the con game being waged against them by the federal government. Thus in 1967 and 1968, there is plenty of evidence in American newspapers of a growing awareness that something was wrong. Remember, this was the time when LBJ was imposing the Great Society on the United States, just a few years after Mao Zedong had decimated the Chinese economy with his Great Leap Forward.

In the Olwein (Iowa) Daily Register, an editorial from May 19, 1967, lamented "A Diminishing Freedom." This piece, in about 400 words, managed to sum up the fallacy of Social Security and to warn Americans that when they first begin to surrender their "freedom of choice" to the government, they have opened the door to a nightmare scenario. Even then, before the Social Security trust fund had been raided, it was obvious to some people that the scheme presented a huge risk, and that it was a risk that was being forced upon the American people, without any opportunity to "just say no."

"It should be apparent to everyone that social security provides no such choice. Therefore it becomes a form of socialized insurance, perhaps the fore-runner of socialized medicine, socialized plumbers, socialized printers and what have you."

Hmmm. Socialized medicine. Where have I heard that before? Oh yeah, national mandatory health insurance (also known as Obamacare). And as for socialized printers, you might as well start writing the obituary for democracy when that happens. As soon as the government gains control of the press, we have all had it.

But don't think it can only happen in China! The Federal Trade Commission earlier this year presented a series of proposals for how the national government could boost newspapers and TV stations through tax breaks and subsidies and even government-paid journalists to just kind of, you know, help out. Oh yeah, and for a nice Orwellian touch, the non-profit group promoting a government takeover — er, bailout — of newspapers is called "Free Press."

To complete the trifecta of "socialized medicine, socialized plumbers [and] socialized printers," we would just need to find out that "Joe the plumber" has gone over to the dark side. You remember him, right? The working stiff who got candidate Barack Obama to admit that he believes in the fundamental communist idea that "when you spread the wealth around, it's good for everybody." Joe didn't buy it, but many someone else will if the government tells them they can have free plumbing service whenever they need it.

Anyway, back to that editorial in Iowa in 1967, it starts with concerns about Social Security but ends with a general appraisal of American liberty:

"Freedom is a funny thing," the editorialist wrote. " It is granted to only a few in this vast world, and to be among those who enjoy it is really a rare privilege. History has proven, however, that freedom for any length of time is enjoyed only by those who guard it carefully, wisely and diligently."

Regarding America, he noted that "social security, like so many other government programs today, [has] eliminated any freedom of choice..." and he concludes, "We cannot make ourselves believe that our fore-fathers would have strived nearly so hard to set up the 'ideal' government if they could have realized that the individual would eventually lose even a minute portion of his freedom to choose for his own benefit."

Freedom of choice. It isn't in the Constitution, but that doesn't mean it doesn't matter. The Constitution didn't give us our rights, you know; it merely protects some of them. And freedom of choice is one of those rights that the Ninth

Amendment acknowledges and which the government too often doesn't — the rights given to us by, as Thomas Jefferson wrote, our Creator.

As the amendment's authors wrote: "The enumeration in the Constitution, of certain rights, shall not be construed to deny or disparage others retained by the people."

Or, in simpler language that even Congress and the president can understand: "Don't Tread on Me."

But don't be complacent. Don't think slogans will keep you free. And don't — please don't — think the government will.

The rights of the people are only "retained" as long as the people keep up their guard. And as the Iowa editorial writer reminds us, "Once the guard has been let down even the strongest have crumbled."

OBAMA, FDR AND THE MYTH OF 'PERMANENT PLENTY'

December 5, 2010

A few readers took umbrage to my column last week in which I quoted some newspaper articles from the 1960s that found fault with Social Security.

Readers seem to have assumed that I was against Social Security because I quoted some folks who thought that the program was tantamount to socialism.

They were wrong. I was not against it. Far be it from me to bite the hand that will clothe and feed me when I retire. I was just worried about the fact that it seemed doomed to eventually fail — possibly before I retire!

But because of the challenge of my readers, I went back and researched the start of Social Security in the New Deal, and what I found scared me enough that I may now have to change my mind — maybe I AM against Social Security. (Folks, if you want to remain stuck in your current thinking, I strongly

recommend that you not pursue an issue with an open mind —
it CAN be dangerous.)

Indeed, as several readers have pointed out to me, I may
have fallen short of my real goal in looking for "where we went
wrong" when I focused on the 1950s and '60s as the point
where America stopped fighting communism and decided to
embrace socialism.

Reader Rick Spencer, in particular, challenged me to look
to the New Deal for the real answers with this pithy comment:

"I have always declared this national march [to socialism]
to have begun here in the U.S. during the 1930s with the advent
of Social Security when every citizen would henceforth be
considered and did become a financial liability rather than an
asset to the country."

It is hard for people such as myself who will depend on
Social Security for our retirement to imagine that the program
is not in the country's best interests. Nonetheless, there is
plenty of evidence to suggest that is the case. It is also hard to
argue with the historical record that the New Deal was a form of
homegrown "share the wealth" socialism that conflicts with our
core American principles.

Beginning this week, therefore, I am going to push my
historical research further into the past, back even before Social
Security was passed by the Congress in 1935.

As a starting point, let's turn to the commentaries of an
"insider," the author of "The New Dealers," a 1934 book written
anonymously by John Franklin Carter, a journalist who later
headed a secret White House intelligence unit for FDR. A copy
of this book was provided to me by Inter Lake reader Mike
Horn, who noticed that it might contain significant parallels to
our current administration.

Carter unapologetically wrote about the New Deal as a
"fundamental transformation" of the United States — to borrow
the phrase more closely associated with President Obama's
election in 2008.

"We are having a revolution and the revolutionary process
will take from ten to twenty years," he wrote, adding somewhat

cavalierly, "Nobody knows what it will lead to and nobody seems to care."

This reminds me of Speaker Pelosi's infamous declaration that "we have to pass the [Obama health care] bill so you can find out what is in it." But perhaps that is no accident. Carter also provides a description of Franklin Roosevelt at the beginning of his book that may fit our current president and his agenda as well.

"Franklin Delano Roosevelt did not invent the New Deal; he does not own it; it is only by chance that he administers it; it would have come without him and it will go on even if he should cease to be its greatest advertisement."

Could the same be said of Obamacare? Net neutrality? Stimulus money? Bank bailouts? Cap and trade? Amnesty for illegal immigrants? Aren't all of these revolutionary programs merely coincidentally associated with President Obama? Does anyone really think he is the architect of the New World Order that has been sculpted in the first two years of his administration?

Let's be honest. George W. Bush was party to much of the "fundamental transformation" that is under way today, and John McCain would have embraced much of it too, if he had been elected president. Ultimately, the "fundamental transformation" promised by Barack Obama was just a candid admission that "the revolutionary process" cited by John Franklin Carter in 1934 had not been completed in 10 or 20 years, as he anticipated, but was still in full swing.

But most importantly, Franklin — a confidante of FDR — confirms that the New Deal was not just a "cunningly contrived brainstorm" in response to the stock market crash or the Great Depression.

"Its measures are the result of neither spontaneous combustion nor immaculate conception. Its roots, like those of Roosevelt, go back rather far into our unwritten history."

"Unwritten history" is an interesting phrase, and an ominous one. Generally, history is understood to be "all recorded events of the past," as Webster's puts it. So, what kind of history is "unwritten"? What has happened that we don't know about? And who did it? And why?

It suggests almost a conspiratorial view of history, as though powers and principalities were working behind the scenes to influence the direction of human affairs without being seen. But if that were true, then everything we know would be a lie. We would be living in a political equivalent of "The Matrix," where everything that is obvious is false, and everything that is true is hidden.

Do I propose such a theory?

Not yet, but listen to John Carter's explanation for why the New Deal took place. It didn't have anything to do with the Great Depression — it was wired to the closing of the frontier 35 years before!

"The New Deal was necessary. When the American frontier disappeared in the 1890's, it was conceived. The growth of industrial power, of mass production, the fall of the birth-rate, and the end of mass-immigration were signs that it was coming. Theodore Roosevelt, who knew little or nothing of economics, sensed it; Woodrow Wilson, who knew little or nothing of finance, strove to anticipate it... It was caused by one very simple fact: that we can produce more than enough for everybody in this country... The Roosevelt election of 1932 was simply one of a series of psychological explosions involved in adjusting our civilization to the fact of permanent plenty."

Oh my God. There it is — out in the open — undisguised by rhetoric or subterfuge. The liberal mindset which has hijacked our country for the last hundred years is based not on power, not on greed, but on the staggeringly wrong-headed assumption that we live in a world of "permanent plenty."

No wonder socialism seems like a reasonable alternative to capitalism to those who buy into it. Why work so hard when we can just "share the wealth" instead? Indeed, if there really were a source of "permanent plenty," we would be fools not to take advantage of it. However, I have to ask: At what point does reality intrude and get us to admit that "permanent plenty" is a fairy tale akin to Aladdin's magic lamp and the goose that laid the golden egg?

It is unfortunate that we may not hear the truth in our lifetimes. The stimulus package; the endless bailouts for banks, mortgages, even foreign countries; the sweet succor of free health care — these are but the latest manifestations of "adjusting our civilization" to the big lie of "permanent plenty."

Apparently we have not learned a thing since 1934. Because if the New Deal was NOT a "cunningly contrived" response to the Great Depression," then neither was the Obama stimulus bill a "cunningly contrived" response to the Great Recession. And just as John Franklin Carter assures us that Roosevelt "invented nothing in the New Deal," I think we can safely say that Barack Obama did not invent the American Recovery and Reinvestment Act, even though he signed it and took credit for it.

That bill, the massive raid on the future wealth of the American people, was not invented in a few brief weeks by the Obama administration. It was largely the work of the non-profit Apollo Alliance — "a project of the Tides Center," whose chairman is the founder of ACORN. You can follow the connections yourself, but what you will clearly see is that Obama and the Democratic Congress were beholden to outside influences that wanted to create a new economy in the United States and used the stimulus bill to do it. The Apollo Alliance even brags about this on its website. Indeed, they quote Democratic Majority Leader Sen. Harry Reid giving credit to the Apollo Alliance for the American Recovery and Reinvestment Act, with its emphasis on clean energy and green jobs:

"This legislation is the first step in building a clean energy economy that creates jobs and moves us closer to solving our enormous energy and environmental challenges," Reid said. "We've talked about moving forward on these ideas for decades. The Apollo Alliance has been an important factor in helping us develop and execute a strategy that makes great progress on these goals and in motivating the public to support them."

For emphasis, let's repeat: "We've talked about moving forward on these ideas for decades." Or to quote John Carter

Franklin: "Its roots... go back rather far into our unwritten history."

Of course, it is not really unwritten history; it is just untaught and unacknowledged — the history of how, in Carter's words, "generations of idealistic young men [were sent] to Yale, Harvard and Princeton to prepare themselves as the moral aristocracy of the then distant future."

We ARE that distant future, and if we hope ever to find out how we got here — on the brink of bankruptcy in a world of "permanent plenty" — we had better be prepared to decipher the "unwritten history" that holds the answers.

WAS U.S. SHUFFLED INTO SOCIALISM BY NEW DEAL

December 12, 2010

Last week, I explored the notion that perhaps — just perhaps — Franklin Roosevelt's New Deal was part of a larger plan to detour the United States into socialism.

It seems absurd, of course. We all grew up admiring FDR for his wisdom and courage and were taught that he had saved the country from the Great Depression through his government-funded stimulus programs.

But nowadays, with the benefit of hindsight, and with our generation holding the bill for 75 years of "stimulus," "welfare" and "entitlement" programs, it is appropriate to study President Roosevelt's policies with the same intense scrutiny that we apply to President Obama's. They are at root, after all, the very same policies.

Author John Franklin Carter, a friend and admirer of Roosevelt, wrote in his 1934 book "The New Dealers" that the New Deal "was caused by one very simple fact: that we can produce more than enough for everybody in this country."

This is the myth of "permanent plenty" that Carter sets out as fact in his book, and it explains why he thinks the New Deal would have been necessary with or without a Great Depression. But, of course, the Depression made it so much easier.

In the words of President Obama's first chief of staff, Rahm Emanuel, "You never want a serious crisis to go to waste. And what I mean by that is an opportunity to do things you think you could not do before." Emanuel, of course, engineered the passage of the 2009 stimulus bill and the 2010 health-care bill by channeling the American public's fear of the Great Recession into an opportunity to create a second New Deal.

So this is not just a history lesson. These are lessons that must be learned sooner or later by the American public if they don't wish to be turned into a permanent underclass dependent on the "moral aristocracy" (educated at Yale, Harvard and Princeton) that John Franklin Carter proposed as the new overlords of America.

Carter laid the whole plan out in the first few pages of his book.

"[FDR] invented nothing in the New Deal. This is his greatest achievement. He combined ... familiar elements so calmly and with so friendly a smile, that even after a year of the New Deal there are still people who do not realize that a revolution has taken place."

I can trump that. Even 75 years after the New Deal, there are millions of people who do not realize that a revolution took place — silently, bloodlessly, and dangerously. But Carter went a step further. Just one year into the New Deal, he warned that it could not be stopped. Even if Roosevelt were assassinated or defeated in re-election, the revolution would continue.

"Whatever happens, the New Deal will go on — as either a peaceful revolution or a bloody one — for ten, twenty or fifty more years, until it has achieved its purpose."

That is a bold statement — and a scary one for those who pledge their allegiance to the Constitution. But clearly, Carter felt that the New Deal was more important than the Constitution. Now here is a scary question: Has that revolution yet achieved its purpose? Or is it still under way? Is that the real explanation for the agenda of stimulus and bailouts of the last two years?

Each of you must judge for yourself, but after 75 years of life under the FDR progressive revolution, should we be surprised that Congress has declared health care to be a right? Should we be surprised that Congress and the president want to give away American citizenship to illegal immigrants? Should we be surprised that Obama signed into law the greatest overhaul of the banking industry since the New Deal?

Certainly not if you listen to John Franklin Carter: "Slow or fast, the New Deal is moving to establish a better distribution of American abundance, and Roosevelt is simply a symptom of that process and not its cause."

There again, we have the language of socialism — "a better distribution of American abundance." Or you can call it "redistribution of wealth" if you want. Or as President Obama said, "I think when you spread the wealth around, it's good for everybody."

Or as Karl Marx, the father of communism, put it: "From each according to his abilities, to each according to his needs."

Should we be surprised to see American presidents lining up with Karl Marx in their efforts to create a "welfare state" that will redistribute "American abundance" in an effort to create a more just society?

It was surprising to me — because I had never bothered to study the history of the New Deal before. It just seemed like one of those things that the government did because it had to do it. Desperate times, after all, call for desperate measures.

But what if Carter was right, and Franklin Roosevelt was just the "master-of-ceremonies" in the New Deal, and not the "manager" who was behind it. What if he was instituting a program of redistribution of wealth not because of exigent circumstances, but because that was the goal all along? What if the goal was really to expand the powers of the federal government in order to concentrate power in the hands of the few — the "moral aristocracy" who thought they knew better than the rest of us how to apply economic and social justice.

Carter assures us that FDR used the methods of his predecessors such as Grover Cleveland, Teddy Roosevelt and Woodrow Wilson and "the methods of the World War" to promulgate the New Deal reforms. In particular, he saw the usefulness of "spawning ... emergency inter-Departmental Committees, Board and Administrations" and the "wholesale use of publicity and propaganda to win and hold popular support for a prolonged national effort."

It is certainly apropos to note that the New Deal was essentially the start of the massive federal bureaucracy that we have today. The "committees, board and administrations" in their turn spawned endless regulations, rules and loopholes that turned the American citizenry into trained monkeys who learned to jump through hoops for their paltry rewards and a pat on the head. Good monkey. It also has led through the years to an ever-burgeoning executive branch, which now can dictate to the American public without legislative authority on every topic under the sun — whether it's pretending that CO_2 is a dangerous pollutant or pretending that Glenn Beck is a dangerous American.

Yep, with enough "publicity and propaganda" you can convince the majority of people that CO_2, the gas that leaves your mouth when you exhale, is a dangerous pollutant, but that doesn't make it so. And as for Glenn Beck, he is dangerous only to the extent that he pokes holes in the "publicity and propaganda" being promoted by the power brokers in Washington, D.C. He isn't dangerous to America; he is dangerous to the people who run America.

And just who are those people? Who are the forces that envision their task as "moving to establish a better distribution of American abundance"?

We get some frightening clues in John Carter's 1934 book.

"Roosevelt had the benefit of several other great national experiments as useful points of reference for the American New Deal," Carter forthrightly opines. "He had before him the spectacle of the Soviet Union with its recent dramatization of economic reorganization through the Five-Year Plan. He had before him the example of Fascist Italy with its regimentation of business, labor and banking in the 'Corporative State.' He had before him the instances of Kemal, Mussolini and Hitler in restoring national pride and self-confidence to beaten or dispirited peoples."

So there you have it, straight from the horse's mouth. John Franklin Carter, an ally and advocate of the New Deal, a close confidante of FDR — without the benefit of political correctness — told the unvarnished truth. The New Deal was modeled after the examples and policies of Stalin, Hitler and Mussolini — the poster boys for communism, national socialism and fascism.

Carter even goes so far as to compare the National Recovery Administration created by Roosevelt to the Soviet "GPU," the State Political Directorate which was the precursor of the more infamous KGB and which created the infamous Gulag system for political prisoners in the Soviet Union.

Remember, these associations between the New Deal and fascism or communism are not my idea, or even Carter's idea — it's in the historical record, and the admiration society went both ways. Hitler told the American ambassador that the New Deal represented "the quintessence of the German state philosophy." Mussolini said admiringly of FDR that "America has a dictator" and wrote in a review of Roosevelt's book, "Looking Forward," that FDR's rhetoric and proposals were "reminiscent of the ways and means by which fascism awakened the Italian people."

Looking backward, the question is what will awaken the American people out of the slumber into which they have fallen? After 75 years of "revolution" and "redistribution of American abundance," we don't need a New Deal any longer — we need a fresh deck.

NEW DEAL? MANY DID
DARE CALL IT SOCIALISM

December 19, 2010

Perhaps the most important lesson of Franklin Roosevelt's New Deal is what it reveals to us about the sweep and scope of history — and how easy it is to bury truth under the winds of change.

Today, FDR is considered one of the best presidents ever. A survey of presidential scholars performed by the Siena College Research Institute five times since 1982 has consistently placed FDR as the "top all-time chief executive." Other surveys of the experts consistently rank him in the top three.

That is what historians say, but what does history say?

The more you look at the contemporary record, the less confidence you can have that Roosevelt should be judged as anything less than an American dictator who charmed the country into surrendering its sovereignty and cut us loose from our constitutional moorings. It wasn't just Republicans who said so at the time either — it was Jeffersonian Democrats; it was the Supreme Court; it was the local newspaper.

In fact, Roosevelt was much more openly called a socialist in the early years of his first term than President Obama is today. But both have embraced programs and principles of socialism, and should be judged accordingly.

Frankly, if you want to understand the battle between left and right that is raging today, if you want to understand the rise of the Tea Party, if you want to understand the agenda of President Obama, then you almost have to dig up a Rosetta Stone from history that puts the language of Roosevelt's New Deal side-by-side with the language of socialism and the language of the Democratic Party. Such a Rosetta Stone exists in the contemporaneous newspaper accounts of the 1930s.

Take a look, for instance, at the following Associated Press story from June 1935 and see if you can connect the dots between President Roosevelt, President Obama and the socialist agenda.

As published in the Sandusky (Ohio) Register, the story bore the headline, "Roosevelt Urges Share-Wealth Taxes." The subhead noted that "Big Incomes are Targets of Message."

In some ways, this is of course similar to our current debate over the so-called Bush tax cuts. Up until recently President Obama too has been urging share-the-wealth taxes on big incomes. But as a result of the mid-term elections, he has stepped back and has now reached a compromise agreement that would keep taxes at their current rate. The significance of that compromise has yet to be fully analyzed, and it is possible that Obama got more than he gave. But not all Democrats see it that way. Many of them continue to push for tax increases on those with incomes above $250,000 a year, or at least $1 million if that isn't possible.

The clamor of Democrats for higher taxes ultimately raises the question of just why some politicians think the government is entitled to a bigger share of rich people's income. Perhaps the question can be settled by the AP's rather blunt reporting from 1935.

The first paragraph of the Sandusky, Ohio, story said flatly that Roosevelt's "share-the-wealth" tax program was "based on the philosophy that big fortunes are created by collective rather than individual effort." A paragraph or two later, we read that the president called his initiative a "sound public policy of encouraging a wider distribution of wealth."

A follow-up story by the Associated Press described the tax plan as "intended to break up great fortunes and reduce large incomes." Imagine that.

Apparently my caution last week in hesitating to say outright that FDR had steered us on a path to socialism was unnecessary. It was obvious from the start to those who had to live under the New Deal. Just listen to the code words: "share the wealth," "collectivism" and "wider distribution (read 'redistribution') of wealth."

Collectivism, the notion that the group is more important than the individual, is the backbone of socialism, communism and fascism. Little wonder then that FDR and his backers admired Mussolini, Hitler and Stalin, as acknowledged by John Franklin Carter in his sympathetic 1934 book "The New Dealers."

Indeed, as my research proves, both left and right in the 1930s acknowledged that Roosevelt's policies had socialist tendencies. And what is more important to us, those socialist tendencies have been continued and intensified for the past 75 years.

The five-point program proposed by Roosevelt in 1935 is certainly eerily familiar to those who are following the current political debate. The program included raising death taxes, raising taxes on incomes above $1 million a year, and raising taxes on business. Again, that should of course sound familiar. The first two were cornerstones of the program being pushed by House Democrats last week in opposition to the Obama-McConnell tax compromise.

It should also be noted that the politics of the New Deal were not unlike the politics of the Obama Deal — FDR proposed this package knowing full well that he could not win approval of it at the time. But he won political points for it nonetheless, and then got to play the role of conciliator. Likewise, President Obama has been pushing for an end to the Bush tax cuts for the past two years, campaigned strenuously on it, and only gave up out of political necessity.

But please, let's not mistake pragmatism for ideology. In both FDR and Obama we are confronted with presidents who have conscientiously and deliberately aimed to dismantle the American market economy in the service of ideals that are foreign to our republic.

A Dec. 18, 1933, story in the Huntingdon, Pa., Daily News, reported on a speech made in London by George Lansbury, the leader of the opposition Labour Party in the House of Commons, who lauded FDR for taking the United States in the direction of worldwide governance and global socialism.

"Every step he takes from month to month appears to me to bring the United States nearer to the ideals of Socialism. The President is minimizing competition among individuals and minimizing individual profits."

Imagine that!

Well, as they say, it takes a socialist to know one.

Of course, it is doubtful that many Americans, then or now, would intentionally sign on to an agenda of less competition and less profit — or in Karl Marx's famous words, "From each according to his ability; to each according to his need."

But Lansbury was right. Socialism DOES diminish competition, because there is no need to strive to be better when you are already having all your needs met while doing nothing, or next to nothing. And yes, under socialism there will be less profit, too, because with everyone taking it easy, there will be less success, and less to share.

Socialism, in short, is a recipe for disaster.

That is just what Roosevelt gave us, whether you call it the New Deal or the same old dole. You may as well just be honest and call it socialism because there is no reason to call it free enterprise. Freedom is an individual right; not a corporate one. I cannot be free as an individual if I am forced to do what is good for the collective.

Alexander de Tocqueville warned of this in 1840. He predicted in "Democracy in America" that we would eventually reach a stage in which the "collective" good was considered more important than the individual. At such a time, the government would arrogate to itself the ability to make decisions for each of us individually. It started even before the New Deal, and was perhaps perfected with Obamacare, with its "individual mandate" that we must each purchase health insurance.

But there is no reason for us to be silent. The small community newspapers of the 1930s were never silenced. Here is one more example, from an editorial in the Bluefield Daily Telegraph in West Virginia, circa September 1934:

"The failure of all [the Democrats'] depression cures, which were for the most part such as to curtail individual liberty and personal freedom contrary to the constitution, constitute a great disappointment to the voters, and the high-handed coercive manner of the administration program as stirred a formidable resentment."

As Tocqueville cautioned, "The true friends of the liberty and the greatness of man ought constantly to be on the alert to prevent the power of government from lightly sacrificing the private rights of individuals to the general execution of its designs."

Or put in specific terms: "The true friends of liberty" must fight against any government or any president — no matter how popular — who "sacrifices the private rights of individuals" for the benefit of the collective good. Period.

'LIBERTY ... IS NOT SAFE': A CONTINUING DEBATE

January 9, 2011

H.L. Mencken, a famous writer of the first half of the 20th century, is often credited with having said: "Nobody ever went broke underestimating the intelligence of the American public."

So far as I can tell, he never actually said that, which may just give more credit to the validity of the dictum itself. However, he did write something very similar in an essay entitled "Notes on Journalism," published in the Chicago Tribune on Sept. 19, 1926.

"No one in this world, so far as I know," said Mencken, "...has ever lost money by underestimating the intelligence of the great masses of the plain people."

What is surprising is that the next line has been largely forgotten through the passage of time: "Nor has any one ever lost public office thereby."

The greatest proof of this latter point would seem to be the re-election three times of President Franklin Roosevelt by great majorities, despite the overwhelming evidence of his disregard for the Constitution, the rule of law and the inalienable rights set forth in the Declaration of Independence.

Consider the evidence: Roosevelt, who essentially became president for life, massively expanded the federal government beyond its constitutional restraints; he tried to pack the Supreme Court in order to gain control of the judiciary; and he asked for and was granted massive new powers by Congress with the Reorganization Act of 1939, thus forever changing the balance of power between the three branches of government.

It's hard to believe that Roosevelt convinced the country to go along with such nonsense 75 years ago, but he certainly didn't convince everyone. To browse through the historical record is to be struck, time and time again, by just how vehemently and loudly people shouted out that Roosevelt was leading the country to ruin.

Listen, for instance, to Ogden Mills, the former secretary of the treasury, speaking to an economic forum in New York in May 1934 about the dangers of the New Deal:

"The social and economic planning that has been enacted into law during the last 12 months has been presented to the people as novel, progressive and liberal," he said. "It is not novel... It is not progressive since it reverts back to the economic despotism of the Middle Ages. It is not liberal since it means the end of individual liberty. In part or in whole ... it has been tried repeatedly throughout the course of history. Everywhere it has failed."

Nor was this Herbert Hoover Republican alone in his criticism of FDR. Democrats were equally vocal in their defense of liberty. One such was former Sen. James A. Reed of Missouri, who said in a Constitution Day address in Chicago in 1934 that the Roosevelt administration was "violating the safeguards of liberty set up in the Constitution and doing by force what the basic law of the republic specifically prohibits."

It is perhaps not coincidental that Mencken, that harshest judge of politicians, had only kind words for Sen. Reed when he had retired from the Senate in 1929. He saw Reed as virtually a lone defender in the Senate against the excesses of government.

"It is a great pity that there are not more like him. The country could use a thousand, and even so, each of the thousand would find a thousand mountebanks in front of him," Mencken wrote of Reed in the American Mercury. "The process of government among us becomes a process of pillage and extortion. The executive power is in the hands of a gang of bureaucrats without responsibility, led by charlatans without conscience. The courts, succumbing to such agencies as the Anti-Saloon League, reduce the constitutional guarantees to vanity and nullity. The legislative machine is operated by nonentities, with frauds and fanatics flogging them. In all that vast and obscene mob there are few men of any solid ability, and fewer still of any intellectual integrity. Reed was one. He had both."

That intellectual integrity, along with Reed's respect for the Bill of Rights and the Constitution, was no doubt what led him to speak up, several years after his own day in power had passed, and condemn the vast expansion of government under the New Deal.

He was legitimately frightened about the direction of the country, and condemned Roosevelt for it, just as he had spoken against fellow Democrat Woodrow Wilson during that president's administration. What mattered to him more than party loyalty was national loyalty — and particularly loyalty to the Constitution.

What he said back on that Constitution Day in 1934 might not have been popular among Democrats of the time, but it certainly strikes a chord for all patriots who believe in the principles of limited government.

Speaking at the Chicago World's Fair, he told the many in attendance that "Liberty — the spirit of the Constitution — is not safe in this republic today."

"The framers of the Constitution had seen enough of paternalistic government," Reed said. "They had studied the pages of history — they knew that power feeds on power, and that when government once asserts the right to control labor, the property or the habits of the citizens, it has entered upon the old and bloody road of despotism."

Reed did not name Franklin Roosevelt personally in his speech, but there was no doubt who he perceived as the greatest threat to liberty in our long history as a nation.

"Can it be that those we have trusted with power, and who swore to support and defend the Constitution against all enemies, foreign and domestic, now stand foresworn and are plotting the destruction of the great Magna Charta of our liberties? Fortunate it is that we are beginning to realize that the liberties gained by the struggle of the centuries are imperiled, and that the Constitution is the great bulwark of liberty. Such it was intended to be by its authors. Such, please God, it may remain, despite assaults of foreign foes and the conspiracies of domestic traitors. The Constitution of the United States is the keystone of the arch of liberty. Destroy it and liberty is dead."

Yet, despite the loud cries of Reed, Mills and many others, America sank further and further into the age of "paternalism" that they decried. Why? How? What sheep's clothing did the wolf wear to gain power over the innocent people of the nation? Reed provides the answer, in words that easily explain the despotism of the nanny state and make it clear how completely we have been conned by those who "only want to help us."

As Reed warned, The despot's "countenance is wreathed in smiles, and in honeyed words he protests his love for the people — an infinite desire to shield them from harm and guide them to the high plains of prosperity. But in the end the tyrant has struck with an iron hand."

In a front-page editorial that quoted Reed and Mills, the Centralia [Wash.] Daily Chronicle of Sept. 20, 1934, reflected on the nation's newfound attention to the Constitution as a terrified response to the New Deal.

"From all sections of the country there [are] being published speeches delivered by prominent men on the Constitution of the United States. There has never been a time since its adoption in 1787 that there has been so much interest in its contents and its incorporated principles. Attached to the original draft and a part of it are ten separate paragraphs called the Bill of Rights.... Study the Bill of Rights in the light of the present governmental plans to force the people to do certain specific acts and you will then understand why the thoughtful men and women of the country are so deeply concerned over the regimentation now going on."

The dangers of the New Deal were thus plainly laid out just one year after it started. Liberty itself was seen to be in peril. Statesmen of great stature were willing to speak out and say so, and yet America slumbered for the next 75 years with self-serving somnambulance. We walked liked zombies from one government handout to the next, until finally we woke up and found ourselves being handed an order to buy health insurance.

That was the final straw. On top of the government bailouts, the stimulus bills, the endless giveaways, there was the indignity of Obamacare. Finally the sleeping beast awoke again and threw off its chains. The American people yearned for liberty, and once again they sought it in the Constitution.

It is no accident that the House of Representatives has opened its new session with a reading of the complete U.S. Constitution for the first time in the history of Congress. That document is our lifeblood. It alone can restore our nation to health, and our future depends on understanding how badly the liberty it protects has been abused in the past.

Some have called the reading of the Constitution a stunt or cheap theatrics. I suspect those are the same people who say the Constitution is irrelevant when Congress makes laws. Sadly, for the past 75 years the Constitution has indeed been made largely irrelevant by the federal government it was intended to control.

But today, thanks to the Tea Party movement, America has revived from its long slumber and once again has a chance to restore the Constitution to its rightful place as the tether on ambitious men. If we are lucky — if we are worthy — then in future centuries, the period between the New Deal and Obamacare will be known as the long interregnum when the Constitution was nearly — but not quite — forgotten.

WHITE-HOT FREE SPEECH IS NOTHING NEW

January 16, 2011

A popular myth that has arisen in recent years — and been intensified by the rhetoric over the recent shooting in Tucson — is that somehow politics is more polarized or more heated these days than it was in times past.

That such a notion could gain any credence, especially among the so-called educated class of writers and national leaders, is astounding.

In my research into the political climate of first the 1960s and then the 1930s, I have seen indisputable evidence that American politics has long been vociferous, personal and hard-hitting.

The Literary Digest in a report on its presidential poll of 1932 had this to say:

"The campaign has plunged into its bare-knuckle stage — the crisis of that quadrennial fever which disrupts American life, and throws the best of neighbors into a cat-and-dog feud until the passing of election day releases them from the spell and allows them to see what jolly good fellows they've been shaking their fists at.

"This fever now seems to be raging according to the best traditions. No more front-porch stuff. Vigorous campaign touring by both candidates and their oratorical aides. Slathers of rhetoric leaping out of the nation's radio sets. Everybody hot and bothered. Parliamentary amenities put aside. Attack, counter-attack. Irritability. Censure. Sarcasm. Whispering campaigns. Nerves on edge. The country itself on edge. We are at the ticklish stage in this campaign."

Don't forget, that was before Franklin Roosevelt had been elected and before the New Deal had even been announced. But yet, there was plenty of heated rhetoric, irritability and "attack, counter-attack." And trust me, despite the editorialist's expectation that the political rhetoric would settle down after the 1932 election, it didn't. Rather, it just got worse as the Great Depression dragged on and as FDR revamped the entire U.S. economy.

Nor do we need to stop our historical survey in the 1930s. Vitriol and white gasoline have been a part of political rhetoric from the first. Is it not still taught that one of our Founding Fathers, Alexander Hamilton, died in a duel with Aaron Burr over longstanding political grievances? And what about the portraits of Abraham Lincoln as a monkey that were featured in newspapers across the entire nation, north and south.

Listen, for instance, to this 1864 plea in the Allen County Democrat newspaper of Lima, Ohio:

"Democrats, with a conscription of a most odious character menacing the people, do not lower your standard one inch or abate your opposition to the measures of this infamous and detestable administration one jot."

On the front page of the Mountain Democrat from Placerville, Calif., in the same year appeared this snippet: "What bigotry and blindness it was for the heathens to throw themselves under the car of Juggernaut to be crushed to appease the wrath of their false gods. And in this enlightened day, what folly it is for the American people to offer themselves as sacrifices to promote the ambition of Lincoln."

These are examples picked at random of the kind of attacks that have been part and parcel of American politics from the beginning. You can find similar attacks on Thomas Jefferson, Teddy Roosevelt, John Kennedy, and George W. Bush. The fact that such attacks continue to be made against President Obama is neither a sign of racism nor of radicalism, but of the same old "cat-and-dog feud" that cannot help but be waged by free men and women in defense of their liberty.

In a recent column, I quoted former Sen. James A. Reed referring to Franklin Roosevelt's New Deal and other policies as "the conspiracies of domestic traitors."

That's pretty strong language, but what made it rather extraordinary from our perspective is not its intensity, but that Reed, like Roosevelt, was a Democrat. I might venture that all the talk we hear of how "polarized" the political climate is today is because, in former times, it was principle that guided rhetoric rather than partisan loyalty.

Can you think of any Democrat today who is willing to publicly rail against his party's "big government" policies? Montana's Sen. Jon Tester fashions himself as an independent Democrat, for instance, but it seems like the only time he is independent is when his vote isn't needed to push forward the progressive agenda.

That kind of timidity wasn't seen in the 1930s. Real debate, uncleansed by political correctness, was the standard. President Roosevelt was attacked from within his own party vociferously, and in no uncertain terms. But he and his advisers could give as good as they got.

When Sen. Huey Long of Louisiana mounted a credible third-party bid from the left-wing of the Democratic Party on FDR in 1935, Roosevelt and his Cabinet and advisers attacked

Long's "share-the-wealth" agenda before finally co-opting it as their own.

Numerous advisers of the president such as Gen. Hugh S. Johnson, the administrator of the National Recovery Administration, Postmaster General (and old political hand) Jim Farley, and Sen. Harry Byrd were loosed by FDR to denounce Long.

Byrd called Long a "supreme demagogue" and said, "He has made himself dictator of his state." Johnson said Long was a preacher of "destruction" and that "Hitler couldn't hold a candle to Huey in the art of the old Barnum ballyhoo."

Six months later, Huey Long was assassinated by a lone gunman. To this day, no one has blamed either Harry Byrd, Gen. Johnson or FDR for the killing. By the same token, it is wrong to blame anyone but the gunmen and their accomplices for modern assassinations. Strong speech may be "irritating," as the Literary Digest suggested back in 1932. It may even be offensive, but it is not murder — it is rather the basis of all our civil liberties.

Do not think that the King of England approved of being called a tyrant in 1776. Do not think that Lincoln approved of being called a tyrant in 1864. Do not think George Bush approved of being called a usurper when he was declared the winner of the 2000 presidential election. Do not think President Obama approved of being called a usurper in 2008 when his birth status was questioned.

But do not imagine an America where we cannot speak our minds. Do not imagine an America where political speech has to be politically correct speech before it can be heard. And do not imagine an America where you and I have to agree with each other all the time.

That is not America. That is the end of America.

IN PRAISE OF A FORGOTTEN HERO

January 30, 2011

The premise of John F. Kennedy's book "Profiles in Courage" was that true political courage is found when politicians take a principled stand that turns their assumed friends into sworn enemies.

Kennedy (or his ghostwriter) told the stories of eight senators who had crossed party lines or ignored their own political fortunes in order to do what they thought was the right thing.

I suppose the fact that Kennedy only came up with eight stories for his book out of all the hundreds of senators who had served till that time could be evidence that political courage is relatively rare.

Or maybe it is just easy to overlook because the people who exhibit it are often going against the grain, and are thus not always immediately — if ever — recognized as heroes. Sometimes they are publicly repudiated such as Sen. Joe Lieberman, the Democratic senator who vociferously supported President Bush in the war on terror. Other times they are belittled and trivialized such as the Republican establishment has tried to do with Sarah Palin and Ron Paul.

Often they are forgotten by history altogether.

Such is the case of Bainbridge Colby, the constitutional attorney who was briefly secretary of state under Democrat Woodrow Wilson. If you don't like Sarah Palin, you will most assuredly despise Bainbridge Colby.

Colby was a vociferous opponent of the Soviet Union, even though Russia had been President Wilson's ally in World War I, shortly before Colby took office. It was Colby who crafted the statement in which American recognition of the Lenin regime was denied, a policy which continued for 13 years until Franklin Roosevelt took office.

Perhaps that was what turned Colby against FDR. In the 1932 campaign, Colby had gone on a speaking tour supporting Roosevelt against President Herbert Hoover. Colby and

Roosevelt were both upper-crust New Yorkers and probably had an affinity for one another. Indeed, Colby had been a supporter of FDR's cousin Teddy Roosevelt in his failed 1912 campaign to regain the presidency as a Progressive.

But Colby foresaw the dangers of communism when it was still in its infancy, and he must have been doubly incensed when FDR not only recognized the Soviet Union but imported some of its social policies to the United States under the name of the New Deal. He spent the next several years campaigning against Roosevelt nationwide.

In 1934, he told the American Coalition of Patriotic Societies, meeting in Portland, Maine, that "the overturn of our institutions, including the Constitution, is the avowed goal" of FDR's immediate advisers. And in words that will be familiar to those of you who have fought against the indignity of Obamacare, he decried the "imposed regimentation" that will "take the place of American ingenuity and enterprise."

He complained that "bureaucratic control, even of our going out and coming in, is to weigh down the land once known as the land of the free." And Colby, like the Tea Party in 2010, argued that the American people must turn to the congressional elections "to save our beloved country from the enemies which are within the gates."

"Congress is democracy's arena under the Constitution. The elected representatives of the people are the spokesmen of democracy in America. But when I say Congress, I mean a true Congress, a self-respecting Congress, not a rubber-stamp Congress such as Congress proved itself in the last session.

"When I say representatives of the people, I do not mean the servile and herded majority, incapable of function as representatives, which in the last Congress allowed the executive to originate its measures and then passed them without reading or scrutiny."

Does this sound familiar? This is the underground stream of liberty that has nurtured our republic for hundreds of years — these are the torrents that spring up from Samuel Adams and George Washington and Benjamin Franklin and wash over all patriots still today.

"Read the bill!" Where have we heard that before? "Represent the people!" Where have we heard that before? This is the Tea Party movement rising up 65 years before George W. Bush took office and nearly 75 years before Barack Obama pledged to "fundamentally transform" America.

And when Bainbridge Colby concluded his speech, we can hear more echoes that are still heard today. Just as Barack Obama has his Valerie Jarrett and Bill Ayers and the rest of the Chicago mafia, so too did FDR have his "brain trust" from Eastern academic circles, including Rexford Tugwell, the advocate of agricultural planning who learned a lot of his tradecraft from the Soviet Union. Colby took dead aim at Tugwell, who had just then been promoted to undersecretary of the U.S. Department of Agriculture.

"The country takes notice [of this] distinguished promotion," Colby wryly said, pointing out that it was Tugwell, who declared " 'there is revolution in our midst,' and who out-Russias Russia in his contempt for our popular morality, our public school education, and our religion, which ... he says, 'clings to ethics long ago outworn.'"

Take heed. A lot of folks are once again saying there is a revolution in our midst — folks like Van Jones and Mark Lloyd and Cass Sunstein and President Obama — and like Tugwell, some of those folks have contempt for our popular morality and our religion.

Indeed, the description of Tugwell is reminiscent of President Obama's analysis of those poor backwards folks of Pennsylvania who still don't get it that big government is their friend.

"It's not surprising then that they get bitter," Obama told a fund-raising dinner in San Francisco in 2008. "They cling to guns or religion or antipathy to people who aren't like them or anti-immigrant sentiment or anti-trade sentiment as a way to explain their frustrations."

Or they cling to the Constitution.

Which may be what worries folks like Paul Krugman of the New York Times and Keith Olbermann, formerly of MSNBC, who miss no opportunity to blast the Tea Party movement as hate-filled and vitriolic. These are educated people who know quite well that the Constitution doesn't allow big federal government, and that therefore the superstructure of the New Deal and the welfare state is illegal. They encourage us all to return to the state of wakeful sleep that has existed for the past half century, because that is good for their progressive agenda.

Perhaps the last time before now that the American public had been fully engaged in an earnest desire to protect their political liberties was indeed the era of the New Deal, when not just Republicans but Democrats spoke out passionately against government encroachment.

In 1935, Bainbridge Colby said this: "The political party founded by Thomas Jefferson, and elected on a platform which proclaimed the liberties of which I speak, has converted the American Republic into a socialist state and enveloped it in a mesh of tyrannous and bureaucratic rule which has no counterpart save among the peoples of Europe, now sunk under the autocratic sway of unresisted dictatorship.'

" 'As a Democrat,' he went on, 'I would venture to remind the heady and nonchalant innovators of the moment, who are officiating as instruments of the Democratic Party, and usurping its name, that the government of the United States was established to get rid of arbitrary, discretionary executive power...'

"The Democratic Party cannot nor will it turn from legal regulation to executive regulation, from law to personal power, without rending itself in twain and divorcing from its ranks countless thousands who have a fixed attachment to its historic principles.

"Such Democrats do not intend to abandon the foundations of liberty and just government. Nor will they at the behest of anyone, or under the pressure of a needlessly, and I sometimes think a wantonly, prolonged depression renounce the birthright of democratic government and turn back to the most discredited models of government known to history."

No doubt, those who support bigger government and find the foundation of their progressive agenda in the work of Franklin Roosevelt will cringe at the words of Bainbridge Colby.

No doubt if asked who was the traitor against his country, FDR or Colby, they would not hesitate to point at the man who defended the Constitution against the New Deal.

But who had more political courage? The president who pandered for votes by dismantling the Constitution and auctioning it off piece by piece to garner funds for his New Deal? Or the loud-mouthed friend of liberty who didn't just shut up and go along to get along?

My vote is with Bainbridge Colby, a forgotten hero.

The Billings, Mont., Gazette eulogized Colby after his death in 1950 as "an independent liberal" who was "often called a 'radical' during the years when he was a conspicuous figure in the political life of the country."

It is the "independent" label more than the "liberal" label that defines Colby's political perspective, and just like the "independent conservative" Sarah Palin, it was his independence that made the mainstream media label him as a "radical." True independents eschew labels and embrace principles, and both Palin and Colby are principled defenders of the U.S. Constitution.

As the Billings Gazette said about Colby:

"He was too intelligent to permit his sincere and constructive liberalism to be used to further the designs of those who would weaken or betray the free institutions of our constitutional government."

Accordingly, Colby spent most of his career outside of government; so too may Palin. They may never be seen as giant figures of history, but both of them carry the banner of 1776, and thus cannot be ignored. If they never achieve greatness themselves, they still stand on the shoulders of giants — those immortals who shaped the Constitution of the United States of America.

For true patriots, that is enough.

THE 'RATIONAL' EXUBERANCE OF SPENDING OTHER PEOPLE'S MONEY

February 6, 2011

To sink or swim? That is the $15 trillion question.

It's now up to the American people to decide whether the American experiment in self-government will stay afloat through reason and sacrifice or else sink into oblivion as a result of self-deception and greed.

For a long time it looked like greed would win — not the supposed greed of people who succeed through hard work and smart decisions, but the greed of those who want something for nothing, who think that life owes them a good education, nice house, nutritious meals and an easy ride.

That certainly is not what was intended when the United States of America was founded. In fact, it is the opposite of the principle of liberty espoused by Samuel Adams, Thomas Jefferson and Ben Franklin. It matters little whether the people looking for a free ride are royalty or the so-called proletariat. In either case, the free ride comes at the expense of the labor of someone else, usually the middle class, and thus at the expense of their liberty.

So whether it is a king living the life of luxury in a palace or it is a welfare mother using food stamps and government handouts to subsidize 60-inch flat-screen TVs, Xbox game systems, and brand-new automobiles, it is a reflection of the exact same sense of entitlement. The king and the welfare mom both think they don't have to work, and you do.

Fortunately, we don't have to work for the king anymore, but we still have to work to support those who don't want to work for themselves and for those who think they are entitled to more than they can afford.

For a while, the system even seemed to work. That was thanks to the Baby Boom after World War II. With more and more people entering the work force, the tax base kept growing fast enough to pay for the also rapidly increasing entitlements that federal law granted to everyone lucky enough to be born in America.

But that was then; this is now.

Now we have a shrinking or stagnant work force and a growing list of obligations — in particular the burgeoning obligations of a national debt rapidly approaching $15 trillion.

Ironically, one of the causes of the declining tax base in the last 30 years that has led to the debt crisis is the liberal abortion policy that has resulted in something like 50 million potential taxpayers not making it out of the womb alive (or in the case of partial-birth abortion, not for long).

But even under the best of circumstances, eventually every budget runs out of money. When this happens in a family or a business, dire decisions are made. Purchases long anticipated are delayed or done away with altogether. Employees are laid off. Vacations are canceled. Yard sales are held. Everyone understands that you can't spend money you don't have.

But that is not the model for national governments. In fact, thanks to Keynesian economics, spending money you don't have is actually encouraged. The worse off you get, the more money you spend.

It might even work — for a while.

Except for one fly in the ointment — human nature.

Because we do not just have to spend money to meet our current debts. As a result of the greed factor, we also have to spend money on new debts that are incurred by the spiraling expectations of the welfare class for more privileges and more fulfillment of "human rights."

And of course because the middle class is not a bunch of dummies, they eventually see the allure of being paid not to work, or being subsidized to obtain goods and services that are otherwise unrealistic. Thus the welfare class grows exponentially with the amount of money being allocated. Eventually you reach a point of absolute insolvency, at which time the system collapses.

The only chance to avoid this fate is to face facts — something which human nature seems to stubbornly resist.

That, dear friends, is where we find ourselves in the year 2011. And it is now up to our beloved representatives in Congress to either introduce the American public to fiscal reality or to sign our economic death warrant.

Republicans in Congress seem to understand this — at least some of them do. Democrats, on the other hand, seem to think the debt star hurtling toward Earth is just more pie in the sky. They will keep spending other people's money until they are flattened.

It's probably unfair to blame either Republicans or Democrats at this point. It is for the most part an almost universal delusion that we can justify spending money on any "good cause" for the simple reason that it is "good." If families operated under such a simplistic premise, then we would eat lobster and filet mignon every night instead of hamburgers and spaghetti.

The problem, in essence, is that under the pressure of socialism's plaintive wail in the 19th century, we slowly began to replace economic necessity with social justice as the basis for our spending decisions. That transition became much more rapid with the New Deal, and today is as devilishly fast as any expressway to hell.

A few statesmen have resisted the temptation to buy votes with government lucre, but they are few and far between. One who might, in hindsight, be classed as a great president was Democrat Grover Cleveland, who served two terms as president (from 1885-1889 and from 1893-1897) and won the popular vote three times.

Cleveland was noted for his commitment to classical liberalism, especially for the principles of limited government and constitutional protection of individual liberties. He was also noted for his honesty, courage and integrity. It is these characteristics which seem to be lacking in many of today's leaders.

Pay attention especially to Cleveland's words from 1887 when he vetoed a bill to provide Texas farmers with a government handout to assist them in times of drought. You can be sure the president did not hate Texas farmers, but apparently he was not convinced that spending money on a "good cause" was always necessary and in the best interests of society. In fact, he expressly thought it might hurt society, as he wrote in his veto note:

"I feel obliged to withhold my approval of the plan, as proposed by this bill, to indulge a benevolent and charitable sentiment through the appropriation of public funds for that purpose. I can find no warrant for such an appropriation in the Constitution, and I do not believe that the power and duty of the General Government ought to be extended to the relief of general suffering which is in no manner properly related to the public service or benefit. ... Federal aid in such cases encourages the expectation of paternal care on the part of the Government and weakens the sturdiness of our national character, while it prevents the indulgence among our people of that kindly sentiment and conduct which strengthens the bonds of common brotherhood."

Although Cleveland was proven correct by history, his point of view unfortunately did not prevail — to the point where we now — all of us to some extent — depend servilely on the "paternal care ... of the government" for our well-being, and have watched the "bonds of common brotherhood" be replaced with the handcuffs of forced charity.

And the best that the Republicans in Congress can come up with to slay the debt dragon is a measly $32 billion. Pathetic. Of course, that is $32 billion more than the Democrats are going to offer.

Trouble is, the only way to cut more than that is to summon up those qualities that Grover Cleveland was noted for — honesty, courage and integrity. Someone has to tell the American public that there is no such thing as a free lunch. A few of us know that already, but so many people are eating at the public trough that they can't be bothered with a lesson in harsh economic reality.

In 1776, the American people rebelled against a king — demanding that he stop exploiting their labor for his wealth. Today, the American people will either rebel against the tyranny of entitlement which chains them to the federal government, or else they will succumb to the same sad fate that befalls all who sow the wind.

They will reap the whirlwind.

WHY DO BAD THINGS HAPPEN TO GOOD COUNTRIES?

February 13, 2011

It's hard to be a hero.

First you have to recognize a threat — then you have to analyze the threat, consider possible responses, marshal your resources and eventually ACT — with no assurance of success.

It is this last element which ensures that heroes are few and far between. If we knew that we would prevail against evil, foolishness or just plain stupidity, then we would all jump into the fray to grab our share of immortality.

But with no assurance of success, most of us just sit on the sidelines and do what people on the sidelines always do — criticize the folks who are trying to make a difference.

That makes sense as a matter of self-preservation, I suppose. Heroes have a relatively high mortality rate, after all. But what if the choice is not so simple? What if you had a choice between trying to be a hero and possibly dying ... or doing nothing and almost certainly dying? What would you do then?

That is essentially the choice facing the Congress of the United States — and by extension the rest of us — as we look into the maw of a $15 trillion national debt. Survival or death? Those are the high stakes involved for our country, and yet most folks in Congress are still reorganizing the deck chairs on the Titanic. Rep. Paul Ryan, R-Wis., had the audacity to initially propose just $32 billion in cuts from the president's $3.8 trillion budget. Remember, that massive budget is funded with only $2.2 trillion in revenue and $1.56 trillion in borrowing. In other words, more than 40 percent of everything the U.S. government plans to spend this year is someone else's money.

To help you grasp this concept, just write down your own annual household income on a piece of paper and multiply that by 1.7. If you make $50,000 a year, that means following the congressional spending plan you would actually be able to spend $85,000. That's a handy chunk of change. It will make it oh so much easier to pay off your bills.

But on the other hand, since it is borrowed, you will have to make plans to pay it back — and since there is no possible way you can pay back $35,000 if you make $50,000 a year and expect to continue spending at the same rate as the previous year, the inevitable result for you and your family is bankruptcy._ That is the inevitable result for the U.S. government, too — except they call it by some other fancy name since the federal government can't technically declare bankruptcy. I just like to think of it as COLLAPSE.

But most politicians and most pundits are going about their everyday business as if nothing were wrong.

There are one or two exceptions — most notably, freshman Sen. Rand Paul, R-Ky., and Ohio Rep. Jim Jordan, chairman of the Republican Study Committee. Paul and Jordan have stepped forward with proposals for massive cutbacks in the federal budget to try to make our spending consistent with our revenue. These reality-based plans, however, conflict with long-ingrained entitlements and feel-good programs that politicians are afraid to touch.

To many people, it seems evil to talk about cutting funding for the Corporation for Public Broadcasting or the National Endowment for the Arts. To others it seems evil to talk about cutting military spending. But you can't be a hero if you are afraid to do battle. Every enemy has its proponents, and so it is with spending. You cannot make a cut without hearing a loud squeal in return.

But if you want to be a hero, you have be willing to fight the dragon, and slay it. You can't worry about the dragon's feelings. You can't talk about dragon rights. And you certainly can't feed the dragon. But that is what President Obama is doing. Even though he has talked about the huge problem caused by the national debt, he plans to expand it. Most recently he is ramping up an effort to spend billions in borrowed money on high-speed rail service and high-speed wireless broadband services.

Well, slow down, Mr. President. You are going in the wrong direction.

Which brings us to another hero: The Reverend Frank Scott, who is famous for going in the right direction.

The name may not be familiar, but most of you have seen him and heard him. He preached that the individual has to try to make a difference and not wait for some higher power to rescue him from his circumstances. In short, he said: "Don't pray to God to solve your problems. Pray to that part of God within you. Have the guts to fight for yourself. God wants brave souls. He wants winners, not quitters. If you can't win, at least try to win. God loves tryers."

Still don't recognize the Rev. Scott? He wasn't talking about the sinking U.S. economy when he said, "Sitting on our butts isn't gonna help us," he was talking about a sinking ship — literally. And not the Titanic either, but rather the S.S. Poseidon.

Yep, the Rev. Scott is a fictional character played by Gene Hackman in the original 1972 film "The Poseidon Adventure," about an ocean liner that is overturned as a result of greed. Hit by circumstances that are unusual, but by no means unpredictable, the vessel winds up capsized in the middle of the Atlantic Ocean with only several dozen survivors left in the dining room. It's not exactly the equivalent of a budget crisis, but it nonetheless provides some valuable lessons for how to handle yourself when things go topsy-turvy.

The Rev. Scott, it should be noted, did not think of the solution to his problem on his own. He was trying to do a good deed by bringing a crewman down into the dining room when a small still voice (played by character actor Red Buttons) whispered in his ear, "Isn't it better to go up?"

It turns out that when you are in a boat that is upside down there is no point in standing still; you have to take action in order to have any hope of survival. The Rev. Scott quickly adapts, and immediately asks the other survivors to follow him into the unknown, with no certainty of survival. But that just makes him unpopular. The ship's purser, the senior officer left alive, has convinced most of those in the dining room that the problem of an upside-down ocean liner in the middle of an ocean is not really that bad. "Help is on the way" is his mantra. "Help will be here any minute."

Of course, the people who listen to the purser all die. There is no help on the way. The only help comes from those who, as the reverend notes, "have the guts to fight for [themselves]."

The Rev. Scott and his nine followers have no guarantee of success as they begin their perilous journey through the ship's innards to try to reach the hull and possible safety, but it is a plain sight better than doing nothing and being drowned without a doubt.

That should be obvious, but the purser can't stop thinking about the way things used to be — about when he was in charge of a luxurious floating hotel, complete with bands, a movie theater, stores and the good life. He doesn't want to give up any of that, just as some good people don't want to give up their federal subsidies for the arts, their funding for Energy Star, Family Planning, high-speed rails — you name it.

But if you follow the people who want to spend more money, you will drown. The only chance we have is to follow the people who are telling us unpleasant truths. Listen to the Rev. Scott talking about the ocean and imagine that he's talking about a sea of red ink instead: "The sea will keep pouring in. We'll keep settling deeper. We may even go under... before we cut our way out. But it's a chance. We might make it..."

Fifteen trillion dollars is a lot of red ink. There is no guarantee that we can ever cut our way out of it, but if we start right now — cutting massively, pitilessly, unflinchingly — there is at least a chance. We might make it.

DEMOCRACY OR CHAOS?

February 20, 2011

Following the momentous political eruption in Egypt, President Obama told the world, "I am confident that the people of Egypt can find the answers, and do so peacefully, constructively, and in the pursuit of unity that has defined these last few weeks — for Egyptians have made it clear that nothing less than genuine democracy will carry the day."

This, of course, is supposed to be an applause line.

"Genuine democracy" in the Middle East — what could be better?

Well, almost anything.

Let me explain.

First of all, the United States of America is not a democracy. By plan, design and intention, the Founding Fathers rejected pure democracy and instead instituted a democratic republic. Note the order of those two words. Our system of government is democratic only as a description, an adjective, a modifier of The Republic.

We are a democratic government because we have self-rule — but we have successfully defended that self-rule for 234 years because we are a republic. It is the republic which is enshrined in the Constitution of the United States, not a democracy, and it is the institutions and traditions of the republic which protect us from the vagaries of the moment. A pure democracy, on the other hand, cannot resist the winds of change, and bends to every mood and movement like straw in a slight breeze.

That would be well and good IF mankind were uniformly well-intentioned and consistently an influence for good. Then, it would be safe to turn a nation's future over to the whims of the public will.

But if we can agree that mankind too often follows the path of least resistance and thus is quite capable of being seduced by a convenient profit at the expense of an inconvenient principle, then we can see the danger of pure democracy. The profit may be financial or it may be power, but in any case the sacrifice of principle for self-gain has only one result — chaos.

We have seen the results of such power shifts time and time again in history. And no matter whether they come under the name of democracy or not, it behooves us to study not just the ideals of a so-called freedom movement, but also the reality of outcomes.

It is instructive, as a starting place, to return to the French Revolution of 1789. Like the Egyptian insurrection, it largely took place on the streets of the capital. The storming of the Bastille prison and the march on Versailles provided the spark needed to overturn a long-standing monarchy and to establish a republic, but what followed was not liberty, equality and fraternity; it was disorder, chaos and terror. Indeed, in the absence of democratic institutions, without the groundwork of an already established power structure, the French Revolution quickly devolved into the Reign of Terror, during which as many as 40,000 people were slaughtered.

Of course, there is a huge difference between the French Revolution and the American Revolution, just as there is a huge difference between democracy and a republic.

In France, the established power base dissolved practically overnight, leaving a power vacuum that was filled by ambitious men who, to use my previous phrase, were "quite capable of being seduced by a convenient profit at the expense of an inconvenient principle."

In America, on the other hand, while we did have a Revolution, it did not happen overnight, but over the course of five long years. Nor were we fighting to overturn the monarchy, but to separate ourselves from it in order to continue to develop the form of self-government which we had already established over a period of decades. This was not mob rule seeking to overturn a government, but rather a group of organized militias fighting on behalf of a Continental Congress to defend the colonial governments against an imperial power that was based thousands of miles away.

To confuse Egypt and the American Revolution is a dire mistake. To fail to see the similarities between Egypt and the

French Revolution is to miss the whole point of what is happening in Cairo. Yes, the protests in Tahrir Square were a manifestation of the urge toward democracy, but in its worst form — mob rule. They no more ensure a period of freedom for the Egyptian people than did the Russian Revolution ensure freedom or prosperity for the Russian people.

Indeed, the Russian Revolution was actually two separate revolutions, which may presage what we can expect in Cairo. The February Revolution in Russia, a spontaneous uprising of the people against the czarist regime, was well-intentioned and motivated largely by hunger and poverty. It is the equivalent of what we have seen in Egypt's own February revolution, with the collapse of the Mubarak regime.

But the fall of the czar left a power vacuum as well, and power did not magically wind up in the hands of the people. The "democratic" revolution of February 1917 only created an opportunity for those who were positioned to seize power for themselves. Thus the October Revolution followed just as surely as autumn follows summer, and the long winter of the Russian people under communist dictatorship began.

Democracy, in other words — especially in the form of street riots, protests or demonstrations — does not automatically lead to self-government or a better life. Indeed, if we are to assume that, at a minimum, democracy means some form of "majority rule," then street riots such as we have seen in Egypt, Tunisia, Jordan, Bahrain, Yemen, Iran and elsewhere in the Middle East cannot even be said to be any form of democracy. Allowing a vocal minority to grab power by being unruly is not democracy. It is revolution, yes. It is insurrection, yes. It is rebellion, yes. But it is not democracy. And it is certainly not a democratic republic, where people's rights are protected, where power is shared, and where minorities are protected but not pampered.

If 2 million people camped out in Tahrir Square to oust Mubarak — fine. That tells us what 2 million people think. But it does not tell us what the wishes of the majority of Egyptians is for the future of their country. It only tells us that a vocal minority can obtain power through fear and intimidation.

Which brings us to Wisconsin.

Yep, right here in the good old USA, we are seeing an effort to legislate from the streets — to create a "people's power" movement that will dissuade established authorities from taking action that will nominally "hurt" the people.

But don't be fooled. The people who will be hurt in Wisconsin by the governor's plan to restore budget sanity are not "We the People," but rather "We the Special Interests." This is about teachers' unions and other public-service unions trying to protect their slice of the pie when most of the American economic pie has vanished altogether. The Wall Street Journal compared what is happening in Wisconsin to the "welfare state riots" seen recently in France or Greece.

Indeed, this is likely to be the first of repeated protests, as entrenched special interests are forced bit by bit to relinquish their stranglehold on state and federal budgets as America navigates its way back to economic reality. In Montana, the same special interests intend to march on the state Capitol on Monday. The Montana teachers' union, no doubt inspired by the Wisconsin uprising, is joining with the "Montana Organizing Project" (part of the left-wing Alliance for a Just Society based in Seattle) to "rally to save education and public services."

Don't believe it. This is a rally to intimidate legislators and scare the public. Fortunately for us, Montana isn't in desperate financial straits like Wisconsin and other highly unionized states, but the future begins right now. The public-sector unions know what kind of trouble is coming, and so should you.

But in the meantime, we are going to have to listen to tiresome rhetoric about the noble cause of the people who are trying to block government action that is long overdue. For instance, Wisconsin Democratic Sen. Bob Jauch, said, "The story around the world is the rush to democracy. The story in Wisconsin is the end of the democratic process."

Of course, Jauch is right, but the scary part is that he has no understanding of why he is right. The "democratic process" he is talking about is something quite different from what is taking place on the streets of Madison. The democratic process in America is the election of representatives and executives to make and apply laws for the good of "we the people," not to guarantee permanent benefits and entitlements for a narrow class of people such as government employees.

The teachers on the streets, and their Democratic allies in the state legislature of Wisconsin — both of whom went AWOL from their assigned posts — are trying to prevent the democratic process from going forward because they fear the result. What is happening in Wisconsin is not democracy; it is chaos.

And if any liberal can't see that because they support the cause of the teachers, let them consider how they would have reacted if a similar uprising had occurred in August 2010 when nearly 2 million Tea Party advocates gathered at the mall in Washington, D.C. Suppose those people had marched on the U.S. Capitol and occupied it. Suppose they had refused to disperse when ordered to do so by legal authorities. Suppose the president had ordered the military to break up the demonstration because it was disrupting public order in the nation's capital. Suppose that the military had refused to fire upon the demonstrators and they thus gained additional power and prestige. Suppose that eventually our president had been forced to resign because of foreign and domestic pressure, and that a new compromise government was established to appease the Tea Party Movement.

No, that is not democracy. It is the end of the constitutional republic. Rome's republic ended. The First French Republic ended. Don't be so sure that ours won't do the same. When power shifts to the street from the statehouse, you can bet that the end is near.

ATHENA IS A FITTING SYMBOL FOR THE TEA PARTY

April 10, 2011

Where did the Tea Party come from?

No doubt doctoral dissertations will be written to answer that question for many years to come, but I would like to propose an answer which like all great truths is more poetic than practical.

In my mind, it is a classical myth which best sheds lights on the birth of this modern-day movement. Indeed, it could be argued that the Tea Party sprang full-grown out of the American body politic exactly like Athena did from the forehead of Zeus.

Remember, Athena arrived not just fully formed but girded for battle.

That description also applies to the Tea Party, which leapt into existence in 2009 with remarkable strength — almost unparalleled for a fledgling movement in the history of our country. From the start, it has also been under steady attack, yet has managed to defy all predictions and rise to power rapidly, without any central organization or the authoritarian impulse that often accompanies such power.

First in April and then on July 4 of 2009, there were spontaneous uprisings throughout not just the small towns of America, but also in the major cities. The Town Hall Offensive in the summer of '09 caught politicians by surprise, as more and more they were being held accountable by the voters who had given them power in the first place. There were also huge, peaceful rallies involving hundreds of thousands of people which drew the derision of the media and the celebrity left, but through it all there was a steadfastness of purpose and clarity of vision that ultimately led to the mid-term election victories of 2010.

Talk about the warrior spirit!

Something has been awakened in the average America-loving American, and it will not be easily defeated. But nor should it be confused with what the left likes to caricature as a gun-totin', Bible-thumpin', science-fearing right-wing fringe movement. Forget your stereotypes. The guns and Bibles that decorate the homes of many Tea Party advocates are the same guns and Bibles that were at the root of our nation's birth in 1776. If you do not know their power, then beware, because they give the movement unbelievable strength.

It is no accident than the Tea Party takes its inspiration from the nation's Founding Fathers; they are the Zeus from which our Athena was born. Indeed, the Tea Party is a perfect personification of Athena. Yes, the goddess of warfare — capable of heroic endeavor — but also the goddess of wisdom — and therefore able to use her strength, strategy, and skill to achieve victory often without force. Most importantly, the Tea Party embodies that balancing aspect of Athena that makes her the goddess of civilization itself — the patron of Athens, and thus of the entire Western world.

So just as the spirit of the French Revolution was personified by artist Eugene Delacroix as a woman in his painting, "Liberty Leading the People" (based on the Roman goddess of liberty) I propose that the Tea Party should henceforth be associated with the spirit of Athena.

Whether Western civilization can be saved at this point is an open question. That should not surprise anyone. Civilization is a fragile enterprise, and there have been many times before when the West has nearly collapsed. The entire period of the Dark Ages was a perilous interregnum out of which we may easily never have risen. Later, there was the onslaught of the Ottoman Empire into Europe that was stopped only at the Battle of Vienna after two hundred years of battle. Most recently the Nazi assault came perilously close to snapping the back of Western Civilization and replacing it with a primitive hero worship that recognized no individual liberties and threatened the entire world.

But what should be clear to everyone is that if the West is to persevere and indeed prosper, it will be up to America to carry the torch — the same torch held high by the Statue of Liberty in New York Harbor. But Liberty cannot defend herself simply with ideals. Someone needs to take up the sword (or yes, the gun) to keep her safe.

That's where Athena comes in. She is protected by her aegis or shield, which is the equivalent of the breastplate of righteousness. But she also carries a thunderbolt, and in my mind both the shield and the weapon represent the power of truth — to protect and enlighten — and ultimately to defeat the forces of darkness.

Perhaps it is that raw power of Athena which frightens opponents of the Tea Party. Indeed, it may be no accident that much of the power of the Tea Party movement has been embodied in women warriors such as Sarah Palin and Michelle Bachman — who speak proudly of both their faith and their country. Strong women are at the very heart of the conservative movement, just as they are at the heart of civilization itself.

Mock them — and their values — at your own risk.

DON'T FEAR THE WOMEN WARRIORS! THEY ARE HERE TO HELP!

April 17, 2011

The usual complaints were heard about my column last week from the usual suspects — How dare I! What was I thinking? How could I! What kind of an idiot am I?

It seems that, according to these folks, I was wrong to compare the Tea Party to Athena — the Greek goddess of war and wisdom.

And what exactly was wrong with the comparison? That's simple. Two words: Sarah Palin.

Or in this case four words: Sarah Palin and Michele Bachmann.

You see, at the end of a metaphoric explanation of how the traits of the Tea Party movement mirrored the birth of Athena full-grown from the forehead of Zeus, I mentioned those two Republican women as examples of modern women warriors who symbolize the strength and wisdom of the Tea Party.

Imagine that!

It turns out that some people — some otherwise supremely tolerant liberal people — don't like strong conservative Republican women such as Palin and Bachmann.

I'm not the first to notice that, but I thought that as a follow-up to last week's column, it would be instructive to consider some further examples of conservative women who have wielded the thunderbolt of truth and the breastplate of righteousness against the establishment forces of "business as usual."

One person who should scare anyone who is afraid of strong women is Ayn Rand. Coincidentally, the long-awaited film version of her most famous novel "Atlas Shrugged" has just hit the movie theaters. That novel too features a woman warrior — by the name of Dagny Taggart — who rebels against a United States government that has grown fat and feral — a dangerous combination that threatens to crush private entrepreneurship, individual creativity and the American dream.

Taggart would make a better candidate for president than either Palin or Donald Trump, and certainly much better than the usual timid Tims and unmitigated Mitts who seek the GOP nod. But that is fodder for another column.

As for Rand herself, she was one of the best-selling authors of all time, the inventor of her own philosophy, and a woman who like Palin was not afraid to say what she thought. Since she was a vigorous opponent of communism, socialism, and nanny statism, her outspokenness meant that she was vilified 60 years ago the same as Palin is today.

In a famous review of Rand's prophetic novel "Atlas Shrugged," conservative convert Whittaker Chambers called the book "sophomoric" and "remarkably silly." Rand scholar Mimi Reisel Gladstein notes that when the book appeared in 1957, "reviewers seemed to vie with each other in a contest to devise the cleverest put-downs," calling it "execrable claptrap" and "a nightmare" that was "written out of hate" and showed "remorseless hectoring and prolixity."

This is comparable to the name-calling used against Palin — and more recently Congresswoman Bachmann. The only difference is that history has already proven Rand correct and made her assailants look like the socialist stooges they always were. Palin awaits vindication through what is very likely to be either the collapse of our country or its return to a constitutional republic at the prodding of the Tea Party. Smart money seems to be betting on the former.

Are there differences between Rand and Palin? You bet. Huge ones — most notably, the fact that Rand was a rabid atheist and Palin is a devout Christian — but that does not mean they are not both representatives of the same philosophical movement — a movement based on individual freedom, the free-market economy and constitutionally limited self-government. Indeed, Rand's continuing relevance to the Tea Party movement validates the thesis of last week's column — that the Tea Party's sudden appearance as a remarkable force in American politics was possible because its roots run deep.

It is also instructive that attacks on both women tend to be visceral, personal, and dismissive. The attempts to marginalize Palin as an unintellectual boob can only be properly understood when paired with criticism of Rand in basically the same terms, even though Rand was a devoted student of history, philosophy and classical literature. Palin is a relatively easy target, but Rand not so much so. In fact, Rand had every aspect of an intellectual except for one — she was not a liberal — and thus she was dismissed as a freak and a fool.

There is much more to explore on this theme, and I intend to devote at least two more columns to powerful conservative women who have been warriors in the service of liberty.

In the meantime, I will take a break from the written word on Monday when I address the Flathead County Republican Women during their noon luncheon at the Red Lion in Kalispell. That seems like a fitting forum to continue this discussion of the principles of the Tea Party, the powerful women who preceded it, and the importance of strong individuals if we hope to avoid being forced into a collective grave.

Oh yes, and rest assured, if there are any Democratic groups that want to hear about the principles of limited government that are at the root of the Democratic Party, I would be happy to speak to them as well. The free exchange of ideas requires first of all a willingness to share them, and second a willingness to hear them. If we only converse with those who agree with us, we can neither grow nor effect change.

PARTISANS? OR PATRIOTS?

April 24, 2011

(The following column was adapted from a speech I gave to the Flathead County Republican Women.)

I prefer not to speak at partisan events in general because I do not want to be viewed as a partisan. The problems we face in America are not partisan; they are fundamental.

At its root, the crisis in America today is a crisis of values, a crisis of institutions, and a crisis of the Constitution. When we try to shift blame from one party to the other, we ignore how we got here — and how we can get out.

I am not so naive as to believe that Democrats are always wrong, and Republicans are always right. In fact, Republicans have been at fault in many of the worst excesses of the past 100 years — and in some ways they are even more culpable because they traded their core principles for votes or for campaign contributions in issue after issue — corporate welfare, entitlement spending, illegal immigration, government expansion. There is hardly one major issue where Republicans can differentiate themselves from Democrats on a consistent basis.

Ultimately, therefore, I have sought solutions to our national crisis outside of the two-party structure. I am confident there is no actual partisan Democratic agenda to "dumb down" our citizenry or to use public schools and college campuses to indoctrinate young people into following a left-wing agenda. Nor is there a Republican agenda to lower our quality of life by sending jobs offshore and by bringing more and more illegal immigrants into our country to stretch our limited resources ever more thin. Those are not partisan agendas — they are just facts of life.

Indeed, as a result of the research I've done for this column, I have become aware of an assault on American values and institutions that has been waged not just from overseas, but also from our nation's capital, for decades. I have also become something of a student on the Constitution, although I don't have it memorized by any means. And I have turned increasingly to history for guidance as I try to find arguments that will persuade the unconvinced that the freedom we enjoy in the United States is not just exceptional, but also exceptionally fragile.

To save the country from its massive challenges, I would prefer that we could all stop seeing each other with a D or an R after our names, and start seeing a P — for patriot. It doesn't matter to me whether our liberty is defended by a Democrat or a Republican — as long as it is defended with honor. And let us remember that defending our liberty means defending our Constitution. It is that document which protects our inalienable rights against the whims and evils of government.

Again, I have to tell you that I have been disappointed by both Democrats and Republicans when it comes to upholding the Constitution with honor. More and more it seems like the Constitution is viewed as an impediment to "social justice" instead of the best proof in human history that "social justice" is actually obtainable. Legislators write laws because they think they have an obligation to "protect" us all from poverty, from sickness, hunger — when in fact the only things they are supposed to protect us from, according to the Constitution, is foreign aggression and the government itself.

The biggest obstacle to restoring America as a small "R" republic seems to be that much of our society has been trained to think that social justice can only be achieved by means of collective action — that the group has to guarantee or ensure success for the individual. But what our Constitution and our Declaration of Independence made clear, however, is that true social justice only occurs when the individual is free from the pressure of the collective. Social justice should mean ensuring that everyone has the opportunity to succeed AND the freedom to fail. That is a true constitutional republic.

For me, the Tea Party movement is really all about re-establishing that fundamental truth in our society. And in some ways the challenge facing freedom-loving Americans today is even greater than the challenge facing our Revolutionary War brethren. For more than 100 years, our society and our citizens have been conditioned to believe that government is there to help. But, as Ronald Reagan once said, the nine most terrifying words in the English language are: "I'm from the government and I'm here to help."

We need less government. Indeed, we need the kind of government that a Democratic president once envisioned when he said: "A wise and frugal Government, which shall restrain men from injuring one another, shall leave them otherwise free to regulate their own pursuits of industry and improvement, and shall not take from the mouth of labor the bread it has earned. This is the sum of good government."

Or as President Jefferson said on another occasion: "The sheep are happier of themselves, than under care of the wolves."

It is just such thinking, which extends from the Declaration of Independence to Ronald Reagan and beyond, that led me to surmise in a recent column that the Tea Party movement springs from the very bedrock of our national being, and thus, appeared in 2009 to be born fully grown like Athena from the forehead of Zeus.

Indeed, it is because of the well-developed philosophy of limited government that fueled our nation's growth for its first hundred years that the Tea Party movement has such power and such vibrancy. It was not Rick Santelli, with his "rant heard round the world," that created the Tea Party — it was the American character itself that made the Tea Party a necessary response to a government that had lost its way, a government that no longer represented the hopes and aspirations of the people, a government that saw itself as more important than the Constitution.

So now I have taken inspiration from the symbol of Athena and have found proud women warriors for truth, justice and the American way in both some contemporary leaders such as Sarah Palin and some historical figures such as Ayn Rand. It is probably not coincidental that both women have been the subject of vicious attacks — not because they are women but because they are right, and ferociously so, unyieldingly so.

Does that mean they are right about everything? Of course not. Does Sarah Palin occasionally misspeak? No doubt. Did Ayn Rand have a tendency to come off as a self-important, self-obsessed boor? I'm afraid so. But I'm not interested in their personalities or their human frailties. I'm interested in their willingness to stand up to what passes as the "accepted wisdom" of their day, and boldly, proudly reject that wisdom of the day for the more eternal truths that have been tested and proven in the furnace of history.

Too many of us today keep silent — remain unhappy sheep under the care of wolves — when the only noble thing is to speak up, to speak out — to stand for principle, no matter what the cost, no matter what they throw at you.

Those of us who like Sarah Palin like her exactly for that — because she cannot be cowed into silence, because she forcefully rages against complacency. If you think you would like Sarah Palin better if she were muzzled, that says nothing about Sarah Palin, but it says a lot about you.

AMERICA IN GOOD HANDS WITH MAMA GRIZZLIES

May 15, 2011

Believe it or not, a candidate has come to my attention who actually has a spine — someone who wants to get a grip on Congress and restore sanity to spending.

She is one more of those strong conservative women I have been writing about in recent weeks. You may not have heard of her, but she is a true American hero. Just listen to her stump speech — listen to her tell the truth to the voters:

"You warned those who served you in Washington that you were disturbed by the high cost of government. Your warnings were heeded. You ALMOST received the tax cuts and other economies you demanded. Then something happened... Congress went on a spending spree with your money... spending more than ever before ... The result was inflation. Prices soared higher and faster than incomes. I am convinced this inflation was unnecessary and could have been avoided. Now then. Are you going to send men and women to represent you in Washington who are so easily provoked into panic? Who will plunge you into bankruptcy, waste your money and mine? Then tax you again and again until you are destitute? Or are you going to elect men and women who are determined to regain control of the purse strings in Congress? Representatives who will eliminate waste, and balance the budget, while keeping you free and secure?"

So who is this brazenly outspoken candidate who wants to balance to budget and, by the way, also wants to "liquidate the United Nations," "consider going back to the gold and silver standard," pass a bill "protecting our states' rights from the Supreme Court," and get the government "out of competition with privately owned business"?

Michele Bachmann? Sarah Palin? Meg Whitman?

No, none of the above — and chances are, it's someone you've never heard of — but that doesn't mean you can't learn from her. No, she's never held political office before, but she is grounded in American values and American traditions and does not mind "seeming overzealous in [her] patriotism."

That's my kind of woman — and my kind of candidate. In fact, she embodies the virtues that Sarah Palin talks about when she refers to common-sense conservative women as "Mama Grizzlies."

So without further ado, let me have the honor of introducing you to Jean Walterskirchen, candidate for Congress from Montana and a woman ahead of her time — way ahead.

In fact, Walterskirchen's campaign slogan was "Freedom at Stake in '58" — as in NINETEEN fifty-eight.

And the spending binge she was talking about in her stump speech had happened because Congress was frightened by the Soviet launch of the Sputnik satellite. But that "spending spree" in the 1950s was infinitesimal compared to what happened when Congress panicked in 2008 and 2009 — when Congress and the presidents (both Bush and Obama) spent well over a trillion dollars RE-acting to a so-called crisis.

Clearly, Walterskirchen's fears more than 50 years ago about where the country was headed were not unfounded. Nor would I consider the timing of Walterskirchen's warning within one year of the 1957 publication of Ayn Rand's "Atlas Shrugged" to be entirely coincidental. Both women were tireless warriors, who like the Greek goddess Athena came equipped with not just wisdom but the torch of liberty — and their words still burn bright with the thunderbolt of truth today.

I was actually introduced to this fine American, Jean Walterskirchen, not too long ago by her daughter Helen Neumunz, who spends her summers in the Flathead, and who shared with me a copy of a speech from 1958 that was used by her mother in her campaign against Lee Metcalf to represent Montana in the U.S. House of Representatives.

Some of you may have even known her, though she died in the late 1960s. Born in Butte and longtime resident of Missoula, she was a dedicated Republican and had served as president of the Missoula County Republican Women's Club as well as on the state Republican Central Committee. She was certainly well known throughout Montana, and some members of her family still live here in the Flathead. But she was a politician by accident, not by design. She ran for Congress because she saw something wrong and wanted to fix it, rather than because she longed for power or prestige. Indeed, I think she took her greatest pleasure from her family, not from politics, which may be why she was awarded the title of Mother of the Year for the state of Montana in 1961.

But it is her stump speech from 1958 that singles her out as a great American, ahead of her time, unafraid of taking a stand, and always standing on principle. If she were alive today, I have no doubt that she would be a leader of the Tea Party movement

— and could very easily have run on the same platform she used in 1958.

Listen to her:

"My slogan — Freedom at Stake in '58 — sums up my entire philosophy. It is a goal from which I will not be diverted nor compromised. I am and always have been a dedicated American believing that our Constitution is the greatest document ever written by man. Because it safeguards our God-given rights and freedoms."

She warned those who had ears to hear:

"You choose to vouchsafe your freedoms or lose them depending on HOW you vote. Choose wisely the men and women who are to serve you. Get to know exactly where they stand and WHAT they stand for. The pages of history reveal many never-to-be-forgotten experiences through which great nations have been forced. Nations which enjoyed abundance, religious freedom, peace... and then suddenly were plunged into slavery because of their apathy and complacency.

"Our country, unfortunately, is in an era of complacency."

That was written 63 years ago, but is still true.

Walterskirchen was fully aware of where we were heading:

"Our prosperity has been threatened because we have based it on a false philosophy of economics. A philosophy which ruined Italy and Germany and paved the way for dictators. We need a one hundred cent dollar. Worth a dollar. Remember, you are government, and you and I can, and should demand that wasteful spending in government be stopped. We should demand a reduction in taxes for everyone. Business needs this relief from the heavy tax burden to expand facilities. Thus providing more jobs. The worker needs more take home pay..."

Time and time again, Walterskirchen was proven right by history — the danger of communism, the failure of "progressive" education, the foolishness of going bankrupt while sending billions overseas in foreign aid to countries that aren't even our friends.

In at least one instance, unfortunately, she was proven dead wrong:

"I also believe," she said in 1958, "that America will never accept the socialized medical program, advocated by social planners, and shall resist such a catastrophe in our country."

Ladies and gentlemen, the catastrophe is upon us. America did accept socialized medicine — or at least Congress is trying to force us to accept it, though 26 states are resisting with all their might in the federal court system.

It is lamentable that Jean Walterskirchen, R-Mont., was never elected to Congress, but her truth goes marching on. Balanced budget — or profligate spending? Less taxes — or more? "Loving America first, last and always" — or viewing America as a tainted, repressive imperial power?

It's unlikely that Republicans will find a standard bearer as powerful, clear-thinking or plain-spoken as Jean Walterskirchen — but history has proven her right.

So now, we have a choice. Follow Obama — or follow Walterskirchen. For me the choice is clear. I'm with the Mama Grizzly.

A TALE OF TWO STRONG CONSERVATIVE WOMEN: YEP, IT CAN HAPPEN HERE

May 22, 2011

A famous 1935 novel by Sinclair Lewis, titled "It Can't Happen Here," envisioned the arrival of a fascist regime in America in the guise of a voluble, charismatic president named Buzz Windrip.

It was supposedly written as a warning against Huey Long, the Louisiana populist who was gaining a national following for his "share the wealth" politics, but was widely acknowledged to be a conniving, back-stabbing demagogue.

Curiously, Long was assassinated just before the book was released, but it remained as relevant as ever because President Franklin Roosevelt was himself just as glib, just as charismatic, and just as authoritarian as either Huey Long or Buzz Windrip. And did not FDR — just like President Windrip in the novel — promise quick, easy solutions to the Depression that involved consolidating power in the executive branch, reshaping the Constitution, and creating a cult of personality around the heroic president himself?

I can't say for sure whether Sinclair Lewis ever recognized the similarities between Windrip and Roosevelt, but I am confident that his wife Dorothy Thompson did.

You've probably never heard of Thompson, one more of those women warriors who have a huge influence on public policy and public discourse, but are ultimately dismissed as irrelevant. An example in modern times, of course, is Sarah Palin. Her ability to crystallize opposition to Democratic and left-wing policies in a few words is best noted, perhaps, in her use of the phrase "death panel" to describe the inevitable necessity of providing nationalized health-care under a triage system that will ensure that taxpayers' money is not being "wasted" on the old and infirm.

Palin was blasted for her "incendiary" rhetoric in that case, although upon closer scrutiny her analysis turned out to be essentially accurate. Obamacare did include a plan for panels that would determine which kind of medical care was appropriate for which kinds of patients. Those with a low survival rate need not apply.

As everyone knows, Palin is one of the most popular women in modern public life, yet she is marginalized, minimized and micro-analyzed at every step of the way. Thompson, too, underwent something of a similar process in the 1930s, especially after she started writing a column of political commentary in 1936.

She wrote extensively about the dangers of Stalinism, Nazism and Fascism, both inside and outside America, and thus was known as "something between a Cassandra and a Joan of Arc." Indeed, she was one of the first people to recognize the danger of Hitler's political philosophy and urged action against him years before World War II. Indeed, way back in 1931, before Hitler had even ascended to power, Thompson did a lengthy interview with him that resulted in a book called "I Saw Hitler." Although she thought that Germany would reject Hitler because of his personal weaknesses, she was fully cognizant of the danger of his agenda, and tried to warn the world.

In addition, throughout the 1930s, she was one of the loudest voices warning America not just of the dangers in Europe, but of the dangers in our own political system. In 1937, as President Roosevelt was attempting to push his leftist agenda through Congress, Thompson wrote that what FDR was after was "a tremendously centralized government, with a power and authority vested in the president, not far from equal to the power and authority vested in Mussolini and Stalin."

In that same column, she noted that FDR's program was "profoundly revolutionary," yet the mainstream media and the "powers that be" were silent about what was under way. It seemed to her that "We are going to be cajoled into revolution, with the pretense that it is all innocuous, and really not at all important."

It is eerily similar to the movement under way today by the Obama administration to "fundamentally transform" America. While the press pretends nothing unusual is happening, it has been people like Sarah Palin who have been asking the obvious question — "Fundamentally transform it into WHAT?"

Of course, Palin is dismissed by the mainstream media and much of the political establishment as some kind of a weird throwback to the days when America was a proud Christian nation, grounded in moral principles and honor. To that, Palin pleads guilty — or, as she says, "We don't need to fundamentally transform America. We need to restore America."

Thompson, raised by a Methodist minister and his wife, would certainly have understood Palin. They were cut largely from the same cloth, although Thompson couldn't so easily be dismissed as a simple-headed conservative woman by the intelligentsia and academia — she did after all have the imprimatur of being Sinclair Lewis's wife, so she had to be taken seriously by the left. Nonetheless, she had so many traits in common with Sarah Palin that it is probably no mere coincidence.

She called herself a "liberal conservative," which sort of stands as a bookend to Sarah Palin's self-avowed role as a "conservative feminist." In both cases, they take the best of both worlds, and act as lightning rods of criticism from all angles.

Thompson was declared by Time Magazine in a cover story in 1939 to be, along with Eleanor Roosevelt, one of the two "most influential women in the U.S." In Palin's case, she probably shares the stage somewhat uncomfortably with Michelle Obama, but in truth I think Palin is actually a bit more powerful than this First Lady.

But even with their acknowledgment of Thompson's role as a significant opinion-molder, it should be noted that Time Magazine then, like Time Magazine today, was not above injecting some "spin" into the article to make readers less likely to take Thompson seriously.

Indeed, the cover story bore the dismissive title "Cartwheel Girl" in reference to a story of how Thompson had once done immodest cartwheels in front of her mother's Methodist lady friends when she was about 10 years old. The article also referred to her "plump pair of legs," noted that "for a woman she seemed surprisingly intelligent," and then concluded by reminding us that she is a "plump, pretty woman of 45, bursting with health, energy and sex appeal."

Time magazine also found it helpful to mention that Thompson had flunked her teachers' examination in English grammar and noted that "Mrs. Lewis still has to correct her speech." Goodness gracious, could the sabotage be any more self-evident? Almost the same as the attack on Sarah Palin because she speaks with a folksy dialect that has been identified as having a Northern Minnesota origin. It just doesn't pay to be a powerful political woman, whether it's in the 1930s or the 2010s. You may be speaking the truth, but heaven help you if you do it with an accent or a misplaced modifier.

But at least one bit of analysis from that Time Magazine article did capture the essence of Dorothy Thompson, and explain her popularity:

"Liberals have regretfully come to the conclusion that she is a conservative, a fact which she freely admits. Conservatives do not altogether trust her... Radicals hate & fear her, think she is a potential Fascist herself. But to those Americans who live in the smaller cities and towns and especially to the women, Dorothy Thompson is infallible — not so much because of what she thinks as because of what she is. To these women she is the embodiment of an ideal, the typical modern American woman they think they would like to be: emancipated, articulate and successful, living in the thick of one of the most exciting periods of history and interpreting it to millions."

The same description, almost word for word, could be applied to Sarah Palin.

The lesson: Strong conservative women have been part of the American political fabric for decades. They've also been subject to the same misogynistic attacks that in essence are intended to put a woman "in her place."

Well, the place for women such as Dorothy Thompson and Sarah Palin in American politics is still up for debate. So far, they have not risen to the position of ultimate power such as happened in England with Margaret Thatcher or in Israel with Golda Meir, but you dismiss them at your own peril. Like Athena, they prefer to guide with wisdom — but when pressed, they are willing to go to war for their principles.

Don't mess with the Mama Grizzlies.

PUTTING PRINCIPLE AHEAD OF POPULARITY

May 29, 2011

Last week, I had the pleasure of introducing many of my readers to author Dorothy Thompson for the first time.

Thompson, who died in 1961, started her career before World War I as a suffragette working to win American women the right to vote, then briefly worked as a social worker. After the war, she sailed to Europe and began a stint as a foreign correspondent in Europe, where she had the reputation for always being in the right place at the right time during a chaotic period of history. Later, she became an on-air commentator on world events and wrote a charming column about domestic life in the Ladies Home Journal for many years.

But it was her career from 1936 to 1958 as a newspaper columnist that ensured Thompson not just a place in the history of journalism, but also in the history of ideas. She is frankly one of the most penetrating thinkers I have ever encountered, writing with ease on every topic of world politics — often puncturing those in power and elevating those without a voice.

Last week, I wrote about some similarities between Thompson and Sarah Palin, and I would like to expand upon that to some extent this week. Of course, it should be plain that Thompson and Palin are women of different eras, who made different choices, and are by no means exact parallels, but they are both fearless conservatives who put their principles ahead of their popularity. It should also be noted that Palin, in addition to her political career, is herself an on-air commentator and a hugely popular author (selling more than 2 million copies of her book "Going Rogue"). And although Palin chose not to continue a career in journalism, her college degree is in fact in communications, with an emphasis in journalism.

But those are relatively trivial similarities. What really cements the case for me is reading Thompson's conservative analysis of national and world politics. Time after time, she boldly defends the Constitution, common decency and common sense against the platitudes of politicians and the perennial assault of assumed progress. She was certainly akin to Sarah Palin as a defender of Western civilization, and if she had lived today she would have been mocked just as mercilessly.

A few examples should suffice.

You remember how, during the last presidential campaign, it was Sarah Palin who unflinchingly drove home the point that Barack Obama was a socialist.

"Senator Obama said he wants to quote 'spread the wealth.' What that means is he wants government to take your money and dole it out however a politician sees fit," Palin said in October 2008. "But Joe the Plumber and Ed the Dairy Man, I believe that they think that it sounds more like socialism. Friends, now is no time to experiment with socialism. To me, our opponent's plans sounds more like big government, which is the problem. Bigger government is not the solution."

Of course, the left-wing media (oops, I mean the mainstream media) said Palin was an extremist for such views — despite the fact that Barack Obama had the most liberal voting record in the Senate, and thus was essentially a self-avowed... (drum roll, please!) ... socialist. Naturally, liberals in Congress and in the media were offended by Palin's blunt assessment.

What, then, would they have made of Dorothy Thompson's bold assertion in a 1938 column that "Strict followers of the Moscow Party Line may call themselves 'Liberals,' or 'Progressives,' or 'Democrats,' or 'New Dealers,' or even 'Republicans.'" Thompson pointed out that the hopes of communism for victory in a country such as the United States was not through organizing its own political party, but by having their adherents spread throughout society and by "boring from within" as they penetrated every kind of social organization.

It goes without saying that Thompson was proven correct years later when communists were found to have infiltrated throughout not just all levels of American society, whether in academia or the arts, but also into our very government.

Thompson's many, varied and broad attacks on the Franklin Roosevelt administration make Palin's occasional forays against the Obama administration seem like child's play, it is true, but Palin takes much more heat for her modest criticisms compared to the very direct attacks on FDR that Thompson waged almost weekly for years.

In 1937, when FDR threatened to reorganize the Supreme Court in order to bend it to his will, Thompson wrote a brilliant column that challenged both the public and the president. She likened the president's plan for the nine justices to "decapitation" and compared it to the situation in Moscow where "political inconveniences are bumped off," which in the slang of the day meant to be murdered.

Of course, Palin would be soundly criticized if she referred to any presidential action as "decapitation." You remember what happened when she had the audacity to put some congressional seats in the "crosshairs"! Scary stuff!

But Thompson, like Palin, did not take her marching orders from folks who thought the best response to a socialist takeover of the country was to shut up and enjoy the handouts.

Thompson noted in her sly way:

"I am positively startled by the vigor of my objections [to FDR's plan for the Supreme Court]... For along about now the American people, who are seldom interested in anything for more than two weeks, will begin to say, "Oh, let the President do what he likes. He's a good guy."

It is just such lackadaisical acceptance of the "fundamental transformation" of America that the left-wing media has proposed for the American public in today's political battle. And it is because of Palin's loud and lingering insistence that America should be "restored" to its former constitutional ideals — not transformed — that she has been caricatured as a "cocky wacko," (Sen. Lincoln Chaffee) a "Nazi" (comedian Joan Rivers) and "profoundly stupid" (MSNBC host Chris Matthews).

The vehemence of the attacks on Palin from the left would not have surprised Thompson, who also spoke her mind as a conservative woman and thus outraged both her friends and enemies.

I think of one column she wrote about communist-hunting Sen. Joseph McCarthy in 1952, who had won a landslide primary victory in Wisconsin despite being "repudiated" and "denounced" by his own party and by "the nation's intellectuals." Thompson warned that despite the wishes of the establishment GOP and the national media for him to just go away, the McCarthy victory revealed "considerable about the present American temper."

Her description of the GOP repudiation of McCarthy is certainly reminiscent of the national Republican Party's hand-wringing over the "wacko" Tea Party movement that is largely populated by people who vote for Republicans.

Thompson wrote that, "All sorts of explanations have been offered [for McCarthy's victory] to avoid the simple and obvious one: That Americans regard the fight against Communists and their sympathizers as the preeminent issue in this campaign, and they are not squeamish about the tactics used, as long as something is done."

Ditto the Tea Party's insistence on fiscal sanity, whatever the political cost. You can call them names all you like, but the Americans behind the Tea Party movement are doing what they believe is best for their country and their children.

Again, Thompson, like Palin, spoke out in defense of the common folk and common sense. She was willing to make politically incorrect assessments because she viewed them to be true, and because she was not beholden to the powers that be. And she, like Palin paid a price. In this same column about McCarthy, when she called him "an asset to the Republicans," she noted, "We have said it against the enraged cries of many readers, the denunciation of our personal friends, and our own regret. But objective analysis tells us that this country (and its independent voters) is moving away from the 'liberalism' that has held sway for twenty years."

Of course, history proved Thompson wrong. To her regret, I am sure, liberalism continued to hold sway throughout her lifetime, and became even more dominant in the years after her death. One of the clearest signs of that victory of liberalism is that it is considered bad manners to even bring up Sen. McCarthy without prefacing his name with an adjective such as "reviled," "repudiated" or "disgraced."

In fact, just by quoting Dorothy Thompson's quasi-defense of McCarthy, I expect to be branded as a crypto-Nazi, a fascist or a right-wing troglodyte. That's just the way liberals express their tolerance of ideas they don't agree with.

Oh well, the more things change, the more they stay the same.

WHAT'S FOR LUNCH? WHATEVER THE MAMA GRIZZLY WANTS!

June 5, 2011

A lot of people wonder why I like Sarah Palin so much.

No, she isn't polished. No, she isn't sophisticated. In fact, she can best be summed up with an anagram of her last name: Palin is Plain. Plain-spoken. Plain dealing. Plain and simple.

Does that mean she is not smart? Hardly.

Does it mean she is not competent? Hardly.

Does it mean she is dangerous? Only if you think complicated lies are better for the country than the plain truth.

Because what Palin and a lot of other conservative women bring to the table is a passion for honesty, simplicity and righteousness. That's not something you learn in college. It's something bred into the bone.

As Alexis de Tocqueville observed more than 150 years ago, in a simpler era, "The Americans ... have not required to extract their philosophical method from books; they have found it in themselves."

Thus, Palin, unlike many other modern politicians, does not need to be told what she believes. She does not need to put her finger in the air to see which way the wind blows. Nor does she revise her right and wrong to adjust to the latest fashion.

She is who she is — take it or leave it.

Yeah, she comes with a lot of baggage, too — she is a patriot who is grounded in American values and has an abiding love of our country. In other words, she is not politically correct. That's fine with me. As long as she knows that America is the last best hope for liberty, then I trust her to be on the right side of preserving our freedom.

About the worst anyone has been able to say about Sarah Palin is that she resigned from the governorship of Alaska. This is presumably a bad thing because we have been deprived of enjoying the prurient pleasure of watching Democrats in Alaska spend taxpayer money endlessly investigating trumped-up allegations of wrong-doing against Palin.

But let's face it, Palin is not the first public official to resign in order to pursue a higher goal. Often, for governors or senators, that goal is to run for president. That may even be Palin's goal. We don't know. But clearly, if she had remained in office, she would have been bogged down in petty politics aimed almost entirely at diminishing her national image so that she would be crippled as a presidential candidate.

Anyone who can't understand that is simply not paying attention to the way the national media and their left-wing allies operate. By thinking outside the box, Palin avoided a long, drawn-out political battle that would have done neither her nor Alaska any good.

It's probably not what she wanted for herself or for Alaska, but as the ancient Chinese general Sun Tzu recommended in "The Art of War," "According as circumstances are favorable, one should modify one's plans."

She did so, and lived to see another day.

She also managed to infuriate the people who hate her so much, which is part of her simple charm. She always seems to be able to outthink and outflank the self-appointed intellectual elites who sneer at her countrified grammar, her down-home dialect and her womanly wiles.

The very next line in Sun Tzu's famous manual of military strategy may explain much of Palin's mastery of the political battlefield: "All warfare is based on deception. Hence, when able to attack, we must seem unable; when using our forces, we must seem inactive; when we are near, we must make the enemy believe we are far away; when far away, we must make him believe we are near."

Case in point... the magical mystery "One Nation" bus tour that Palin embarked on last week to the consternation of the major media, the establishment Republican Party, and the pygmies currently running for the GOP presidential nomination. They were angry that they did not KNOW she was going to do a bus tour. They were angry they did not know WHY she was doing a bus tour. They were angry they did not know HOW she had outwitted them. They were just plain angry.

This is also straight out of the Sun Tzu playbook. As a strategist, Palin knows that her only chance of taking the high country of the White House is to use the strength of her enemies against them. And she has done that masterfully the past week.

"If your enemy is of choleric temper, seek to irritate him. Pretend to be weak, that he may grow arrogant."

Have the media and establishment ever looked more arrogant and irritated than last week when Sarah visited the Lincoln Memorial, Gettysburg, the Liberty Bell, Ellis Island, the Statue of Liberty, Bunker Hill and other patriotic sites? How dare she!

At every step of the way (or should I say "every turn of the bus"?) Palin has done what SHE wanted, and not what the press or the GOP establishment wanted her to do. She is the very model of Tocqueville's idealized portrait of the American woman, who even while a young girl, "already thinks for herself, speaks with freedom, and acts on her own impulse... The vices and dangers of society are early revealed to her; as she sees them clearly, she views them without illusions, and braves them without fear; for she is full of reliance on her own strength, and her reliance seems to be shared by all who are about her."

Well, all except those who hate her, or mistake her twang for stupidity. She is not stupid. Whether she has read "The Art of War," or just understands its principles intuitively, doesn't matter. Either she is a cunning genius or she has a stunning natural talent for being right. The "One Nation" bus tour proves it. Certainly Sun Tzu would be proud of her for marching into the Northeast, where she is supposed to have no popular support, and taking it by storm.

"Attack [your opponent] where he is unprepared, appear where you are not expected," said the Chinese general.

Palin's sudden assault on the political scene after months of dormancy — her near-instant acceleration from zero to 60 in a globe-warming bus and two SUVs — has left the conventional wisdom of the pols and pundits in tattered disarray. They have tried to counterassault, but just made themselves sound whiny and afraid as they seized on Palin's exhaust fumes from their caravan behind the bus and tried desperately to weave them into a blanket of serious charges.

We've heard the media complain about virtually every aspect of the bus tour, even ridiculously claiming that Palin was putting reporters' lives at jeopardy because they didn't know where she was going, so they might do something stupid to try to keep up with her.

We've heard liberals who would loudly support anyone's right to burn the U.S. flag as a matter of principle roundly criticize Palin because she had dared to show a stylized representation of the flag on the side of the bus and thus broke the "law." (She didn't.)

We've heard politicians grumble that she had rained on Mitt Romney's parade by visiting Massachusetts while he was announcing his hopeless quest for the presidency in neighboring New Hampshire. (Poor Mitt!)

We've heard her denounced because she plainly ISN'T running for president, but just wants to make money. And we've heard her denounced just as vociferously because she plainly IS running for president, and refuses to say so!

We've even heard her and Donald Trump blasted for eating pizza with a knife and fork. Dastardly knaves!

In other words, we've heard all kinds of whining about how Palin won't play by the rules, darn her. All of which — taken together — means that she is just plain smarter than the average bear — mama grizzly or otherwise.

She eats what she wants... when she wants... the way she wants. So let the tourists with the cameras and reporter's notebooks beware. You are on the menu.

AS WE GO OVER THE CLIFF, JUST WHO IS IN THE DRIVER'S SEAT?

June 12, 2011

A few months ago, I asked the question, "How did we get here?"

If you have to ask where "here" is, then you may as well not read this column. But if you, too, believe that "here" is the end of the road for Western civilization, then you may as well read it and weep.

I have explored a few possibilities already to explain the collapse of American values and American traditions in the past 50 years (which roughly correspond to my own life span up till now). Most of them seem to be linked to the phony Marxist philosophy of "redistribution of wealth," whether in the guise of the New Deal, the Great Society, social justice or "the myth of permanent plenty."

It is almost — but not quite — unbelievable that such a fundamentally un-American philosophy should have taken root in such a short time not just among radicals and revolutionaries, but among the very institutions that are the pillars of our society. There is no way that you can simply conclude that Franklin Roosevelt was a Marxist or that Lyndon Johnson was a communist, yet the policies of both presidents played into the hands of the enemies of capitalism and democracy.

How could that be?

Forces are clearly at work that operate behind the scenes, or at a much deeper level than is ordinarily apparent, to shift America from a nation governed by a Constitution to a nation governed by an agenda. That means movement from a land of free and responsible people to a land of prisoners who do not even know there is a prison.

In a sense, we have reached that stage which C.S. Lewis referred to (in his book of the same name) as "The Abolition of Man" — a time when mankind has severed its ties to the Creator in a kind of dangerous declaration of independence that leaves her vulnerable not to divine retribution, but rather to human intervention.

As Lewis wrote in 1943, about the time all of this was getting under way in earnest, "The final stage [occurs] when Man by eugenics, by pre-natal conditioning, and by an education and propaganda based on a perfect applied psychology, has obtained full control over himself."

It is thus to ourselves that we must turn if we wish to answer the question, "How did we get here?"

The problem is that when man obtains full control over himself and thus declares God irrelevant, if not dead, we can no longer assume any truths to be self-evident. That all men are created equal is just a hypothesis. That all men have certain unalienable rights is an assertion without any predicate. That "life, liberty and the pursuit of happiness" have any inherent value is an unproven proposition.

Indeed, instead of taking for granted certain fundamental propositions about the worth of the individual, the importance of right action, and the value of honor, mankind finds itself in the position of being manipulated to serve that which is convenient rather than that which is constant.

"For the power of Man to make himself what he pleases means, as we have seen, the power of some men to make other men what they please." That is how Lewis describes it. He addresses in particular the ability of educators to mold future generations into anything at all — untethered to values, morality or higher purpose beyond that which the educator wishes to instill.

Lewis notes that educators in every generation have sought that power, but concludes that "the man-moulders of the new age will be armed with the powers of an omnicompetent state and an irresistible scientific technique: we shall get at last a race of conditioners who really can cut out all posterity in what shape they please."

If we have really reached that stage when mankind has thrown off religion and reduced all aspiration to that which is merely "rational," then perhaps that explains the decline in Western civilization for the past hundred years. It certainly fits the bill. Have we not turned our values and our education over to secular humanists and turned our back on God?

And if we cannot easily see the face of God, do we really think we can see in any better focus the faces of these superior creatures who are molding us and our society into "what shape they please"?

I think not. That is why it is so hard to answer the question, "How did we get here?" No doubt we have been steered from the high point of human dignity, as immortalized in the Declaration and Constitution, to the suicidal precipice of Marxism and social justice, but no one can say for sure how it happened. All we know for sure is that, for most of us, it is not our hand on the steering wheel.

Lewis put the dilemma of progress severed from eternal values perfectly:

"Man's conquest of Nature, if the dreams of some scientific planners are realized, means the rule of a few hundreds of men over billions upon billions of men. There neither is nor can be any simple increase of power on Man's side."

As Lewis concludes, "Each new power won by man is a power over man as well. Each advance leaves him weaker as well as stronger. In every victory, besides being the general who triumphs, he is also the prisoner who follows the triumphal car."

Clearly, for the past 100 years, mankind has been taught to see itself as driving the car. Our education, our politics, and our religion have all encouraged us to value progress, and to envision mankind as the engine of progress.

But it is time that we all ask the question of ourselves — are we truly driving the car? Or are we walking behind in shackles? Do we as individuals have more dignity than our grandmothers and grandfathers? Or less?

If you think you are better off than Thomas Jefferson and George Washington, then I wish you the best in your brave new world. But if you agree with me that you are worse off, then ask yourself why. You might even want to pray about it.

AN EDUCATION IN HOW THINGS WENT SO WRONG

June 19, 2011

There was a man who once said, "Give me a lever long enough and a fulcrum on which to place it, and I shall move the world."

The likelihood that most people in our country have no idea who said it, and — even worse — probably no idea what it means, can be attributed to the fact that someone (or really, some group of people) recognized the truth of that saying and put it into action.

Last week I asked, "How did we get here?"

This week, I can reveal that "here" is at the end of a long lever named "progressive education." With any luck, we may even determine what the fulcrum is that allowed "progressive education" to uproot American society and to a large extent Western Civilization in less than 50 years.

That's a lot to chew on in a weekly newspaper column, but I'll give it my best shot. I can guarantee you up front, however, that I won't settle it all this week, so let's just start with the big picture.

As I noted last week, there seems to be a movement afoot to shift America from a nation governed by a Constitution to a nation governed by an agenda. What the agenda is shouldn't matter to people who love their freedom, but I think anyone who has been paying attention to the past century knows that it is not a strictly partisan agenda. It doesn't matter whether Republicans are in power or Democrats — the agenda keeps moving forward either way, directing us all toward what is touted as a more "enlightened," a more "socially conscious," and a more "open and tolerant" society.

Those are all delightful attributes except when you have to trade your freedom to gain them, and when you are seeing the Constitution undermined as part of this social agenda, you can bet that the ultimate goal is less freedom for the individual.

Upon casual observation, this is sometimes hard to fathom because the common wisdom suggests that mankind has gained more and more freedom over the past 100 years. To a large extent, that is true for individuals but not for society as a whole. As a result of the various social revolutions of the past century, individuals have been either legally or morally encouraged to engage in free love, drug experimentation, gender-bending relationships, and to reject tradition and authority in almost every aspect of their lives.

So how does that translate as less freedom?

The clue is in the phrase "legally or morally encouraged." Think of that encouragement in human society as a cattle prod, and you will start to get the picture. No doubt the cow that is being led to the slaughterhouse has a certain feeling of freedom. After being cooped up in a trailer or a pen for a lengthy period, the gate is opened and a breath of fresh air reinvigorates you as you stumble toward the light. You don't know whether to turn left or right, but whenever you turn right, you feel the jolt from the cattle prod, so you choose to turn left. Besides, everyone else is turning left as well, so you are comfortable with your choice as you wind your way to the hammer punch to the head that will end all your troubles.

Of course, human beings are not cows, but the herd instinct is not exclusive to bovines either — the instinct to avoid pain, to follow the easier course, and to do what you are told means that people can be steered almost as easily as cattle. This is particularly true if they surrender the main advantage they have over cows — namely a knowledge of history, an awareness of where they come from and how they got where they are now.

Cows don't know they are being steered. Unfortunately, most people don't either anymore — because they have surrendered their moral compass as the necessary trade to enjoy the forbidden fruits of a world without right and wrong.

This brings us back around to our starting point — that huge lever of progressive education which has invisibly and swiftly tilted the entire world. If you don't know what progressive education is, that is roughly the equivalent of a flounder not knowing what the ocean is. Indeed, you and I —

and our society as a whole — are so much a product of progressive education that it is to be forgiven if we take it for granted as much as a fish does water.

In essence, other than in a few hundred private schools and among home schools, there is no such thing any longer as traditional education — the kind of education that insists on students learning not just the fundamentals of knowledge, but also the moral, religious and cultural underpinnings that give that knowledge meaning and significance.

Progressive education does not believe in moral, religious or cultural absolutes, but rather only believes in questioning those absolutes and replacing them with relative truths, i.e., convenient lies. Indeed, we need to consider whether the proponents of progressive education have always been "intending to make a clean sweep of traditional values and start with a new set," as C.S. Lewis put it in his 1943 book, "The Abolition of Man."

The evidence is certainly there, for those who have the patience and willingness to look for it, but to do so means you must be willing to jettison your own easy acceptance of the one absolute in progressive education — "doing your own thing."

To further study the precepts of progressive education will take another column, at least, but let us begin by taking a quick look at "A Novel Method of School Teaching in Chicago," a May 1900 newspaper column by Milton B. Marks on the "University Elementary School, conducted by Prof. John Dewey of the University of Chicago.

Marks was much impressed with Dewey's revolutionary pedagogical techniques, and noted that, "The casual observer would probably make neither head nor tail of the class instruction as it is carried on in this school, and would conclude that the children were enjoying a perpetual holiday."

If that sounds familiar, it should. It was the philosopher Dewey who developed progressive education as a practical movement, and after he left Chicago, he headed to Columbia University, from which he oversaw the complete overhaul of the education industry as practiced not just in America, but throughout the world.

But it is clear the groundwork was already laid in 1900.

"A school without books: This seems almost a misnomer," noted Marks in his laudatory report, "but the children who attend Prof. John Dewey's University Elementary School have little use for books. The schoolrooms are not treated as places in which to learn and recite lessons, but are really visiting rooms where teachers and pupils meet to compare experiences and to exchange questions and ideas."

Or as another brief report from 1900 said in the Stevens Point (Wis.) Journal, the John Dewey school in Chicago is "where children are permitted to grow up and acquire knowledge with the least possible interference from those in charge of them."

If you wondered where the mess started, you need look no further. As Archimedes, the author of the quote with which we began today's column, also said, "Eureka! I have found it!"

THE PAST IS PROLOGUE;
THE FUTURE IS BLEAK

June 26, 2011

It was rightly said some years ago that the Constitution is not a suicide pact. Too bad the same cannot be said about modern American education.

Unfortunately, the seeds of our own potential destruction as a nation and culture have been sown into the fertile ground of our high schools and universities for at least the last 100 years.

How can that be? Don't we spend billions of dollars every year to train our young people to be prepared to enter society and take their part as the future leaders of the country?

Well, no — actually we spend billions of dollars every year to teach our young people to question the value of our society; to doubt the legitimacy of our history; and to mistrust our leaders, our traditions and our laws.

It wasn't always so.

Education has not always worked against the values of America.

In a presentation made to the 1894 convention of the National Education Association by Professor S.G. Williams on "How to Teach the Teachers," for instance, it was decided "in the discussion [about] the 'little red schoolhouse,' or the country school, that 'good morals and good manners constitute an essential part of an educational equipment. The inoculation of patriotism, of respect for law and order, of whatever tends to make a good citizen, is of as much importance in a small as in a large school. Regularity, punctuality, obedience, self control, are as necessary in the country as in the city school.' " [Cited from the annual report of the proceedings in a 1902 newspaper article.]

In other words, in 1894, education still had the function of promoting the well-being of society and not the now-too-common function of promoting self-indulgence rather than self-control.

So what happened?

Essentially, the mission of education was intentionally shifted from what it always had been — a means to pass information, values and traditions from one generation to the next — into a system which encouraged students of each generation to insist on inventing anew everything it believed. Ironically, therefore, although this new pedagogy was called by the name of progressive education, it had the actual effect of making progress not just unlikely, but impossible.

If previous generations had stood on the shoulders of giants, each generation since 1900 has stood on the quicksand of moral relativism while whacking at the legs of the aforementioned giants to bring them down to our own Lilliputian size.

As noted previously, the primary blame for this unfortunate transition falls on John Dewey, the socialist educator and philosopher who wrought a revolution by insisting that we teach children what they want to learn instead of what they should learn. His influence on American culture was immense and surprisingly immediate. Just a few years after his experimental elementary school opened at the University of Chicago, he was being imitated and lionized throughout the culture.

Essentially, what the progressive education movement wanted to accomplish — and largely did accomplish — was to jettison traditional values and replace them with transient values (those which each generation or even each student adopted individually). This meant that society was no longer tethered to what the philosopher C.S. Lewis calls The Tao — "the doctrine of objective value, the belief that certain attitudes are really true, and others really false, to the kind of thing the universe is and the kind of things we are."

It does not require a Christian concept — or even a deistic one — to follow Lewis's argument in "The Abolition of Man" that mankind either accepts certain values as bedrock, or else all values are clay to be shaped this way and that depending on the intention of our teacher. Because, yes, values do come down to teaching, and teaching comes down to values.

There is no doubt that John Dewey understood this. He was not stupid. It was plain to everyone that the "new education" meant a farewell to old values and a discovery process that would lead to unknown ends.

"We agree," Dewey once said, "that we are uncertain as to where we are going and where we want to go, and why we are doing what we do."

Time magazine in 1958 put it this way:

"In a kind of country-club existentialism, Dewey and his boys genially contended that the traditional ends of education, like God, virtue and the idea of 'culture,' were all highly debatable and hence not worth debating. In their place: enter life adjustment. The Deweyites thus transformed conditioning techniques into ends in themselves... Within the schools, discipline gave way to increasingly dubious group persuasion. 'With teen-agers,' one high school principal said proudly, 'there is nothing more powerful than the approval or disapproval of the group. When the majority conforms, the others will go along.' It would not easily occur to the modern educationists that such blind fostering of group pressure is a travesty of free democracy."

In other words, by that time — after a half-century of progressive education — our schools had been turned into a kind of institutionalized "Lord of the Flies" environment where novelty and experimentation have taken the place of civility and tradition, and where the group crushes the individual — and the voice of reason.

Even in 1933, progressive educator Irwin Edman, one of the "Dewey boys" at Columbia University, had already thrown in the towel in an article in the Billings Gazette entitled "A Progressive Calls a Halt," in which he lamented that "the progressive education turns out often to be a dangerous form of sentimentalism."

In particular, he points out: "The world did not begin yesterday, and the past is not a rubbish heap.... The past is full of techniques and habits, already developed, that we at our peril dispense with. If we were really to overthrow the past, we should have a brand new world with a complete set of ignorant fools in it who would have to learn everything from the beginning again.... It is almost fantastic that professional educators should have come to talk of the past as an attic full of useless lumber. It is rather the fountainhead of all that we have and are."

Edman's warnings, alas, were not heeded. We could turn again to the editorial in Time magazine in 1958 for proof of where things stood 25 years later:

"The poor performance of their students has proved the [progressive] educationists wrong. U.S. high school students are plain ignorant of things grammar school students would have known a generation ago. Years of barren discussion courses in English have made a whole generation chronically incoherent in the English language. Cut off from any but the most obvious contact with his tradition... the student has lost his sense of history."

Nor should we try to pretend that the intervening 50-plus years have changed things for the better. We are still the children of Dewey, and still re-inventing the world each generation with a little less success. The bold assertions of Time magazine in 1958 are validated in cold, cruel statistics from the latest National Assessment of Educational Progress that was administered by the U.S. Department of Education. According to those test results, only 12 percent of high school seniors are proficient in history. Most fourth-graders could not identify a picture of Abraham Lincoln. Only 22 percent of eighth-graders could adequately explain the system of checks and balances.

But maybe that is the goal. It certainly looks that way when you read the July 4 issue of Time magazine not from 1958, but from this year, and see a picture of the United States Constitution that is being shredded for a cover story that asks about our sacred founding document, "Does It Still Matter?"

The answer to that question is, yes, it still matters, but only for as long as We the People can fight back against the people who C.S. Lewis called "The Conditioners" — those educators, authors and intellectuals who want to erase (or shred!) the traditions and values that got us here and replace them with the artificial values that they have determined to be for our own good.

No, the Constitution is not a suicide pact — but neither can it protect our society from being killed from within. When all of the underpinnings have been eaten away, there is nothing left but collapse.

EDUCATION: 'IT'S A HIDEOUS MESS, BUT IT'S OUR MESS'

July 3, 2011

We have spent the last two weeks surmising that the lever that pushed America from the land of the free to the "land of the free lunch" in a short five decades was progressive education.

The "novel method" of teaching invented by John Dewey before 1900 aimed to educate children by letting their own interests, rather than society's interests, dictate their course of study. This was roughly the equivalent of the 1912 musical education method perfected by Professor Harold Hill as "The Think System" ("You don't have to bother with the notes!") and was just as much of a con job, although John Dewey had a real pedigree so he had a much easier time staying ahead of the authorities than did "The Music Man."

You would think that America would be dismayed and disgusted with Dewey as education and civic understanding declined throughout the century, but rest assured that was not the case. Indeed, America has been mostly as happy with Dewey's "new education" as the fictional parents in River City, Iowa, were when they first heard the caterwauling of their precious children showing off their new musical prowess. It was a hideous mess, but it was OUR hideous mess.

By 1930, progressive education was already an established force in society. An article in the Altoona Mirror from that year, declared, "This new education, which is revolutionizing both private and public school methods, is not a passing fad."

Indeed, it was not. And it WAS revolutionary, although most people did not notice or care that education had switched from being a method of reinforcing social conventions and standards to uprooting them.

As Miss Hilda Orr told a meeting of Altoona English teachers back in 1930, "Progressive educators seek to develop in children the social and cooperative spirit rather than aggressive, competitive and exploiting qualities.... The leaders seek to abolish the evils of the competitive marking system which is so apt to produce in brilliant children self-consciousness, conceit and selfishness and in the slow-minded child a sense of failure, inferiority and injustice."

Of course, what the breathless Miss Orr failed to notice as she rushed giddily into her brave new world was that the new system she touted would teach smart students that there was no value in excellence, and encourage slow students to conclude that bad was good enough.

Thus, progressive education had two primary faults that together ensured the decline of culture — first, it put the curriculum in the hands of the student, resulting in children learning what was convenient rather than what was necessary;

second it removed any incentive to achievement, replacing rugged individualism with tepid collectivism.

It is no wonder, then, that as the American education system increasingly incorporated the ideas of Dewey into the classrooms in the first 50 years of the 20th century, something had to give. The sheer force of that huge lever on our society had to cause a giant shift in our values and our knowledge base. Yet despite the growing influence of progressive education from 1900 to 1950, it can also be argued that America's power and influence grew exponentially throughout those decades.

That is certainly true, but at some juncture a tipping point was reached. Perhaps it was when the first generation taught with the principles of progressive education started taking their place on school boards across the country, or perhaps it was when those same people started to occupy Congress, the Supreme Court and the presidency. Putting people in the seats of power who had already been molded by "progressive education" meant that it would become increasingly difficult to halt the revolution.

Moreover, the most important people in the country who had an interest in education — the parents — were also largely ready to turn their children's future (and thus their country's future) over to the educators who not only preached "the evils of competitive marking," but also the evils of competitive marketing — namely the free enterprise system that resulted in equal opportunity for everyone, but unequal results depending on one's abilities. How unfair!

Yep, progressive education was a necessary predecessor for America's plunge into willing acquiescence to progressive economics — also known as socialism. Thus, we are close to a solution to our initial question: "How did we get here?" We have exposed the lever of progressive education as the mechanism by which Americans were primed to surrender the blessings of liberty in exchange for the bonds of socialism.

It remains only to find a fulcrum large enough to allow the dangerous lever to do its work. If it exists, no doubt it shall be found somewhere in the prosperous 1950s, after which American tumbled into a downward spiral that has not ended to this day. No doubt, also, like progressive education, it shall be hidden in plain sight. They who have eyes to see, let them see.

EDUCATION OR DISRUPTION?

July 10, 2011

Over the past several weeks, I have endeavored to chart the growth of progressive education in America in the first half of the 20th century.

At times, it seemed like the entire country was blind to the scope of the changes that were under way, but that was not exactly the case. As usual, there were a few people who understood the revolution, and happily supported it because they considered American capitalism — indeed, American constitutionalism — to be a flawed system. Many more people supported it because they didn't know any better. They were just going along to get along.

But there were other people who were alarmed by the headlong rush into socialism that seemed to accompany the "new education" — as America launched first a "progressive era" to accompany its new progressive education, and then the New Deal to institutionalize in economics the non-competitive philosophy that educator John Dewey and his brethren preached in schools.

By the mid-century point, after the United States had demonstrated the continuing practical value of its core values by preserving freedom in both Europe and Asia, it almost appeared as though the old patriotic love of country would prevail and the attempt to fundamentally transform the social consciousness of America through education would fail.

Indeed, some people thought the victory was won. In 1953, the Brownsville Herald in Texas was editorializing that what it called Deweyism was really "The Great Delusion":

"We know what the effects of progressive education have been with regard to education. The Gallup Poll reports that nearly 40 percent of adult Americans do not know what a tariff is; one in four has not the faintest idea of the meaning of inflation, filibuster is Greek to half the nation's voters; to two-thirds of them, jurisdictional strike is meaningless; only four out of ten know what the Electoral College is. John Dewey thought he had found a shortcut to a system that would train students to think. It has not worked."

Moreover, and most importantly, the editorial writer gleaned a most important and subtle result of the loss of the "old-fashioned teachers [who] had insisted on the value of discipline, both mental and moral" — namely the vacuum in the classroom that was left when the Three R's were no longer paramount. The ingenious victory of "progressive education" came about because it replaced discipline with indoctrination.

The editorial writer put it this way: "So long as the instruction in the schools was limited strictly to the essential skills and the Three R's, there was little indoctrination of the youngsters with 'social consciousness,' the 'democratic way,' and a lot of other junk that is foisted upon young minds today."

As the editorial went on to explain, the prejudice of the new education against competitiveness was sowing the seeds of our own destruction in a world that remained dog eat dog, however much we tried to convince ourselves that we were socially conscious vegetarians.

"Under the present system children are taught that competition is not good, only to find out when they become adults that they are in a competitive world. No sooner do they discover this vital point than they become easy marks for those who feel that the competitive, free enterprise system is bad and that competition should be eliminated by the force of the government."

Of course, it is no mystery who would argue that the free enterprise system is bad — socialists (or put plainly, communists) or for those who fancy themselves a bit more intellectual: followers of Karl Marx. This really gets down to the crux of what we have been looking for — an explanation of how American values could have been subverted in a relatively short time span from rugged individualism to weak-kneed collectivism.

The answer, it turns out, has been staring us in the face.

"It is only natural," the editorial concluded in 1953, "that the children brought up in this sort of environment will look upon the competitive system with a jaundiced eye and turn to the government for the solution to their problems."

As prescient as that statement seems, it is hard to imagine that anyone in 1953 could actually imagine that in 2011 the competitive system would have come into such disrepute that teachers would in good conscience have been able to take part in "grade-raising parties" to fake a quality education in the name of affirmative action, but that is apparently just what happened in Atlanta over several years.

Nor is there really any difference between the criminal enterprise in Atlanta and the national education program sponsored by George W. Bush known as No Child Left Behind. Both have the purpose of graduating students in order to make the system look good rather than because the students are actually educated.

Such a system is based on the false premise of "equal results" that is part of the mythology of social justice, and which in the past five or six decades has replaced the American creed of "equal opportunity." It is here where "progressive education" and "social justice" intersect that we can identify the fulcrum that was used to fundamentally transform America in a brief few decades. Call it complacency. Call it conformity. Call it arrogance.

It was our own character traits of tolerance and openness that made it possible for enemies of the American way of life to work from within to destroy it, and then to encourage the rest of us to thank them for it.

And behind it all, there was a nearly universal attempt to scrub American traditions out of education and replace them with a traducement of our values. Traducement, according to Webster, means "to expose to shame or blame by means of falsehood and misrepresentation." I can think of no more accurate assessment of the indoctrination of American students that has taken place since the 1960s, in particular.

American education had by that time became a tool for ridiculing American values, not for teaching them. Is it any wonder, therefore, that those values have begun to erode? Yet because those who hold positions of power today were products of that indoctrination, it is hard to even get them to admit the problem, let alone fix it.

Nor is this an attack on individual teachers or schools; almost all of them are striving honestly to provide what they believe is a good education. It is what they themselves were taught to believe that contains the seeds of our destruction because no society can propagate itself into the future under the premise that all of its root traditions, values and beliefs are suspect.

Education is about continuity; revolution is about disruption. What we have had in the schools for the past 50 years is not education, but disruption. Society is in the balance, and the tipping point may long since be past.

How America Dropped the Baton

July 17, 2011

Every culture is either self-propagating, or by definition it is self-destructive. Culture has no meaning and no value unless it is passed on to the next generation.

Think of it as a generational relay race, with the belief systems of a group of people being the baton that is passed on from runner to runner. You can imagine the mayhem that would be caused in a race if at each hand-off, the runners stopped and debated the shape, size or color of the baton. If each new runner insisted on dictating revisions to the baton before carrying it forward, this would slow things even further. Not only would the team lose the race, but ultimately the baton would not look anything like what it was when the race started.

Under such circumstance, the idea of culture as a set of shared beliefs and values, passed on from father to son, and mother to daughter, would be meaningless. And if each runner taught his or her successor to despise the baton as unworthy, then sooner or later the baton would be dropped, and the culture would end.

It is this picture which must inform our discussion of education as we try to understand why the America of 2011 looks nothing like the America of 1911. Somewhere along the way, the baton of proud American traditions, brilliant accomplishments and upstanding virtues became a thing of shame and ridicule. Our schools, teachers and yes our parents have more and more questioned our long-held values, and have substituted expedient excuses for eternal truths.

Whether such a dangerous agenda was externally imposed or merely a form of accidental suicide, I don't know. But I am convinced that the proof that such a change took place is just as self-evident as those Jeffersonian truths that mankind for the past 100 years has been so eager to hide from.

You can either believe J. Edgar Hoover or you can believe Nikita Khruschev, two icons from the 1950s — one a proponent of free enterprise and Americanism, the other an advocate of totalitarian communism. But what is funny is that it doesn't matter which one you believe because they were in total agreement that America was in danger of losing its identity, its values... its cultural baton.

Hoover and Khruschev each acknowledged that there was an effort underway to destroy capitalism and the American way of life. And though both men have tarnished reputations nowadays, in the mid to late 1950s, they were at the pinnacle of their power and were certainly among those in the best position to know whether America was under attack.

Hoover, the director of the FBI during five pivotal decades, wrote in the Elks Magazine in August 1956, "We must now face the harsh truth that the objectives of communism are being steadily advanced because many of us do not recognize the means used to advance them... The individual is handicapped by coming face to face with a Conspiracy so monstrous he cannot believe it exists. The American mind simply has not come to a realization of the evil which has been introduced into our midst."

This was at the tail end of the so-called McCarthy era, when Sen. Joseph McCarthy argued that there were communists in positions of power throughout our government and elsewhere in society. McCarthy had already been shamed into silence, but Hoover never gave up his belief that America had been infiltrated by those who would destroy it.

In this belief, he may have received comfort from a quote widely attributed to have been uttered by Khruschev, the Soviet dictator, 3 1/2 months before his visit to the United States in late 1959.

"We can't expect the American people to jump from capitalism to communism, but we can assist their elected leaders in giving them small doses of socialism, until they awaken one day to find that they have communism."

Like I say, there is no way to ascertain whether Khruschev actually said those exact words, but they certainly represent a common thread (and threat) of communism since at least the time of Lenin. And it is Lenin who perhaps holds the key to how the "monstrous" conspiracy unleashed in the United States took hold.

"Give me four years to teach the children and the seed I have sown will never be uprooted," Lenin famously declared.

In the transmission of the baton of culture from one generation to the next, education is everything. Obviously Lenin understood that. Heck, even the simplest stone-age tribal group understands that. Every tribe ever encountered in history has held one fact as true — our way of life is the best. That is the glue that holds individual cultures together. It is also the guarantor of diversity. And as soon as a culture begins to doubt the validity, indeed the primacy of its traditions, then that culture has begun to die.

Perhaps Lenin understood that; perhaps not. But certainly the Soviets as a whole, and the communists and Marxists who supported them, were well aware that if America could no longer wholeheartedly teach its children that the American way of life is the best, then we were doomed.

Indeed, the communists were so confident of victory that Khruschev publicly declared in 1956, "Whether you like it or not, history is on our side. We will bury you."

It turns out that the Soviet Union had its own problems, but the collapse of the Soviet Union does not preclude the collapse of the American republic. And what Khruschev saw as the inevitable tide of history is still slowly playing out.

Perhaps no greater proof of the collapse of American values can be found than in the transition that occurred in the 1950s or 1960s about who Americans perceived as their enemy.

In the late 1940s and early 1950s, following the remarkable tectonic shift of geopolitical power that occurred in World War II, Americans turned to Hoover's FBI and the House Committee on Un-American Activities for guidance about how to protect and preserve our values against communist intervention. By 1969, however, following the social revolution of the 1960s, that House committee's name had been changed to the House Committee on Internal Security, and by 1975 it had been dissolved altogether. No longer could it be assumed that Un-American Activities were bad. They were merely alternative ideologies that we could learn from.

Such relativistic thinking would have been inconceivable to our Founding Fathers. There was no alternative view possible of "unalienable rights," nor should there be. One could not wage war against King George III by trying to see his point of view, nor would victory in World War II have been possible if America had waffled on the evil of the Third Reich.

But when in the 1950s and 1960s, America began to surrender its own absolute certainty in its self-worth and substituted a form of re-education that might just as well have come from Mao's China, we were on the path to collapse that has led us to the somnambulistic, hedonistic 21st century. No longer was the enemy communism, but rather the nasty people like McCarthy and Hoover who preached against communism.

Syndicated columnist George Sokolsky, in an article about education in 1952, asked: "Are Marxists to start our children's careers with their environmentalist doctrines which exclude religion as superstition, patriotism as chauvinism, morals as comparative and ethics as a bourgeois notion?"

He no doubt thought that the question was merely rhetorical, but the answer now seems obvious. Yes, yes, yes and yes! Marxists, or their innocent dupes, did control the education system to a remarkable degree, and thanks to the long lever of John Dewey's system of "progressive education," which started before 1900, and the fulcrum of the collapse of American certainty that happened sometime in the 1950s, we were entirely open to all of the elements of indoctrination that Sokolsky tried to warn us against.

The results would have delighted Khruschev and Lenin, and mortified Thomas Jefferson and J. Edgar Hoover. Turns out that this "shovel-ready project" was taking place at the proposed burial site of America. Lenin had planted his seeds, and the learning tree would sprout its dark fruit just a few years later — in the radical 1960s that re-shaped America for good.

DR. BILL AYERS: OR HOW I LEARNED TO STOP BOMBING AND DESTROY THE SYSTEM FROM WITHIN

July 24, 2011

By the mid-1960s, all hell had broken loose in the American education system, most obviously in the universities that were at the center of the Vietnam War protest movement, but more subtly in the public school system as well.

And since the universities that were exploding with radical ideologies in the 1960s were also the furnace in which future educators were forged — there was an inevitable long-term effect on what teachers taught their students about American traditions, values and beliefs. The anti-American fervor on college campuses during the Vietnam era was the fuel that led teachers to give up their traditional role as the builders of culture and turned them instead into termites that ate away at the foundations of our society.

That disconnect between American idealism and American youth may ultimately be how progressive education was able to shift the paradigm in America, and no better poster boy exists for the transformation of American education from a cultivator of good citizens into an incubator of radicalism than Bill Ayers.

You may remember Ayers from his tangential role in the 2008 presidential election. It turns out that he was an early supporter of Barack Obama and had helped the future president get jobs on two boards that divvied up millions of dollars in education and anti-poverty grants.

That wouldn't have been a problem except for the fact that Ayers is best known for blowing things up. As a founding member of the Weather Underground, he turned to violence in the late 1960s as an approved tactic for bringing about social change.

That may have been the most dangerous thing Bill Ayers did in the turbulent Sixties, but it is certainly not the most effective technique he found for changing America from a capitalist nation to a communistic one.

For that you need to look at where Ayers spent his time both before and after his bomb-throwing period — namely at schools and universities — and on those boards doling out big bucks to effect social change through education.

Ayers was at the University of Michigan when Students for a Democratic Society was founded in 1966, and he participated directly in the radicalization of SDS that led to the violent revolutionary group known as the Weather Underground. Ayers and his cohorts bombed the Pentagon, inspired riots in the streets, and encouraged violent uprising in order to bring about a new socialist world order.

You can get a taste for Ayers' style of politics from a January 1970 report by syndicated columnists Robert Allen and John Goldsmith on a four-day meeting of the national council of the Weatherman faction of SDS which took place in Flint, Mich.

After his now-wife Bernardine Dohrn had worked up the crowd by bashing them as "wimpy on armed struggle" and reminding the assembled revolutionaries that "violence is our aim and motto," Ayers got his turn to go macho, giving karate lessons that were "accompanied with such encouraging remarks as 'It is necessary to take up arms and resort to violence in order to fight and destroy the pigs'" (namely the police and establishment leaders).

Probably no one reading this column today would condone or accept such rhetoric, unless they were themselves avowed revolutionaries. But make no mistake about it, that rhetoric was standard fare on the campuses of the 1960s. For at least a decade, it was common college wisdom that America was evil and that you couldn't "trust anyone over 30."

Well, a lot of those folks over 30 were what we today call "the greatest generation," the American men and women who sacrificed life, limb and our national treasure in order to preserve liberty for their children. It would no doubt take a major psychological study in order to ascertain what factors came into play in the post-war years to explain how the "greatest generation" allowed their children to rip apart everything they themselves had worked so hard to secure.

But for now we can simply surmise that the generation which had given up so much in order to ensure that their children would enjoy liberty's bounty was also somehow psychologically circumscribed from imposing ANY significant restrictions on that precious liberty, and thus created a generation characterized by an overwhelming sense of entitlement, narcissism, and ultimately ingratitude. For lack of a better name, call it the Bill Ayers Generation.

The "older generation" no doubt didn't understand the Bill Ayers Generation, and that probably went for Ayers' own father, too. Thomas G. Ayers was president and later chairman and CEO of Commonwealth Edison. In other words, he was a major industrialist, and part of the system of capital and wealth creation that his son and the Weather Underground sought to topple. Again, the psychological implications are enormous, and the story of the Ayers family was no doubt duplicated in millions of other Baby Boomer families across the nation.

By letting their children do whatever they wanted instead of grounding them in the same wholesome principles with which they themselves had been raised, the "greatest generation" was engendering a generation of experimentation, rebellion and decay. The children and grandchildren of that generation are the ones left holding the bag these 50 years later, and the bag is empty rhetoric. "Hope and change" has replaced "blood, sweat and tears."

Of course, the people who have been selling hope and change for the past 50 years, in one form or another, are hopeful that you will not notice the gap between reality and rhetoric.

They are also no doubt hopeful you will not follow the trail of evidence that links progressive education, revolutionary politics and the decline of America, but it's all laid out in plain sight — often in the words of Bill Ayers himself.

Ayers was a key author of "Prairie Fire: The Politics of Revolutionary Imperialism," which was distributed while he was a fugitive from federal charges in 1974.

There is much to learn in this book, which candidly describes the plan for revolution in America, but let's just close with what the book tells us about education, the field which Ayers entered in 1966 and in which he later became a distinguished professor with a wide influence on contemporary pedagogic thinking.

Here, in a discussion of "busing" students to achieve racial "equality," Ayers and his co-authors give away the game:

"The real question is: Who will control the schools? The design of the state is control of the child's education, whether in the integrated or segregated school."

That was the real question, and it still is: "Who will control the schools?"

Bill Ayers tried and failed at violent revolution, but he never lost sight of his goal — he just changed tactics. In an assessment of the Cuban Revolution in "Prairie Fire," the authors noted that, "The revolution has launched an offensive to transform education and culture into powerful revolutionary tools."

In future columns, we will explore just how Ayers and his colleagues launched an offensive in the 1960s and beyond to "transform education and culture into powerful revolutionary tools" right here in America, and how they succeeded.

EDUCATION OR VIOLENCE: THE TWO-PRONGED REVOLUTION OF BILL AYERS

July 31, 2011

When the Students for a Democratic Society organization was wracked by a schism in the summer of 1969, Bill Ayers sided with the faction that favored widespread revolution across the face of America. It is instructive that the newly formed SDS council honored Ayers with the title of secretary of education.

Based on his later career as a distinguished professor of education at the University of Illinois, it is a title he took seriously — it's just too bad that so many others have ignored it, and what it tells us about Ayers' plans for our country.

In another time, in another revolution, he would have been called the commissar of propaganda. But the goal was the same — to shift popular opinion against the capitalist economy, traditional morality, and self-determination — and to bring about social change through indoctrination rather than violence.

That, of course, is a long-term goal. It cannot be accomplished overnight, and since Ayers was part of a revolutionary movement that was impatient for change, he had to take a back seat while his colleagues tried bombs, rather than books, as their weapon of choice to bring down the establishment.

But that does not mean he wasn't using his time well. Indeed, there is plenty of evidence that Ayers always thought that education was the key to social change, even when he became discouraged by society's resistance to his ideas.

Way back in 1966, Ayers was working with his girlfriend Diane Oughton at the Children's Community School in Ann Arbor, where they taught using the Summerhill method, a progressive system that allowed students to set their own curriculum. All lessons were optional, and students were free to do whatever they wanted.

For all the reasons you would expect, the Children's Community School failed within a couple of years, which helped to spur Ayers to pursue other means of revolutionary change.

In a 1970 analysis of Ayers and Oughton, UPI authors Lucinda Frank and Thomas Powers wrote that by late 1968, Ayers was speaking out about "the failure of education to change people." He is quoted as saying, "We are tired of tiptoeing up to society and asking for reform."

That no doubt explains the transformation of Ayers from a gentle teacher who encouraged students to "do their own thing" to a harsh revolutionary who used bombs in an effort to force people to do whatever he wanted them to do — namely to reject capitalism.

But we should be clear that while Ayers adopted violence, he never abandoned education. Indeed, unless Ayers was truly schizophrenic in his outlook, he thought that education and violence could serve the same end — revolutionary change — and he proved himself on more than one occasion to be willing to switch tactics as necessity dictated. The only thing he has never done is renounce his dream of a socialist revolution.

In fact, Ayers wrote as recently as last year, "Every revolution is impossible until it occurs; after the fact, every revolution seems inevitable."

It may seem a coy sentiment, but during the bold 1960s, Ayers and his fellow radicals were much more transparent about their loyalties and their priorities than they are today. In a January 1970 column by Robert Allen and John Goldsmith, a friend of Ayers by the name of Ted Gold gave his plan for what would follow their hoped-for destruction of the American government.

"An agency of the people of the world would be set up to run U.S. society and economy after the defeat of U.S.

imperialism abroad," he told a crowd at the national Weatherman revolutionary council held in Flint, Mich., in December 1969.

One listener asked with apparent nervousness, "Does that mean that if the people of the world succeed in liberating themselves before American radicals make the American revolution, then Chinese, Africans, and others will take over here and run things for white America?"

The dedicated revolutionary Gold didn't miss a beat. "Well," he said, "if it takes fascism to bring about the American revolution, I guess we'll have to have fascism."

Yes, those were refreshingly transparent times. There was never any need to wonder what kind of "fundamental transformation" these revolutionaries had in mind for our country. Indeed, in 1970 the group issued a "Declaration of a State of War" against the United States government — and Gold was not just talking the talk. He died, along with Terry Robbins and Ayers' girlfriend Diana Oughton, in New York City in March 1970, as "glorious heroes of the revolution," when a nail bomb they were building exploded prematurely instead of at the military dance it was intended to shatter.

Forty years later, Ayers and his revolutionary wife, Bernardine Dohrn, honored those "heroes" in a commemorative essay as "beautiful and committed young people who believed fiercely in peace and justice and freedom." They forgot to mention fascism.

Ayers was perhaps the primary intellectual force behind the 1970s revolution, and he was a key author of "Prairie Fire: The Politics of Revolutionary Imperialism," which was distributed while he was a fugitive from federal charges in 1974. The book was dedicated to Gold, Oughton and Robbins, as well as dozens of other radicals including Sirhan Sirhan, the convicted assassin of Robert Kennedy.

It is doctrinaire communist propaganda, and since Ayers continues to stand behind his revolutionary writings, we can gain insight into what this longtime instructor of young educators actually believes. If you wondered why so many modern schools have become a cultural war zone where traditional families, traditional religion and traditional values are mocked and ridiculed, you need look no further than the agenda of Bill Ayers. Here is one small, but vital, example out of "Prairie Fire":

"The modern male-run nuclear family, when we tear away the veil of sentimentality, is the basic unit of capitalist society. Capitalism and the modern family matured together historically, feeding each other's development. In the family, women both reproduce the labor force and begin the socialization process of the new generation, which is essential to the productive system and the functioning of society."

Did you catch that? Women's role as mother and educator in traditional families is "ESSENTIAL ... to the functioning of society." Given the desire of Ayers and his socialist allies to overthrow capitalism society, it is no wonder that for the past 50 years, there has been a deliberate, debilitating, deadly attack on the traditional nuclear family in schools, churches and legislation. This "nuclear" bomb has done much more damage to society than any mere explosive.

It's not all one man's fault, of course, — whether Ayers or Dewey — but it's obvious that there's been a sea change in American values over the past 50 to 100 years. Anyone who can't see it — or who claims there was no damage done by rejecting the heritage that made America great — is himself but one more example of collateral damage, one more victim of the time bomb that Ayers, the "secretary of education," happily planted many years ago.

'THE PURPOSE OF EDUCATION' — AND THE FAILURE TO PURSUE IT

August 14, 2011

It would seem obvious that how we educate our children is also how we preserve our culture. It is the solid foundation that allows us to even speak of a culture — a shared experience that defines who we are.

If that is the case, then modern education has failed.

Because for the past hundred years, the solid foundation has cracked, the shared experience has shrunk, and our culture extends no farther back in the past than to the last Harry Potter movie.

Yet some people act as though education is beyond criticism — simply because the purpose of education is to teach. But that misses the point of criticism — and of education.

As Martin Luther King Jr. wrote in "The Purpose of Education" when he himself was a student at Morehouse College, "Education must ... train one for quick, resolute and effective thinking... We are prone to let our mental life become invaded by legions of half truths, prejudices, and propaganda... I often wonder whether or not education is fulfilling its purpose. A great majority of the so-called educated people do not think logically and scientifically. Even the press, the classroom, the platform, and the pulpit in many instances do not give us objective and unbiased truths."

Can we get an Amen? Thank you, Rev. King, for the lucid thinking and the clear warning: If you are looking for objective and unbiased truths, don't look for them from "the press, the classroom, the [political] platform, and the pulpit."

I have written often about how the press is pursuing an agenda of "half truths, prejudices and propaganda." And it is obvious from polls that show an approval rating as low as single digits for Congress that most Americans no longer trust politicians to do the right thing. As for preachers, these days many of them seem to be as changeable as the wind, following the path of least resistance from their parishioners rather than the path of greatest insistence from their God.

But once again we must ask ourselves how did we get to this point? How did the politicians, the preachers and the press get so far off kilter?

And there is no doubt what the answer has to be — the shift in the purpose of education from 1900 when America was still a strong, tradition-based society to 1947 when the Rev. King was already seeing "half truths" in the classroom all the way to 2011 when education has become a vehicle for social change rather than the conduit of self-evident truth.

Everything that was taken for granted in schools 100 years ago is taken to the garbage dump today. Ask yourself: Do public schools still have the courage to promote the brilliant accomplishments of America and Christianity? Or do they toss our traditions aside for the Golden Calves of multi-culturalism, relative truth, and the propaganda of social justice?

The answer, of course, is that as an institution — not necessarily as individuals — modern education has joined with Karl Marx, Jeremiah Wright and Bill Ayers in questioning the value of America's contribution to society and the worth of our founding principles.

Of course, that is because most educators do not teach objective truth any longer — which ultimately means truth that is based in what C.S. Lewis called the Tao, the moral underpinnings of natural law that allow us to make judgments unashamedly.

Without the Tao, we cannot say "this is bad" or "this is good." And, of course, even if individual teachers DO know what is right and wrong, they are not supposed to teach that to their children any longer because the Tao implies some sort of religious viewpoint, some acknowledgment that mankind is not jetsam and flotsam in the turbulent eddies of nihilistic infinity. Thanks to the ACLU and other similar organizations, the mere acknowledgment of a higher power, a deeper meaning in life, has become not just unconstitutional, but also un-American.

That leaves teachers in the position of letting students make their own "relative" judgments about history, politics, and right and wrong instead of teaching them what mankind has always known to be true. And, of course, this has a huge impact on the future of the culture with which these students have been entrusted. Every absolute has been jettisoned and replaced with a merely convenient truth.

Think about what that means.

Whether you like your own child's teachers or not, they are neither permitted nor equipped to pass on the "objective and unbiased truths" that Martin Luther King took for granted, as did Thomas Jefferson and the Founding Fathers.

With the educational system now totally untethered from the Tao, we are still providing knowledge to students, powerful knowledge, but without any guidance in how to use it. It is the equivalent of providing a loaded gun to a baby. You can see the result last month in Greece, last week in London, and coming soon to a rowdy mob near you.

Martin Luther King recognized the danger of this kind of half-education instinctively, even as a teenager. That should not surprise us, as King was well-grounded in the Tao, having grown up as the son of a preacher and a proponent of individual responsibility and traditional morality. King's argument in his 1947 paper on "The Purpose of Education" when he was just 18 years old parallels in brief form the argument of C.S. Lewis in "The Abolition of Man" that education freed of the moorings of morality is reduced to mere propaganda.

Though educators may resist this notion — though some parents may wear blinders — it is inarguable that what schools pass on to children today is a wholly different world view than what was provided to Martin Luther King, who as a black man knew just how dangerous a society that ignored the Tao could be to individual liberty.

No wonder he wrote the following words:

"To save man from the morass of propaganda, in my opinion, is one of the chief aims of education. [But] we must remember that intelligence is not enough. Intelligence plus character — that is the goal of true education. The complete education gives one not only power of concentration, but worthy objectives upon which to concentrate. The broad education will, therefore, transmit to one not only the accumulated knowledge of the race but also the accumulated experience of social living.

"If we are not careful, our colleges will produce a group of close-minded, unscientific, illogical propagandists, consumed with immoral acts. Be careful, 'brethren!' Be careful, teachers!"

I think it goes without saying that Martin Luther King Jr. was not against education when he wrote these words, nor should anyone mistake my words for a personal attack on teachers. No one is against teachers. No one is against schools.

But what we want is what every culture expects — whether Native American, Southeast Asian, Muslim, or African — an education system that promotes the values, traditions and beliefs that make the culture unique, and which ensure its survival.

Short of that, just what is the point?

THE REVOLUTION YOU MAY NOT EVEN KNOW HAPPENED

August 21, 2011

Revolutionaries, by the very nature of their task, face a peculiar challenge that creates inherent risk in their enterprise, and thus necessitates that they be ready to change tactics frequently.

It is easy to understand why. To achieve their goal of overthrowing the government or ruling system, they must have a public campaign to persuade the masses, yet everything they do publicly may also be used against them by the government which they oppose.

If they give up the public campaign and just wage a private battle, they are almost certainly doomed to failure by their own small numbers and the brute strength of entrenched power. Yet if they go public, they expose themselves to the risk of arrest or even death in the worst-case scenario, or the more subtle risk of public rejection should their revolution prove to be unpopular with the "downtrodden masses."

Just such a choice confronted the Students for a Democratic Society back in 1968 when they were seeking to overthrow the U.S. government and the capitalist system. For a while it had seemed like the propaganda of the street would win the war. Americans grew their hair longer. They wore their skirts shorter. They enjoyed the fruits of free love and readily available psychedelic drugs. Even Mrs. Robinson was ready to throw caution to the winds. The button-down generation had come unglued.

But then something strange happened. Nixon got elected. The Vietnam War continued. Jim Morrison, Janis Joplin and Jimi Hendrix died. Charlie Manson killed. Maybe the revolution wasn't quite as ready for prime time as Bill Ayers and his fellow conspirators in SDS had hoped.

It was around this time when Ayers, fresh from being named "Education Secretary" for the new radical branch of SDS, went underground in the Weatherman organization, along with his girlfriend Diana Oughton, his future wife Bernardine Dohrn, and a small cadre of dedicated revolutionaries. Instead of encouraging street demonstrations and teach-ins to rally public opinion to their cause, they switched tactics and planted bombs. As part of their campaign for the violent overthrow of the U.S. government, they bombed the Capitol, the Pentagon, the State Department, and even themselves. (Oughton and two other radicals died in their Greenwich Village apartment when a bomb they were assembling prematurely exploded.)

By the middle of 1970, the Weather Underground had actually declared war on the United States. This declaration is instructive in several particulars about the nature of the revolution that they sought, and the tactics they would pursue.

"We've known that our job is to lead white kids into armed revolution," the declaration read by Dohrn asserted. "Ever since SDS became revolutionary, we've been trying to show how it is possible to overcome frustration and impotence that comes from trying to reform this system. Kids know the lines are drawn: revolution is touching all of our lives. Tens of thousands have learned that protest and marches don't do it. Revolutionary violence is the only way."

The declaration referred to the deaths of Oughton, Ted Gold and Terry Robbins in the N.Y.C. townhouse explosion several times and promoted them as martyrs for the cause. It also noted that 10 of the 12 Weatherman leaders who were under indictment for their conspiratorial activities had outwitted the system.

"Terry is dead, Linda was captured by a pig informer, but the rest of us move freely in and out of every city and youth scene in this country. We're not hiding out but we're invisible...," the statement claimed. "We fight in many ways. Dope is one of our weapons. The laws against marijuana mean that millions of us are outlaws long before we actually split. Guns and grass are united in the youth underground... If you want to find us, this is where we are. In every tribe, commune, dormitory, farmhouse, barracks and townhouse where kids are making love, smoking dope and loading guns — fugitives from Amerikan justice are free to go."

In other words, the revolutionaries had recognized that they could never overturn the power structure by talking their fellow citizens into joining them in armed rebellion for political purposes, but they could turn them into outlaws by corrupting them. If these hip revolutionaries could seduce the masses with sex and drugs, then they could count on their support when they fought to topple the system that tried to regulate sexual morality and to outlaw drugs.

That strategy in and of itself shows that the revolution sponsored by Bill Ayers and Bernardine Dohrn was not some naive childish prank. Their very success in corrupting the morals of the American republic using the "weapons" of sex and drugs in the 1960s and '70s proves that they were the equals of Lenin and Che as revolutionary strategists. Once the moral values of the country had been surrendered to the revolution, it was inevitable that the political values would follow. Thus, feel-good personal morality led like clockwork to feel-good public policy, and the system was gradually milked of billions of dollars in a Marxist transfer of wealth from the haves to the have-nots. And most of this occurred long after the last bomb was set by the Weather Underground.

Bombs were a matter of convenience, but revolution was a matter of conviction — a conviction which neither Ayers nor his wife Bernardine Dohrn have ever renounced. Indeed, as Dohrn read in her Declaration of War, "For Diana Oughton, Ted Gold and Terry Robbins, and for all the revolutionaries who are still on the move here, there has been no question for a long time now — we will never go back."

Elsewhere, in the declaration, the revolutionaries note that their parents falsely believed that "the revolution was a game for us. But the war and the racism of this society show that it is too f---ed up. We will never live peaceably under this system."

Those words were written in 1970 when Ayers, Dohrn and the other Weatherman leaders were fugitives. In 1980, they turned themselves in. Federal charges against Ayers and the others were dropped. Prosecutors had determined that evidence against the revolutionaries had been gathered illegally by the FBI. But also, times had changed. You didn't need a weatherman to know which way the wind blew — America was a new place. The young radicals of the early 1960s were starting to run things, and the old America of Lawrence Welk, Guy Lombardo and Kate Smith was now singing a new tune.

There was no need for the Weather Underground to stay underground any longer because their radical agenda was now being implemented above ground. The seeds in other words had sprouted. As a result, the revolutionary propagandist Bill Ayers got off scot-free. Bernardine Dohrn had to face Illinois state charges and was fined a paltry $1,500 and placed on three years probation for her part in a deadly conspiracy to overthrow the government of the United States. In other words, they beat the system.

But it is wrong to assume that in the years following 1980, they somehow embraced capitalism, the Constitution, and the American way of life.

Just the opposite. Although they both settled down to outwardly normal lives (he as an educator and she as an attorney), numerous statements and writings in the intervening years prove conclusively, in their own words, that they never gave up their contempt for the country they live in. Thus, although they did not continue to pursue violent overthrow of the government, it is safe to assume that they remain committed to their pledge to "never live peaceably under this system." They do not live "under" the system; they live within it — as agent provocateurs.

Indeed, for anyone who has read his book "Fugitive Days," it is plain that Bill Ayers remains a dedicated Marxist radical whose aim is to bring about what has been called elsewhere "fundamental transformation" of the United States of America, and what is better known as revolution.

I think it is inarguable that they accomplished their goal. A theory about how they did so will be put forth in next week's column.

REVOLUTION WENT FROM VIOLENT OVERTHROW TO CO-OPTING THE SYSTEM

August 28, 2011

Does any legitimate authority really think that communists targeted the U.S. public education system as a means to transform the American character from rugged individualism to comfortable socialism?

You bet. Let's start with the U.S. Congress.

Back in 1969, the Committee on Internal Security (in the House of Representatives) issued a report on "SDS Plans for America's High Schools." It was readily apparent to the congressmen who signed this report that America faced a severe challenge from the young revolutionaries who publicly proclaimed themselves to be Students for a Democratic Society, but privately vowed to transform America into a socialist utopia:

"Basic to SDS is the idea that contemporary American society is corrupt, evil and oppressive — and must be destroyed. To reform it, they insist, to change it for the better, is impossible. SDS says our Nation's system of government and traditional values must be destroyed."

Therefore, according to the House committee report, the immediate goal of SDS back in 1969 was "to wreck our educational system," and said that "the high schools in the United States are clearly targeted by the radical left, and particularly SDS for 'activism.'"

The report went on to note that, "Many of the SDS leaders have publicly declared themselves to be revolutionaries dedicated to the Marxist-Leninist ideology. For example, Mark

Rudd, William Ayers, and Jeffrey Carl (Jeff) Jones, leading national officers of the SDS, publicly identified themselves as revolutionary communists during a televised interview over station WJW-TV in Cleveland, Ohio, on August 30, 1969."

Ayers, of couse, is of especial interest these days because he is a reputed friend of President Obama, but we should be more interested in him because of his long and respected career as a professor of education. How, after all, does society tolerate as a teacher someone who wrote this about the typical high school student: "Imperialism oppresses him by jailing him [in school] and the only thing to do is break out and tear up the jail [school]."

That is just one of many inflammatory statements about education in the SDS manifesto known as "You Don't Need a Weatherman to Know Which Way the Wind Blows," which Ayers co-authored. Moreover, SDS publicly declared its intention to foment militant resistance to school authority as a "means to overthrow [the] system" (as stated in the "high school resolution" passed at the SDS National Council meeting in Boulder, Colo., in 1968). So it is easy to see why Congress was concerned about SDS back in 1969.

But the congressional report didn't quite get it right. The real threat of SDS to high schools had nothing to do with violence. Yes, there were isolated incidents on high school campuses, but for the most part militancy never took hold the way it did on college campuses in the 1960s. Nonetheless, SDS's intention of radicalizing the nation's high schools was a real and long-term threat.

That's because the SDS strategy for America's schools was two-fold from the beginning. More important than violent demonstrations was the plan to indoctrinate students to believe that America was a "sick" society that exploited workers at home and abroad. They did so, at first, with teach-ins and revolutionary propaganda. But later, they discovered it was much more effective to change the way students thought by changing the way they are taught. That meant working from within the system, and explains why Bill Ayers pursued his career as an instructor of teachers. It also helps to explain why much of the curricula in high schools today resembles a self-criticism session reminiscent of Mao's Cultural Revolution.

But what it doesn't explain is why America has accepted Ayers and other revolutionaries as respected leaders of our country instead of self-avowed traitors who should hang their heads in shame.

Remember, the leaders of SDS were dedicated revolutionaries who had declared themselves the sworn enemies of America, democracy and capitalism. Yet in the past 20 to 30 years, many of these same people and their fellow radicals who vowed to destroy the U.S. government, economy and educational system have become deeply embedded within those very institutions.

Maybe we should not be surprised. Working undercover was always part of the SDS strategy. In 1969, the group published a "Work-in Organizers Manual," which instructed radicals on how to infiltrate business and industry in order to revolutionize society by giving up their summer vacations and spreading the party line while working on assembly lines.

An Aug. 1, 1969, report in Time Magazine on this strategy quoted an unnamed SDS leader as saying, "For SDS people, there is no summer vacation. We see ourselves working 18 hours a day forever. We're in this for a lifetime."

If that doesn't scare you, nothing will, but try this on for size:

In a documentary entitled "The Weather Underground," SDS leader Jeff Jones is seen in a film clip responding to an incident of alleged police brutality against protesters back in the 1960s.

Jones boldly declares, "The power belongs to the young people and the black people in this country. Come on! We gotta build a strong base and someday we gotta knock those m-----f-----s who control this thing right on their a--."

That was bold and colorful revolutionary rhetoric, but isn't that exactly what they did? Didn't they go ahead and build a strong base out of what Time magazine called "community organization projects, propagandizing and planning," and knock this country right on its butt?

Jones seems to have instinctively realized that the social changes brought about in just a few years in the mid-1960s were evidence of a huge power base that was largely untapped for political purposes. It was that recognition which fueled the new strategy developed by SDS and later the Weather Underground to not just fight the system, but to infiltrate it and work from within to fundamentally transform it.

If you don't think it worked, then you don't know who Jeff Jones is today. After his arrest by the FBI in 1981, Jones mainstreamed himself — first as a journalist and then as an environmental consultant. Today he operates Jeff Jones Strategies ("Consulting for Good Causes") but like his fellow revolutionary Bill Ayers, he has not renounced his militant past ("I do not regret my militant opposition to racism and the Vietnam War"). Instead, he has learned to work more effectively to change the system by owning it rather than overthrowing it.

On his website, Jones says he is "committed to the idea of building a partnership of workers, environmentalists, business, government, social and environmental justice advocates" — in other words he is still working for the communist revolution, but is now doing it without bombs.

In fact, Jones was one of the founders of the Apollo Alliance, which is a coalition of unions, community action groups like ACORN, and environmental groups aiming to push social policy as far left as possible — as fast as possible. They accomplished that goal in 2009 when the federal stimulus bill was passed by Congress and signed into law by President Obama just weeks after he took office. It turns out that the Apollo Alliance wrote large portions of the law, which is officially called the American Recovery and Reinvestment Act.

That means a guy who was arrested 30 years ago for his part in a revolutionary movement to overthrow the U.S. government now played a huge role in a law that had the effect of bankrupting the U.S. government.

And for the most part, no one even cares. That's why I state confidently that the revolution sought by Jones and Ayers has already succeeded.

IS AMERICAN DECLINE THE PRODUCT OF CHANCE OR OF DESIGN?

September 5, 2011

Look around and ask yourself if the United States of America is growing stronger or weaker.

If you think it is stronger than it was 20, 30 or 50 years ago, then God save you when you figure out what is really going on, because you are going to be very angry when things start to fall apart.

If you think it is already crumbling, then don't stop there, but ask yourself how it happened. How did the country, in just a half a century or so since the end of World War II, go from the mighty defender of freedom with a standard of living unequaled in history to the miserable paper tiger we are now?

Do you really think that happened by accident?

Or is it not possible, indeed even likely, that the collapse of the American giant occurred because there were forces underfoot that recognized our Achilles' heel and struck at it?

I suppose it is hard to believe that a system as complex and powerful as the American government, not to mention the entire American economy, could be brought down by the directed action of a few revolutionaries, but virtually every revolution in history has accomplished a similarly gargantuan task against great odds. Revolution starts with a manifesto, or a statement of ideas, created by one or more people. It then either proceeds or dies based on the ability to turn those ideas into action.

I think, if we go back and look at the manifestos of the 1960s youth revolution led by Bill Ayers and the Students for a Democratic Society, we will discover that — unbeknownst to most of us — their revolution has long since achieved most of its goals.

In previous columns, we have talked about the desire of SDS to bring about a revolutionary transformation of education into a tool for fighting against the traditional culture, economy and government of the United States. But that was just one

317

front in a multi-pronged assault. Let's step back and look at the big picture rather than get caught up in polemics about the quality of education in America.

The education system per se is still as strong as ever in the United States when compared to education in other countries. You can't fault American educators for doing a bad job at educating; they are for the most part superb. This is not an issue of American ingenuity we are talking about, but rather a question of American naivete. The issue is not how well students are being taught — but WHAT they are being taught — and why we as a society have capitulated to our own debasement.

Sure, most of us have trudged forward with blind acceptance of American exceptionalism and a complacent view of our ability to remain atop the heap of nations, but others have worked tirelessly to use our boundless generosity as a tool to turn America into an exceptional failure. It is our unwillingness to take seriously that threat which has made us so vulnerable.

Indeed, because of our naivete, it is widely regarded as a foolish waste of time to even entertain the notion that those 1960s radicals were a danger to the government of the United States. How could those anti-establishment termites have possibly brought down the most powerful country in the world?

Perhaps that question should be addressed to someone familiar with pest control rather than to the "giant intellects" that populate our national media, government and academies. Then the answer would be clear. Tiny termites bring down houses one bite at a time. And what is true for wood is also true for the world. Whether you see them or not, you ignore them at your own risk.

That was the case in Russia before World War I, Germany before World War II, and Iran before the Islamic Revolution. Such examples have not been lost on the new American revolutionaries. It was not armed rebellion that won those wars for the radicals; it was propaganda and the promise of hope and change

That's why, back in 1969, the radicals in America were not just taking to the streets. As we saw last week, they were also infiltrating industry, high schools and other institutions in order to work from within to turn people against the government and against capitalism. And they were also thinking way beyond any one strategy for achieving their goal of "world communism."

As Time Magazine noted in its Aug. 1, 1969, issue: "Activists not attracted by the call of the assembly line have focused on community organization projects, propagandizing and planning. In Boston, 200 radicals are attending a nine-week 'Movement School,' at which they are to develop a 'critique of American society' and plan future tactics."

It would be wonderful if we could dig up the notes for that "critique of American society," and find a blueprint for the future tactics that would be employed to achieve a classless society, wouldn't it?

In fact, a contemporary source does exist which provides just such a critique and blueprint. In the June 18, 1969, issue of New Left Notes, you can read the revolutionary manifesto signed by Bill Ayers, Bernardine Dohrn, Mark Rudd, Jeff Jones and seven other members of the radical SDS faction known as the Revolutionary Youth Movement.

This document was called "You Don't Need a Weatherman to Know Which Way the Wind Blows," after a line in a Bob Dylan song, and it tells everything you need to know about the goals of the communist revolutionaries who wanted to overthrow the U.S. government from within.

For Bill Ayers and his friends, the central point of understanding is that the United States is an oppressor nation and an imperialist nation whose wealth was derived from exploiting the masses both at home and abroad. We need not take time now to explore the absurdity of calling the United States an imperialist power when history plainly shows the opposite, but it would be interesting to know how many people accept this terminology today as self-evident. That would be an indicator of just how successful the SDS revolution has been from a propaganda point of view.

Ayers and his fellow radicals declared, "It is the oppressed peoples of the world who have created the wealth of this empire and it is to them that it belongs; the goal of the revolutionary struggle must be the control and use of this wealth in the interests of the oppressed peoples of the world."

In other words, the primary goal of Ayers and SDS was not ending the war in Vietnam as a naive reading of history might presume, but rather the Marxist goal of "redistribution of wealth." Mind you, this is not just about helping the poor people of America, because as the "Weatherman" document plainly spells out, even the poor people in America (described as the "enslaved masses") have a "material existence very much above the conditions of the masses of people of the world."

Therefore, what the Weathermen sought was very explicitly "international revolution," a movement of wealth outward from the United States to the control of the "oppressed people of the world." Just such a shift of wealth has of course occurred in the past 50 years, and it's possible to imagine that it occurred randomly, but it is much more reasonable to envision a scenario whereby it occurred as part of an intentional strategy to bleed the American treasury dry.

If such a strategy had been implemented, it would explain the three main aspects of the American decline of the past 50 years — the loss of capital and jobs overseas; the draining of billions of dollars into foreign aid and foreign wars; and the geometric increase of domestic entitlements to vastly unsustainable levels. Although the government agents and politicians who implemented these policies may have been unwitting pawns, there is no doubt that they played perfectly into the hands of the revolution championed by Bill Ayers.

We'll see how next week.

'HOW DID WE GET HERE?'
FINALLY, HERE'S THE ANSWER

September 11, 2011

Lots of people resist the notion that the horrible things that have gone wrong in the United States could possibly have been the outcome of a planned rebellion.

I don't purport to be able to delineate how such a plot could have been accomplished, but the evidence is irrefutable that the radical left of the 1960s outlined a strategy for bankrupting the United States "empire" and that is just what happened. If it happened by accident, then the guardians of our country were guilty of gross malfeasance in turning a blind eye to the step-by-step draining of our treasury.

More likely though, it happened on purpose, just the way it was proposed to happen. You can see the blueprint in the 1969 manifesto called "You Don't Need a Weatherman to Know Which Way the Wind Blows," written by leaders of the Students for a Democratic Society such as Bill Ayers and Bernardine Dohrn.

Here it is in a nutshell:

"The goal is the destruction of U.S. imperialism and the achievement of a classless world: world communism. Winning state power in the U.S. will occur as a result of the military forces of the U.S. overextending themselves around the world and being defeated piecemeal; struggle within the U.S. will be a vital part of this process, but when the revolution triumphs in the U.S. it will have been made by the people of the whole world."

So the 1960s radicals who are most associated with working to end the war in Vietnam really did not oppose the war — they just opposed the United States in the war. In other words, they were not pacifists; they were traitors.

This strategy of forcing the United States to "overextend" itself militarily around the world was part of a worldwide communist game plan that the 1960s radicals adopted as their own. They credit Chinese communist Lin Piao and Cuban guerrilla Che Guevara with the initial insights that led them to embrace the Vietnam War as an inevitable step in the collapse of the United States.

Here, they quote Lin Piao:

"U.S. imperialism is stronger, but also more vulnerable than any imperialism of the past. It sets itself against the people of the whole world, including the people of the United States. Its human, military, material and financial resources are far from sufficient for the realization of its ambition of domination over the whole world. U.S. imperialism has further weakened itself by occupying so many places in the world, overreaching itself, stretching its fingers out wide and dispersing its strength, with its rear so far away and its supply lines so long."

Forget about the anti-imperialist rhetoric. You can agree with me that the United States is the exact opposite of an imperial power and still see the accuracy of Lin Piao's argument from a practical point of view. There is no doubt that the United States since World War II had used its military forces globally in a way that was unthinkable in previous eras. You and I probably see the U.S. military as a force for good — not empire building — in Europe, Korea, the Mideast, Japan and elsewhere, but there is no doubt that our treasure has been depleted, our resources diminished, and our strength dispersed as a result.

Thus, Bill Ayers and his fellow revolutionaries in SDS and the Weather Underground seized on the idea of what Che called "creating two, three, many Vietnams" in order to "mobilize the struggle so sharply in so many places that the imperialists cannot possibly deal with it all. Since it is essential to their interests, they will try to deal with it all, and will be defeated and destroyed in the process."

Can anyone say Lebanon, Somalia, Kosovo, Iraq, Afghanistan, Yemen, Libya and Syria? Not to mention the old favorites in Korea, Germany and Japan. Nor can we forget the unnamed war on the U.S. border with Mexico.

Yep, the "Weatherman" manifesto had it right. It WAS "essential" to U.S. interests to fight against communism and oppression in various parts of the world, and we DID try to "deal with it all," even though realistically we probably should have known all along that we could NOT possibly succeed. Here you have the classic strategy of the ancient Chinese general, Sun-Tzu, of using an enemy's superior force against itself. Or for those who like a more direct analogy, it is the equivalent of jiu-jitsu, the Japanese martial art that turns an enemy's superior strength into a weakness.

We don't have to agree with the communist rhetoric of Ayers and his colleagues in order to see that they were fundamentally correct about the impact of the United States overextending itself militarily abroad. The cost of being the world's policeman had to be accounted for somewhere at home, even if without explicit acknowledgment. Thus, U.S. involvement in military campaigns overseas was good for communist revolutionary goals because it would create unrest at home. The "Weatherman" manifesto foresaw that "the condition of all workers is worsened through rising taxes, inflation and the fall of real wages" as war payments deplete the ability to pay for domestic entitlements. It is this economic impact on the people at home that makes SDS a proponent of war abroad.

"The more the ruling class is hurt in Vietnam, the harder people will be pushed to rebel and to fight for reforms." All you have to do is elide the word Vietnam and substitute Iraq and Afghanistan and you will see the fruition of this strategy in contemporary America — overextended, bankrupt and embracing socialist reforms like Obamacare.

The unified field theory of rebellion as envisioned by the Weather Underground saw support for the "liberation movements" in Vietnam, Africa and elsewhere as one way to ensure social chaos in the United States with the ultimate aim of upheaval and rebellion. In other words, war abroad was good because it ensured revolution at home.

As explained in the "Weatherman" manifesto, "The huge defense expenditures — required for the defense of the empire and at the same time a way of making increased profits for the defense industries — have gone hand in hand with the urban crisis around welfare, the hospitals, the schools, housing, air and water pollution. The state cannot provide the services it has been forced to assume responsibility for, and needs to increase taxes and to pay its growing debts while it cuts services and uses the pigs to suppress protest. The private sector of the economy can't provide jobs, particularly unskilled jobs. The expansion of the defense and education industries by the State since World War II is in part an attempt to pick up the slack, though the inability to provide decent wages and working conditions for 'public' jobs is more and more a problem."

That last paragraph is the perfect summation of where we are as a country, and since this series of articles began with the question, "How did we get here?" I think we have to answer that we got here because we got out-thunk by a handful of smart-aleck college students who went underground as fugitives and then went even deeper underground when they resurfaced 10 years later.

In essence, the revolutionaries who foresaw the collapse of the "empire" in 1969 patiently drilled down into the establishment that they so despised and then waited. Waited. Waited. Little by little their dream has been fulfilled. The state can no longer provide the services it has promised. The private sector can't provide jobs. The public sector, which picked up the slack, has overextended itself with jobs that can't be afforded, unemployment benefits that never end, health care that can't be paid for, and debts growing at an unsustainable pace.

"How did we get here?" You now know the answer.

RECIPE FOR DISASTER: AYERS, ALINSKY, CLOWARD & PIVEN

September 25, 2011

When last we left the revolutionary Bill Ayers, he was furiously scribbling the "Weatherman" manifesto in 1969 and learning how to build nail bombs while actively encouraging not just one, but "two, three, many Vietnams," in an effort to bring down the United States government.

It was obvious, after examining the words of "You Don't Need a Weatherman to Know Which Way the Wind Blows," that Ayers and his allies in the Orwellian-named Students for a Democratic Society (You know the routine: "war is peace," "freedom is slavery," "communism is democracy"!) were waging a two-front war of violence against America which they hoped would topple the government by over-extending its resources.

But the war of violence proved to be far too controversial for it to achieve its goals. Turned out the public was not as keen on nail bombs as Ayers and his fellow radicals were, and when it was revealed that the Weatherman splinter group of SDS had intended to blow up a dance hall on a military base, violence lost some of its allure. Nor was a public that was already tired of the Vietnam War likely to be enamored of the notion of the U.S. fighting multiple wars around the world. This strategy only worked if — like Ayers and SDS — you wanted to collapse the United States to begin with. Since most Americans during the Vietnam War era — including most of the protesters — actually loved their country, they weren't likely to fall for the SDS strategy of bringing about "world communism" by luring the U.S. into unwinnable, unpopular wars across the globe.

But fortunately for Ayers and Co., they actually had another element to their plot to bankrupt the U.S. government and bring about a social revolution — and this element proved to have much more staying power than the Vietnam War.

In their own words from the "Weatherman" manifesto, they explained that drawing the U.S. into multiple costly overseas wars would go "hand in hand" with a domestic strategy also intended to bankrupt the U.S. Treasury.

That strategy saw an opportunity to take advantage of what it called "the urban crisis around welfare, the hospitals, the schools, housing, air and water pollution."

These social services and social protections were a much easier sell to the American public than either bombs at home or wars abroad, but they had just as dangerous an impact on the viability of the American government. Thus, promoting more and more "entitlements" and insisting on more and more "social justice" was part of the same revolution that led inexorably to nail bombs and multiple Vietnams.

As envisioned by Ayers and his co-authors in 1969, once the public gets acclimated to being guaranteed a growing panoply of social services such as welfare, medical care and housing, "The state cannot provide the services it has been forced to assume responsibility for, and needs to increase taxes and to pay its growing debts while it cuts services..."

That — as Ayers was smart enough to see — would lead inevitably to social turmoil and financial disaster, and thus might precipitate the communist revolution that SDS hoped would topple the United States government.

We may still get to see if they were right — because that is exactly where we are today. One step ahead of us is Greece, but the growing number of entitlements in our federal budget has already made us an economic basket case, with no cure available except the unthinkable: massive cutbacks in spending that would lead to huge social unrest.

While it seems fantastic that this ragtag group of revolutionaries could have been so far-sighted as to have actually planned the tremendous growth in the welfare culture of the United States, and thus put us in this position, it is certainly not out of the question.

Indeed, by the time that the "Weatherman" manifesto was published in New Left Notes in June 1969, the basic strategy for bankrupting the U.S. as a means of forcing social revolution was already 3 years old. Nor was it the product of long-haired hippies, but rather the work of two serious academics whose call to action was published not in some obscure communist journal, but in a highly visible publication called The Nation, which has been in continuous publication since 1865.

In the May 2, 1966, issue of The Nation appeared an article entitled "The Weight of the Poor: A Strategy to End Poverty." Written by the husband and wife team of Frances Fox Piven and Richard Cloward, the article proposed a means to force income redistribution in the United States by means of creating a political crisis that would leave the government with no alternative other than surrendering to economic blackmail.

It seems that Cloward and Piven (as they are now generally referred to) recognized that American society's urge to take care of our poorest members could be used by an "organized" welfare class to leverage a "guaranteed annual income and thus an end to poverty."

That would happen by enrolling not fewer people in welfare programs, but more! It seems that the more people who are getting financial assistance from the government, the more power those people would have as a group. Cloward and Piven foresaw that a "massive drive to recruit the poor ONTO the welfare rolls" would challenge the resources of even a wealthy nation like the United States, leading to "a profound financial and political crisis."

This could only happen, Cloward and Piven declared, if "cadres of aggressive organizers would... come from the civil rights movement and the churches, from militant low-income organizations like those formed by the Industrial Areas Foundation (that is, by Saul Alinsky) and from other groups on the left."

It's certainly interesting that Cloward and Piven acknowledge the role of Saul Alinsky in their blueprint for revolution. Alinsky, after all, is the godfather of community organizing, Chicago style, and it was community organizing, not guns, that eventually won the revolution of the 1960s for the left. But the two strains of radicalism existed side-by-side for at least five years.

Cloward and Piven wrote their "Strategy to End Poverty" in 1966, and Cloward co-founded the National Welfare Rights Organization that same year to begin the work of turning welfare into a government obligation or a social "entitlement." Meanwhile, the "Weatherman" manifesto was published in June 1969 declaring that over-extending social services and military commitments was the key to overturning the U.S. government. That same year in August, Time magazine wrote that "Activists ... have focused on community organization projects, propagandizing and planning" how to "revolutionize society and plan future assaults on the established order."

In 1970, the SDS splinter group called Weatherman went underground and began a futile campaign of bombings, bank robberies and guerrilla tactics that became increasingly irrelevant. This turned out to be a near disastrous detour for the radicals, and would have been the end of communism in America were it not for cooler heads that prevailed. In 1971, Alinsky wrote his seminal book "Rules for Radicals" in which he tutored radicals that in order to achieve their revolutionary goals they needed to "work inside the system" and act more like neighbors than activists. This was the turning point.

It took Bill Ayers and his wife Bernardine Dohrn another decade to recognize that Alinsky was right and they were wrong, but eventually, in 1980, they emerged from the underground, put on suits and skirts, attended graduate school and law school, and promptly went to work "inside the system" to gnaw away like termites at the system they had declared war against years before. With their new tactics — and new allies — they would eventually prevail, or come close to it, as America tilted precipitously toward democratic socialism and the welfare state.

WHY CARE ABOUT AYERS?

October 2, 2011

Some people say that writing a series of columns about 1960s revolutionaries is a waste of time. They say that radicals like Bill Ayers weren't that popular to begin with and are completely irrelevant by now.

On the first point, I certainly agree. There's no reason to think that Ayers had popular support for his revolution back in 1969 when he was preaching the triumph of "world communism" from his SDS pulpit. He was and is out of the mainstream, with little likelihood to convince people to support him and his desire to overthrow the U.S. government.

But when you say he is irrelevant, that's where I draw the line. How can he be irrelevant when the revolution he sought so earnestly has come about?

If Ayers is irrelevant, then so is Barack Obama. If Ayers is irrelevant, then so is Hillary Clinton. If Ayers is irrelevant, then so are dozens of top-level players and consultants in and out of the Obama administration such as Cass Sunstein, Anita Dunn, Valerie Jarrett, Carol Browner and Ron Bloom. All of those people — Obama, Clinton and the rest — have ties to radical organizations either dating to the 1960s such as SDS or Saul Alinsky's Industrial Areas Foundation or to later socialist organizations that shared the goal of dismantling American society and rebuilding it as a socialist state. You merely need to read their own words to see that none of this is secret. The evidence is all over the Internet. Their hatred for "bourgeois" America is transparent, visceral and unmistakable.

Indeed, the whole point of quoting extensively from Ayers' own writings for the past several weeks has been to establish the remarkable parallels between the revolution he and his contemporaries envisioned and what has actually taken place. Their stated goal as members of Students for a Democratic Society, and later the Weather Underground, was "the destruction of U.S. imperialism" and ultimately the imposition of a new socialist state that would dictate the "control and ... use of the wealth of the Empire for the people of the whole world."

You would have to be severely lacking a sense of irony not to appreciate the fact that while America has not yet fully committed to its newfound role as leader of the socialist world, we have nonetheless embraced liberating Libya and other Third World countries from their imperialist oppressors, using our "ill-gotten" wealth to bail out Europe not to mention Africa and Asia — and of course creating a welfare state that provides housing and health care for all, and even tuition breaks for illegal aliens!

Indeed, with everything going so far left so fast, one has to imagine that the unrepentant revolutionary Bill Ayers could finally echo the words of Michelle Obama just a few years ago when she said: "For the first time in my adult lifetime, I'm really proud of my country."

I guess it's no accident that the Obamas should come up in a column about Bill Ayers and his wife Bernardine Dohrn. After all, they seem to share some of the same hopes and aspirations.

Forget about the actual personal and political connections between Obama and Ayers. Forget about the meeting in 1995 at Ayers' home in Chicago where Obama launched his political career. Forget about Obama's role as president and board member of the Chicago Annenberg Challenge non-profit that was started in 1995 by Ayers to promote education "reform." Forget about the fact that they served together for three years on the board of the Woods Fund of Chicago, an anti-poverty foundation that promoted welfare "reform" and redistribution of wealth. Forget about the fact that, in "The Manchurian Candidate," author Aaron Klein documents that Obama and Ayers worked together as early as 1988 when Obama was invited to join the Alliance for Better Chicago Schools that was created by Ayers' wealthy industrialist father, Thomas Ayers.

Forget about all that, if you can. Because it's irrelevant whether they actually conspired together. What matters is not how they worked together, but how they have long shared a common dream and were part of the same network for social justice in Chicago — from the 1980s until at least 2002 — whose goal was to "fundamentally transform" America.

Nor do you have to go back to the dark ages of the 1980s to find evidence that President Obama has a common agenda with communist Bill Ayers and socialist Saul Alinsky. You just need to read his speech last week in Denver, where he justified raising taxes on the wealthy to pay for programs for the poor. He said "we're not doing this to punish success," but "those of us who have done well should pay our fair share" to keep the nation strong. In other words, taxing the rich is a patriotic duty in order to accomplish Obama's goal of redistribution of wealth.

You shouldn't be surprised. President Obama said much the same thing when he was still a candidate in 2008 talking to Joe the Plumber on the campaign trail:

"It's not that I want to punish your success. I just want to make sure that everybody who is behind you, that they've got a chance at success, too... My attitude is that if the economy's good for folks from the bottom up, it's gonna be good for everybody. If you've got a plumbing business, you're gonna be better off ... if you've got a whole bunch of customers who can afford to hire you, and right now everybody's so pinched that business is bad for everybody and I think when you spread the wealth around, it's good for everybody."

That "spreading the wealth around" thing — I may be mistaken, but I think it's the same as what Bill Ayers called the "control and ... use of the wealth of the Empire for the people of the whole world." Another word for that, by the way, is socialism, which is why it is pointless to criticize me or anyone else for suggesting that President Obama is a socialist.

It's funny how words have a way of pinning people down. Can't really get away from them once you have uttered them. That goes for Texas Gov. Rick Perry and his ridiculous comment that people who are against giving benefits to illegal immigrants are "heartless" just as much as it does to Obama for wanting to "spread the wealth around."

It is also a beautiful, lovely coincidence that just as I was preparing to write this column, another liberal Democrat — this one running for Congress in Massachusetts — used virtually the same rhetoric as Barack Obama to characterize her desire to take from the rich and give to the poor.

Elizabeth Warren is a Harvard law professor who worked for President Obama not too long ago trying to protect us poor little consumers from those evil millionaires on Wall Street we keep hearing about. Now she is trying to unseat Scott Brown and take back "the Kennedy seat" for liberals.

On Sept. 21, she was talking to a house full of supporters and said this:

"There is nobody in this country who got rich on his own. Nobody. You built a factory out there — good for you. But I want to be clear. You moved your goods to market on the roads the rest of us paid for. You hired workers the rest of us paid to educate. You were safe in your factory because of police forces and fire forces that the rest of us paid for. You don't have to worry that marauding bands would come and seize everything at your factory and hire someone to protect against this because of the work the rest of us did.

"Now look. You built a factory and turned into something terrific or a great idea — God bless! Keep a big hunk of it. But part of the underlying social contract is you take a hunk of that and pay forward for the next kid who comes along."

I bet you didn't know that was the social contract you had signed on to when you were born in the United States of America, did you? But Bill Ayers knew it, and so did Barack Obama. It's all the same theory of "social justice."

I doubt that Elizabeth Warren has ever worked with Bill Ayers (like President Obama did) or studied with Saul Alinsky (like Hillary Clinton did) but she is nonetheless a product of 1960s radicalism and one more proof that Ayers and Co. may have lost a skirmish or two, but they won the revolution.

And yet the magical mystery media manages to make the whole mess disappear just as quick as you can say Jeremiah Wright. Nothing to see here. Move along!

ARE THE CONDITIONS READY FOR REVOLUTION?

October 9, 2011

So at last we have come full circle. The revolution that started on the streets four decades ago, then went underground, has returned to the streets once again.

You've probably become aware of the "Occupy Wall Street" movement that has spawned spin-offs in Los Angeles, Philadelphia, D.C. and supposedly a thousand other cities including Missoula, Montana.

What you probably didn't know is that it was exactly 42 years ago this weekend when the Weatherman revolutionary organization took to the streets of Chicago to "bring the war home" — namely the war of communist-inspired "workers" against the oppressor imperialists.

The protests — called "Days of Rage" — were intended to use opposition to the Vietnam War to galvanize a true communist revolution in the streets. It was supposed to be the culmination of a resolution that came out of a National Council meeting of Students for Democratic Society the year before that demanded direct action to bring down the system.

Indeed, the resolution was titled enthusiastically (if sophomorically) "The Elections Don't Mean Sh-t — Vote Where the Power Is — Our Power Is In The Street."

But it turned out that the power of the Weathermen was not in the street. The Days of Rage protest was a dismal failure, resulting in a change in strategy for the next 10 years that led Bill Ayers and his fellow Weathermen to throw bombs from the shadows instead of leading protests in the streets. Then in the early 1980s, when Ayers, Bernardine Dohrn, Mark Rudd and other Weather Underground fugitives came up for air, a new strategy emerged that would put 1960s radicals into suits and skirts and "mainstream" them into positions of power and influence where they could "create the conditions for the development of a successful revolutionary movement and party," as they wrote in their 1974 manifesto "Prairie Fire."

Anyone who doesn't think they were earnest about their vow to make a lifetime of war against the "imperial U.S." simply hasn't been paying attention. These people were not playing games when they took to the street or started throwing bombs, and they are not playing games today. They are deadly serious.

You can certainly read many recent writings and utterances by any of the Weather Underground radicals to see that they remain committed to revolution, but it is their appearances in 1969 that provide the blueprint to their lifelong goal of revolution and exactly what it would entail should they ever gain power.

According to Lucinda Franks and Thomas Powers, writing for UPI in 1970, when Bill Ayers attended a protest organization meeting in November 1969 in Washington, D.C., he was asked what the Weatherman program was.

"Kill all the rich people," Ayers answered. "Break up their cars and apartments."

"But aren't your parents rich?" he was asked.

"Yeah," Ayers said. "Bring the revolution home, kill your parents, that's where it's really at."

Nor were they just talking in the abstract about the pleasure of killing rich people. Indeed, Bernardine Dohrn — who is now Bill Ayers' wife — is quoted in the same article by Franks and Powers as exulting in the deaths of Sharon Tate and her Hollywood friends who were victims of the brutal Manson Family murders of 1969.

"Dig it!" Dohrn is quoted as telling 400 people who had gathered in Flint, Mich., in December 1969 for a "war council": "First they killed those pigs, then they ate dinner in the same room with them, then they even shoved a fork into a victim's stomach! Wild!"

It is such rhetoric, such a gleeful account of symbolic cannibalism by the poor against the rich, that makes it hard to swallow the nonsense spouted last week at the Wall Street protest by none other than Frances Fox Piven, the co-author of the 1960s strategy to destroy the federal government by bankrupting it through entitlement programs.

Piven enthusiastically assured the crowd of mindless drones who had occupied Wall Street because they had nothing better to do (like go to a job) that the nation's financiers and bankers are not just greedy and thieves, "but they are also cannibals... because they are eating their own — US!"

That kind of rhetoric is typical of what is being heard across the country, including from the president and Democratic leaders, about the business community on Wall Street and elsewhere. It is impossible not to interpret the vitriolic attacks on capitalism as the latest phase of the same Marxist propaganda that created 70 years of slavery in Russia, killed 60 million people in China and turned North Korea into a basketcase. But that doesn't mean the gullible among us won't be lapping up the rhetoric with the same intensity that a dog goes after its own vomit.

But forget emotion; let's just look at the facts.

This latest plan to occupy "enemy territory" started quietly on Sept. 17 in New York. An agitprop poster featuring a variation of the old Soviet hammer and sickle and the red star of communism shouted that, "Wall St. belongs to us," and proclaimed, "Let the U.S. Days of Rage begin."

That latter slogan was a reference not to Bill Ayers and SDS (who are supposedly irrelevant these days) but to those so-called "Day of Rage" protests in the Mideast, which have brought down three governments so far.

The goal of the protesters in the "Occupy Wall Street" movement (or at least their unacknowledged leaders) is no different than what it was in Cairo or Tripoli. Indeed, Wade Rathke called the Occupy Wall Street movement an "anti-banking jihad," using the rhetoric of Islamic holy war to warn bankers that violence was coming. No surprise, Rathke, the founder of ACORN "community organizers" got his start as a foot soldier in Students for a Democratic Society, the precursor of the Weather Underground.

Rathke, Piven and the rest of the "generals" of this jihad want nothing less than the collapse of the American government and economy, and though they might not put President Obama in a cage the way Egypt did with President Hosni Mubarak, they would certainly do much worse to President George W. Bush should they ever get their hands on him.

This protest that started on Sept. 17 was not unanticipated. It has been contrived by labor leaders such as Steven Lerner of SEIU (the Service Employees International Union), who said as long ago as March that he was planning to disrupt Wall Street in order to "destabilize the folks that are in power," "put banks on the edge of insolvency," and "cause a new financial crisis."

It is also supported by people such as Van Jones, the former green jobs czar in the Obama administration, who "coincidentally" was holding a conference in Washington last week that had the misleading name of "Take Back the American Dream." The real emphasis wasn't on the American Dream at all, but on "taking" wealth — not taking it BACK, mind you, but taking it AWAY — from those who had earned it. And that's the same emphasis you find it Occupy Wall Street.

It's no wonder, therefore, that Jones told MSNBC's Lawrence O'Donnell (himself a declared socialist): "You are going to see an American Fall, an American Autumn, just like we saw the Arab Spring. You can see it right now with these young people on Wall Street. Hold onto your hats, we're going to have an October offensive to take back the American dream and to rescue America's middle class."

Maybe so. I mean the communists and socialists definitely need to get the middle class on their side or the whole movement will fail, so now it is just a question of how smart we in the middle class are. Are we paying attention? Do we understand the difference between "hope" and "change" yet? Or can we still be played for suckers?

ARE YOU REALLY FOR REVOLUTION?

October 17, 2011

"This is WHAT democracy looks like," chanted about 1,000 protesters as they plotted their Occupy Philadelphia strategy a couple of weeks ago.

Not sure if they meant the mindless chanting, the threats of violence and intimidation, or the raucous anarchy of the street, but in any case, they are correct. This IS what democracy looks like, whether it is the democracy of the Occupy Wall Street movement, the democracy of Cairo during the Arab Spring, the democracy of the Bolshevik revolution in 1917 or the democracy of 1789 during the French Revolution.

For those who are history challenged, let's look beyond the slogans of these "democratic movements" and see what the result of such "popular" uprisings has been.

Since former comedian and now social activist Roseanne Barr has been promoting her faux presidential campaign recently by suggesting that bankers and other wealthy bastards should be beheaded, we should probably begin our historical

survey with the granddaddy of all democracy movements — the
French Revolution — which delivered the people's judgment at
the end of the sharp blade of a guillotine.

Supposedly inspired by the American Revolution, the
French Revolution of 1789 led directly to the Reign of Terror of
1793-94 during which as many as 40,000 people were killed.
Reflecting the Orwellian nature of language during
revolutionary periods, these murders of French citizens were
accomplished by the deceptively named Committee of Public
Safety.

Speaking of the power of words to lull you to your death,
there can be few examples more misleading than the slogan of
the French Revolution. The failure of Robespierre and his fellow
Jacobins to deliver either "liberty, equality or brotherhood" —
as promised — should be all the proof you need that slogans
can't be trusted to protect human rights. What slogans do
achieve is mobilizing the people on the street into a political
force, and then manipulating that political force into a tool that
can be used to agitate for social change. But the change that
comes is never liberty; it is never equality; and it is certainly
never brotherhood. Instead it is rage.

You can see the face of that rage on the streets in America
now. The Occupy Wall Street movement is supposed to be
about economic "justice" and fairness for the little guy.
Unfortunately, it doesn't really have anything to do with justice
— it is just another case of the "have nots" taking what they
"have not" earned from those who have.

The "justice" of that process is accomplished, by the way,
not through courts or laws, but through brute force. Perhaps
Ron Bloom — the Obama administration's manufacturing czar
— was thinking of street justice for Wall Street in 2009 when he
said, "We know that the free market is nonsense. We know that
the whole point is to game the system... [and] we kind of agree
with Mao that political power comes largely from the barrel of a
gun."

Guns are sometimes needed in revolutions, and sometimes
not, but in either case, the revolution usually starts with
slogans, followed by protests, and then may or may not advance

to the gun stage depending on how much fear the protests can create through the power of intimidation.

The Russian Revolution (which coincidentally was another October Revolution) started out with slogans and protests, too, just like "Occupy Wall Street." Of course, life in 1917 Petrograd was a lot harder and a lot more desperate than it is today in Philadelphia or New York — but the ruffians on the streets don't care about that because they don't study history. If they did, they might be more apt to follow the Russian example and overthrow Obama's czars who have imposed absurd and unwieldy regulations on banking and business instead of trying to destroy the capitalists who actually have the capacity to create wealth — and jobs.

But the protesters don't know anything they didn't learn on Twitter. Revolutionary slogans fit nicely into the 140-character format of Twitter, and with the Internet they can spread just like the "prairie fire" that both Mao and 1960s revolutionary Bill Ayers used as their metaphor for grass-roots revolution.

But is there really anything "grass roots" about what is happening on Wall Street or in other urban areas across the country where thousands of protesters are gathering for their own version of the Greek riots? Heck no. Not unless you think "flash mobs" are really spontaneous outbreaks of crime and violence. They are not. They are the result of planning and networking. Social media and the Internet have made it possible for revolution to spread like "prairie fire" across the urban landscape, but that doesn't mean there aren't people and groups wielding matches who are directing the mob.

Which brings us to Egypt, Tunisia and Libya in 2011. The Arab Spring is more accurately called "Days of Rage" because its purpose was to channel anger into a weapon. Another word for this is rioting, and in case you wondered, yes rioting IS what democracy looks like.

That's because democracy or "rule of the people" is not only heir to the flaw of "tyranny of the majority," but also — and less frequently noted — "tyranny of the loud minority." Democracy is about scaring other people off the street. One way to do that is to "occupy" the street with smelly, loud violent people who are willing to call other people names, shout them down and if necessary throw a punch at them or even behead them. That's why our Founding Fathers rejected democracy, and instead instituted a constitutional republic where minorities are protected by the rule of law.

That's also why it was always dangerous for Americans to wholeheartedly endorse the street movements in Cairo and Tunisia. Yes, we support the rights of people to govern themselves, but we need to recognize the extraordinary difference between the rule of the people through law and the rule of the mob through force.

The rule of law is the last thing that "democratic" movements are interested in; they want change, and they want it now. Ayers and his gang of radicals tried to use violent street protests in 1968 and 1969 to disrupt the rule of law in Chicago, and there is no reason to think the same tactic won't be tried again in 2011 or 2012.

Listen for instance to the rhetoric of an unidentified Occupy L.A. speaker who discounts suggestions that "nonviolence" can bring about change.

"No, my friend. I'll give you two examples: French Revolution, and Indian so-called Revolution. Gandhi, Gandhi today is, with respect to all of you, Gandhi today is a tumor that the ruling class is using constantly to mislead us. French Revolution made fundamental transformation. But it was bloody. India, the result of Gandhi, is 600 million people living in maximum poverty. So, ultimately, the bourgeoisie won't go without violent means. Revolution! Yes, revolution that is led by the working class. Long live revolution! Long live socialism!"

At this point in the speech, the crowd breaks out into cheers. It is those cheers which should scare you, along with the fact that the national media and Nancy Pelosi are among those cheering.

Here's the bottom line: Anyone who supports the America of the Founding Fathers and Martin Luther King cannot with good conscience also support a movement that advocates the violent overthrow of capitalism. If you cannot worship both God and Mammon, by the same token you cannot overthrow capitalism and leave liberty standing.

Yet there are literally hundreds of examples on the Internet of protesters in the Occupy Wall Street movement confirming that they are socialists and that they are violent. Anyone who supports them and is not also a socialist or pro-violence has lost the right to be taken seriously.

ONE PERCENT LOGIC; 99 PERCENT BULL

October 23, 2011

The Occupy Wall Street movement has been aptly described as "Anarchists for Totalitarianism."

Given the logical inconsistency of such a movement, the OWS folks have to be glad there is no official theme song yet; otherwise, the repetitive mindless chants emanating from Zuccotti Park would all have to end with "If I only had a BRAIN!"

Think of the level of education that has to exist for grown men and women who believe the government is controlled by oligarchical conspirators intent on enriching themselves to then put at the top of their demands a more powerful government that will control banks, dictate profits, regulate income and ensure prosperity for all!

It is unlikely that any of the street protesters would recognize the dysfunctional Orwellian logic of "Anarchists for Totalitarianism." Indeed, they seem to have begun their movement by building on the boneheaded rhetoric of Karl Marx, who declared that "property is theft."

From there, it is but a short circuit to the electrifying notion that rich people are BAD! And VERY RICH people are VERY BAD! Which, from what I can tell, about sums up the Occupy Wall Street movement.

Indeed, although the Wall Street haters have studiously avoided making any coherent demands (perhaps they are simply incapable of being coherent?), it would seem that their movement can be encapsulated by the catchphrase, "We are the 99 percent."

This ubiquitous slogan, which paints Occupy Wall Street as a reasonable, mainstream movement, exposes it at the same time as the dangerous aberration it really is.

The "99 percent" theme is dressed up in a number of variations, but it always comes down to pitting this overwhelming majority of 99 percent against the lowly 1 percent minority, who — we are told repeatedly — are responsible for all the treacherous villainy on earth. Even when it appears that violence or evil has been done by the 99 percent, turns out that the devilish 1 percent "made them do it," to paraphrase Flip Wilson.

But really what we have here when you come right down to it is something called "scapegoating." It is the MANY blaming the FEW for all their troubles, and is no different than the traditional anti-Semitism that has seen Jews blamed for all the problems of the much more plentiful Christians, Germans, Moslems and other groups whom they live amongst. Why? Well because the Germans are the 99 percent, which means that if anything goes wrong, they get to blame the Jews, er, oops, I mean the 1 percent.

Nor, sadly, is this just a metaphor. If you actually care to know the facts instead of just siding with Occupy Wall Street because it "feels right," you can Google "anti-Semitism in Occupy Wall Street" to find lots of examples of demonstrators blasting Jews or "Zionists" for their own troubles. A few that have gotten national attention:

— "I think that the Zionist Jews who are running these big banks and our Federal Reserve, which is not run by the federal government, I think they need to be run out of this country." This was announced in a TV interview by a woman who was a substitute teacher in Los Angeles. She was subsequently fired, although several other teachers who have made similar comments remain on the payroll.

— "You're a bum, Jew." This caustic comment was spoken ironically by someone who was camped out on the street with no apparent means of support!

— A black protester claimed, "The smallest group in America controls the money, media and all other things. The fingerprints belong to the Jewish bankers. I am against Jews who rob America. They are 1 percent who control America."

So, yeah, the slogan "We are the 99 percent" may make you feel good, but it doesn't feel very good for the 1 percent, and in a country that has made an art out of teaching our children not to be bullies, it's almost funny that we apparently feel OK about kicking that miserable, miserly 1 percent until they turn over all their money.

Yep, that 1 percent must be pretty bad, so let's go directly to the source, and find out why. Here is the straight scoop from the "We Are the 99 Percent" website:

"We are the 99 percent. We are getting kicked out of our homes. We are forced to choose between groceries and rent. We are denied quality medical care. We are suffering from environmental pollution. We are working long hours for little pay and no rights, if we're working at all. We are getting nothing while the other 1 percent is getting everything. We are the 99 percent."

WOW. That's pretty horrible, isn't it!

Except of course, it isn't true. How many people do you know that have been kicked out of their homes? Some certainly, but 99 out of a hundred? Absurd! And those who DID lose their homes had the misfortune of not being able to PAY for their homes! That's not UN-fair, but rather the natural conclusion of failing to live up to your obligations.

And the rest? Do you really think 99 percent of Americans can't pay for their groceries? And among those who ARE indeed too poor to buy groceries, aren't most of them getting Food Stamps? Denied medical care? Just go to any emergency room in the country and demand it! You'll get it, and it will be free because America's taxpayers (the 53 percent) have a hard time saying no to the tax freeloaders (the 47 percent), but that is another story.

If you want to know the truth, it turns out that the so-called "99 percent" is really the 1 percent — namely the loud-mouthed, whiny 1 percent trying to blackmail, steal or expropriate the wealth of the rich 1 percent by boldly and falsely claiming they represent the untapped power of the nation's 98 percent who are staying home minding their own business.

ANARCHY AND EXPERIENCE: CAN PEOPLE STILL LEARN FROM THEIR MISTAKES?

October 30, 2011

Anarchy is a great place to visit, but I wouldn't want to live there.

Hopefully, the thousands of Americans toying with anarchy in the current Occupy Wall Street movement will eventually grow to feel the same.

I understand that there is an appeal to not being answerable to any authority — at least until you want to know who's going to take care of it when you are robbed, raped or assaulted by those lawless bums who don't share your same high principles.

At that point, order is much preferable to chaos. Yet we might agree that lawlessness IS in some ways the pristine blank slate on which all of mankind's eventual accomplishment's have been written. At some point in every society we throw everything out and start over, and that essentially is a point of anarchy.

But from there, things can go in either one of two ways. Because lawlessness is essentially a vacuum, it is most likely that power will fill that vacuum in the most direct way possible — through brute force. We just watched that on a tiny scale with the death of Gadhafi in Libya, but we have also seen it on a much larger scale repeatedly in history through the example of opportunistic tyrants such as Napoleon and Hitler.

On the other hand, every once in a while, anarchy (or something close to it) can be replaced with a new order — a new social contract — but that requires "enlightened self-interest," a state of mind so unlikely to prevail in anarchic conditions that instances of it are mostly the stuff of fiction such as Edward

Bellamy's "Looking Backward" — or even science fiction — such as Robert Heinlein's "The Moon Is a Harsh Mistress."

There is one prime example in history, however, of enlightened self-interest that shows mankind to be capable of learning from a failed social experiment without pivoting into tyranny first.

I am talking about the U.S. Constitution, and the decision by our forefathers to hold a constitutional convention to improve their common lot rather than giving in to the more banal self-interest that leads to civil war and tyranny.

The constitutional convention of 1787 was essentially an acknowledgment that the laws and systems in place following the successful American Revolution were not working, and needed to be tossed. In essence, the Articles of Confederation codified a kind of lawlessness or anarchy. With no strong central power, the states were under no particular compulsion to act civilly to each other, nor without a strong central government could much of anything get done. The Articles didn't even establish a real nation per se, but only a "firm league of friendship."

No wonder that only a decade later, in 1787, the citizens of the United States — also known as "We the People" — began the Constitution with the proclamation that they intended "to form a more perfect Union."

It would not be hard to make a more perfect union than the mess that existed under the Articles of Confederation, but yet we have to assume that the folks who gave us the Articles had done so with the best of intentions.

So what had changed?

Well, here — for the sake of brevity — we need to adopt a philosophical point of view, rather than a historical one. Let us say that what had changed is that our Founding Fathers had gotten an education — courtesy of hard knocks and experience.

That, as much as anything, is what makes those early Americans worthy of so much respect. Unlike politicians today, they did not dig in their heels and defend the status quo simply because they had voted for the status quo 10 years earlier. The status quo sucked, and by admitting it, they took bold action to change things and make a better world.

Which brings us to Occupy Wall Street.

On one hand, the protesters and demonstrators envision themselves as the equivalent of our forefathers because they recognize that "the status quo sucks." It would be hard to find anyone who didn't agree with the occupier's complaints about federal bailouts of big banks and corporate greed.

But where Occupy Wall Street falls down is that it doesn't have a plan to create "a more perfect union" when the current system collapses. Instead, it has "high hopes" and an earnest desire to improve life for all mankind.

No doubt that the French Revolution had "high hopes" too before it collapsed into mass murder. No doubt the Russian Revolution had high hopes before it descended into the madness that led to the deaths of millions. Even Mao's Chinese Revolution in 1949 had high hopes. Probably very few people could have predicted the deaths of up to 40 million people in the next 25 years from purges and "re-education" under Mao's leadership.

It's easy NOT to imagine such a bloody conclusion to any revolutionary movement in America — because we are "different" — but the very things which make us different, which shield us from the insanity of mass murder and civil war — are the things which Occupy Wall Street wants to tear down. The freedom to be different. The freedom to achieve success without feeling guilty. Most importantly, the freedom to fail.

If you support Occupy Wall Street and don't support the collapse of the government and capitalism, then please re-evaluate now. The thing that our forefathers had going for them was the ability to learn from their mistakes. The only hope we have today is the ability to do so, too — and quickly.

I do see one glimmer of hope in the prairie fire revolution that has been lit across the American landscape today. It seems like many of our fellow citizens are learning the lesson that our great-grandparents knew by heart — life is not fair, but that doesn't mean you have to give up.

In story after story, I have read about how communistic high hopes have had to bend to reality the tent city now known as Occupy Wall Street.

Some protesters tried to get the organizers of Occupy Wall Street to "share the wealth" from their $500,000 bank roll, but the organizers held tight to the money they had collected. They were now the 1 percent, and they saw that the money would just be wasted if it were divvied up among the protesters instead of put to a higher and better use.

More recently, the kitchen staff of Occupy Wall Street went on strike because they were angry about working 18-hour days to feed ungrateful "professional homeless people" and ex-cons who were being lured to Zuccotti Park by the promise of free food. A security volunteer said the cooks felt "overworked and underappreciated."

Imagine that! Maybe those cooks will be joining the Tea Party movement next, which already has figured out that giving money to people who haven't earned it creates a sense of entitlement that will rapidly drain life and spirit out of a nation.

If we are looking for common ground, that is a better place to start than anarchy.

WALTER VROOMAN, ECONOMIC EQUALITY, OCCUPATION WALL STREET AND OTHER LOST CAUSES

November 5, 2011

As we watch the swirling turbulence of social upheaval that is known as Occupy Wall Street, there is a temptation to credit it with good intentions (change for the better) and then to wish for its success (hope against hope).

Such movements of hope and change have arisen repeatedly in modern history. The change is always temporary. The hope is always illusory. Yet we as a society remain as gullible as ever — serial offenders who fall victim time and time again to the con game of economic equality because who, after all, could be against equality?

Well, that's pretty simple really.

Anyone who is in favor of fairness has to be against equality. You should watch New York University law professor Richard Epstein explaining "The Good Side of Economic Inequality" to a mostly stunned PBS reporter to get schooled in why inequality actually is the spur which encourages economic growth. Or check out broker-investor Peter Schiff as he challenges Occupy Wall Street protesters to tell him how much of his money they want the government to take away from him.

This really should be Economics 101 to an educated nation, but the problem is we aren't an educated nation — not really. Instead of No Child Left Behind, our national education slogan should be No Liberal Shibboleth Left Behind. The problem with teaching economics in high school is that we would run the very high risk of having our children turned against capitalism by teachers who prefer socialism. That already happens now, of course, but not overtly.

But let's face it, this is nothing new. The United States has been facing a steady stream of economic reformers, educators and socialists seeking to dismantle capitalism for at least a hundred years. One man who embodied all three of those components — reformer, educator and socialist — was Walter Vrooman, a name of absolutely no import today, but who might be deemed the patron saint of lost causes even more so than St. Jude. Indeed, Vrooman presided over one lost cause after another till he died a broken man who had even stolen from his own wife to pay for his socialist schemes.

As he lay on his deathbed at the age of 35 in 1904, here is how the Fort Wayne Morning Journal-Gazette described him:

"Vrooman crowded into 20 years more socialistic activity than any other man in this country, and in the furtherance of his schemes, all of which failed, he has expended sums estimated to amount to millions. This included part of his wife's fortune."

The Joplin [Mo.] Daily Globe wrote about the dying Vrooman that he had spent $10 million in socialistic schemes, and that, "This vast sum has been drawn from the pockets of more or less intelligent persons by a remarkable linguistic ability."

I suppose that "linguistic ability," which the paper also labeled "his plausible tongue," could convince even the canny that he wasn't as bad as he seemed. Maybe that's why the Daily Globe ended its story rather generously by noting, "It has never been charged that Vrooman was dishonest — he was merely impractical."

That summation may very well be applied not just to Vrooman, but the entire history of socialistic enterprises. Has a well-intended solution to mankind's eternal problems ever been less practical than socialism — a philosophy which accounts for every eventuality except human nature? And yet hundreds, thousands, millions are enticed to "fall for it" out of an honest, misplaced desire to "do good."

Poor, earnest Walter Vrooman was dogged in his efforts to bring economic equality to the world, and thus was a fitting progenitor of the Occupy Wall Street movement that proposes such grand schemes as a guaranteed income without the need to work for it, a cap on income (without any explanation why people will work as hard when they don't get paid for it) and a free education (as if they really wanted one — see above!)

The socialistic rhetoric which Vrooman employed 100-plus years ago is almost indistinguishable from that which is heard today among those who want something for nothing. Listen, for instance, to this speech from 1887 as reported in the Boston Daily Globe. It was titled, "Why are the Toilers Poor and the Idlers Rich?"

Vrooman told his audience of 4,000 on the Boston Commons, "The workers build great houses and palaces that the idlers live in, while they must be content with a cheap shanty or a crowded tenement... We cannot have the benefit of the wealth we have created; we know it is by some trick we are kept out of it, and the object of this meeting is to find out how it is done. The wealth of the world is robbed from the producers, and wasted and squandered by idlers."

Or — as we have it today — the 99 percent are doing all the work, and the 1 percent are just unfairly appropriating that which does not belong to them.

Except, fortunately, we have the very instructive historic example of just what happens when wealth winds up in the hands of a socialist do-gooder like Mr. Vrooman. Time after time, Vrooman convinced wealthy people to help out the 99 percent by investing or lending or giving away their money to further one of Vrooman's schemes. And time after time, Vrooman left town with nothing to show for his dream of economic equality except an opportunity to learn from his mistakes. Alas, he never took advantage of that opportunity.

There is certainly a lot for the rest of us to learn though — starting with the fact that socialism doesn't work, and never has. Nor does it ever seem to stray far from the impulse to violence and intimidation.

The Boston Globe, writing about Vrooman shortly before his death, noted that "Mr. Vrooman first came into prominence when the Chicago anarchists threw the bomb in Haymarket Square [in 1886]. He was then a poorly clad youth, and gained public notice by protesting against the convictions of Spies, Parsons, Lingg and others. Vrooman was arrested several times for incendiary speeches in Kansas City, Mo., and St. Joseph."

Interestingly, the Haymarket affair is a nexus of various socialist and revolutionary movements in America. The protest where the bomb was thrown at the Chicago police occurred on May 4, 1886, and later inspired the May Day protests which continue to this day under the banner of socialism and communism. Eight police officers died in the violence that ensued after the bomb exploded, and ultimately four of the anarchists who were at the protest were convicted and executed for inciting the violence even though none of them had thrown the bomb.

Vrooman was just 17 at the time of the Haymarket riots, and was 18 a year later when he spoke in New York in September 1887 at a rally organized to protest the death sentences for the anarchists.

"These men who have seen so much misery and such outrages may have been hasty and made mistakes, but their only crime was free speech... It is a conspiracy of the ruling classes to put down the laboring classes. They are going to hang seven representatives of labor in Chicago," The World newspaper quoted Vrooman as telling a crowd of "fellow wage slaves."

The outrage Vrooman expressed is not unlike that which was heard last week when police fired non-lethal rounds at an Occupy Oakland crowd to disperse them after they refused to leave a park when ordered to do so. When one of the protesters was seriously injured, the cry of police brutality went up, as it always does from those who provoke the police by breaking the law.

Vrooman's words could have been uttered in regard to either event, and as intended they still have the effect of bringing sympathy on those who broke the law. Yet the "99 percent" does not have a free pass to do whatever they will. They must be held accountable lest we fall from the freedom of a lawful society to the bondage of lawlessness.

Which reminds me: It was Bill Ayers and the Weathermen revolutionary socialists who blew up the statue of a Chicago policeman in Haymarket Square in 1969 just before the "Days of Rage" protests. Yep, that Bill Ayers. The tentacles of socialism are long and deadly, and if you follow the clues from 1969 to 2011, you don't need a Weatherman to know which way the wind blows.

Vrooman, Ayers, the Weathermen, Occupy Wall Street and the anarchists in Haymarket Square all have one thing in common. They want to impose economic equality on a world that uses inequality as the fuel that drives us to success. Inequality, not bailouts and handouts, is what provides us the opportunity for growth. In a world where everything is equal, or where everything is easy, there is no reason to achieve anything. Imagine no incentives. It's easy if you try.

Occupy Wall Street is the ultimate lost cause — not because it cannot win, but because if it does, we are all lost.

DON'T BE AFRAID TO SAY IT: 'WE ARE THE 1 PERCENT'

November 20, 2011

It is time to stand up and be counted.

I am the 1 percent.

Let's be plain about this. Though I have a good job and a good paycheck, I have virtually no wealth, no savings and no need for tax shelters. I have substantial debt. My family owns three vehicles, the newest of which is a 1999 Ford Windstar worth about $2,000. That's our "good" car. If it breaks down, we would have to go further into debt to fix it or replace it. I cannot afford to put my three children — the oldest of whom is in high school, the youngest in diapers — through college. We vacation 20 miles away in Whitefish because we can't afford airfare or gas for a long trip. We live in a hundred-year-old house without central heating and we are happy to have it. Sometimes we do look with envy at our neighbors' houses that have modern plumbing and electric systems that don't short out when you run the pancake griddle and the space heater at the same time, and sometimes we do wonder why we can't own a brand-new SUV like so many other families do. But envy is cheap; SUVs are not.

So what we do is get by. We are fortunate that I make enough money to support a family of five with food, clothes and a roof over our heads. That's for now, but I'm 56 years old. In six years when my middle child graduates high school, I will be eligible to collect Social Security, but I won't be qualified to retire — not with the paltry sum that I've been able to set aside in my 401(k). If I am lucky, I'll still be working here at the newspaper. But if not, they say that Wal-Mart likes to hire the elderly. My wife, who attended school in China and speaks Mandarin as her primary language, intends to enter the work force by then to support me and our youngest child, but even if that is possible, it's unlikely we would ever have a chance to raise our standard of living substantially.

Times are tough. And it's not just us. It's families across this country, from coast to coast. We scrimp and scrape and we get by. We don't have stocks. We don't have safes. We don't have dividends or trust funds. But we've got something more important. We've got our honor. We've got our integrity. We've got our decency. And we've got our common sense.

Which is why I say, now and forever, I am the 1 percent. I won't turn my back on my fellow Americans who have succeeded. I won't let the mob take away my honor by turning me against those who have a better material existence than I do.

As Emerson explained succinctly, "Envy is ignorance." Material success only matters to those who have lost their way spiritually. The 1 percent and the 99 percent are the same people with different clothes. And if I try to take the clothes off my brother's back, just what kind of neighbor am I? What kind of human am I?

Wealth is not the issue; justice is. There will always be a 99 percent and a 1 percent, but that is not unjust. It is simply a fact of life. Injustice occurs when the 99 percent threaten the 1 percent because they outnumber them. Injustice occurs when the 99 percent use their majority status to commandeer the wealth of the 1 percent.

And if I stand by and let that happen, then I am unjust. So I will stand with the 1 percent. Even though I don't have much money of my own, I cannot stand by and watch the wealth of my brethren be stolen. That is not the American way; it is the communist way. In America, what is mine is mine and what is yours is yours. So even though I have no money, I will proudly proclaim that I am a capitalist.

I will proudly proclaim that I am Dolores Broderson.

Do you know her? You should. She is the 78-year-old woman knocked down a flight of cement stairs in Washington, D.C., by a mob of "Occupy D.C." protesters earlier this month. Her crime? Nothing. She was just collateral damage. She's not rich. Not by a mile. In fact, she is a retired special-education teacher from Detroit. She lives on a pension, and she paid $350 to ride a bus for 11 hours to attend a dinner sponsored by the Koch brothers and Americans for Prosperity. Yeah, those Koch brothers — the billionaires who think they should have a right to use their own money to support the causes they believe in — such as prosperity.

And notice it is not Prosperous Americans for this or that. The Koch brothers don't need an organization to brag about their wealth, or to get more wealth. Trust me, they could sit back and enjoy life without lifting a finger. It is not a group FOR Prosperous Americans; it is Americans FOR Prosperity. It is about the Koch brothers and thousands of others celebrating success and fighting for the principles they think will lead to the most wealth for the most people. In other words, it is about the American Dream — start with nothing and end up with something big like Bill Gates, or maybe just end up with enough to get by and be happy like me.

Or like Dolores Broderson. She doesn't have a lot of money, but she has principles and a belief in an America where everyone has a chance to succeed. So what was her crime that led the mob from Occupy D.C. to go after her and other people attending the Americans for Prosperity dinner?

"I think they thought we were all rich or something," she said.

In other words, they thought she was part of "the 1 percent."

That's scary, isn't it? But it gets to the root of why Occupy Wall Street is a fundamentally anti-American movement. Targeting and dehumanizing a small group of people in order to motivate revolution is the stuff of Russia or Germany, not the United States of America. It usually starts small, like the attack in Washington, but eventually — if it is encouraged by those in power — it reaches the level of a pogrom or a mob attack on an entire population of people who are seen as dangerous to the interests of the majority. That mentality is fueled by anti-Semitic and incendiary rhetoric such as "Jewish bankers," "Humanity vs. the Rothschilds," "It's Yom Kippur: Banks should atone!" and "One day the poor will have nothing left to eat but the rich."

The sad news is that all of those slogans were found not at a 19th century pogrom and not in Nazi Germany, but at Occupy

Wall Street events. One particularly vicious display of anger had a man dressed as Christ (complete with a crown of thorns) carrying a sign that read, "I threw out the moneylenders for a reason." This is the original blood libel — combining the myth that the Jews had killed Jesus with the claim that Jewish bankers are evil, dangerous overlords.

So if you want to make a difference in this country, do yourself a favor. Step away from the 99 percent, and join the 1 percent. Stand with those who are being maligned. Stand with the Jews. Stand with Dolores Broderson. Stand up and be counted.

We are the 1 percent.

ECONOMIC INEQUALITY AND THE ENDURING MYTH OF 'EASY MONEY'

December 4, 2011

Thanks to winter weather and a handful of belatedly plucky mayors around the country, the Occupy Movement has gone into semi-hibernation, but don't imagine you've seen the last of it.

And please don't be so naive as to think you saw "the first of it" when it was unleashed on the country on Sept. 17 as a supposedly "spontaneous" combustion of anti-capitalist rhetoric and pro-entitlement socialism.

There is absolutely nothing new about class warfare, nor about the inclination of a certain sector of the American public to blame their misfortunes on "income inequality."

I have no doubt that "income inequality" exists, but how, after all, could it not? Though we are "created equal," and were all endowed equally with certain "unalienable rights" by our creator, we do not have equal abilities, equal ambitions, or equal luck. That means some people who start with little or nothing accomplish much, and often acquire much, and that some other people who start with a silver spoon in their mouth end up with a tarnished reputation and sink like a lead balloon.

Instead of bewailing the fact of unequal outcomes, however, we should really be celebrating it. This is not just the American way; it is the inevitable result of natural law when mankind is allowed to flourish with freedom instead of endure under the yoke of government mandate.

And yes, unfettered capitalism — the bain of the "Occupy" crowd — is the proof of that. It rewards effort and risk, and allows all of us a chance to excel, though few of us do. The question is why wouldn't we cheer on the successes of those who make it to the top of our economy just as we cheer on those who prevail in other endeavors?

Remember, there can only be one best student in a class of 100, one best team after the Super Bowl, one winner of the National Spelling Bee, and so too there can only be 1 percent of people who wind up in the top 1 percent of income. And unless you are a socialist, there is no need to fret about that. Income inequality is what makes capitalism possible, and make no mistake, capitalism is the engine that made America great.

Think about it. If all the money were distributed equally between all the people, then it would be impossible for mankind to engage in any enterprise without government management. No one individual would have enough money to open a factory, a farm, a quarry, or even an outhouse, nor would any two individuals be allowed to band together to better themselves as that would leave the poor singletons at a distinct disadvantage.

Yep, it would be government for all, and all for government — and therein lies the rub, for in that endless empowerment of government what mischief may come, must give us pause. All government management is, after all, by definition "government mis-management." It is also ipso facto a diminishment of each individual's liberties, and thus can only be rightly applied with "the consent of the governed," as Thomas Jefferson worded it in the Declaration of Independence.

But although bigger government is antithetical to the America spirit of liberty, it has been propounded as the solution to income inequality at least since the time of Karl Marx in the mid-19th century. And in the United States, there have been proponents of big government solutions to poverty and social inequality at least since the end of the 19th century.

Indeed, the presidential election of 1896 was fought largely over populist themes trumpeted by Democrat William Jennings Bryan as he sought to push "easy money" into the economy to benefit the little folks. He sought to eliminate the gold standard and replace gold with silver as the guarantor of paper money. Indeed, he claimed that 16 silver-backed dollars could be printed for every one dollar backed by gold, and because of the way the U.S. Treasury operated in those days, this would have meant more money in the hands of farmers and others in the "99 percent."

Bryan, of course, despite his fiery rhetoric about mankind being crucified "upon a cross of gold," was not elected president, and the class warfare he represented was more or less submerged for many years until the Great Depression in the 1930s.

Not coincidentally, it should be noted, the late 19th century and early 20th century was a period not just of income inequality, but also of tremendous growth in America. Those two things seem to go together, hand in glove. And just as so much of the wealth at the end of the 20th century was created by men and women who opened the high-tech spigot that has changed our way of life, so too the end of the 19th century was a period of unprecedented wealth for those who brought to fruition such modern indispensables as railroads, electric lights, the automobile, the telephone and the airplane.

If Occupy Wall Street is envious of the top "1 percent," you would have found an even more seething opposition to the wealthy industrialists at the turn of the previous century. Instead of being known as the filthy rich, they were the "robber barons." Men such as John. D. Rockefeller, Andrew Carnegie, J.P. Morgan, James Buchanan Duke, Edward Henry Harriman and Cornelius Vanderbilt were enormously wealthy as a result of astute investing, and their lifestyle was far beyond what even kings in a previous era would have expected.

This inevitably led to envy and to demands for "redistribution of wealth" from the rich to the poor, but consider three points before you condemn the wealthy.

First, almost all of these men had reached the top 1 percent from humble beginnings. Carnegie's first job was in a bobbin factory; he later became a messenger boy. Rockefeller was the son of an elixir salesman who supposedly bragged, "I cheat my boys every chance I get. I want to make 'em sharp." Harriman started out as an errand boy on Wall Street at the age of 14, and by the age of 22 he was a member of the New York Stock Exchange.

Second point: Consider the benefit of these men to society at large. Rockefeller revolutionized the petroleum industry, without which very little of the remarkable lifestyle of the 20th century would have been possible. Carnegie financed innovations in the steel industry that made the miracle metal cheaper at a time when the nation was being crossed with railroads and dotted with skyscrapers. J.P. Morgan was the genius behind such consummately American institutions as General Electric and U.S. Steel. Think of the jobs, the opportunities, and the advancements that were made possible by the "income inequality" that had given these men a platform upon which to launch their great enterprises.

Nor did these men's legacy get buried with them in the cemetery. John D. Rockefeller is regarded as the richest man in history, but he also developed modern philanthropy, and his foresight and generosity has funded untold numbers of charitable ventures, including as just one instance the University of Chicago. J.P. Morgan helped establish the Metropolitan Museum of Art, an invaluable resource for the preservation of the world's culture and art. Cornelius Vanderbilt founded Vanderbilt University, and James Buchanan Duke founded Duke University — two of the greatest institutions of higher education in the world. Andrew Carnegie, of course, devoted much of his fortune to the establishment of libraries, universities and charities across the country, many of which still bear his name.

Thank God for income inequality. If we all worked for the government, the world would be a glum gray prison with no way out. Instead, we all have a chance to enrich ourselves and our world by making the most of ourselves that we can and by refusing to be limited by anyone else's poverty of imagination.

TEDDY, BARACK AND THE VISION OF AMERICA

December 11, 2011

President Barack Obama and I spent a rare day on the same page last week when both of us pondered the similarities between the economic conditions at the beginning of the 20th century and the beginning of the 21st century.

Unfortunately, the page might well have been written in two different languages because we came to two utterly different conclusions based on the same evidence.

I've been looking at the late 19th century and early 20th century as a parallel to our own time. Both eras have been characterized by complaints about "economic inequality" and yet both have also seen tremendous advancement in the living conditions of the poor. And both eras were also characterized by a tremendous increase in wealth among people who were able to take advantage of either the industrialization of America, in the earlier instance, or the technology boom in our own day. In my mind, that raises the legitimate question whether or not an increase in "economic inequality" is the necessary price you pay if you want to improve conditions for the lower class.

But President Obama, in his by-now-familiar strategy of class warfare, suggests that "economic inequality" is instead a burden on society that must be lifted through some form of redistribution of wealth — what we traditionally call socialism. The president used a speech on Dec. 6 to begin what seemed like his re-election campaign, and he pointedly gave the speech in Osawatomie — the Kansas town where Teddy Roosevelt had challenged America 101 years ago to ensure that everyone in our great country got a "square deal."

Obama pointedly drew parallels between the two eras as well, but whereas I find hope in those parallels, he sees only despair. Indeed, he seems to agree with the rhetoric of Occupy Wall Street that the top 1 percent are somehow cheating the "bottom" 99 percent out of their just deserts, and have been getting away with murder — or close to it — for at least a hundred years.

To make his case for economic "reform," President Obama quoted that famous Roosevelt speech from 1910 as the supposed cornerstone of what can be accomplished in 2012, but he quoted it quite, shall we say, judiciously.

He did report correctly that Roosevelt had said: "Our country means nothing unless it means the triumph of a real democracy... of an economic system under which each man shall be guaranteed the opportunity to show the best that there is in him."

But he did not quote the former president when he assured his listeners, "When I say I want a square deal for the poor man, I do not mean that I want a square deal for the man who remains poor because he has not got the energy to work for himself. If a man who has had a chance will not make good, then he has got to quit... Give him a chance, not push him up if he will not be pushed."

President Roosevelt, or as he was known also, Col. Roosevelt, made repeated reference to the military system as an exemplar of what he expected from society.

"I ask that civil life be carried on according to the spirit in which the army was carried on [in the Civil War]. You never get perfect justice, but the effort in handling the army was to bring to the front men who could do the job. Nobody grudged promotion to Grant, or Sherman, or Thomas, or Sheridan, because they earned it. The only complaint was when a man got promotion which he did not earn."

Imagine that! A system where everyone has equal opportunity "to show the best there is in him," but also to "quit," to fail to "work for himself," and to "not be pushed." A system where people do not get promotions or benefits they did not earn. Such a system as envisioned by Theodore Roosevelt actually does exist, but not in the philosophy of President Obama. It is called free-market capitalism, something which the president derided last week.

"It doesn't work. It has never worked," he said.

Well, sorry, but it does work — when it is allowed to work. But for the past 100 years, the government has replaced freedom with regulation. In a thousand ways, the government has worked to prevent equal opportunity — for capitalists and laborers both — from being allowed to flourish because of the very real consequence (and political fallout) of the unequal results that must inevitably follow.

This government interference is witnessed in thousands of subsidies and allotments that benefit an individual industry (such as "green energy") or an individual investor (such as Warren Buffet). And it is seen in the concept of "affirmative action" which has been distorted into "affirmative oppression" — a program designed to deny equal opportunity rather than to guarantee it. Indeed, the government, for the past 50 to 100 years has worked tirelessly to ensure not only that equal opportunity is in short supply, but more dangerously that the majority of Americans have no interest in taking advantage of it when it does exist. The safety net has grown so broad and so comfortable that there is absolutely no incentive for anyone to even climb up on the high wire at all and take the risks associated with creativity, investment and invention.

Yet despite this experiment in social engineering that seems designed to drive ingenuity out of the American lexicon, we have still seen in the last 25 years an immense development of technology that has also, once again, led to the much feared state of "income inequality."

Yep, there is no doubt that people like Bill Gates and the late Steve Jobs amassed enormous wealth as a result of their individual genius and cunning, and there is no doubt that millions of others in our society have similarly benefited by wise investment in technology stocks, while a huge pool of people without ready access to capital have remained in the "lower" 99 percent of incomes. There is also no doubt that society as a whole has been the beneficiary of the technology revolution to such an extent that the very idea of poverty in our own day has very little relation to what previous generations suffered through.

The late 19th century had a similar jump in the living conditions of all people, as things such as indoor plumbing, electric lights, gas heat and other improvements were making their way into the homes of first the rich, then the middle class, and eventually the poor. Anyone who thinks that such giant steps would have been possible without capitalism, without investment, and without risk-takers is living in a fantasy land, and yet both then and now there have been rabble rousers who would try to convince the poor and working class that they were somehow being exploited by the wealthy.

Let's be clear. The industrial revolution, representing a completely new era in human society, did go through a dangerous period of exploitation and unsafe conditions, but that was quite rapidly dealt with by society as a whole. Indeed, the transition from rural agrarian society to urban industrialization was accomplished almost miraculously within a generation or two — three at most — and brought mankind closer to its pinnacle than to its nadir, as socialists would have your believe.

Yet according to President Obama, America as the land of opportunity doesn't even exist any longer.

"The basic bargain that made this country great has eroded," he said in Kansas. "Long before the recession hit, hard work stopped paying off for too many people. Fewer and fewer of the people who contributed to the success of our economy actually benefited from it."

Really? Does he really believe that? Because if he does, it's no wonder that he wants to radically transform the country. But I, for one, and millions of other Americans alongside me, want to restore the country, and herein lies the battle which is being fought in our schools, in our living rooms, in our politics, and in our streets.

This might well be characterized as the war between the Tea Party and Occupy Wall Street. As much as some people, including President Obama, want to squeeze both those movements into the same reform niche, you cannot do so without the explosive result that you get when mixing matter and anti-matter in the same space.

For the sake of simplicity, let's just say that the Tea Party represents the originalists of American history, the Founding Fathers, and that Occupy Wall Street represents the progressivists, the Rebellious Adolescents who think they have a better idea.

For the Tea Party, the idea of "reform" means to restore the country to its original shape — to re-form that which has been distorted by manipulation, forgetfulness and good intentions gone wrong. To the Progressives, the idea of "reform" means literally to re-shape the nation into a new form altogether, to transform that which they believe has never worked in the first place.

If you think that America and the Constitution never worked in the first place and need to be "re-shaped," then you join Barack Obama, the Progressive Movement and Occupy Wall Street in their task of "fundamentally transforming" America.

If, on the other hand, you think that the original concept of America as sculpted by our Founding Fathers has never been surpassed, then you should stand for the Constitution, stand with the Tea Party, and work to restore our fundamental greatness. It's not too late.

THESE PORT PROTESTERS 'OCCUPY' SHEEP'S CLOTHING

December 21, 2011

As a great man once said, "By their fruits you shall know them." Indeed, Jesus warned that sometimes "ravening wolves" come to you "in sheep's clothing."

The false prophets of doom otherwise known as the Occupy Movement dropped their sheepish disguise last week just long enough to show their true colors as wolves ready to rip with tooth and claw at the innards of American society.

You see, on Monday, Occupy protesters gave up their role as a modified Greek chorus in the collapse of American society and started taking a more active role in dismantling the American economy they so intensely despise.

It was just a flash of fang, a glimpse of things to come, but for those who have eyes to see, it was a worrisome sight indeed when at the behest of the Obama administration's former Green Energy Czar Van Jones, several thousand protesters shut down ports in Oakland, Portland and the Seattle area.

You know... the ports that are the lifeblood of our economy, the point of entry for all those consumer goods that make life so rich for even the poor among us. The ports that are the departure point for all those exports that feed farmers, manufacturers and millions of others who are productive members of society.

Jones had told his troops on Dec. 2 that the Dec. 12 attacks were the beginning of the "post-encampment phase" of the Occupy protests. He also sent his followers to a story by the Agence France-Press news group that told of the coming blockade.

That story said the port protest was a reaction to being evicted from squatters' camps around the country, but it was also being waged for political reasons as well:

" 'We're shutting down these ports because of the union busting and attacks on the working class by the 1 percent,' said Barucha Peller of the West Coast Port Blockade Assembly, of Occupy Oakland, in a statement. 'We are also striking back against the nationally co-ordinated attack on the Occupy movement. In response to the police violence and camp evictions against the Occupy movement, this is our co-ordinated response against the 1 percent.' "

Oh please. The 1 percent don't give a darn about the shutdown of the port by a few hundred protesters, and if they did care they could open the port again in hours.

But who does care, or should care, are the hundreds of workers who lost a day of work because of the Occupy goons. Even more to the point, those who SHOULD care are the American people in whose name this kind of disruption is supposedly being done.

As even the Democratic mayor of Oakland, Jean Quan, said, "They are saying ... they have to get the attention of the ruling class. I think the ruling class is probably laughing and the people of this city will be crying this Christmas. It's really got to stop."

Or does it?

Might it not just get worse?

I imagine the czar of Russia could laugh off a protest or two in 1916, but by February of 1917 he had lost his crown and by the middle of 1918 he had lost his life.

If you think that is an extreme view, you are right. And there is every possibility that the Occupy movement could founder and fail this winter, but only —ONLY — if the American people (yeah, the "99 percent") recognize that they've been taken for a ride by a bunch of socialist thugs.

Or we could be in for a bumpy 2012, as the Obama-emboldened Occupy Movement grabs for more and more power by brandishing the ugly weapons of intimidation and disruption as we enter the coming election year.

Is this just fear-mongering? Call it what you want, but there is no doubt that every radical in America is energized by the successes of the Occupy Movement and prepared to launch greater protests as soon as practical. Time Magazine was not wrong to name "The Protester" as the person of the year, and what "The Protester" wrought in Egypt and Libya could easily happen here as well, much to the glee of those who wish to overturn the established order.

Listen to the words of Pham Binh, a radical activist in the Occupy Movement, writing in the Links International Journal of Socialist Renewal:

"Occupy is a once in a lifetime opportunity to re-merge the socialist and working-class movements and create a viable broad-based party of radicals, two prospects that have not been in the cards since the late 1960s and early 1970s."

Binh concludes that "the most basic and fundamental task facing socialists is to merge with Occupy and lead it from within... Out of clouds of pepper spray and phalanxes of riot cops a new generation of revolutionaries is being forged, and it would be a shame if the Peter Camejos, Max Elbaums, Angela Davises, Dave Clines and Huey Newtons of this generation end up in separate "competing" socialist groups as they did in the 1960s... Above all else, now is the time to take practical steps toward creating a broad-based radical party that in today's context could easily have thousands of active members and even more supporters."

In other words, the Occupy Movement could be just the beginning. If you favor radical transformation of America into a socialist state, then pick up your sheepskin and drape it over your shoulders. For now, it is safe for wolves to walk among us, speaking soothing words about the "99 percent" and about fairness, while sharpening their claws in readiness for the day they can pounce on the "1 percent" and devour the freedoms that make the 1 percent possible.

But the wolves cannot stay under cover for long. "A good tree cannot bring forth evil fruit, neither can a corrupt tree bring forth good fruit."

Pay attention. Open your eyes, people!

"By their fruits, you shall know them."

ONE HUNDRED YEARS OF SOLICITUDE: FROM TEDDY TO BARACK

January 8, 2011

In the past year, I have sought answers to the question of American decline — how exactly did we come to the point of audacious despair that led us to jettison our cherished traditions and values and embrace mediocrity as the new excellence.

This exploration has taken me from the know-it-all superiority of John Dewey's progressive education to the dangerous radicalism of terrorist Bill Ayers — from the "New Deal" of FDR to the "Great Society" of LBJ — and finally from the incipient socialism of Teddy Roosevelt in 1912 to the insidious socialism of Barack Obama in 2012.

And don't blame me for making the connection to our current president — that was done not by me, but by President Obama himself, when he visited Osawatomie, Kansas, last December to draw comparisons between himself and Teddy Roosevelt — and between the complaints of "economic inequality" one hundred years ago and those heard today in the Occupy Wall Street movement.

It turns out that those comparisons between then and now provide the Rosetta stone that lets us once and for all decipher the American decline as the work of do-gooders who allowed their own worst fears to shape our ever-worsening national nightmare.

To adapt a phrase from the great South American novelist Gabriel Garcia Marquez, we can proclaim with sadness that the last century in America has been "one hundred years of solicitude."

As defined by Merrian-Webster, solicitude is "an uneasy state of mind, usually over the possibility of an anticipated misfortune or trouble." The second definition refers to it as "attention accompanied by protectiveness and responsibility."

Could any word better describe the American ethos that has evolved over the past 100 years? Is not the nanny state the exact manifestation of "protection and responsibility" that is foisted upon a formerly sovereign citizenry as a result of "an uneasy state of mind... over the possibility of ... anticipated misfortune or trouble"?

There's never really been any doubt that President Obama and his fellow progressives think they have a responsibility to protect us all from our own foolishness and misfortune — but Teddy Roosevelt helps put into perspective exactly where that Big Brother-ish concern came from and why, little by little, Americans have almost completely surrendered their independence in exchange for government handouts and the illusion of a "safety net."

In large measure, it was Teddy Roosevelt who set the stage for the increasing size of government in the 20th century, and the increasing role it played in the everyday lives of Americans. And the speech he gave at Osawatomie in 1910 is considered the cornerstone of that philosophy.

Professor George E. Mowry, author of the 1946 classic "Theodore Roosevelt and the Progressive Movement," said that the Osawatomie speech was "the most radical speech ever given by an ex-president ... His concept of the extent to which a powerful federal government could regulate and use private property in the interest of the whole and his declarations about labor, when viewed [with]... the eyes of 1910, were nothing short of revolutionary."

Indeed, Roosevelt's ideas were not just considered revolutionary by mainstream Democrats and Republicans of the day, but even by the Socialist party itself, which was in full swing then.

In an article published in the Van Wert (Ohio) Daily Bulletin on Oct. 30, 1912, author James Boyle, who had been private secretary to President McKinley, marveled at the transformation of Roosevelt, who had served as vice president under McKinley and had now "lost his bearings" and become at the very least an "unconscious Socialist."

"It is interesting and somewhat instructive," Boyle notes, "to know what the Socialists now think of Theodore Roosevelt. The 'Appeal to Reason,' the most extreme and the most widely circulated of the Socialist papers — of which [Eugene] Debs, the Socialist candidate for president, is one of the editors — in speaking of the Chicago Bull Moose platform, declares that 'many of Roosevelt's theories are so radical that they make the Socialists gasp with amazement.'"

If the socialists were amazed by Roosevelt's transformation, the gilded aristocrats of the New York Times were absolutely astonished. In 1913, the year after Roosevelt came in a respectable second place as a third party candidate for president (a feat never matched), the Times devoted well over

30 column inches to an editorial entitled "Roosevelt's Super-Socialism."

It was a response to Roosevelt's article on "The Progressive Party" that had been published in The Century Magazine and which, as the Times saw it, laid out Roosevelt's form of socialism for all to see.

"Mr. Roosevelt achieves the redistribution of wealth in a simpler and easier way [than Karl Marx]. He leaves the land, the mines, the factories, the railroads, the banks — all the instruments of production and exchange in the hands of their individual owners, but of the profits of their operation he takes whatever share the people at any given time may choose to appropriate to common use... Marx left Socialism in its infancy, a doctrine that stumbled and sprawled under the weight of its own inconsistencies. Mr. Roosevelt's doctrine is of no such complexity. It has all the simplicity of theft and much of its impudence."

This theft is, in essence, the basis of the modern socialistic state that we have become — the theft of taxation on those who have built up society in order to fund programs to benefit those who have contributed little or nothing to society. It's no wonder that President Obama has adopted Teddy Roosevelt as his economic guru.

Of course, neither Obama nor Roosevelt publicly accept the title of socialist — except when they do. For Mr. Obama it was when he told Joe the Plumber that "when you spread the wealth around, it's good for everybody." For Mr. Roosevelt it was when he said, "The goal is not socialism, but so much of socialism as will best permit the building thereon of a sanely altruistic individualism, an individualism where self-respect is combined with a lively sense of consideration for and duty toward others, and where full recognition of the increased need of collective action goes hand in hand with a developed instead of an atrophied power of individual action."

In other words, Roosevelt just wanted enough socialism to turn you and me into people who do what he wants us to do. It's either socialism or it's fascism, but one thing it is not is Americanism. Maybe we should call it by the politically neutral term of "social engineering," as really that is what "progressivism" is — a movement to herd mankind forward by using government to guide and protect us because of the solicitude of our overseers who are worried just what might happen if we are left to our own devices.

Like it or not, this is where we have gotten 100 years later — with just the kind of government that Teddy Roosevelt promised us when he spelled out the goals of the Progressive Party: "It will be necessary to invoke the use of governmental power to a degree hitherto unknown in this country, and in the interest of democracy, to apply principles which the purely individualistic democracy of a century ago would not have recognized as democratic."

Marx called it the "dictatorship of the proletariat." I just call it dictatorship.

WHAT WE KNOW, AND WHAT WE THINK WE KNOW: POKING AROUND THE PROPAGANDA FACTORY

March 18, 2012

The president has started his re-election campaign in earnest recently by touting the wonderful state of the economy, his brilliant energy policy, popular health-care reforms, and respect for American traditions and liberty.

If you were nodding your head approvingly throughout that first paragraph, finding yourself in perfect agreement with the accomplishments attributed to the president, then consider yourself the latest victim of Edward Bernays.

Who? I thought David Axelrod was the mastermind in charge of President Obama's feel-good re-election campaign.

Yeah, sure, Axelrod is good. After all, he's the guy who asked, "Are we going to have a country where hard work pays and responsibility is rewarded, or the schemers are the ones who get rewarded?" and actually thought the answer would help Democrats.

That kind of double talk is staggering in its audacity. BUT IT WORKS! The general public doesn't take time to do an analysis of the comment; they just agree or disagree with it — or think they do. The only response possible to Axelrod's question is: Yes, we want a country where hard work pays. No, we don't want a country where schemers are rewarded! End of story.

And since Axelrod is working to re-elect President Obama, then he must be the candidate who is FOR responsibility and AGAINST rewarding schemers, right?

No, he is the candidate with the best ability to manipulate voters by using techniques that ignore truth and exploit emotion. And that brings us back to Edward Bernays, the father of modern propaganda techniques.

Bernays worked for Woodrow Wilson, the president who was re-elected because he "kept us out of war" and then promptly took us into World War I, where 117,000 American soldiers were killed in action. It was Bernays who helped come up with the justification of "bringing democracy to all of Europe," and was delighted to find out that the American public could be easily manipulated with slogans and blatant falsehoods.

Although rarely acknowledged today, he laid the groundwork for modern political propaganda and in particular is the godfather of progressive techniques for pushing public opinions such as those used by moveon.org and Media Matters.

Here in a nutshell is the Bernays philosophy as outlined in his seminal 1928 book titled "Propaganda":

"The conscious and intelligent manipulation of the organized habits and opinions of the masses is an important element in democratic society. Those who manipulate this unseen mechanism of society constitute an invisible government which is the true ruling power of our country... We are governed, our minds are molded, our tastes formed, our ideas suggested, largely by men we have never heard of... In almost every act of our daily lives, whether in the sphere of politics or business, in our social conduct or our ethical thinking, we are dominated by the relatively small number of persons... who understand the mental processes and social patterns of the masses. It is they who pull the wires which control the public mind."

So now, let's consider the president's re-election campaign themes in light of our awareness that there are certain unscrupulous people who believe they can control your mind, shape your beliefs, and get you to vote however they want — regardless of your own best interests or desires.

And be aware, they do this, in large measure, right out in the open, by blatantly lying, distorting the truth, and deflecting your attention with scandals, controversies and distractions.

President Obama engaged in this technique personally last week when he gave a speech on energy policy and made a number of outrageous claims. In order to refute the charges of Newt Gingrich and others in the Republican Party that the president is responsible for high gas prices, the president made the following claim:

"Do not tell me that we're not drilling. We're drilling all over this country. There are a few spots we're not drilling. We're not drilling in the National Mall. We're not drilling at your house. I guess we could try to have, like, 200 oil rigs in the middle of the Chesapeake Bay. "

So now, according to the president, if you are for more drilling for oil — if you are for lower prices at the gasoline pump — you should vote for President Obama. Except he knows, and you know, and everyone else knows that it isn't true.

Despite the president's implication that he has authorized drilling everywhere but your back yard, just the opposite is true. His administration has fought drilling — and the oil industry in general — at every turn. This administration has refused to open the Alaskan National Wildlife Refuge to drilling. It stopped issuing permits for drilling in the Gulf of Mexico, even after a judge ordered it to resume doing so. And it goes well beyond that. The Obama administration has not approved any new oil refineries, for instance. Plus, it has done everything in its power to prevent the Keystone Pipeline from being built.

But other than that, Obama is pro-oil, pro-drilling and pro-consumer — as long as the president or David Axelrod says so. You have no choice but to go along with what you are told (or should I say, sold?). After all, in the words of Edward Bernays, "It is they who pull the wires which control the public mind."

And it's not just about oil or energy policy. Not by a long shot. Once you understand the audacity of propaganda, you'll see it everywhere. Consider the following frequently heard justifications for a second term for President Obama (and the unspoken truths behind them):

• Unemployment is down (as long you don't count the people who are most discouraged about the chance of finding a job and have therefore stopped looking for work).

• Inflation is low (if you don't count the commodities that are increasing in price most dramatically like food and gasoline).

• The right to use contraception is under attack (except it really isn't unless you think you have a right to free contraception, paid for by people who oppose it for moral or religious reasons).

• The right to religious freedom is being protected (by forcing people to pay for things they oppose for religious reasons).

• Your freedom to vote will be defended zealously (even if you are an illegal alien).

• The war in Afghanistan is being won (unless you mean by us).

The unfortunate, sad, heart-breaking truth is that politicians can say almost anything they want, no matter whether it is true or not, and still be elected and re-elected.

It's not their fault for wanting to enjoy the fruits of power; it's our fault for not doing a better job of vetting them and looking behind their campaign slogans. Maybe the only way to prevent the wrong candidates from being elected is to pay less attention to what they do say, and more attention to what they don't say.

DO WE NEED AN AMENDMENT TO PROTECT OUR LIBERTY?

July 15, 2012

Just when you think there is no possible solution to the mess facing our country, you discover that the solution has been around for more than half a century.

No doubt a handful of my readers have heard of "The Liberty Amendment," but I never had until I was reading a syndicated column in the Feb. 10, 1952, issue of the Valley Morning Star of Harlingen, Texas.

This particular paper was one of 10 daily newspapers published by Freedom Newspapers Inc., a partnership that was based on belief in "a system of natural law." That same belief in natural law is what led to the Declaration of Independence and the U.S. Constitution, but that is another story.

For now, I want to focus on this particular column by Willis E. Stone about a "Proposed 23rd Amendment" as it would have existed in 1952. Stone had actually proposed the amendment in 1949, but it was first introduced in Congress in 1952, and over the years starting with Wyoming in 1959 was endorsed by nine states. As recently as 2009, Rep. Ron Paul of Texas (yes, THAT Ron Paul) introduced the amendment as House Joint Resolution 48.

The Liberty Amendment has evolved somewhat since 1952, but that initial kernel which I read about in Stone's column was enough for me to realize that a structure has existed for more than 50 years that would have put fetters on the federal government so that the very idea of Obamacare would be recognized as anathema to a free and united people. The Supreme Court wouldn't have been able to meretriciously invent new government powers to try to convince us that a little bit of slavery is a good thing.

Here's the text of this remarkable philosophical construct, which now is like a vestigial appendix that merely reminds us of what once was and what could have been:

"The government of the United States shall not engage in any business, professional, commercial or industrial enterprise in competition with its citizens except as specified in the Constitution, nor shall the Constitution or laws of any state, or the laws of the United States, be subject to the terms of any foreign or domestic agreement which would abrogate this amendment."

Or as John Lennon might have said, if he were a conservative: "Imagine there's no socialism; it's easy if you try."

A large part of that long-ago column by Willis Stone dealt with trying to convince the average reader that he would be better off with the amendment. As he put it, "Briefly, the answer is: taxes would be reduced about 45 percent, the personal freedom of each citizen would be multiplied many times, and the peace of the world would improve."

The astounding thing to note from his column though is that on the basis of the federal budget from 1950, "the hidden costs and losses of the federal corporations [that would have been banned by the amendment] consumed a total of more than 10 billion tax dollars."

Yep, $10 billion. That was the crisis then.

Today we spend almost $10 billion every week just on the interest on the national debt, and massive amounts of that debt has been accrued just exactly by the government becoming involved in "business, professional, commercial or industrial enterprise[s] in competition with its citizens."

We call those enterprises by various names, but basically if the federal government is engaged in some enterprise that doesn't involve building roads or mailing letters, they have almost certainly gone beyond their constitutional restraints. You can look for examples in Medicare, Medicaid, the Department of Education, the Department of Energy and of course the Affordable Care Act (which is the final step in ensuring that health care will be endlessly more expensive to taxpayers).

Getting rid of those institutions and expenses would probably be impossible now. Just as Europe has seen its population protesting and rioting over the possibility of losing entitlements, so too would America erupt in massive turmoil should we suddenly decide to bring back the liberty that our Founding Fathers had envisioned for us.

Is that a conundrum? People rioting to forestall a return to liberty? Not when you realize that their liberty had been bought with a comfortable life. Many a wild animal has been tamed with a nightly steak dinner. So too can free men and free women be caged easily by the promise of creature comforts.

Because one thing is certain. Liberty is worthless without a correspondence of responsibility. So too is a Constitution.

Note: You can read the entire history of the Liberty Amendment at http://libertyamendment.org/

Do nation's watchmen now stand guard in vain?

July 15, 2012

Last week, I mentioned that I had found a column about the "Liberty Amendment" in a newspaper owned by the Freedom Newspapers group, and noted that Freedom Newspapers and its owner R.C. Hoiles were worth a column of their own.

Well, here it is.

I first became aware of Hoiles last year when researching information about the influence of progressivism on our public education system. Hoiles was one of the strongest voices against educator John Dewey and progressivism, and I quoted an editorial in one of Hoiles' newspapers that called Deweyism "The Great Delusion." As noted by the editorial writer, possibly Hoiles himself, "Progressive education is producing students who can't think and who can't read, write, spell, or figure with facility."

Even more significant was the conclusion of the editorial writer that, "Under the present system children are taught that competition is not good, only to find out when they become adults that they are in a competitive world. No sooner do they discover this vital point than they become easy marks for those who feel that the competitive, free enterprise system is bad and that competition should be eliminated by the force of the government. It is only natural that the children brought up in this sort of environment will look upon the competitive system with a jaundiced eye and turn to the government for the solution of their problems."

In 1953, when this was written, maybe the jury was out. But now that we have lived through the conversion of our mid-20th-century manufacturing-based economy to the 21st-century welfare-based economy, there is a guilty verdict hanging over the head of progressivism for anyone to see.

Unfortunately, the "jaundiced eye" predicted by Hoiles or his surrogate has grown so diseased that at least half the population of the United States no longer has eyes to see. Socialism — free stuff — is now considered the birthright of Americans even more than liberty. Unfortunately, this uniquely American form of socialism masquerades as "social justice" and thus wears the cloak of respectability. Instead of government acquiring the means of production, the overseers merely acquire the means of producing wealth in the form of taxation policies that soak the rich and pay off the poor. The honest socialists call it "redistribution of wealth"; the deceptive ones call it a progressive tax policy.

In the meantime, people like R.C. Hoiles are few and far between these days, especially in the media. His conviction that the country needed newspapers that "believe in moral principles and have enough courage to express these principles" might well confound the entire faculty at any school of journalism in the country, especially his oft-expressed belief that "every fact of existence — if it is a fact — is immutable, irrevocable and eternal" and that "moral facts are no less concrete and timeless than physical facts."

This is the same conception of natural law that motivated and empowered our Founding Fathers as they set about to bring forth "a new nation, conceived in liberty, and dedicated to the proposition that all men are created equal." Without a belief in "immutable" moral facts or laws, you cannot hold any truths to be "self-evident," nor can rights be "unalienable" as proposed by the Declaration of Independence. It is therefore a certainty that R.C. Hoiles was a direct descendant philosophically of Thomas Jefferson, George Washington and the other Founders.

If his ideas now seem "quaint" or "silly," that is only because we as a nation have lost our connection to what William Faulkner called "the eternal verities of the heart" or what Hoiles called the "fundamental moral laws... [that] govern human behavior."

More and more, as I study the decline of the American republic in the 20th century, I see that life preservers were thrown out repeatedly to the populace by patriots such as Hoiles, but they were most often thrown back with disdain. If it feels sometimes like we are now losing the battle to preserve our way of life, including our liberty and prosperity, perhaps the truth is even more dismaying.

Perhaps, the war is already lost. We may just not have been able to bring ourselves to acknowledge that distasteful fact. After all, the clarion call of Hoiles and people like Barry Goldwater and Ronald Reagan who were manning the bulwarks 50 years or more ago should have been as urgent an alarm as that sounded by Paul Revere in 1776. Instead, American slumbered.

More and more, it looks as though the barbarians have long since advanced past the gates, and that we are now an "occupied" nation. Call it the Land of the Freebie. Or the Home of the Braying. Or just call it "The Great Delusion" and give Hoiles the final word. He has earned it.

AN AMERICAN HERO
FROM ANOTHER WORLD — 1962

July 29, 2012

The past couple of weeks I have been exploring how America in the 1950s and '60s had a chance to stop the juggernaut of bigger government from crushing the spirit of free enterprise, and for the most part missed the opportunity.

It's been a nostalgic, if not exactly a feel-good, look back at a simpler era when good and evil were understood to have real meaning, and the folks fighting for right did not have to justify themselves in the public square.

Coincidentally, for the past few weeks, I have been working on putting together a special section of the Daily Inter Lake that focuses on Northwest Montana 50 years ago. That collector's edition will be published in Monday's paper and features 46 pages from the 1962 "Progress Edition" published by the Inter Lake. I highly recommend it to our readers for a chance to brush up on your local history, as well as to enjoy a real "feel good" moment about our shared American traditions.

As part of my research in putting together the "Back to the Future" section, I stumbled upon an editorial page from Feb. 11, 1962, that I thought was worthy of comment. It demonstrated that even a small-town newspaper could be a forum for big ideas and for defending our country against attacks both foreign and domestic.

In particular, I noticed an editorial entitled "Governor's Last Speech." It explained that a speech by Gov. Donald G. Nutter had been broadcast posthumously following his death about 10 days earlier in a plane crash.

The Inter Lake editorial writer said that the speech "pointed out some things we feel bear repeating" and then lamented that "there are pieces of logic that must be played over and over and over again so that they soak into our heads, which sometimes are pretty dense."

I must admit that I sympathized with both the governor and the editorial writer. Too often I feel like I am reduced to repeating in this column bits of logic that should be truisms, but which seem startlingly fresh and even unconvincing to some readers — things like "American patriotism is good" and "communism is bad."

I suppose Gov. Nutter must have felt the same way when he spoke out against the United Nations, as he did in this final speech. He was probably considered a "right-wing kook" and an extremist because he stated plainly that the United Nations "has become little more than a forum for our enemies." Remember, this was back in the day when little old first- and second-graders like me were carrying our milk cartons to raise money for UNICEF right along with our pillow case for collecting candy on Halloween.

But Nutter was a man of principle, not expediency. In fact, I learned that he was the only governor in the nation who did not proclaim United Nations Day. Instead he had proclaimed Oct. 23 as "United States Day" in Montana. How refreshing! According to the Inter Lake, Nutter explained that he would "support any organization of nations dedicated to Christian principles and promoting freedom and liberty for all people, everywhere."

Today, of course, no governor could make such a statement. He or she would be considered a bigot for promoting "Christian principles" to the exclusion of Muslim or communist principles. I have heard this criticism myself many times, to which I have asked in response, "If a person or a country or even a church cannot promote their own principles, then what is the point of having principles?"

Gov. Nutter was obviously a man of principle, who did not hesitate to stand for what he believed. He had enlisted in the Army Air Forces in World War II and as a B-24 pilot had flown more than 60 combat missions. After a brief career in business, he enrolled in law school and also pursued a political career that led to his being elected governor in 1960. Due to the plane crash that killed him and five others, he only served one year in office — leaving us to ponder what impact he might have had on the course of our nation's future had he been able to convince his fellow citizens that the United Nations and socialism were dangerous to the Americanism of our Founding Fathers.

In his final speech, Nutter intoned, "There are those among us who believe some other form of government is better, that socialism in its ultimate degree — communism — has something to offer."

That certainly remains true to this day — perhaps even more so than in 1962. Witness the rise of the "Occupy" movement last year, and the casual acceptance of socialist programs in our federal government for decades. Indeed, those who have comprehended the growing danger to our republic can only read Nutter's final words with fear and trembling:

"What does all this mean to you and me? Just this: through selfishness, greed, complacency and apathy, we can cancel out all of the sacrifices made by us, by our fathers and by our forefathers.

"Through failure to exercise our constitutional rights and perform our duties to protect this nation, we can and will drift away from our great heritage."

The judgment of the 50 years that have passed since these words were written is not kind to our generation or to the one before it. Can we honestly say that we have upheld and defended the Constitution? Can we make the case that we have protected our nation from enemies both foreign and domestic?

I doubt that Gov. Nutter, an American hero, would think so. Nor would another American hero, John Kennedy, who wrote and delivered a better known address, and who also died an untimely death the following year.

It was President Kennedy who said, in his inaugural address, "that the torch has been passed to a new generation of Americans — born in this century, tempered by war, disciplined by a hard and bitter peace, proud of our ancient heritage — and unwilling to witness or permit the slow undoing of those human rights to which this Nation has always been committed, and to which we are committed today at home and around the world."

Sounds to me like the senator and the governor were, in many respects, on the same page. Kennedy was famous for telling Americans that they must ask what they could do for their country — AND for the freedom of man. Nutter was asking the same thing. One was a Democrat and one a Republican, but they were united in their love of country.

How far we have come from 1962, and yet how desperately we need to get back to it. Perhaps we can sum up our plight best with another quote from President Kennedy's inaugural address:

"The world is very different now. ... And yet the same revolutionary beliefs for which our forebears fought are still at issue around the globe — the belief that the rights of man come not from the generosity of the state, but from the hand of God."

It is this precept which fuels everything I believe in — and which makes me today neither a Republican nor a Democrat, but a liberty-loving American.

A MIRACLE DRUG FOR WHAT AILS US? MAYBE, MAYBE NOT ...

August 5, 2012

I'm not sure why people insist on thinking that our current political environment is the worst ever, but it isn't.

Strongly held beliefs were not just invented when Barack Obama was elected — and whether you look at the founding of our country or any significant decision point since, what you are most likely to find is a nation that struggles mightily to come to consensus, and oftentimes fails to do so.

Remember that only a third of the original colonists were also revolutionaries, so even from the start we were a nation divided. That hasn't ever really ended, and if you think that observation conflicts with Lincoln's famous dictum that "A house divided against itself cannot stand," then you are taking the very short view of history.

Lincoln was right, but he didn't provide a timetable. Neither did Jesus, who originated the phrase in Mark 3:25. But whether it takes 10 years or 50 — like some civil wars — or fully a thousand years like the decline of the Roman empire, it is indisputable that failure to find common ground will inevitably result in collapse and chaos. This is not just idle speculation; it is moral law.

Of course, I suppose that sounds like a death knell for our American republic, which is divided today under President Obama, just as it was divided 10 years ago under President Bush, but there may be an antidote available against political division — it's just a bitter pill for some to swallow.

I found a reference to this cure on an editorial page in the Daily Inter Lake from 50 years ago. It was the same page where Montana's Gov. Donald Nutter was lauded for his posthumous speech blasting the United Nations, socialism and communism. In fact, there were several references to this cure on the opinion page from Feb. 11, 1962, most colorfully in a small reprint from Life Lines magazine titled "Miracle Drug of Patriotism." Here it is, in full:

"There is a wonder drug that will work miracles for the spirit of America. It is patriotism — patriotism pure and simple. It is a national disgrace — an individual disgrace as well — if strong men can be made weak and compromising by the collective efforts of those in our society who wish to gain from less effort, less principle, more timidity, more 'something for nothing.' This is the spirit — lack of spirit is a better term — that can cause our nation to be less productive, less effective, more fearful of conflict, more ready to compromise and even for defeat.

"But the miracle drug of patriotism can work wonders here! This is the drug that is being discovered by many Americans — and, happily, many young men and women among them. This wonder drug gives rise to pro-Americanism. It sweeps aside the cobwebs of mistaken thinking. It gives our people hope for the future — their future — the future that can be for America.

"Now is the time, if ever, for unabashed patriotism, for unapologetic patriotism that holds America high in the world. We can win for freedom if we will but make the necessary effort."

It is obvious without any further context that the author of this prescription was already somewhat demoralized, just as many of us are today, and just as Gov. Nutter was when he wrote in 1962 that "through selfishness, greed, complacency and apathy, we can cancel out all of the sacrifices made by us, by our fathers and our forefathers... and ... drift away from our great heritage."

Yet there appeared to be — even in the middle of the Cold War, when communism was at its most terrifying pinnacle worldwide — an answer to everything that could destroy us, an answer in the form of this so-called "miracle drug of patriotism."

The enemy, mind you, was not Russian communism, or Chinese communism. Thanks to Truman and Eisenhower and Kennedy, those had been put in their place. Yet, even in 1962, the most dangerous enemy of America was an enemy within — an enemy that worked without guns or missiles to reshape the nation into a place where "strong men can be made weak and compromising by the collective efforts of those in our society who wish to gain from less effort, less principle, more timidity, more 'something for nothing.'"

I don't know about you, but these are words that still speak to me. They are not just an historic footnote, but rather a prophecy. I do believe that this enemy has already succeeded at making our nation "less productive, less effective, more fearful of conflict, more ready to compromise and even for defeat."

Yet the answer is not surrender. The answer is education and Socratic questioning. Do you, does anyone, really want the weaker America of "less effort, less principle [and] more timidity"? Heaven forbid. Yet isn't that what we have wound up with?

That being the case, we are indeed in a precarious position. I'm not sure whether the "miracle drug of patriotism" can save the patient any longer. After all, a lot of our patriotic fervor these days seems to be reserved for touting that very same "something for nothing" philosophy which worried Life Lines back in 1962. And pro-Americanism these days is probably unconstitutional because it promotes a place of "national origin." Don't our schools and universities these days teach that all nations, all cultures, all philosophies are equal?

Yet I remain an optimist. I remain convinced that if enough good people speak the truth fearlessly, and accept the price of speaking that truth without concern for self, then eventually truth will prevail. I believe that Americanism as devised by

Jefferson, Adams, Madison, Washington and those other revolutionaries is still worth living for, and worth dying for.

That doesn't mean America itself will survive all its woes. But if Americanism cannot stand in America, then eventually it will rise on another shore. For though a house divided cannot stand, neither can truth be destroyed. It will always rise again like a phoenix out of the ashes. In the long view of history, what matters isn't America; it is Americanism._

1962: 'EXTREMISTS' WARNED IN VAIN AGAINST SOCIALISM & SURRENDER

August 12, 2012

One last shot from 1962 and then I am finished.

We started out two weeks ago by encountering the tragically shortened term of Gov. Donald Nutter, who had gained fame the previous year by refusing to proclaim United Nations Day in Montana, declaring it instead to be United States Day.

If you want to give yourself a headache, just try to imagine how much better the world would be today if the United States had not surrendered its hard-earned moral authority to an international body of rogues and thieves.

But, of course, Gov. Nutter didn't manage to persuade many people to re-examine America's relationship to the United Nations, and even if he had lived past the first year of his term as governor, he wouldn't have had any more luck. Back then, they called people like Nutter — people who put their country first — extremists. Come to think of it, they still call them the same thing, and sometimes just for good measure they call them dangerous extremists.

One such extremist was prominently featured on the editorial page of the Daily Inter Lake, along with Gov. Nutter, in the Feb. 11, 1962 edition. He was a syndicated columnist, and just as Thomas Sowell is considered a crackpot by some of our contemporary readers, so too was this columnist considered a crackpot as well. His name was Barry Goldwater.

Sen. Goldwater, a Republican from Arizona, was then in his second term in the U.S. Senate and was noted for his 1960 book "The Conscience of a Conservative," which helped set the agenda for the Reagan Revolution 20 years later. Although Goldwater became the Republican presidential nominee in 1964, his loss against Lyndon Johnson was inevitable following the assassination of John F. Kennedy.

But two years before, with Kennedy in between the Bay of Pigs fiasco and the October Missile Crisis, Goldwater was a well-reasoned voice for staying tough on communism. His column in that February newspaper was an impassioned plea for his country not to abandon him and go soft on this worldwide enemy.

"In my travels throughout the country, I find more and more conscientious Americans wondering why this nation does not declare victory over the forces of international communism as our cold war purpose," he wrote.

"I find growing dissatisfaction with a foreign policy based on the optimistic but naive, conception that we can have peaceful coexistence with an enemy which has sworn to destroy us. I find open resentment at the insistence of foreign policy spokesmen that a national program of foreign aid, disarmament and extreme deference to the United Nations is sufficient to the challenge which faces freedom in the world today."

Imagine that. A politician who doesn't simply spout feel-good bromides, but demands solutions that actually match the significance of the problem. Worldwide communism was THE existential threat to freedom in 1962, and Barry Goldwater said so. He was also smeared for saying so, just as today Michele Bachmann is smeared for saying that the existential threat to freedom in 2012 is Islamic jihad and the Muslim Brotherhood.

Goldwater wrote, "I am disturbed when our leaders attribute this concern solely to the work of radicals and extremists. This is not the time to decry an excess of patriotism among the American people." How very disturbed then must Goldwater have been to hear his Republican successor, Sen.

John McCain, call Rep. Bachmann's warning about the threat of the Muslim Brotherhood "specious and degrading."

What is degrading is a United States senator who won't face up to the possibility that enemies of our country will use any and all methods to demoralize us, to divide us, and to destroy us.

For the final perspective on this, let's turn to Mr. R.O. Waller, who wrote a letter to the editor in the Feb. 11, 1962, edition, entitled "What About Super Patriots?" Perhaps Mr. Waller, as a former chairman of the Republican Central Committee in Flathead County, was himself tired of being called an extremist — or maybe he just didn't like what people were saying about Gov. Nutter and Sen. Goldwater.

In any case, Waller began his letter like this:

"Maybe what we should do first is to define what we mean by 'extreme' right and 'extreme' left in our country's make-up. Just who are the 'extreme' righters and who are the 'extreme' leftists?"

This was, of course, merely a rhetorical flourish, as Mr. Waller was just setting up his target. In the extreme left, he lumped Americans for Democratic Action, the Farmers Union, "the more radical labor unions," and finally "some of the college eggheads who advocate government control of our free enterprise system and the expansion of the welfare state, deficit government spending and increased taxation."

This set of "extreme" left-wing goals sounds uncomfortably familiar to an observer of 21st century politics — and it doesn't sound so extreme anymore. In fact, it sounds mainstream. Government control of free enterprise? Expansion of the welfare state? Deficit spending? Higher taxes? Aren't those all part of the Democratic agenda — and too often the Republican agenda?

Mr. Waller went into much more depth about the platform of the "extreme" right — mostly opposition to what he called "unwise government policy" that in general gave more power to the president and to international bodies and less power to Congress and to the people. He challenged higher taxes, the United Nations and a power structure that showed favor to "questionable subversive elements in this nation" and thus made it extremely difficult to "obtain conviction of known enemy agents working against the U.S. government."

This all sounds deadly familiar today, as does this warning that concludes Waller's letter:

"Some people are tempted to accept 'federal aid' in one form or another — in the mistaken belief that they are getting something for nothing. Citizens should remember that politicians cannot give them anything from Washington that has not first been taken 'from them (the taxpayer) in taxes... The hour is late — but, it may not be too late to save our form of government and our way of life, our freedom and all that goes with it, if thoughtful men and women in all walks of life and political beliefs will act in unison in opposition to socialistic government trends."

The hour is later still today, and if those citizens who oppose "socialistic government trends" have indeed banded together in the form of the Tea Party movement, they have been met full force by the "Occupy" movement and by those who support socialism.

In these two movements, we see that the same battle that consumed Sen. Goldwater and R.O. Waller is still under way 50 years later. The outcome is far from settled. But if you are confident that you don't need to do anything to protect and defend our Constitution — if you are sure that your liberty will be preserved by the government without your insistence or participation, then we are all one step closer to losing that Constitution and that liberty.

Maybe we have at last gotten to that point which Benjamin Franklin foresaw when he warned us in 1787 that the Founding Fathers had given the American nation a republic... "if you can keep it."

RELIGIOUS FREEDOM IS FINE
AS LONG AS IT STAYS IN CHURCH

September 9, 2012

I have written before about Freedom Newspapers, the chain founded by R.C. Hoiles, which operated under a set of moral principles espoused by Hoiles and published frequently in his newspapers in the 1950s and '60s.

Freedom Newspapers used three "guides" in making decisions about what is "moral or immoral — good or bad — helpful or harmful to the human race."

Those three guides were the Decalogue, more commonly known as the Ten Commandments; the Sermon on the Mount preached by Jesus (considered by Hoiles to be "an exposition of the Decalogue"; and the Declaration of Independence (called "a political expression of the Commandments" in the Freedom Newspapers' credo).

Plainly this is an expression of faith and an expression of religious belief — in other words an example of the "free exercise of religion" guaranteed to all Americans under the First Amendment. If you didn't agree with Hoiles, you didn't have to read his newspapers — or work for him — but it was plainly understood that Hoiles had a perfect right as an American citizen to use his own means to promote his personal religious beliefs.

But that was then.

Nowadays, Hoiles would very likely have been hauled into court for trying to force his employees to honor religious traditions they might not agree with.

Forget about the First Amendment — or the ancillary rights and responsibilities of free association. Forget about the opportunity everyone has to quit a job they don't like or to start their own newspaper where they can promote their own belief system. All that matters in the post-modern, post-Christian world we live in today is that if my beliefs offend anyone in the public square, then I have to exercise my religious freedom by shutting up.

Don't believe me?

Well, listen to what Obama administration attorneys argued in a federal court in Michigan last month. According to them, a private business that isn't obviously a religious organization has no right to exercise religious freedom.

The case was brought against the Affordable Care Act by the Thomas More Law Center on behalf of Legatus, the nation's largest organization of Catholic business leaders, as well as Weingartz Supply, a family-owned business that sells and services outdoor power equipment. The plaintiffs, who have a moral objection to abortion, objected to being ordered by the federal government to provide abortifacients for their employees as part of the health-care mandate.

Big Brother (er, I mean the Obama administration) didn't care. They said that Weingartz Supply Co. by definition is a "for-profit, secular employer, and a secular entity by definition does not exercise religion." They argued that Weingartz as the owner of the corporation has no right to "impose his own personal religious beliefs on the corporate entity's group heath plan or its employees."

This is an extreme view of entitlement that may very well be upheld by our topsy-turvy justice system. Employees are entitled to whatever the government says they are entitled to, and employers are entitled to shut up. Or do I repeat myself?

R.C. Hoiles would have had plenty to say about this. Among the principles he espoused was the notion that all people were "born with certain inalienable rights" and that these rights were "the endowment of the Creator and not the gift of a transient state."

Something similar to this did indeed appear in the Declaration of Independence, the founding document of our nation, but as every schoolchild knows, the Declaration has no force in our modern jurisprudence, and no standing in our government. Elsewise, the government could not grant or take away rights, as it so gleefully does on a regular basis. The Creator has not only gotten short shrift in the recent Democratic convention, but in the very institutions and bulwarks of our society.

Hoiles had a very good argument why the government could not restrict the rights of a group of people such as a corporation or a union if the individual members of that group already enjoyed the same rights.

"|n all of recorded history, men have banded together for certain reasons — to hunt, to play, to trade, to build. In a voluntary association, such as the one that publishes these newspapers," he wrote, "each man exercises his rights through the group."

He argued that a group of people still had all the same rights as an individual, and that no group of people — no matter how large — could take away anyone else's rights.

His argument for "a single standard of conduct" was buttressed by no less an authority than Thomas Jefferson, the author of the Declaration of Independence, who wrote, "I know of but one code of morality, whether it be for men or for nations."

In Hoiles' view, it would be oppression to force someone to work for Weingartz Supply Co. or for any employer whose views were anathema to the employee. But, by the same token, it would be oppression for the government to force Weingartz to surrender its own moral views in favor of those espoused by the government.

Yet that is just what the Obama administration proposes by ordering Catholics and other business owners to provide and pay for services that they find morally abhorrent.

The ultimate irony, of course, is that if the Justice Department prevails in its bid to outlaw religious belief from the private sector, it will only be doing half the job. Good folks like Weingartz will be banned from "imposing" their moral beliefs on their employees, but all of the unkind (pre-conversion) Scrooges in the world will still be free to spread their toxic venom of faithlessness.

Doesn't seem fair, does it? But then again, it isn't meant to be.

ADVICE FOR GOP: DON'T CHANGE YOUR MESSAGE, CHANGE THE MAP!

November 18, 2012

Winning the presidency isn't about who you nominate, but about who votes — and most importantly about where they live.

The Democratic Party has recognized this, and turned it to a huge advantage in winning the last two presidential elections, and creating what appears to be a virtual lock on the presidency into the foreseeable future by dominating the Electoral College map.

This demographic domination by Democrats has many components, but one in particular that is easy to recognize is the growing success of the Democratic Party in winning over Latinos — the fastest growing bloc of voters in the country. Combined with the increasing number of minority voters as a whole, and their proclivity to vote Democratic, this has put Republicans in an almost untenable position. No matter how many individual citizens vote Republican, if minority voters in largely populated states continue to swing heavily toward Democrats, then an Electoral College victory by Republicans grows more and more remote.

Perhaps this sense of helplessness is what has persuaded many voters, presumably Republicans, to embrace the idea of secession from the United States as a way to restore their confidence that they will not just become increasingly irrelevant as the culture changes and the vision of the Founding Fathers is brushed aside.

But face it, secession is not an answer. As an intellectual exercise, it is intriguing to talk about what the Founders intended when the several states joined together to form the United States of America, and clearly Thomas Jefferson at least envisioned that states would retain the right to remove themselves from the union as a way to restrict the appetite of the federal government for more and more power.

As a practical matter, however, the issue of secession was settled once and for all by the Civil War when President Lincoln waged a bloody battle to protect the Union and to keep it whole. There is no right of secession any longer because the federal government says there is no right, and the feds ultimately determine what rights the states have both through the power of courts and the power of guns.

On the other hand, neither the courts, nor guns, nor even the Constitution itself can stop human beings from aspiring to independence, striving for freedom, or seeking "to effect their Safety and Happiness," as the Declaration of Independence would have it.

So, if secession is outlawed and revolution is folly, what mechanism remains available to the several states and their people to achieve the liberty that our Founding Fathers asserted in 1776? How, in other words, can the discontented states "provide new Guards for their future security" while still remaining conjoined with the other states that don't feel threatened by an ever tightening federal chokehold?

The answer, once again, is demographics — and the ultimate solution was once again provided by the genius of the Founding Fathers as embedded in the United States Constitution.

I am referring to the much maligned Electoral College itself, the very institution that seems to guarantee Democratic victory.

Unless the Republicans are willing to permanently cede the presidency to the Democratic Party, they need to develop a new strategy for winning in the Electoral College that takes advantage of their own strengths and doesn't try to win at the Democrats' game.

In other words, if Republicans expect to remain relevant, they don't need to change their message, or their messenger; they need to change the electoral map.

Remember that the number of Electoral College votes awarded to states is based on congressional representation, which in turn is based on the U.S. Census. Increase your population, like California and Florida, and you will increase your electoral votes. Watch people flee your borders, and see your state's importance decline a la New York, Michigan and Pennsylvania.

There are two ways that Republicans can take advantage of this unique electoral system — one long-term and one short-term. Both methods rely partly on human nature, and partly on harnessing the anger that would lead a million people in the past 10 days to sign online petitions stating they want to secede from their beloved United States.

The truth is that people can restore our nation to its founding principles and they can do so without leaving their country — all they need to do is leave their state!

Put another way: To change the future, change your demographics. If the Republican Party, for instance, could encourage 50,000 reliable Republican voters to move to Ohio over the next four years, they could probably compete in that crucial state in 2016. Likewise Florida. Likewise Colorado. That is the short-term solution.

It sounds crazy, but it just might work.

Remember, the original signers of the Declaration of Independence pledged their lives, their fortunes and their sacred honor in order to fight tyranny and promote liberty. But they were committing revolution and putting their very lives at risk. Moving from California to Colorado only requires an adventurous spirit.

Remember also that the vast majority of the original colonists had been part of a mass exodus that was much more dangerous, much more risky and much less certain of a positive outcome when they sailed from England, Ireland, and the rest of Europe to seek a new life in the New World. If unhappy Republicans decide to abandon Blue states and head to the Red states, they are only engaged in what the signers of the Declaration enshrined for them — the pursuit of happiness.

Indeed, human nature declares that for small-government Republicans to remain in California, they are doing harm to their own persons. Most of them who have the capacity would eventually migrate across the border to Arizona or Nevada or Utah or Montana anyway — just because of their own self-interest in lower taxes, greater safety and increased liberty. Isn't that the same urge which liberal Democrats tell us justifies the migration of Mexicans illegally across the southern border?

If enough Republicans were to follow their self-interest so that they can live in Red States where there is less regulation and less government, they will accomplish two effects — first, they will swell the ranks of Republican voters in those states where they move. This will allow Republicans to have a chance to win electoral votes in the swing states immediately.

Secondly, they will increase the overall population in those states, so that all Red states which are so enlarged will have greater congressional representation following the 2020 Census and greater clout in the Electoral College starting in 2024. That would ultimately make the swing states less significant, and would make a Red state Republican victory more and more likely — hopefully bringing with it a dedication to stripping back the power of the federal government to manageable proportions.

Call it the Nonviolent Revolution of 2024 — using brains rather than bullets to achieve a counter-transformation of America back to its founding principles.

And if 12 years seems like a long time to wait for a plan to come to fruition, remember that it took 11 years for the seeds planted with the Declaration of Independence to come to fruition in the U.S. Constitution in 1787.

If we want the Constitution back, we had better start working on it today.

A DECLARATION OF SANITY: DON'T GIVE UP RIGHTS

February 10, 2013

What part of "self-evident" don't Americans understand?

Or more to the point, I suppose, what truths in the Declaration of Independence are left that Americans actually DO understand?

Somehow, in 237 years, we have gone from declaring the NECESSITY of dissolving political bands with England and explaining proudly why we must do so ... to the current pusillanimous acquiescence to tyranny which we are assured by the villains in Washington, D.C, is better than the alternative.

Don't you believe it. The alternative, ladies and gentleman, is freedom.

After describing the unalienable rights to "life, liberty and the pursuit of happiness," and how a just government works to secure these rights, Thomas Jefferson went on to state unequivocally: "That whenever any Form of Government becomes destructive of these ends, it is the Right of the People to alter or to abolish it, and to institute new Government, laying its foundation on such principles and organizing its powers in such form, as to them shall seem most likely to effect their Safety and Happiness."

Nothing in there about how a desire to preserve the Union trumped "Safety and Happiness." That's because free men don't put the government first, and their own "Safety and Happiness" second. "Just government" has only one purpose — "to secure these rights" of life, liberty, etc., and failing to do so, it has given up its legitimate claim to power.

That was not only the case in the American Revolution either. The United States government has frequently championed the rights of self-determination for other people as well, whether the oppressed nations of Eastern Europe during the Cold War or the nations of North Africa during the so-called Arab Spring.

Yet the establishment politicians and mainstream media mock those who yearn for unfettered liberty in our own country. Take, as just one firm example among many, the Second Amendment. It's about as clear as the water in a Rocky Mountain stream: "A well regulated militia being necessary to the security of a free state, the right of the people to keep and bear arms shall not be infringed."

The key words of that amendment are "shall not be infringed." There is no wiggle room there for people who want to restrict certain kinds of rifles or handguns, or determine how many rounds are permissible for each type of weapon. To be precise, "shall not be infringed" means shall not be limited, restricted, modified, undermined or encroached upon. Could that be any plainer?

Nor can anyone argue that because the authors of the Bill of Rights included a specific assumption in the amendment about the value of a well regulated militia, that the right to keep and bear arms can therefore be ignored or abridged if modern folks disagree with the Founders about what a "well regulated militia" is. No matter how you change the meaning of the stated assumption, it does not change the definitive conclusion: "...the right OF THE PEOPLE to keep and bear arms shall not be infringed." That can only be changed by a further amendment to the Constitution.

Yet we see United States senators and the president and vice president, who have all taken oaths to protect and defend the Constitution, working overtime to infringe, restrict, limit, abridge and all but eliminate the RIGHT to keep and bear arms! They do so on behalf of a sincere belief that restricting firearms will increase the individual security of our citizens.

But the stated assumption or purpose of the Second Amendment, in its very own text, is that the people's access to firearms is intended not to protect individuals from harm, but to ensure "the security of a free state." And clearly, the Founders considered a free state to be vulnerable to some sort of threat.

What exactly could they have meant?

Well, if you thumb through the Constitution, you will find over 200 references to either "state" or "states." Other than references to "the United States" and two references to "foreign states," all of the other uses of the word state refer to the individual states in our diverse country. It is therefore safe to assume that the reference to the "security of a free state" also refers to the individual states in the United States. Moreover, the militia was understood at the time to be a military unit organized at the state level.

Therefore, when the Second Amendment was passed, its intention was obviously to provide for the security of the individual states, not for the security of the federal government known as the United States. That being so, we must ask who or what was considered a threat to the individual states. The answer surely was not England or Canada, but rather the federal government itself.

Remember, the entire purpose of the Constitution was to enshrine limited government, and the Founders tried to provide clear directions that the rights of the individuals and the individual states should always take precedence over the insistent bullying of the federal government except in cases where the Constitution plainly spelled out federal supremacy. If in doubt that this is true, citizens are advised to read the Ninth and 10th Amendments. YOU are supposed to have the power, not the federal government.

Which brings us back to Thomas Jefferson, independence and the "right of the people to alter or abolish" any form of government which is destructive to the ability of the people to secure their rights.

We as Americans have always understood that we have certain God-given rights, and we had better be willing to fight and die for those rights, or else we will surely lose them. Jefferson put it this way:

"We hold these truths to be self-evident, that all men are created equal, that they are endowed by their Creator with certain unalienable Rights, that among these are Life, Liberty and the pursuit of Happiness. —That to secure these rights, Governments are instituted among Men, deriving their just powers from the consent of the governed, — That whenever any Form of Government becomes destructive of these ends, it is the Right of the People to alter or to abolish it, and to institute new Government..."

What I don't understand is just when we — proud Americans, freedom fighters, defenders of liberty — lost these supposedly unalienable rights for ourselves. We are told that because President Lincoln prevented the Southern states from seceding over slavery, the people of the United States of America no longer enjoy the right of self-determination that we still promote whole-heartedly for Egypt, Cuba and North Korea.

No matter how bad things get, we are stuck with it — stuck with politicians and judges who abuse the Constitution, stuck with "repeated injuries and usurpations," stuck with a shriveled Second Amendment. No matter how the rights to life, liberty and the pursuit of happiness are abridged or truncated, we should just smile and be grateful for a federal government that knows better than we do.

And considering the leviathan nature of the federal government, that just may be true. For all practical purposes, we the people now serve the government and not the other way around.

Of course, it is a matter of faith — and history — that no government instituted among man can stand for long without "the consent of the governed." What we now must determine is whether the governed — we the people of the United States of America — will consent to tyranny or not.

On that, the jury is still out.

FDR, OBAMA AND THE NEED FOR OPPOSITION

March 17, 2013

Some time ago, a reader presented me with a yellowed newspaper clipping from 1936, which seems to grow more relevant every day.

It is a syndicated column by Frank R. Kent of the Baltimore Sun and was written just after the re-election of President Franklin Roosevelt.

I'd never heard of Kent before, but if you look him up on the Internet, you will find that he was a lifelong Democrat and early supporter of Franklin Roosevelt, who got a wake-up call sometime during FDR's first term and then spent the next 10 years dumbfounded that the American people were so easily bamboozled out of their birthright.

Kent was a Jeffersonian Democrat, who believed in small government, a balanced budget and states' rights, and when he saw the direction Roosevelt intended to lead the country he put his heels in the ground and fought back with all his will. Nor did he apologize for being a critic of the president.

As he said, "The more power Mr. Roosevelt has, the more need there would seem to be for critical opposition."

Kent's column is a welcome reminder that the horror conservatives feel today at the willful blindness of their fellow citizens is nothing new. Indeed, I am more and more impressed by the similarities between our current regime and that of Roosevelt.

President Obama, although from a very different background than FDR, governs from almost the same sense of privilege. Both presidents embraced the most impoverished as their power base, but seem to feel more comfortable personally when surrounded by millionaires and celebrities. And in both cases, the poor have been willing to forgive a multitude of sins in their privileged leaders as long as the rhetorical alms kept flowing from the fount of noblesse oblige.

Indeed, it is the unworldly patience of the poor which allowed FDR to maintain power for so long while accomplishing so little of real value for the economy, and the same patience for President Obama which allowed him to maintain high popularity ratings throughout his first term even while his policies were dismantling the American dream.

But, really, how popular is President Obama? As popular as FDR after his first term? Probably not. His positive ratings have hovered mostly around 50 percent, and now are even a few points lower. Yet because of the media echo chamber constantly touting him as the Great Leader opposed only by small-minded Republican extremists, he should come with a warning like the one that is printed on the rear-view mirror: "Politicians may be smaller than they appear on television."

Kent was infuriated by the same treatment given to FDR by the journalists of his day, and began his column with an excoriation of journalists who were more Democratic cheerleaders than champions of truth.

"The curious impression seems to have been created among some of Mr. Roosevelt's more exuberant journalistic spokesmen that there was no one in the country opposed to him at all and that his election was unanimous."

Sound familiar?

We saw the same expectation among journalists in 2012 that after President Obama was re-elected, everyone would get in line and back his programs wholeheartedly because, after all, "the people have spoken!"

But let's not forget that Obama's massive victory gave him just a hair over 51 percent of the popular vote, and a 4-point margin of victory in all. Compared to Roosevelt's 61-37 trouncing of Gov. Alf Landon, it almost seems like President Obama would have been wise to keep quiet about mandates and "the will of the people" and just stay out of trouble for four years. But of course that isn't going to happen.

Indeed, the first thing we heard from the White House and its supporters was that Republicans ought to start compromising in order to stay relevant. No real explanation of how they were going to be relevant by giving up and sounding like Democrats, but that was the order of the day.

But even in 1936, when Roosevelt really did win by a landslide, there were opponents like Frank Kent who could not sacrifice principle just to be popular, no matter how much pressure was brought to bear on them.

And pressure there was, in the form of what Kent called "a lot of nonsense about a new 'era of good feeling,' in which Mr. Roosevelt's critics will join his admirers, and all anti-New Dealers promptly get behind the President... A nice sentimental, slushy time is to be had by all. No discordant note is to be sounded. Everybody is to sing in the angel chorus, with robes, harps and haloes provided by jolly Mr. Farley, who has promised there are to be no reprisals and is beamingly modest and magnanimous."

Substitute Mr. Axelrod for Mr. Farley and we pretty much have the game plan for the first six months of the post-re-election Obama administration. The angel chorus is heard nightly on MSNBC, touting President Obama's "charm offensive" while a harpist approximates the "thrill going up Chris Matthews' leg."

Apart from the rhetorical flourish that Mr. Kent achieved in his column, it is significant that the political situation he describes is approximately the same as what we face today.

Those who opposed FDR were painted as "malodorous millionaires," "oppressors of the poor," and "creatures of entrenched greed" just as Republicans today — and especially conservatives — are casually dismissed as minions of the evil "1 percent," haters of the poor, killers of grandma, and racist Nazis who only oppose President Obama because he has darker skin than they do.

Kent pointed out that most of the 16.5 million people who voted against Roosevelt were "very average American citizens who deeply distrusted the wisdom of the Roosevelt policies — and still do." He also noted that "it is a little sudden to rush them into an 'era of good feeling,' where they are expected to pledge cooperation with a man whose direction is uncertain and support a program before they know what it is."

I hear echoes of Pelosi's "we need to pass the bill to find out what is in it" from the Obamacare debate of the first term in Kent's warning from 1936, and I can only wonder what other legislative monstrosities the president might think he can wring out of a demoralized Republican majority in the House.

Heck, looking around, I think he can achieve almost anything he sets his mind to, no matter how unthinkable it would have been just 10 years ago. We are slouching toward Bethlehem (or is that racing toward Armageddon) at a breakneck speed, and every time a Republican stands up and defends the principles on which our country was founded, he or she is surrounded by a pack of ravening journalists intent on cutting their feet out from under them. If you don't support the "new orthodoxy" of America's liberal establishment, then you are a danger to the country or, as Kent described it in 1936, "disgruntled losers... full of bile and bitterness."

Rush Limbaugh famously said of Obama in early 2009, "I hope he fails," and was widely assailed as unpatriotic for not getting behind the president and wishing him well. Limbaugh has amply defended himself on that charge, but Kent's column about FDR is perhaps the best description I have read for why a president must earn support, not just expect it as a spoil of victory. It is also a perfect prescription of what would have to happen in a second Obama term for the country to have any hope of progress.

"Those who opposed him from conviction will hope sincerely he makes it possible for them to support him. If now, with added power and prestige, he sloughs off his shrill radical advisers, devotes himself to getting us back on an even keel, abandons his vengeful attitude toward business, and restores orderly administration, he will have a right to expect and will be entitled to the support of those who opposed him... Such support under such conditions would not only be due but it would be merely enlightened selfishness to give it."

Let's hope that is the future of a new, reunited America.

RESTORATION AMENDMENT: PUTTING THE GENIE OF BIG GOVERNMENT BACK IN BOTTLE

March 24, 2013

A recent letter to the editor got me thinking about the origins of our great country, and how far astray we have gone from the principles enshrined in both the Declaration of Independence and the Constitution of the United States of America.

Like many other patriots before him, this letter writer had invoked the 10th Amendment to the Constitution as a charm or incantation to ward off the dangerous power of the federal government and to restore the rights of the people and the states. But the fact of the matter is that the Ninth and 10th amendments, which explicitly preserve the sovereignty of the people and the states as the originators of the Constitution and the government which it formed, have no practical value. Historically, they have been ignored, and they offer no specific remedy or mechanism by which the states and the people's rights can be preserved and protected.

For a long time, I have thought that the only hope for our country to continue as a bastion of freedom is to return to the original principles of the Constitution. But how exactly could you do so? An amendment demanding that the Constitution be interpreted according to the plain language in which it was written seemed too vague, just another lost cause like the 10th Amendment. An amendment throwing out case law as it applied to the Constitution and declaring a clean slate seemed hopelessly academic.

What was needed was an amendment which both stated plainly its intended goal — to strip the federal government of the power it has grabbed without authority over more than 200 years — and at the same time provided a clear mechanism for restoring America to the principles envisioned by the founders.

Passing such an amendment might be impossible, or it might not. There would certainly be resistance, but how long could that resistance stand in the face of an American people who demanded their Constitution back?

Besides, the alternative is helplessly watching the United States of America continue its suicidal lunge into tyranny.

So, for the sake of liberty, and in honor of the many patriots who have died over the past 226 years to preserve and protect the principles of that sacred Constitution, I am today proposing the Restoration Amendment, an honest effort to put the genie of big government back in the bottle.

While the wording is no doubt in need of refinement, I am fully happy to send it out in the world to make its own way and see what becomes of it. It's purpose is to do to the federal government what Henry David Thoreau proposed we should do with all our lives: "Simplify, simplify."

The Restoration Amendment

Preamble: "Whereas this nation was founded as a union of sovereign states, we the people of the United States of America do hereby affirm and declare that this Constitution created a combined federal government to serve the states and not to rule them. Therefore, from this time forward, let it be understood by all officials, officers, judges and justices within these United States that the individual sovereign states do retain and preserve all those legislative rights and responsibilities which they possessed when they entered the union, with this exception only — that the federal government is authorized to create and administer laws and regulations as expressly directed by this Constitution to fulfill the mandates established by the several states when they joined together under this Constitution or as established by later amendment."

Article 1: "If a power is not expressly granted to the combined federal government of these United States by this Constitution, then that power cannot be exercised, acquired, or enumerated without specific amendment to this document. Therefore, all laws and interpretations of laws which have resulted in the federal government imposing its will on the states or the people without specific authorization from this Constitution or its amendments shall be declared null and void on a date exactly two years following ratification of this amendment by the states in order to allow for an orderly restoration of power back to the states."

Article 2: "In accordance with Article 1 of this Amendment, all federal laws and regulations currently in place shall be subject to judicial appeal and review to ensure that a specific authorization exists in the Constitution that provides a legal framework for that law to be imposed upon the several states and their citizens. If a court finds that no language in the Constitution specifically authorizes the law or regulation, it shall be declared null and void."

Article 3: "All new federal laws and regulations created after the date of ratification of this Amendment shall include a note setting forth the constitutional provision under which they are authorized as an appropriate use of federal power. Such legislative notes shall be subject to judicial review to confirm that such constitutional authorization is valid. Authority shall never be gained from subsequent judicial ruling but only from the expressly worded provisions of the Constitution and its amendments."

Article 4: "The several states shall each retain full sovereignty according to the will of the people as expressed in their individual constitutions. Except in those few instances where the Constitution of the United States expressly grants the federal government power over the states, each state shall make its own determination on how to regulate people, commerce and morals."

Article 5: "Interstate commerce shall be freely ventured without control by the federal government except that the federal government shall be empowered to ensure that each state must treat commerce with all other states on an equal basis. The federal power to regulate interstate commerce as expressed in this Constitution in Article 1, Section 8, shall not be interpreted to allow the federal government any power to tax, regulate or mandate any transaction beyond those powers which are elsewhere explicitly granted by this Constitution and its amendments."

Article 6: "The right of the people to move freely from state to state shall not be infringed."

Article 7: "The power of the federal government or any of its component parts to promote or provide for the general welfare of the United States shall not be construed to mean that the federal government has any powers of regulation, taxation or conscription beyond those explicitly granted in this Constitution or its amendments. The federal government's interest in the general welfare of the United States does not obligate the nation to provide for the specific welfare of each or any individual citizen of the several states."

There you have it. It's longer than I would like, and shorter than it probably needs to be. Perhaps someone can condense it down to a few sentences, but when attempting to secure liberty, it appears to me that there is no excuse for leaving open to interpretation that which can be expressly stated in the first place.

It is, after all, liberal interpretations of our Founding Fathers' conservative ideas which have gotten us into this mess in the first place.

If you have suggestions or comments on how this amendment can be refined, please send them to me. You don't have to tell me that it is a pipe dream; I already know that. But as Thoreau said in "Walden," "If you have built castles in the air, your work need not be lost; that is where they should be. Now put the foundations under them."

RESTORING THE CONSTITUTION — WITH A LITTLE HELP FROM MY FRIENDS

March 31, 2013

Last week, I somewhat audaciously proposed a "Restoration Amendment" to free the U.S. Constitution from decades of judicial precedent and neglect and return it as much as possible to the original intent of our nation's founders.

Among the reactions from readers, two in particular prevailed. Many readers were grateful for the effort and pitched in with their own ideas for how the federal leviathan could be tamed, but many others were dismal and dismayed — certain that any honest effort to reform the nation was already a lost cause, and that the Constitution was already good enough if only people would follow it.

Probably all of us who are concerned about the state of the union can find a certain amount of sympathy for those who have essentially surrendered to the inevitability of decay and destruction of the principles of liberty enshrined in the Constitution. But that does not mean we should accept that destruction gladly. Let's take the tenor of our fight rather from the Irish poet Dylan Thomas, who urged his readers to "rage, rage against the dying of the light."

Certainly, that spirit of resistance is alive and well in America, whether it is called the Tea Party or something else.

The point is that for those of us who have taken the time to study our nation's founding documents, it is impossible to accept the modern federal state as anything but a mockery of that which was intended by George Washington, Thomas Jefferson and James Madison.

Therefore, we continue to look for solutions that will restore the Constitution to its original purpose as a document to regulate the joint relationship between separate sovereign states, and not a roadmap for federal control of every aspect of our individual lives.

I'll highlight a few of the proposals from readers this week, and expect to return with a revised version of the Restoration Amendment in a future column after incorporating some of these new ideas into it. But one thing is certain, the American genius for invention is alive and well, and so is the thirst for liberty.

Inter Lake reader "Pete" pointed out that education ought to be specifically addressed in a Restoration Amendment. After all, when the Constitution was written, there was no federal involvement with education at all, nor is there any constitutional authority by which the Department of Education can be deemed legal. Pete sees a very good reason why such a federal role would never have passed muster with our Founding Fathers: "How can we expect to have free-thinking citizens when they are indoctrinated by the STATE?" he asks, concluding forcefully, "I would prohibit federal involvement in education — period."

Absolutely. If the prior language of the Restoration Amendment is not strong enough to make it clear, then by all means we should include a provision that specifically bars Washington, D.C., from imposing its belief systems on the individual states or, for that matter, the individual students.

Pete also wanted to see a provision that declared that the "individual states bear no fiduciary responsibility to those states who choose to live beyond their means," raising the specter of state bankruptcy, which is certainly a real possibility for California and other profligate spenders. On the other hand, it is hard to imagine how the union could exist with a mongrel mix of bankrupt and solvent states. I'll have to think about that one.

"Helen" reported that there was a law passed in 1803 that said that citizens did not have to follow any law made that was unconstitutional. That wouldn't work without some fine-tuning, but maybe one article of the revised Restoration Amendment could state the right of every American citizen to challenge the constitutionality of every law if they were willing to bear the cost of such a lawsuit. One of the most annoying aspects of common law that prohibits the public from challenging unjust and unconstitutional laws is that they have to prove "standing" and rarely can. In a true constitutional republic, every citizen should have standing when defending the people's Constitution.

"OhMy" envisioned a provision that would restrict the ability of any government to take more than 10 percent of a citizen's wealth or earnings. That, or something else like it, might make for a healthier, freer society, but it would be beyond the scope of the Restoration Amendment's intent to put things back the way they used to be. Although the income tax was a later amendment to the Constitution, and its legitimacy has been challenged by some, that fight must remain for another day.

Several readers, including "Paul," proposed a paragraph that "specifically states that the Congress as a group and the federally elected politicians as individuals and federal bureaucrats as individuals cannot exempt themselves from the rules and laws that they impose on the rest of us." I have no doubt that such a provision would be adopted by acclamation by the general public, but getting the elites of Congress to vote for it strikes me as about the same likelihood as Marie Antoinette manning the barricades during the French Revolution.

"Ol' Jim" took controls on our elected and unelected officials a step further and proposed that any member of Congress or judge who proposes an unconstitutional bill, or subverts the Constitution in any way "shall immediately be removed from office and banned from further government service of any sort for a period of not less than 120 years." He also specified that, "There can be no 'compelling government interest' allowing violation of the terms of the U.S. Constitution."

"HTC" likewise argued that the amendment must make clear "that any justice who violates these clear restrictions has committed an impeachable offense that requires the people's elected representatives to convene a 'constitutional court' to decide if removal from office is indeed appropriate." He is right that some such conveyance of justice must be included in order to ensure that the provisions of the Restoration Amendment are followed through, but I am pessimistic about the ability to codify such a process in a way that incontrovertibly protects it from mischief and subversion.

HTC also called for a process to enable recall elections of representatives and senators in the face of such violations. Although representatives have never been subject to recall (perhaps because of their short two-year term), senators were indeed subject to recall under the original Constitution because they served at the pleasure of the state legislatures, which appointed them until the 17th amendment was ratified in 1913.

"Scott" shared a number of interesting ideas, but most significant to re-establishing the primacy of the states, as it existed prior to the Civil War, would be establishing a legal process of nullification by which states could overturn federal laws or Supreme Court rulings that are antithetical to the beliefs or morals of the individual states. This, it seems to me, would help to establish the sense of "we the people" as the sovereigns of the Constitution, instead of "we the five black-robed justices" that we have been increasingly stuck with as the arbiters of our rights and responsibilities the past 50 years.

Well, there you have it — a grab bag of ideas all aimed at giving the people more power and the politicians less. You may say I'm a dreamer, but I'm not the only one.

THE STRUGGLE FOR POWER
AND THE COST OF CONSCIENCE

September 22, 2013

Nothing about the political battle between conservatives and liberals is new — not the passion, not the beliefs and not the absolute certainty on both sides that the country is doomed.

You could go back to the nation's founding, and you would find similar disputes such as we are engaged in today. Alexander Hamilton and Thomas Jefferson waged a fierce fight over the notion of a central bank, for instance, and the same underlying themes were apparent then that are now being discussed regarding the need for federal oversight of health care, education, law enforcement, marriage and virtually every other element of daily life.

The essential distillation of the argument comes down to this: Freedom versus big government.

Jefferson believed in an innate moral sense that he and others called natural law. This inner wisdom could be trusted to guide most people to govern themselves, while in Jefferson's mind, government at its best existed only to ensure that when bad people (or bad governments) worked to deprive others of their basic rights, there would be some power marshalled to restore balance.

Hamilton, on the other hand, like all good liberals, thought that people would make a muck of it if they were given their free hand. He thus saw the role of government as essential to protect the people not just in rare instances, but on a recurring and routine basis. It is arguable that the nation might have turned in an entirely different direction had Hamilton not met an early demise at the hands of Aaron Burr, but maybe not. Because over the course of the past 225 years, the dour paternalism of Hamilton has seen a genuine resurgence while the boyish optimism of Jefferson has been sent a-packing by one after another do-gooder who thought average folks just aren't very good at managing their own lives.

Jefferson's freedom-lovers haven't entirely given up the fight, but to some extent they've gone to ground. The Tea Party you always read about isn't nearly as scary as MSNBC's bomb squad makes them out to be. Other than the occasional Koch Brother, in fact, the Tea Party seems more or less impotent. That's one of the problems of the Jeffersonian model in the modern age — its proponents have a natural fear of large government, and by extension, large organizations. They'd rather take care of their problems on their own, which means showing up as part of a mass movement is largely foreign to their make-up.

Liberals, on the other hand, rather enjoy wielding power in bulk. They truly believe they know better than you and I, and they are convinced that their well-meaning laws, regulations, agencies, bureaucracies and reforms will keep herding us sheep toward a better life, even if one or two of us have to be sacrificed as mutton along the way.

When enough liberals get together, they call it Occupy This or Occupy That, and they feel pretty successful when they get to take over a college campus or a city park. I suppose they never thought about the fact that for most of us the verb "to occupy" refers to an invasion — and that's exactly what their nanny government's incessant encroachments into our personal liberties feels like.

If I sound a little bitter, don't worry. It's nothing that a little medical intervention won't solve. And when that Obamacare kicks in on January 1, I'll be able to get a 100 percent reimbursable checkup to find out what ails me. Maybe those government-funded doctors will be able to give me a shot or a pill or just shrink my head so that I fit in better with the small-minded people who run things these days.

And, yes, I understand that a fair number of people out there see me and my love of freedom as the problem — individual responsibility does require a certain degree of orneriness, after all, and a willingness to shrug off the dictates of the majority — but unlike big government, my conscience has no power to conform anyone to my will.

That ultimately is the difference between liberals and conservatives. Whereas liberals seek to wage war on injustice by wielding the power of big government, conservatives wage war against big government by wielding the power of conscience.

Choose your sides carefully. No matter who wins, there will be losers.

'MORAL DECAY' AND THE ROT OF PATERNALISM

September 29, 2013

Last week, I invoked the names of Thomas Jefferson and Alexander Hamilton to trace the roots of American political polarity back to the very foundation of our country.

There is much to recommend both, and we certainly owe Hamilton a debt of gratitude for his contributions to the Federalist Papers and thus for his role in securing our Constitution at a time when our nation was wobbly and transitional.

Nonetheless, with more than 200 years behind us, we can see that Jefferson's vision of limited government secured for us something much more important than a Constitution, and that is liberty.

We still have a Constitution, but the cancerous central government that Hamilton's philosophy unleashed on us has made the concept of liberty increasingly irrelevant in America.

What is liberty when you can be forced by your government to spend endless hours toiling in the Kafka-esque maze of compliance and kow-towing that is our federal government today? As businesses and individuals scurry to curry favor with their masters in Washington, D.C., the nation's wealth is being absorbed into a bottomless drain of regulation and dictate.

And what's scary is that this is the accepted norm. The Supreme Court has joined with Congress and the president to rewrite the very rules which were intended to protect the people. Now the Constitution of the United States of America is an instrument of the government, not a solemn vow of the people. The blessings of liberty have been replaced with the burdens of noblesse oblige.

To accurately reflect the current situation, the Preamble would today have to be phrased something like this:

"We the people of the United States, in order to form a more perfect welfare state, establish social justice, insure domestic compliance, provide for open borders, promote the general anesthesia, and secure the benefits of big government to ourselves and our posterity, do impose and self-validate this Constitution of the United States of America."

That pretty much sums it up, and yet because of the "general anesthesia" that has been so effectively levied upon the people for the past hundred years, what should be the self-evident truth of our sad predicament is instead considered the crackpot invention of rebellious "crazies" like Ted Cruz and Sarah Palin. Think "The Matrix," and you will not be far off.

Of course, all you need to do to see the truth is open your eyes — or read a history book from before 1970 or so. We no longer live in the real world, folks — but it's still there to be rediscovered.

Take this headline from 1969: "O'Connor Cites Moral Decay; Government Paternalism."

That certainly caught my eye when I was doing research on some old-time businesses in Kalispell. The speaker was George O'Connor, then president of the Montana Power Co., who was addressing the Kalispell Rotary Club on Maundy Thursday.

Mr. O'Connor was lamenting the decline of the nation. After praising the invention of America and "200 years of American life under the Christian influence of God-fearing people" and noting that "nowhere on earth has so much progress been made in such a little time," he then concluded that such progress had stopped about 35 or 40 years previously, about the time of the commencement of the New Deal.

"Now maybe it's time we take a look at what we have reaped," he told those Rotarians. "There has been a decay in the Christian philosophy. For the first 150 years our people had great respect for the rights of others; today it is the law of the jungle. Our children were taught to respect the property rights of other citizens; today there are riots, demonstrations, and all we as a nation do is appoint a commission to see what's wrong with our social structure...

"The Supreme Court by virtue of some of its decisions is making it more comfortable for the criminally inclined. Maybe it's time we start going back to church, not just Easter Sunday but every Sunday, and encourage our young people to go because a majority of them are fine young people."

This part of O'Connor's speech is most remarkable not because of its content, but because it happened at all. Whether you agree with his assessment of how Christian philosophy is tied up in our heritage and our success as a nation, you must at least be struck by the fact that in 1969 a major business leader still felt comfortable to promote a moral point of view in public.

This simply doesn't happen any more. Or when it does, such as the public pronouncement recently by the CEO of the Chick fil-A restaurant chain about homosexual marriage, there is an immediate national movement to shame, mock and vilify traditional values and those who promote them. Were the CEO of a major power company to even cite "Christian philosophy" today, he would probably be skirting the law, if not breaking it outright. There is almost no chance that a modern-day CEO of a public utility would declare, as O'Connor did, that during the Great Depression, "Americans turned to a servant, Jesus Christ, and he was our master."

That collapse of the invocation of morality in the public square can be attributed in large part to the growth of central government at the cost of our personal liberty, and perhaps O'Connor sensed that his kind's days were already numbered, for he next lamented the leviathan which government had become.

"But while I'm disturbed by the breakdown in law and order," he said, "I am more concerned about the growing paternalism of government. A government that is getting to be our master. A government that wants to assume responsibility for the type of toothpaste we use, how it is packaged; for the materials in our clothing; wants to tell us how to run our farms;

regulate the pipeline industry; and is an authority on every type of business."

Please don't tell me that we have not lost any liberty. When every choice we make is circumscribed by the government's nanny-state do-goodism, when every business has to serve Washington first and the consumer second, when we have a Congress that wants to make decisions for us about our health care, our cars, and our culture, then we have not only lost our liberty, we have lost the land of the noble free.

Is that important enough to write about? Is that important enough to speak out about? George O'Connor thought so, and he told the Kalispell Rotary just why it ought to matter to them, and ultimately why it ought to matter to us these 44 years later:

"Unless we strive to preserve the things handed down to us; unless we let men run their own businesses and if they are lucky enough make a profit and keep some of it; then there will be no economy in the Flathead, Montana, or our nation."

Let our watchword be liberty, and let us not be distracted by convenience, compromise or derision. Whatever the cost, carry on. That — not a free ride — is the American way.

AMEND IT, OR ELSE …

October 20, 2013

I've written repeatedly about the mostly unspoken constitutional crisis that has enveloped our country for the past 100 years and have even gone so far as to draft a Restoration Amendment to attempt to restore a proper balance between the power of the federal government and the states and individual citizens.

For the most part, I have concluded that serious change of the U.S. Constitution to reflect the original intent of the nations' founders is virtually impossible. Nonetheless, I continue to argue that the only appropriate response to the progressives' decades-long push to "transform" America is to fight back with a plan to "restore" the Constitution's governing principles.

And since the Supreme Court, multiple presidents and the Congress have been unwilling to defend the principle of limited federal government, it is necessary for the people and the states to rise up and reclaim their sovereignty.

The only peaceful way to accomplish that is through amendment to the Constitution, and the only means of amending the Constitution that doesn't require the active participation of Congress is the process described in Article Five of the Constitution whereby two-thirds of the state legislatures may demand that Congress call a "convention for proposing amendments." Under our current 50-state union, that would mean 34 state legislatures would need to submit applications for a convention before it could take place.

Once the convention began, there is no certainty exactly what would take place because such a convention has never taken place yet. In fact, when a few efforts to call a convention got close to being approved by the requisite 34 states, Congress short-circuited the process by proposing amendments on its own, or passing other legislation which seemed to respond to the people's complaints.

The main argument against a convention for proposing amendments is that the convention might exceed the original intentions of the state legislatures and propose amendments not even yet foreseen, or might swing the country in a direction that is dangerous.

This argument fails on two points:

1) The political creativity of the American people did not cease upon the close of the original Constitutional Convention in 1787. Nor did the concept of a republic governed by the people. If the representatives of the American people were to meet as a convention, I have no doubt that they would intelligently debate the future (and past) of our country in a way that would honor our nation's founders. To assume otherwise suggests that we the people are no longer capable of self-government nor worthy of the trust of our posterity.

2) Even if the constitutional convention were to get out of control and propose dangerous amendments that could lead to either tyranny or anarchy, these amendments would still need

to be approved by three-fourths of the states (at least 38 as currently configured) in order to become part of the Constitution. To assume that the states could not be trusted to protect their own sovereignty and their own citizens raises the question of why we trust them with any responsibility at all!

Moreover, if both the people and the states were to concur on a grand scheme to destroy liberty and enthrone tyranny, then wouldn't it be better for We the People to find out now just where we stand?

If you are intrigued by this discussion, I suggest you visit the Outlaw Inn on Monday for the educational seminar being presented by Rob Natelson, a former University of Montana law professor and Republican gubernatorial candidate. He is currently affiliated with the Independence Institute think tank based in Denver.

Natelson is a preeminent scholar advocating an Article Five convention, and in his opinion, there is no chance of a runaway convention. I don't know if he is right or not, but as a pessimist, I am always on guard against the worst possible scenario. It would certainly not surprise me if there were an attempt to hijack the convention, but what do you think is worse: the remote possibility of a runaway convention or the absolute certainty of what we already have — a runaway Congress?

Doing nothing only ensures the status quo — keeping the dysfunctional, power-grabbing federal government we have now. To paraphrase Nathan Hale, "Give me a constitutional convention or give me death."

BANKRUPTING AMERICA: OR, GORBACHEV'S REVENGE

November 3, 2013

It is a well-known fact that Ronald Reagan's military buildup in the 1980s was largely intended to force the Soviet Union to spend money it didn't have on weapons it didn't need. The goal? Bankrupting the Soviet Union and freeing millions of people from the confines of communist totalitarianism.

There were other components of that strategy, including the lesser-known plan to flood the market with Mideast oil in order to bring the price down so that the Soviet Union could not depend on profits from its huge oil and gas reserves to keep up with the cost of military expansion.

As a result, the Soviet empire crumbled. Gorbachev had to cut loose Poland and then the rest of Eastern Europe and finally presided over the death of the Soviet Union.

Unfortunately, communism did not die with it. Nor did the determination of millions of people to see the collapse of the United States under the mistaken belief that poverty in a free society is somehow more oppressive than poverty in a slave state.

Thus, for the past 30 years, forces have been at work to undermine America in just the way that Reagan undermined the Soviet Union. Not in an arms race, because America has no stomach for war any longer — not after one failed venture after another — but by using a cunning strategy that cannot fail to bring us to our knees if the American people continue to think with their hearts and feel with their brains.

In essence, the enemies of America have challenged us to a "conscience race" — just how much do we care about our fellow man? Is the United States really just a heartless oligarchy that exploits the multitudinous poor for the benefit of the greedy 1 percent? Or will we reach into our purse and use our legendary wealth for the advantage of the downtrodden — the homeless, the hungry, the handicapped, the unemployed, the unsung, and the undocumented?

The answer, of course, is obvious. Starting in the 1930s with Social Security and unemployment insurance and continuing right through the introduction of the subsidized health-care insurance program known as Obamacare on Oct. 1, the U.S. Congress has provided a helping hand to any and every cause that can put together a street demonstration, a petition or (these days) a website.

And the enemies of America know this. They are not stupid.

So they are using our compassion as a weapon against us, just as we used the Russians' urge for world dominance as a weapon against them. Call it Gorbachev's revenge. Our enemies know that we truly care about people as individuals and want to assist everyone in achieving a better life, so we have been challenged to do more than we possibly can. This is straight out of Saul Alinsky's "Rules for Radicals," where Rule No. 4 is "Make the enemy live up to its own book of rules."

This is serious business because the rule in America is that every person counts — and so by challenging the government to provide for the well-being of every individual, our enemies are using our own generosity and compassion to bankrupt us.

The point isn't whether or not Americans want to help the homeless, the hungry, etc., but rather what can we realistically do as a government to assist those people? I have heard it described as the lifeboat dilemma. A certain number of people are safe on board the lifeboat, but many more are still in the water — plaintive desperate, and deserving — but if those who are safe give in to their emotions and try to save everyone in the water, then the boat will sink and all will be drowned. Only rational thought can save anyone in such a circumstance, even if our hearts are breaking. But too often, people think with their hearts and surrender to emotions which put them and their loved ones in danger.

That is where we are at as a nation today. It's why we have been bamboozled into accepting the inevitability of Obamacare, which is not really a health-care program so much as a massive redistribution of wealth. It's why this week we are going to start hearing demands from the left that the federal government must restore food-stamp benefits to prior unrealistic levels even though we have no money to pay for those benefits. It's also why Americans are being challenged to commit the capital crime of rewarding illegal aliens with immunity, paid benefits and a path to citizenship.

The goal is to get the United States government to commit as much money as possible toward as many humanitarian causes as possible to the point where eventually the system will collapse.

Of course, it is reasonable for you to be skeptical of such a claim. You should properly ask me for substantiation before you believe it. But it is also appropriate for doubtful readers to be swayed by such evidence when it is presented, and not blindly deny and denounce as ridiculous any suggestion that our way of life is under attack by the enemies of capitalism and democracy.

Those who ridicule ideas they are afraid of are following another one of radical community organizer Saul Alinsky's rules: "Rule No. 5: 'Ridicule is man's most potent weapon.' There is no defense. It's irrational. It's infuriating."

The one-two punch of Alinsky's Rules 4 and 5 is what has turned the United States into a basket case. First our enemies have challenged us to live up to our nation's compassionate ideals; then they have ridiculed anyone who has questioned whether we really have the ability to do so. Tea Party conservatives are painted as monsters because they have the audacity to point out that a 10-person lifeboat cannot save 30 people. This is the obligatory result of a nation thinking with its heart and feeling with its brain.

The only possible way to fight back is with facts, and the fact is that leftists and communists have been straightforward and honest about their goals and their tactics as they seek to topple our government and our way of life.

In 1966, an article entitled "The Weight of the Poor: A Strategy to End Poverty" was published in the Nation, a left-leaning magazine. Written by the husband and wife team of Frances Fox Piven and Richard Cloward, the article provided a blueprint for how to bankrupt the federal government by appealing to the compassionate nature of all Americans.

Cloward and Piven proposed that American society's urge to take care of our poorest members could be used by an "organized" welfare class to leverage a "guaranteed annual income and thus an end to poverty."

The method of this revolution (or transformation) would be through enrolling more and more people onto the rolls of the welfare state, thus redistributing wealth from the rich to the poor and eventually collapsing the system so that something "better" could take its place. The more people who were getting financial assistance from the government, the more power those people would have as a group, in order to force even larger benefits.

Almost all social policy innovations since the 1960s have been incremental steps in the Cloward and Piven plan to bankrupt America by creating "entitlements" that a fair and just tax system could never support. Eventually when the government could no longer meet its payments, the poor would rise up and demand change, whether through violence or the vote, in what Cloward and Piven described "a profound financial and political crisis."

Welcome to the crisis, ladies and gentlemen.

We've managed to borrow $8 trillion in five years in order to assuage our conscience and to assure the world that we really are a compassionate nation. And at the same time, we've invited so many people into the lifeboat that our chance of ever reaching the shores of fiscal sanity is almost non-existent.

At least when the end comes it will probably happen quickly, and we will have the benefit of feeling good about ourselves as we sink what was once the greatest nation in the world.

THE TYRANNY OF BUREAUCRACY

November 10, 2013

Saint Paul noted some 2,000 years ago that the root of all evil is the love of money. A corollary of that prescription might be that the root of all tyranny is the love of other people's money.

It would seem that the power to tax and spend is a lure to potential tyrants as much as putrefying carrion is to bare-toothed scavengers. Other people's money allows any politician to convert the public's own love of filthy lucre into a power base of potential voters. With enough money to dole out of the public treasury, even the most disreputable officeholder can earn the esteem of those on the receiving end of his or her beneficence, thus cementing power and inviting corruption.

I have written before about the warning of Alexis de Tocqueville, the French philosopher, about the danger that would befall American democracy as it grew from its origins of rugged individualism to the inevitable day when the government would grow strong enough to first provide for every individual's needs and then later tell them just what those needs are.

Here is how Tocqueville (in his essential "Democracy in America") described his vision of tyranny in a democratic republic where the average people had surrendered their sovereignty to the whims of the ruling class:

"Above this race of men stands an immense and tutelary power, which takes upon itself alone to secure their gratifications and to watch over their fate. That power is absolute, minute, regular, provident, and mild. It would be like the authority of a parent if, like that authority, its object was to prepare men for manhood; but it seeks, on the contrary, to keep them in perpetual childhood: it is well content that the people should rejoice, provided they think of nothing but rejoicing. For their happiness such a government willingly labors, but it chooses to be the sole agent and the only arbiter of that happiness; it provides for their security, foresees and supplies their necessities, facilitates their pleasures, manages their principal concerns, directs their industry, regulates the descent of property, and subdivides their inheritances: what remains, but to spare them all the care of thinking and all the trouble of living?"

Does that sound familiar? Have we not completely fallen under the sway of de Tocqueville's "immense and tutelary power"? Do not millions of people owe their allegiance to the government for the privilege of receiving food stamps, unemployment insurance, welfare, business or individual tax credits, college loans, agricultural subsidies, and now even health insurance? Is there any branch or even twig of life through which the sap of federal subsidies does not run?

No wonder the Tea Party, with its insistence on turning off the federal spigot, is being painted by progressives as a danger to the national well-being. The national well-being, after all, is a state of stuporific addiction to entitlements and congressionally approved benefits spooned out by thousands of federal bureaus and agencies that prove their worth by keeping the populace in what de Tocqueville called "perpetual childhood."

This role of government as "the sole agent and the only arbiter of [the people's] happiness" is nothing new, though Obamacare has pushed it to a new level. As I said at the beginning of this column, there is something almost satanically appealing about the power to spend other people's money in a bid to make yourself look beneficent. Nor can a politician easily resist the tears of a newborn's mother or the plaintive cries of a family left homeless by fire.

That last example brings to mind the question asked of Rep. Davy Crockett by a Tennessee farmer in the 1820s:

"Where do you find in the Constitution any authority to give away the public money in charity?"

Crockett, you see, had given in to the noble impulse to help those less fortunate than ourselves and had voted to spend federal funds for the relief of families that had been left homeless as the result of a ravaging fire in Georgetown. He never gave a thought to whether such a payment was constitutional or not, but just did it because it felt good. It took his constituent's question to make Crockett examine his own conscience and realize he had erred by authorizing the payment of $20,000 for those homeless families.

As Horace Bunce, the Tennessee farmer, explained to Crockett:

"The power of collecting and disbursing money at pleasure is the most dangerous power that can be entrusted to man... [W]hile you are contributing to relieve one, you are drawing it from thousands who are even worse off than he. If you had the right to give anything, the amount was simply a matter of discretion with you, and you had as much right to give $20,000,000 as $20,000. If you have the right to give to one, you have the right to give to all; and, as the Constitution neither defines charity nor stipulates the amount, you are at liberty to give to any and everything which you may believe, or profess to believe, is a charity, and to any amount you may think proper.

You will very easily perceive, what a wide door this would open for fraud and corruption and favoritism, on the one hand, and for robbing the people on the other."

If it was not evident in the 1820s, it is most certainly self-evident now. With a bow to Lord Acton, "Money seduces, and other people's money seduces absolutely." As Horace Bunce predicted, the federal government has become nothing more than a conduit for redistribution of wealth. To deny that truth is to live in a fairy-tale world where America remains the champion of freedom and the economic engine of the world.

If we ARE the economic engine of the world, we are permanently stuck in first gear, thanks to the crush of regulations, mandates and red tape that Congress has imposed on business. And if we ARE the champion of freedom, it is the freedom to do what we are told to do by the federal government or else pay a fine, tax or penalty (or whatever Justice Roberts decides to call it this time).

An editorial in the Daily Inter Lake in 1924 lamented that one-twelfth of the population of the United States was then supported by some component of government — federal, state or local. That was just jobholders and their dependents, and that percentage may be approximately the same today, but when you add all the people who are supported by the government through benefits and entitlements, the number quickly doubles or triples. Millions of people are beholden to the gargantuan government, which is often criticized but never willingly diminished.

As the 1924 editorial writer noted, the number of people dependent on government "seems needlessly large but is one of the penalties we pay for government by bureaucracy and it will continue to increase until there is a return to comparative sanity, of which there is no indication at the present time."

Amen. And just as the Tea Party spokespeople today are branded as radicals for proposing smaller government, in 1924 it was noted that: "To single out any activity for comment is to provoke the ire of some organized minority whose favor was curried by its creation and whose clamor of defense would send the over-timid congressmen scurrying for cover if repeal was mentioned."

We have indeed at last reached the era prophesied by that long-ago editorial writer, who worried about a bureaucracy that would "supervise every conceivable activity from the cradle to the grave" — and would be able to do so in perpetuity thanks to "the passive acquiescence of the great majority that permits the condition to exist without serious protest."

To paraphrase Edmund Burke, "The only thing necessary for tyranny to prevail is for good men to do nothing."

PROGRESSIVES & PATIENCE:
A LOOK AT HOW WE GOT OBAMACARE

December 8, 2013

Obamacare didn't happen overnight.

For the last 75 years, progressives have trotted out the idea of compulsory health care or subsidized national health insurance every decade or so, been defeated, and then gone back to the drawing board.

Their tenaciousness finally paid off in 2010 when Congress by the narrowest of margins passed a bill with no Republican votes, and President Obama signed into law his "signature" achievement. No wonder Vice President Biden took the opportunity on that occasion to tell the president that passing health-care reform was a "big f---ing deal."

But now that the fruits of national health insurance are starting to be harvested in the form of higher premiums, higher deductibles, and higher taxes (and paradoxically more people becoming uninsured), it might be time to revisit some of the warnings that doctors and politicians shouted for the past three-quarters of a century. Nationalized health insurance might be a big deal, but it is not necessarily a good deal.

You can find strains of the argument for socialized medicine back into the 19th century, but let's give credit for national transformation where it is due and start with Franklin

Roosevelt. Once the president's New Deal had transformed banking, welfare, unemployment, retirement, housing, public works, and labor relations, it was time to move on to health care.

Roosevelt passed on including national health insurance in his Social Security bill of 1935 because of opposition by the American Medical Association, but he didn't give up. In 1938, he called a National Health Conference in Washington, D.C.

A report by D.C. insider columnist Rodney Dutcher describes the program envisioned by Roosevelt in terms that are almost indistinguishable from what passed in 2010:

"New Dealers have in mind a grant-in-aid plan which would encourage states to set up their own health insurance schemes within certain federal standards, the federal and state governments to contribute funds to the general program in each co-operating state. Health insurance systems to be supported by payroll contributions would go side by side with arrangements, especially in rural areas, for setting up new public health services by taxation and local contributions."

No wonder it was so easy for congressional staffers to write up the 2,000-plus page Patient Protection and Affordable Care Act of 2010 — all they had to do was dust off the original proposal by FDR and change a few terms. "Health insurance schemes" became "health exchanges," for instance, and "public health services" became "community health centers."

There was also the same "human theater" that President Obama specializes in when trying to turn political decisions into emotional ones instead. But whereas Obama had "the fainting girl" at his October press conference to reassure us that YES WE CAN sign on to healthcare.gov (it just may take a while!), FDR had what a headline writer for the Joplin (Mo.) News Herald called "Slums Girl."

Florence Greenberg was trotted out at the National Health Conference in 1938 to sell the desperation of the working class in a pitch to convince the AMA to stop fighting the president. Despite the string of (presumably) fake pearls and cunning hair-do she sported for an AP wire photo, Miss Greenberg was plaintive and forlorn as she made the case for why the government should make health care one of "the inalienable rights" of every citizen.

In essence, Greenberg was the 1930s version of the 1980s version of Barack Obama — a community organizer from Chicago's South Side, she was the saddest thing this side of a hobo camp.

The overcome AP reporter gushed that, "Miss ... Greenberg, who never had ridden on a railroad train before she traveled here," told the conference delegates, "my people — the steel workers, the packing house workers, the International Harvester workers, did not know what it means to demand that their needs, their lives, their happiness be considered," but now they are demanding "our government take health from the list of luxuries to be bought only by money."

Gosh, if that girl were still around today, she would have no problem being elevated to U.S. Senate on the basis of her oratory alone, just as President Obama was. Being a friend of the "packing house workers," Greenberg was very likely also a friend of Saul Alinsky — the godfather of community organizers — who was just then trying to organize the meat packers into a political force.

And although every proponent of national health insurance from FDR forward has denied that it is "socialized medicine," it is no accident that the proponents of nationalization of medical care are all avid progressives who see an expanded role for the federal government in almost every aspect of our lives.

Socialism traditionally has meant that the means of production or distribution of a product or service are owned by the government. But that definition is as antiquated as a horse-and-buggy doctor. The overarching power of our massive federal government to direct and command certain results through regulation and legislation is in some ways far beyond anything Karl Marx would even have imagined possible. Controlling the means of production is much more important than owning it, so yes, the term socialized medicine does fit the agenda of the progressive left.

But so does patience.

There is a perhaps apocryphal story told about Norman Thomas, who ran for president six times as the Socialist Party candidate from 1928 to 1948. The story was repeated frequently by Ronald Reagan when he was an actor campaigning against socialized medicine in 1961.

According to Reagan and others, Thomas said "the American people would never vote for socialism" but that "under the name of liberalism the American people will adopt every fragment of the socialist program."

That may not be entirely true yet, but they are still working on it. Rome didn't fall in a day.

GOVERNMENT HEALTH-CARE DIAGNOSIS: DEPENDENCY

December 15, 2013

The claim: The United States is the richest nation in the world, and as a matter of decency should pay for the health care of all Americans who can't afford to pay for their own.

The truth: The United States is not the richest nation in the world; we are the richest debtor nation in the world. We literally owe trillions of dollars — not just in the national debt, but also in unfunded liabilities for various entitlements.

The problem: The United States doesn't really pay for anyone's health care with its own cash supply, but rather requisitions money from individual taxpayers and appropriates it to someone else's medical bill.

The solution: An educated populace. As Thomas Jefferson noted, education gives "to every citizen the information he needs for the transaction of his own business." In this case, such education would help citizens to understand that their business — their personal needs — cannot rightly be advanced at the expense of some other citizen's life, liberty or property.

I have laid it out plainly, yet the plain truth is that for the past hundred years, an agenda of obfuscation has sought to convince Americans to accept compulsory health care —

seemingly incognizant of the fact that compulsion is nothing more than a fancy word for slavery. Demanding that a doctor or a hospital provide health care to those unwilling or incapable of paying for it is forced labor. Taking money earned by one worker and using it to pay for health care for another worker is theft.

It is no coincidence that this leftist agenda has made its largest advances when times were tough. Franklin Roosevelt planted the seeds of a program of national health insurance during the Great Depression in 1938, and Barack Obama reaped the bitter fruit of Obamacare during the Great Recession in 2010. When people are desperate, they will turn anywhere for help — and on the surface, government health care sounds like a huge relief to poor families.

But the fact of the matter is that government interference in health care through massive regulatory authority over the past 50 years, as well as through imposition of Medicare and other federal health programs, has actually been the main impetus for the skyrocketing costs of medicine. And now the unaffordable cost of health care is being used to promote the necessity of government stepping in to "fix" the problem it caused in the first place. Talk about racketeering!

And yes, I understand the generosity of spirit that yearns to lift the burden off the shoulders of our neighbors, but the lever that accomplishes that goal should never be balanced on the fulcrum of government. Rather, it needs to be raised high by the charitable spirit of our people.

That is true for numerous reasons, but two will suffice. First of all, government doesn't care how much it pays for products or services because it is not government's money — it is OUR money. This results in vastly inflated expenses for health care as for other services. Secondly, the beneficiaries of charity are much more likely to take to heart the sacrifice of those who have donated to them than to show even the slightest gratitude for a government welfare program. Informed that their neighbors helped them, most people will work to either pay it back or "pay it forward," but told that the government helped, most people will ask, "What took them so long?"

In addition to that sense of entitlement, government money also creates a sense of dependency because it is institutionalized charity that people grow to depend on, encouraging them essentially not to strive to better their own lives because their immediate needs are already being met with no particular effort. And that benefits only government and politicians, by making them seem like the essential providers of our needs.

That dependent dynamic was addressed by a 1949 editorial writer in The Portsmouth (Ohio) Times, as follows:

"A welfare state is nothing more or less than a society in which everybody looks to the government for everything. The welfare state politicians would like to include health in their program, for the simple reason that nearly everybody would be involved. It would clinch once and for all their proposition that government is the ultimate source of public welfare."

I am not insensitive to the fact that I am currently on the losing side of this battle, but I maintain hope that common sense will prevail in the years ahead. And I believe the fact that Obamacare was passed on a strictly one-party vote has created the very conditions that were foreseen in 1949:

"...in submitting such a proposition, the welfare statists have asked for a showdown. The question is whether or not those who believe the United States prospered became it steered clear of government control in the past, and will prosper in the future if it continues to do so, will be able to defend their position against welfare state politicians."

No one can be sure of the outcome of such a great battle, but as the Affordable Care Act spreads the government's tentacles through every family and every business in America, the warning of that editorial writer 65 years ago still resonates today.

— That "citizens should not become dependent on government except in emergencies."

— That "private enterprise should not be placed under political control."

— That "the people know more about taking care of themselves than their government knows — or cares."

— That "the power to tax is the power to destroy."

Before it is too late, let us hope that our nation's leaders wake up and acknowledge that those principles are the very bedrock on which our country was founded. And if following those fundamental American principles means that we have to sacrifice cheap health care, at least it shall be a sacrifice waged to preserve our liberty, which was bought even more dearly — with blood and sacred honor.

HOW ABOUT 'SHARED RESPONSIBILITY' FOR FREEDOM — PERIOD!

March 2, 2014

You have to hand it to Nancy Pelosi: She was dead-on accurate when she claimed Congress had to pass Obamacare before we would find out what was in it.

The latest case in point is the "Shared Responsibility Payment," which appears in the Patient Protection and Affordable Care Act, but hasn't been widely appreciated for its Orwellian genius until the IRS started to promote it this year.

The "Shared Responsibility Payment" is the penalty U.S. citizens have to fork over to their federal overlords if they fail to accede to the government's order that they purchase health insurance for themselves and/or their families.

You see, it turns out that by taking individual responsibility for my own health care, I am robbing other citizens of their opportunity to get "affordable health care" because part of my premium payment would be used to offset the fact that millions of other people don't pay enough (or possibly anything) for their health-care insurance.

Therefore, the government, in order to protect its Ponzi scheme, assesses me a "shared responsibility payment" — a tax which can then be used to pay those subsidies by which Obamacare distributes wealth from the not-so-rich to the not-so-poor.

Now please realize this example has nothing to do with me personally. I have a very good health-care plan available to me as an employee of the Daily Inter Lake, which I have taken advantage of for 30 years. But that is something I do out of my own free will, and likewise the newspaper has provided this valuable service as a benefit to its hard-working employees because it recognizes the value of doing so.

That is called the free market. It is a far cry from individual mandates and employer mandates and shared responsibility payments. Imagine if the same kind of logic (or illogic) that is applied to health care by the current regime were also applied to other components of our society. At the end of the cash register receipt from your local grocery store, you could expect to see a shared responsibility payment that was taken from you in order to (supposedly!) feed the less fortunate. On every mortgage and rental payment, there would be a percentage set aside as a "shared responsibility payment" to ensure that no one would ever have to be homeless.

It wouldn't matter whether you might personally be inclined to donate a similar amount of money to good causes or not. The choice would be taken out of your hands. Someone — or something, some government bureaucrat — knows better than you where your money can do the best good. And if you thought your family needed every penny of your hard-earned money to ensure that they would be able to get ahead, live a secure life, gain a college education, and perhaps a decent retirement, then you would be mocked, humiliated and shamed as a capitalist roader. That's why they have to take the "shared responsibility payment" from you — because you can't be trusted to do the right thing. Or at least that is what they will try to convince you — through propaganda from the White House, a variety of "social justice" pushers, and the major news media.

You, hard-working American, are the problem. It is your fault that there is hunger, homelessness and income inequality. Your failure to buy health insurance explains why people are needlessly dying in America! And say it loud enough and long enough, and eventually people start to believe it! We may even be almost to that point.

But maybe not. The best hope for stopping the federal government from controlling every aspect of our lives is education. Don't just go along to get along, or you will very likely be going along with all the Chinese killed in the Cultural Revolution, all the people sent to the Gulags by Stalin, and all the freethinkers sent to the guillotine by the Committee of Public Safety during the Reign of Terror.

Isn't it funny how revolution co-opts words and phrases and makes things that are deadly sound like a move in the right direction? Cultural Revolution! Committee of Public Safety! Patient Protection and Affordable Care Act! Shared Responsibility Payment! When you hear words like that, the best advice is grab hold of your freedom and run for your life.

Of course, there is precedent for this failed experiment in forcing people to take shared responsibility for the less fortunate among us. It is called Marxism. "From each according to his abilities; to each according to his means." The only problem with that utopian sentiment is that it destroys what Confucius called "the will to win" and replaces it with the willingness to wallow. A more sure path to decadence does not exist.

Another way to think of the "shared responsibility payment" is as tribute — the money that enslaved people owe to their conquerors as a sign of submission. This was common in ancient times up through the Roman Empire. Failure to make the payments could result in extreme punishments up to and including death because rejection of the "tax" was considered an insult to the emperor. We don't have an emperor, but the federal government has more and more exhibited the imperial trappings that attend to those who rule with a sense of entitlement rather than a sense of honor.

It is not surprising that the most extreme forms of tribute carry with them an explicit admission of indebtedness to the ruling class. The jizya tax imposed by Muslims on non-Muslims up through the 20th century was seen as "a protection for their not being slain," according to Orientalist Edward William Lane.

The "shared responsibility payment" may not go that far, but it is implicitly an acknowledgment that citizens are obligated to do whatever the government orders them to do. Whether you want to pay for your neighbor's health-care plan or not, you must do so. And once the government has conditioned you to do what IT thinks is right instead of what you think is right, well, you can imagine the rest, and it isn't pretty.

IS FREE SPEECH INTENDED FOR EVERYONE? OR JUST LIBERALS?

March 30, 2014

What is it about liberals that makes them so afraid of free speech, free thought and free expression of ideas, especially on college campuses?

You may have heard about the absolute terror which faculty and students at Rutgers University greeted the news that former U.S. Secretary of State Condoleezza Rice had been chosen as the commencement speaker at this May's graduation ceremony.

Professors at both of the college's campuses voted to ask the university to disinvite Rice because of her role in the Iraq War, naming her a "war criminal" for her role in the George W. Bush administration.

Fortunately, Rutgers President Robert Barchi politely declined the request, noting that "These are the kinds of exchanges that every great university welcomes. Like all vibrant intellectual communities, Rutgers can thrive only when it vigorously defends the free exchange of ideas in an environment of civil discourse."

Apparently, Barchi didn't get the memo that the free exchange of ideas in modern America should only include ideas which have been given the stamp of approval by liberals. If it slams America, conservatives or Republicans, you can pretty much say anything you want. If it promotes the Constitution, self-determination, free-market capitalism or the American Transcendental ideal of self-reliance, then be prepared to be called a war criminal, racist or worse.

Conservatives, meanwhile, seem to be able to cope with the idea that liberals have differing opinions without trying to burn them at the academic stake. Take, for instance, the March 7 announcement that Montana State University in Bozeman would be awarding an honorary doctorate to Donna Shalala, who like Rice was a Cabinet secretary who served with distinction.

The only difference was that Shalala served under Democratic President Bill Clinton and the Washington Post has declared her "one of the most controversial Clinton Cabinet nominees" and "one who had been branded by critics as being too liberal and politically correct."

So when conservative Montana heard that Shalala was going to be honored by MSU, did they light torches and pick up their pitchforks to get her banned from campus? Not hardly.

In fact, the news was greeted with a yawn, as it should be. She is an accomplished woman, who in addition to her tenure as secretary of health and human services for the entirety of Clinton's two terms, has also been president of Hunter College, chancellor of the University of Wisconsin-Madison, and for the past 13 years, president of the University of Miami. Whatever you think of her politics — and I think very little of them — there is absolutely no reason why she should not be granted an honorary doctorate in nursing by Montana State University. Let her have her degree and go back to Miami.

But I wonder what Shalala would say if she were asked her opinion of the Rutgers controversy? This, after all, is a woman, who during her tenure at the University of Wisconsin devised a hate-speech code called "Design for Diversity" that was supposed to punish people for making "discriminatory comments" against other people and thus creating "an intimidating, hostile or demeaning environment for education, university-related work, or other university-authorized activity."

Can we all agree that discriminatory comments were made against Condi Rice that undoubtedly created a hostile and demeaning environment for the university-authorized activity of a commencement ceremony? But somehow I doubt that

Shalala will be coming to the defense of Rice, who despite being black does not represent the kind of diversity that liberals want to protect since she is also a Republican.

And if you thought that the Rutgers incident merely represents the kind of close-minded political correctness that is found on left-wing East Coast college campuses, guess again. Last week, the Montana Standard in Butte reported that faculty and students at down-home Montana Tech plan an "unprecedented boycott of the university's spring commencement" in protest of the choice of a conservative couple from Bozeman as the featured speakers.

Greg and Susan Gianforte are co-founders of RightNow Technologies, the software engineering company based in Bozeman which sold in 2012 for $1.5 billion. Inviting them to speak at Montana Tech is a no-brainer because they are living the dream of every engineering student in the world: Take a great idea and turn it into a great venture.

But that's not good enough for the disgruntled faculty and students at Montana Tech, who don't care for the fact that the Gianfortes are also outspoken defenders of their Christian faith and to a lesser extent their conservative political philosophy. The couple has donated money to faith-based charities, including (according to their critics) a Glendive dinosaur museum that promotes creationism.

Apparently, the faculty doesn't see a place for fundamental Christian beliefs in a college that teaches science. How they square that conclusion with the necessity of teaching Newtonian physics, I don't know. Maybe they never heard that Isaac Newton, the founder of modern physics, was a dedicated Christian who was himself a noted creationist.

I suppose after they finish their campaign to ban the Gianfortes from campus, they can dedicate themselves to writing Newton out of their science textbooks.

Fortunately, the chancellor of Montana Tech, Don Blackketter, takes a similar view of the protests as his counterpart at Rutgers.

"It's important to remember what grad commencement is all about," he told the Montana Standard. "It's not political agendas or religious beliefs; it's about sending the graduates off into the world after they've had great accomplishments."

Let's hope that the graduates do not learn from their liberal faculty members that one of those great accomplishments is shutting down free speech.

WHERE DID YOUR CONSTITUTIONAL PROTECTIONS GO?

April 6, 2014

Too bad we spend so much time yelling at each other about which political party is right and which party is wrong. Too bad we get so easily distracted by the slogans and the backslapping. Too bad that myopia is the national disease, because what we aren't seeing down the road is much scarier than who wins THIS election or who votes for THAT bill.

It's all about control — not who's in control, because it really doesn't matter whether Republicans or Democrats win elections these days — but rather just plain simple control. Of you. Of me. Of the economy. Of the military. Of our liberty. Of the world.

The last few weeks have been chock full of horror stories, any one of which would have dropped the jaws of our parents and grandparents, let alone the Founding Fathers who gave us "a republic — if you can keep it," as Benjamin Franklin is reported to have said when emerging from the Constitutional Convention.

In no particular order, let's take a look at three of them and see if we can detect the common unraveling thread:

—A professor from Indiana University is suing the federal government for spying on her and then detaining her at the Indianapolis International Airport after reading emails she had exchanged with a friend from Greece. The customs agents questioned her and the gentleman about the nature of their relationship and apparently cited information they could only have gotten from the emails. No matter what you think of college professors, no matter what you think of national security, no matter what you think of the ACLU (which is bringing the suit on behalf of the professor, Christine Von Der Haar), this case ought to worry every American citizen since we are supposed to be protected against unreasonable searches and seizures by the Fourth Amendment.

— If that one doesn't make you worried, this one should. John Gerald Quinn of Texas was the victim of a SWAT team raid on his house in which he was shot by officers who used a "no knock" entrance on the basis of believing that Quinn might own a legal gun. The fact that the gun was an AK-47 does not make a whit of difference because Quinn is supposed to be protected by the Second Amendment, which ensures his right to keep and bear arms and, yep, the Fourth Amendment against unreasonable searches. I guess the operative phrase in that last sentence is "supposed to be." These days the Constitution is whatever some judge says it is, and more and more of them seem to be saying that it is a vehicle for implementing progressive social change.

— What about this one? Have you heard the story of Justina Pelletier, the sick 15-year-old who has been kept away from her parents for most of the last year because Boston Children's Hospital disagreed with the medical treatment the girl was receiving from a physician at Tufts University. Yeah, you read that right. The hospital has accused the parents of some weird crime known as medical child abuse for following the advice of a doctor! And they basically locked the daughter up against her will in a psychiatric ward for the last year where she has reportedly been denied education, religious services or the medical treatment her family wants for her. "How could that happen?" you ask. Because when the republic slips away, so too do our freedoms. It's no accident that Justina recently said during a rare unsupervised visit, "I feel like a prisoner. Why can't I go home with my parents?" Why? Because for the past 50 years or so the government has worked to abrogate parents' rights and to essentially make children wards of the state. Parents have been cut out of decision-making involving sexual activity, abortion, discipline, education and a host of other areas. The idea of the family unit as the crucial inviolable center of life and of civilization has been all but erased. A man's house is no longer his castle; it is his last refuge, and as John Gerald Quinn knows, it is not very secure. Justina Pelletier, too, cannot feel secure. She may not have studied constitutional law yet, but if she did, she would not recognize the Fifth Amendment, which contains this clause: "No person shall... be deprived of life, liberty, or property, without due process of law." Well, turns out that is not true for the first 14 months. On Monday, we shall see if this tragedy is allowed to continue, since Justina will have yet another day in court, represented by Liberty Counsel.

So there you have it — the sad state of American jurisprudence and the ever shrinking constitutional protections which our forefathers took for granted as their God-given rights. Does it have anything to do with Democrats? Sure, but have the Republicans done anything to stop it? Heck no, and when the Republicans are in power, the downhill slide continues apace.

Don't talk to me about politics. This isn't about politics, any more than the Nazification of Germany was about politics or the Cultural Revolution in China was about politics. It's about power, and you and I are losing it everyday. One day, some of us are going to wake up in prison, and realize we didn't do everything we could have done, to the best of our abilities, to "preserve, protect and defend the Constitution of the United States." In fact, some people — some citizens — are already in prison, real prisons, not metaphorical ones, wondering when the rest of us are going to do something to get them out. It's a question worth asking yourself, too. Or is it already too late?_

EQUAL TIME FOR COMMON SENSE ON 'EQUAL' PAY

April 13, 2014

I've written a couple of columns in a row on some of the more blatant attempts by liberals to shut down free and fair debate on topics ranging from climate change to Christianity.

The techniques employed in this campaign range from name-calling (climate change "deniers," war criminals, homophobes) to actual criminalization of thought (seen especially in Canada with its "hate speech" laws, but working its way into American jurisprudence as well).

But there is also a more subtle approach that probably has more impact on silencing opposition to liberal social policies than sheer intimidation does, and that approach is "the big lie."

Last week, we saw the big lie on full display, as politician after politician bent over backwards to promote the idea of equal pay for women. I should say liberal politicians, because so far as I can tell, the only purpose of this campaign was for liberal politicians to try to make conservative politicians look like bad people by suggesting that somehow they were for unequal pay for equal work.

President Obama and the White House took the lead on "Equal Pay Day" to demonize bosses and businesses. He said that he was fighting for "a simple principle: equal pay for equal work." He then repeated the oft-quoted evidence that suggests an imbalance, an injustice, and impropriety: "Today, the average full-time working woman earns just 77 cents for every dollar a man earns."

Sounds horrible, doesn't it? And it should sound horrible, because it is not just a little lie, it is a "big lie," the kind of lie that is so outrageous no one doubts it is true. And, more importantly, the kind of lie which typical politicians can't afford to vocally oppose because they will find themselves being targeted in the campaign crosshairs as misogynistic Neanderthals.

So what is the lie? Simple. Women do not make 77 cents for every dollar earned by a man in the same job. This has nothing to do with wage discrimination. It has nothing to do with equal pay for equal work. The 77 percent statistic is based on the average salary of all women in all jobs compared to the average salary of all men in all jobs. There is no imputed injustice in the fact that women are paid differently than men who work in different jobs. Nor would there be any justice in creating "equity" in pay between all men and all women. The only way that could be accomplished would be by artificially taking money from one group of people and giving it to another group of people who have not earned it.

This is called "redistribution of wealth." It is a basic principle of Marxism, and if we are surprised to see liberals promoting such an idea in the United States, then shame on us. Just as Sen. Max Baucus admitted in 2010 that Obamacare was intended to correct what he called the "mal-distribution of income in America," almost every social policy introduced by Democrats in the past 50 years has been aimed at taking money from one group of people and giving it to another group of people. You can't even say they are taking money from the rich, because the evidence is clear that they have been taking money from the middle class as well.

So, what exactly would President Obama do if he didn't have conservative Republicans standing in his way? Create a new tax entitlement similar to the "Obamacare" health insurance tax credit (subsidy) or the Earned Income Tax Credit which would simply give women in lower-paying jobs a credit that brought their salary up to the level of the average salary of all men in the United States?

Do I really need to say that such an idea is insane? Yet, there is no other mechanism that could accomplish the intended effect short of ordering that all workers in all jobs shall be paid at the same pay rate, with adjustments based only on the size of one's family rather than one's abilities or one's merit or one's training.

But how many politicians are going to actively oppose the president's "big lie"? Do you know any Republicans who want to face advertising campaigns this fall that accuse them of being "anti-women's rights"? Of course not.

That's why this technique is so effective. It puts conservatives in a box, and makes the truth irrelevant. The so-called Paycheck Fairness Act, which Democrats wanted to pass last week, was a sham. The fact of the matter is that it has been against the law to pay a woman less than a man for the same work in the same job with the same experience since 1963 when the Equal Pay Act was passed.

Moreover, the fake fix offered by the Democrats would be the exact opposite of the fairness promised. It would make it virtually impossible for employers to reward their best employees by paying them more based on performance. What's fair about paying employees based on the job they are asked to do rather than how well they are actually doing it? Nothing, that's what.

But that didn't stop both of Montana's U.S. senators and its governor from pandering to voters over the issue. Sen. Jon Tester put out a statement that Montana's women make on average 76 percent of what a man makes, and he said "We can do better." Yet how? His only solution was equal pay for equal work, but we already have that. No ethical employer is going to offer a woman less money than a man doing the same job with the same experience. And there are almost no cases of people being prosecuted on such charges.

Gov. Steve Bullock goes even further. He claims that in Montana, women earn "only 67 percent of what men do for the same job." That's why, in his first year on the job, he created the Equal Pay for Equal Work Task Force, which recently held an Equal Pay Summit at Montana State University.

The governor claims that in Montana, women don't always "get a fair day's pay for a fair day's work." Maybe he can even find some obscure case somewhere that involved a woman worker making 67 percent of what a male employee made for the same work. No one says injustice doesn't happen on occasion, and when it does, it should be rooted out, but it certainly isn't the rule, and the law already exists to stop wage discrimination. Yet Gov. Bullock says Montana suffers from "a moral failing" because it is treating women differently than men in the workplace.

That is a serious accusation against Montana employers, and should not go unanswered.

My challenge to the governor and anyone else who thinks women don't get equal pay for equal work is simple: Prove it. Don't just keep citing the irrelevant 77 percent statistic, or the even more damning 67 percent statistic. Find actual examples of women who are making less than their male counterparts in the same business with the same experience, and then show how they could not have used the existing Equal Pay Act of 1963 to rectify the problem.

If anyone anywhere could do that, Republicans would demand changes in the law immediately, just as all people would. So why don't the Democrats provide evidence instead of empty rhetoric?

You know the answer as well as I do — politics. I suppose the real question is what are WE going to do about it? Just keep repeating the "big lie" because it suits our own political agendas, or demand responsible leadership that won't exploit people's hopes and fears?

ANOTHER SIGN OF THE TIMES

April 20, 2014

You can call it a symbol or you can call it a coincidence, but I had a phone call on Good Friday which gave me a perfect column for this Easter Sunday.

Kalispell area resident Philip Klevmoen was calling from East Texas to let me know about a news story he was involved in down there in the little town of Hemphill.

Philip is the gentle giant who is responsible for spreading the word of God in the form of the Ten Commandments on storefronts, church buildings, billboards, refrigerator magnets, pretty much any medium you can think of.

He and his wife Suzy have traveled tens of thousands of miles not just in the United States, but in foreign counties as well, to do what they believe they have been called to do — spread the Good News of a living God who loves all people and wants to save them from sin.

Some people don't like Philip — or at least they don't like his message. So it's not unusual for Philip to hear from people who want him to tear down his billboards, or threaten to do so themselves.

This time, the people who want to tear down his Ten Commandments sign — placed on private property owned by pastor Jeanette Golden — is the state of Texas.

Golden put the sign up on her property in August. Not much different than all the Ten Commandments signs you can see throughout the Flathead Valley. Not much different than the Ten Commandments which are honored in several places throughout the U.S. Supreme Court building. But three months later, the Texas Department of Transportation sent Golden a certified letter demanding that she take the sign down because it did not meet the standards of the Highway Beautification Act.

Golden protested, demanding to know how the state could prevent her from posting, on her own private property, a statement of her personal religious beliefs. The state of Texas then explained to her that because the sign included a reference to Klevmoen's website www.Gods10.com, it was commercial in nature.

No problem. Philip agreed to paint over the web address and let Golden put the sign up as "art in the yard." But Texas still wasn't satisfied. They came back and asked Golden to pony up $250 for a permit, plus pay an annual fee of $150.

Enough, she said.

"Too much money to keep it on my private property and I don't know if I'm doing anything illegal and I'm just standing up for what I believe, " Golden told a reporter for KTRE television.

After she did that first interview last week, Golden became a cause celebre, with hundreds and maybe thousands of people stepping forward to support her and the Ten Commandments.

Klevmoen said his organization has placed Ten Commandments signs in more than 30 states and that he has never seen an issue like this come up before.

"I go strictly back to the Word of God and I go back to the First Amendment," Klevmoen said, "and I don't see anywhere in God's law or in the First Amendment where a person would have to pay to put up God's word."

No one has to agree with Philip that Jesus is the path to salvation, nor sympathize with his mission to call America back to the word of God, but you would be hard pressed to dispute his reading of the First Amendment.

Maybe you could make a case for the importance of highway beautification as a social value, but unless there is an amendment in the Bill of Rights that I am not familiar with, highway beautification doesn't rise to the level of an individual's freedom of religion.

Yet everywhere you look, religion is under attack.

This little story from Texas about one woman's refusal to pay a $250 permit fee is one more instance where traditional values are being marginalized by an increasingly secular society that wants Christians to go along to get along.

So, this Easter Sunday might be a good time — a propitious time — to contemplate whether Christians should go along with society or go along with Christ. Don't forget it was Christ's public preaching, along the roadsides and in the cities, which got him into trouble, yet he never hid from the authorities. He told his followers to proudly announce themselves, just as he announced himself when he went into Jerusalem for the Passover meal that fateful weekend nearly 2,000 years ago.

"Ye are the light of the world," he told his followers in the Sermon on the Mount. "A city that is set on an hill cannot be hid. Neither do men light a candle, and put it under a bushel, but on a candlestick; and it giveth light unto all that are in the house. Let your light so shine before men, that they may see your good works, and glorify your Father which is in heaven."

In the context of the many harsh words spoken about both Pastor Golden and Philip Klevmoen because of their love of Jesus and their desire to spread the word of God, it is worth noting that the above passage from Matthew, Chapter 5, follows close on the Beatitudes, including these:

"Blessed are they which are persecuted for righteousness' sake: for theirs is the kingdom of heaven. Blessed are ye, when men shall revile you, and persecute you, and shall say all manner of evil against you falsely, for my sake."

Food for thought, whether you are enjoying an Easter Egg hunt today or not.

LET'S BUILD A FENCE AROUND
JOHN BOEHNER

April 27, 2014

The last few weeks I've explored ways in which liberals have worked to undermine conservatives in the American political scene. This week, let's look at one typical instance of so-called conservatives shooting themselves in the foot.

Examples of this abound, and you will forgive me if I don't make a laundry list of all the ways in which Republicans are played for suckers by Democrats. That would be too painful. Instead, let's just look at the virtual surrender of traditional values expressed by Speaker of the House John Boehner last week while campaigning in his home district in Ohio.

The headline in the Cincinnati Enquirer said it all: "Boehner mocks GOP colleagues on immigration reform."

Say what? Why would the titular leader of the Republican Party in Washington, D.C., make fun of his own party and his own caucus on an issue of huge importance to the future of the country?

Could it be that he has no moral compass? That he, in fact, has no deep understanding of the damage that illegal immigration has done and is doing to this country? That like Jeb Bush, another ersatz Republican, he thinks illegally crossing the border is "not a felony" but "an act of love"? Or that like Vice President Biden he thinks illegal immigrants are "already American citizens."

Well, yeah, it might very well be true that Speaker Boehner is just a political hack, but why exactly do principled Republicans put up with him? Anyone who can explain that — and undo it — may very well have the power to save this country from itself.

But in the meantime we have to put up with Boehner playing up to the liberal cause by suggesting that his fellow Republicans are bad people because they insist on enforcing the law of the land on immigration — and are unwilling to grant citizenship to those who have shown disdain for our laws and our customs

Listen to what Boehner had to say, in a whining voice, to the Middletown Rotary Club on Thursday about the Republicans he leads in Congress:

"Here's the attitude. 'Ohhhh. Don't make me do this. Ohhhh. This is too hard.' ... We get elected to make choices. We get elected to solve problems and it's remarkable to me how many of my colleagues just don't want to... They'll take the path of least resistance."

Hey, John, guess what? Saying no to lawlessness IS making a choice. It is a lot harder choice than giving in to the oh so pathetic argument that big strong America is helpless to do anything to make illegal immigrants leave our country.

Elected to solve problems? How many times have you heard good honest Republicans say, "Let's build a fence to protect our border," just to be mocked by people like the speaker of the House? We can't possibly build a fence that long and that tall, they say, in their best whiny John Boehner voice. Heck, maybe that's why no one has built that Keystone pipeline yet, too — how could we possibly build that big huge oil pipeline all the way from Canada to the Gulf of Mexico? Look at the map! It's soooo far!

Yeah, this isn't your grandfather's America, anymore. People from that generation, or maybe from your great-grandfather's generation if you are under 30, didn't put up with that kind of nonsense. Back in those days, it was a different country. They figured out what needed to be done, they figured out how to do it, and then they did it. End of story.

No need for 10, 20, 30 years of hand-wringing and self-doubt. And no need for "leaders" like John Boehner, who think their job is to work out deals to protect lawbreakers.

Sorry, John. It's not too hard; it's just plain wrong.

A FRONT-ROW SEAT AT THE CULTURE WAR

May 18, 2014

Is it just me, or has the culture war between right and left been escalating wildly over the past few months?

Everywhere you turn, there is another leftist assault on traditional values, as well as the occasional volley fired back by the retreating forces of Christianity and sanity.

This is not a fight about religion; it is a fight about freedom — and believe it or not, the Judeo-Christian tradition provides the philosophical underpinnings of Western culture, which in contradistinction to every other long-lasting culture on the planet, values the individual over the collective, and thus values individual freedom over the whims of the state.

Or, at least, it did. Now, however, we are seeing the fundamental transformation of Western culture and even Christianity itself into a monolithic, totalitarian society in which the state — with the acquiescence of the people — controls all aspects of public and private life.

Call it 1984+30, the nightmare scenario created by novelist George Orwell in his "1984" but with 30 more years to perfect the program. "War is Peace" — check. "Ignorance is Strength" — check. "Freedom is Slavery" — check. But also "Truth is a Lie" — check. And "Law is Oppression" — double check.

It appears that the goal of pro-tolerance agenda being promoted by the leftists is to stamp out diversity. In other words, a "tolerant" society makes room for (or actually glorifies) illegal aliens, oppressive dictators, homosexual marriage, abortion rights, convicted killers, sharia law, unrestricted pornography, teen-age sex and redistribution of wealth, so anyone opposed to these is not just intolerant and outside of the mainstream, but actually subject to shunning and possibly incarceration.

Moreover, the left is intent on co-opting traditional defenders of values such as the Boy Scouts, the Catholic Church, the Southern Baptist Convention and the Republican Party, and turning them into mouthpieces for a form of "tolerance" that not coincidentally turns their own tradition-upholding members into purported agents of hate. I've provided a variety of examples in this column over the past few months. Here are a few more:

Brandeis University in Boston was supposed to award an honorary doctorate to Ayaan Hirsi Ali, the former Muslim, who had written extensively against female genital mutilation, honor killing and child marriage among various Islamic institutions. Perhaps it was brave of the secular Jewish university to have honored a woman who had become so controversial for defending human rights for Muslims, but it was nothing short of cowardly for Brandeis to later say that Ali's spirited attack on Islamic fundamentalism was "inconsistent with the University's core values."

Do the university's core values really include defense of honor killing or of the assassination of Ali's colleague Theo van Gogh, who directed the film she wrote about the abuse of women in Islamic society?

Perhaps Brandeis needs to re-examine its own Jewish heritage and its core values, and find out why they have diverged so radically. The same could be said for almost every institution in America.

Last week, for instance, we saw a pair of stories involving twins that showed that America is becoming more and more intolerant of traditional American values. In one case, boxer Floyd Mayweather publicly declared that he broke up with ex-girlfriend Shantel Christine Jackson "because she got a abortion, and I'm totally against killing babies. She killed our twin babies."

This resulted in outrage against Mayweather, who because he disagreed with the idea of killing his children, was called all manner of vile names and was found by some to be disqualified from buying the Los Angeles Clippers. That last point is especially ironic considering that Mayweather is black, and the Clippers are potentially for sale only because their current owner made racist comments against black men.

The second set of twins involved in the abortion debate are the Benham brothers, who were set to debut their new show "Flip It Forward" later this year on HGTV until it was discovered that the brothers are (shudder!) Bible-believing Christians.

Ironically, they were outed as Christians by a spinoff of People for the American Way, the liberal progressive advocacy group that thinks the way forward for America is to do away with conservatives, if not bodily then by making sure there is no room for their ideas in the town square.

It's not like the Benhams were hiding their light under a bushel. HGTV knew exactly what they were getting. David Benham had led a prayer rally outside the Democratic National Convention in 2012 (not sure if he was in one of those dwindling Free Speech Zones or not!) during which he said that America's Christians must repent for tolerating "homosexuality and its agenda that is attacking the nation" and "demonic ideologies tak[ing] our universities and our public school systems."

David and his brother Jason also oppose abortion, which is not entirely surprising since they are practicing Christians and since their father heads Operation Save America, an abortion clinic protest group.

What it comes down to, of course, is an effort to de-legitimize Christianity and to relegate the Bible to the trash heap of history. People for the American Way and other liberal groups are smart enough to realize that as long as people believe in the Bible, there is a chance that they will start following its rules again. And some people, like the Benhams, have already made their choice.

"If our faith costs us a television show, so be it."

That statement could be the very credo of 21st century Christians, with the words "a television show" substituted variously as "a job," "a college degree," "a relationship," "a friend," or anything else that can be taken away from you.

But how many people are going to make the same declaration as the Benhams? How many will surrender their beliefs for the comfort of "getting along" or the opportunity for a bigger paycheck?

Turns out, all of us have a front-row seat at the culture war. We all have to be rooting for something, and there is no middle ground. The stakes are high; the battle is heating up.

The situation reminds me of the life of Dietrich Bonhoeffer, the young German minister who died in a Nazi concentration camp because of his beliefs. He wrote a book called "The Cost of Discipleship."

How much are you willing to pay?

LET'S UPHOLD (AND HONOR!) THE CONSTITUTION

May 25, 2014

As we celebrate the ultimate sacrifices of hundreds of thousands of Americans who died in the defense of liberty, perhaps it is fitting that we pause for a moment of silence to contemplate the imminent loss of the Constitution which they had sworn to uphold.

Some would say that the Constitution has already been twisted beyond recognition by activist judges, congressional chicanery and tyrannical presidents, but I am willing to give the benefit of the doubt here, and affirm that the genius of the Founders still holds our nation together despite the best efforts of our worst citizens to draw us apart.

You can all provide your own examples of laws that have been passed by the Congress, affirmed by the courts and executed by the president, which on their face would be self-evidently unconstitutional were it possible for such decisions to be based on the plain words of the Constitution rather than the convenience and connivance of our governors. (And no I do not refer to the governors of our states, but rather the governors of our lives — the overseers who tell us what we can and cannot do as supposedly free people.)

But there is one manipulation of the Constitution underway now which is so destructive to our republic that it makes almost everything else which has come before it seem like child's play. The fact that almost no one has even heard of this plot, which is more than halfway to fruition, makes it even scarier.

So what exactly is it?

Something called the National Popular Vote Plan, a proposal which would neuter the Electoral College and thus provide the final nail in the coffin of the republic. You see, the Founding Fathers carefully crafted a mechanism in the Constitution by which a multitude of interests and stakes would be balanced against each other with the precision of a Swiss clock. Alter or remove any one of the basic provisions of governance, and the balance of power is forever shifted. That happened, for instance, when the 17th Amendment passed by the Progressive movement changed the means of electing senators.

Before the amendment was ratified in 1913, senators were elected by state legislatures, thus ensuring that the interests of the state would be represented in Washington, D.C. Rural states could protect their interest in agrarian reform, for instance, by sending a delegation to Washington that would fight for their states' interests, not follow the dictates of a national political party. Any senator who did not adequately represent the state's interests was sent packing. These days, however, senators say whatever they need to say to get elected, then vote however they need to vote in order to curry favor with their party bosses. Ultimately, because senators no longer represent their states' interests, the national government has grown increasingly powerful and the notion of federalism has faded into obscurity.

The National Popular Vote Plan would trump the damage done by the 17th Amendment by extending the popular vote not just to senators, but now to presidents as well, and this time without even the benefit of being a change brought about by the rigorous amendment process. Instead, the National Popular Vote Plan seeks to lure states holding a majority of the electoral votes into forming an interstate compact by which they would all agree to ignore the will of their own states' voters and cast all their electoral votes for the winner of the national popular vote. The clearest signal this sends is that states are meaningless in the United States of America.

Our Founders' federal plan, on the other hand, called for each state to be able to cast votes for a president based on population. The number of electors for each state was the combined total of senators (two for each state) and representatives (apportioned according to population). Each state could determine its own method of casting electoral votes, and it was the pool of electoral votes that determined the winner of the presidency, not the total number of votes cast by individual citizens for one or another candidate. In fact, the Constitution did not even envision a popular vote at all. Instead, it directed that "each state shall appoint, in such Manner as the Legislature may direct" the electors who would choose the president. Originally, some states used an election process; some didn't.

Again, the importance of this cannot be overstated. The Founding Fathers recognized the danger of politicians who could manipulate the affections of the people to gain their power, and created the Electoral College as a cushion that would prevent a demagogue from being swept into office.

But like sophomoric teenagers who yearn to prove how much smarter they are than their parents, mischievous politicians are now hard at work to undermine the work of the Founders. As of April, 10 states and the District of Columbia with 165 combined Electoral College votes have signed on to the National Popular Vote Interstate Compact. That's more than 61 percent of the 270 votes needed to elect a president.

Numerous other states are also entertaining this notion in their legislatures, and as soon as any combination of states with 270 or more electoral votes join together, those states will be mandated to cast their electoral votes for the winner of the national popular vote.

You may well ask what is wrong with that. Besides the problem of tampering with the delicate balance of our constitutionally mandated government, it must be noted that the United States was not created as a democracy, but as a republic. Direct democracy tends over time to diminish the rights of the minority and to solidify the imperious tendencies of the majority.

The most immediate effect is that presidential candidates (and presidents!) will cater to large urban areas even more than they do currently because that is where they will be able to most effectively spend their money to curry votes. If you want Los Angeles, New York City, Chicago, San Francisco, Denver, Philadelphia, Miami, San Antonio, Houston and a handful of other big cities picking your president for you, then by all means get on board.

But if you live in the 90 percent of the country that is going to be ignored from that day forward, you might want to slow down and take a serious look at this deceptively innocent proposal. Ultimately, based on demographics alone, it would probably ensure a Democratic president for the next 100 years or so. That might seem like a tempting reason for Democrats to back the proposal, but I would hope most of them could envision the danger of such a situation and steer clear of experimenting with the Constitution and the fundamental institutions of America.

BENNY, ED AND THE DEATH OF TREASON

June 1, 2014

One of the many signs of the imminent collapse of the United States is that we can't even agree on the meaning of treason any more.

As a former resident of Stony Point, N.Y., where Gen. Benedict Arnold sold his country down the river (the Hudson River) during the Revolutionary War, I have been a student of betrayal for many years. Arnold was so vilified that his very name became synonymous with treason, and every resident of Stony Point knew the story of how Arnold had met with a British officer named Major Andre and passed military secrets to him in order to aid the crown's war efforts against the colonists.

But that was then. Back in the old days when I was growing up before the Vietnam War, Americans were for the most part united in our love of history — and our love of country. We understood that turning secrets over to the enemy made you an enemy, too.

Ah, youth! How innocent I was. Indeed, how innocent WE were!

Because now we have a country that doesn't heap calumny upon the head of a traitor, but rather looks to lionize him, reward him and turn him into a culture hero.

I am speaking, of course, of Edward Snowden — a criminal who makes Benedict Arnold look like a rank amateur when it comes to treason. Snowden is the former National Security Agency contractor who released thousands, perhaps millions, of pages of classified documents to media outlets. Most, but not all, of these documents concerned secret surveillance programs run by various U.S. intelligence agencies.

Now, you may be uncomfortable with the fact that the federal government is performing surveillance on everyone from foreign dignitaries to your Auntie Grizelda, but that doesn't change the fact that this was CLASSIFIED information, the release of which could do (and probably has done) immeasurable harm to our national security. It doesn't change the fact that these programs were duly authorized by the American president and Congress. It doesn't change the fact that Snowden has been accused of espionage by the United States government. It doesn't change the fact that as a result of his independent decisions and actions, Islamic terrorists can sleep easier, knowing just how to avoid detection by programs that previously might have brought them to justice.

Yet despite all that, Snowden is held up in many circles as a hero. If those circles were all in Moscow or Mideastern capitals, it would not be surprising — since they have all benefited from his perfidy. But he is also a hero to many American journalists who think that any secret is a shame, and even to many conservatives who fear the federal government's power more than they do the enemies of our civilization.

Call me old-fashioned, but I will never swoon over a self-declared whistleblower who puts American lives at risk because he doesn't personally approve of policies put in place to make us safer in an ever more dangerous world. Nor do I care that Snowden leaked the secrets to the media, as if that having them publicly available made them less dangerous.

Indeed, Snowden has now provided cover to every spy who follows him. Rather than deliver secrets directly to the Kremlin or Tehran, enemies of America can now follow the Snowden protocol and simply email their dirty secrets to the New York Times. The damage is just as dangerously done, but instead of being hung for treason, the culprit can schedule an interview with Brian Williams on NBC and be nominated for the Nobel Peace Prize to boot.

We live in an upside down world, and the sooner we realize it, the sooner we can get started rebuilding it from the bottom up.

SEARCHING FOR FAIRNESS IN ALL THE WRONG PLACES

June 8, 2014

All right-minded people hate discrimination. It's too bad we no longer know what that is.

The Consumer Financial Protection Bureau, one of the most recent government agencies created by Congress in homage to the oppressive world of "Atlas Shrugged," was in the news last month because it announced (in showy communist self-criticism fashion) that it had been guilty of massive discrimination against its own employees.

What the Consumer Financial Protection Bureau really does is anyone's guess. In essence, it shakes down banks and other lenders and financial companies in an effort to keep the 1 percent on their toes and let them know that the 99 percent can pick up torches and pitchforks anytime they want to and storm the Bastille, er, I mean, the bank. Consider it an outreach program that brings Occupy Wall Street into the halls of power.

The CFPB was the brainchild of Sen. Elizabeth Warren when she was just a lowly socialist Harvard professor. Now she is the senator from Taxachussetts. When she was campaigning for that position, she came up with the slogan later borrowed by President Obama to make the rich feel guilty for their success: "There is nobody in this country who got rich on his own."

Maybe not, but there is nobody in this country who got rich from over-regulation of business either — nobody except politicians, lawyers and bureaucrats. (Come to think of it, that's like one-third of our national economy, isn't it?)

Turns out that bureaucrats getting rich — or at least richer — is what this story is all about. And ironically they are getting their pay raises by shaking down their bosses instead of the banks.

As reported by the Wall Street Journal and other publications starting May 19, the agency has scrapped its system of granting pay raises because discrimination was alleged in how those raises were being allotted.

Supervisors had been giving employees performance evaluations using a rating system that assigned a score of between one and five. A low score meant a low raise or none at all, and a high score meant a higher raise. Simple and straightforward, right?

Not when you take skin color and ethnicity into account. You see, an internal report discovered that 74.6 percent of white employees received ratings of four and five whereas only 65.2 percent of Hispanics received comparable ratings. Only 57.6 percent of black employees received fours and fives.

To the bureaucrats who police other bureaucrats, these numbers are prima facie evidence of discrimination. You see, in a perfect world, all people would score the same on all tests regardless of skin color, ethnicity or gender. In a perfect world, blacks, whites and Hispanics would also perform the same at work and therefore all qualify for the same percentage of top raises.

So the Consumer Financial Protection Bureau decided to go back and give retroactive raises to everyone who received a ranking of three or four and reward them just as if they had scored a five. Which in a perfect world would make perfect sense.

Trouble is, we don't live in a perfect world. We live in a world of imperfection and inequality. That's why in the private sector, some people get raises and some people don't. If you consider skin color in determining how those raises are passed out, then you are guilty of discrimination. But at the Consumer Financial Protection Bureau, if you DON'T consider skin color and ethnicity you are guilty of discrimination.

Believing that a statistical analysis can reveal discrimination is the equivalent of saying that no matter who you hire, no matter what their backgrounds, no matter how dependable they are, they should all perform at exactly the same level as their peers. This is the nightmare scenario of Kurt Vonnegut's dystopian short story "Harrison Bergeron," where thanks to the 211th, 212th and 213th amendments to the Constitution, "Nobody was smarter than anybody else. Nobody was better looking than anybody else. Nobody was stronger or quicker than anybody else."

In the story, that "equality" was achieved thanks to the "unceasing vigilance of agents of the United States Handicapper General." Graceful ballet dancers had to wear bags of birdshot to weigh them down; smart people had to wear headsets that would transmit sharp noises to prevent them from concentrating; beautiful women had to wear hideous masks. Everyone who was above average was assigned some kind of handicap to make sure they didn't exceed average.

And thanks to the likes of Elizabeth Warren, current CFPB Director Richard Cordray and President Barack Obama, the same kind of handicaps are being applied to those employees who loused up the system by being too talented, too smart, or too productive for government work.

Better to keep marginal employees happy than to risk offending anyone by a metric that shows one racial group outperforming another. Cost to the consumers (whose financial interests are putatively being protected by the bureau) of the retroactive pay raises and future pay raises in the next two years: $5 million!

I should mention the utter hypocrisy of Cordray, who in announcing the new policy for raises, tried to pretend that it was not based on the allegations of race-based discrimination, but rather some vague "broad-based disparities in the way performance ratings were assigned."

And one last thought. The statistic cited at the beginning of this story about how many employees received fours and fives in their evaluations WAS outrageous, but not for the reason cited by the agency.

Consider again: Ratings of four and five were achieved by 74.6 percent of white employees, 65.2 percent of Hispanics, and 57.6 percent of blacks. The real problem had nothing to do with race or ethnicity, but with a system that considers it appropriate to label between 57 percent and 74 percent of employees as superior.

Think about it. On a five-point scale, three is average, four and five are superior, and one and two are not up to snuff. In a real world evaluation, you could expect 50 percent or more of employees to achieve an average rating, with perhaps 25 percent above average and 25 percent below average.

There's a reason why not everyone gets straight A's in school, and there should be a reason why not all employees get raises, especially big raises, just for showing up.

WHAT WILL FINALLY BE THE LAST STRAW?

June 22, 2014

There is a name for what the government did to the Washington Redskins last week. It is called extortion.

Extortion, as defined by Merriam-Webster's, is the crime of getting money from someone by the use of force or threats. I much prefer the definition in the 1828 dictionary compiled by Noah Webster himself: "The act or practice of wresting any thing from a person by force, duress, menaces, authority, or by any undue exercise."

You probably heard the story about how the U.S. Office of Patents and Trademarks has canceled the Redskins' trademark on the team name because the team's name and logo is supposedly "disparaging" to Indians.

As the Washington Post said in its coverage, "The ruling's main impact is as a cudgel by an increasingly vocal group of Native Americans, lawmakers, former players and others who are trying to persuade team officials to change the name."

Cudgel. That is another nice word, well-chosen by the Post's reporter. Again from Webster's, 1828: "A short thick stick of wood, such as may be used by the hand in beating."

And make no mistake, it is not so much Native Americans who are wielding this cudgel, but the federal government itself, in a misbegotten effort to beat Redskins' owner Dan Snyder until he gives up his team's 77-year hold on the name and tradition because it offends some small sliver of society.

I can think of no more clear example of wresting a thing from someone by use of "authority" than this attempt at theft through bureaucracy. Remember, this is a mascot that has served the football team since 1937 and on which the team has built its reputation for excellence.

If anyone is disparaged by the use of the Redskins logo, it is the opponents who have many times been put to shame by the team's fierce play on the field. Obviously the team mascot was selected not because people DON'T respect Indians as warriors, but because they do. To argue otherwise turns reality on its head.

What this is all about is nothing more than political strong-arming in order to usher in the brave new world of politically correct and progressively approved social engineering. Divide and conquer. Just as the Obama administration used the IRS to cudgel (again, what a great word to describe the abuse of authority rampant in our federal government) conservative Tea Party groups into either silence or irrelevance as political organizations, so too did the patent office try to silence Redskins owner Dan Snyder from exercising his right to make money by venerating what used to be called without disdain the Noble Savage. For further edification regarding the Nobel Savage, see the novel "Brave New World" by Aldous Huxley. But for frightening parallels to the modern-day tyranny we suffer a long train of abuses under, read "Atlas Shrugged" by Ayn Rand.

Perhaps the closest correlative in Rand's prophetic novel to the extortion being waged against the Redskins is when the weaselly Dr. Ferris visits the inventor-industrialist Hank Reardon to inform him that the government expects him to deliver 5,000 tons of his revolutionary new Reardon Metal in order to avoid being prosecuted on trumped-up charges and having his reputation and business be ruined.

"It should not be difficult for you to see where your interests lie and to act accordingly," Ferris tells Reardon, assuming that his appeal to pecuniary interest will outweigh any inclination of Reardon to do what is right.

"In my youth, this was called blackmail," Reardon says.

Ferris thinks he is on the verge of victory over the inventor and gloats that the government had always known it would defeat him sooner or later because it had passed a series of laws solely for the purpose of bringing to heel those rugged individualists who aspire to live free or die. Here is the excruciatingly accurate passage from "Atlas Shrugged":

"Did you really think that we want those laws to be observed?' said Dr. Ferris. "We want them broken. You'd better get it straight that it's not a bunch of boy scouts you're up against — then you'll know that this is not the age for beautiful gestures. We're after power and we mean it.

"You fellows were pikers, but we know the real trick, and you'd better get wise to it. There's no way to rule innocent men. The only power any government has is the power to crack down on criminals. Well, when there aren't enough criminals, one makes them. One declares so many things to be a crime that it becomes impossible for men to live without breaking laws. Who wants a nation of law-abiding citizens? What's there in that for anyone? But just pass the kind of laws that can neither be observed nor enforced nor objectively interpreted — and you create a nation of law-breakers — and then you cash in on guilt.

Now that's the system, Mr. Rearden, that's the game, and once you understand it, you'll be much easier to deal with."

A nation of law-breakers! Is that really the game? Think about the maze of impossible-to-understand tax laws. Think about the nonsensical 2,000-page Affordable Care Act, and the hundreds of thousands of pages of regulations that it has spawned. Think about carbon credits and all the endless regulations that businesses quixotically spend millions of dollars to obey when it is well nigh impossible to do so. Maybe what they, what all of us, should be doing now is instead writing a new Declaration of Independence, or following the original one:

"We hold these truths to be self-evident, that all men are created equal, that they are endowed by their Creator with certain unalienable Rights, that among these are Life, Liberty and the pursuit of Happiness. —That to secure these rights, Governments are instituted among Men, deriving their just powers from the consent of the governed, —That whenever any Form of Government becomes destructive of these ends, it is the Right of the People to alter or to abolish it, and to institute new Government, laying its foundation on such principles and organizing its powers in such form, as to them shall seem most likely to effect their Safety and Happiness."

We are not safe. We are not happy. The only question now is: How long are we going to take it?

EITHER WE ARE FREE OR WE ARE NOT

July 20, 2014

The Constitution is under assault. So is our way of life. Do you care?

Too many people don't, or at least won't do anything to stand up for it, which is why it's almost a foregone conclusion that the proud experiment in liberty called We the People is about to end in abysmal failure.

Case in point, the June 30 opinion by the U.S. Supreme Court known colloquially as the Hobby Lobby decision. The 5-4 ruling concluded that Hobby Lobby, a regional chain of arts and crafts stores, was permitted to refuse to provide its female employees with insurance coverage for certain forms of contraception because the owners had a religious objection to offering abortifacients as part of the benefit.

This would seem on the face of it to be a blow for freedom. Protecting the religious conscience of Americans from tyrannical abuse is certainly a large part of what our Founding Fathers envisioned when they wrote the Declaration of Independence and then the Constitution.

But the court's ruling does not in any way protect our individual religious freedom; what it does instead is uphold the right of the government to decide for us what religious freedoms we are allowed to have.

A true defense of freedom would have found in favor of the Hobby Lobby corporation based on the First Amendment to the Constitution, the relevant portion of which states that "Congress shall make no law respecting an establishment of religion, or prohibiting the free exercise thereof."

There is no doubt that the Affordable Care Act and the regulations it spawned are laws that prohibit the free exercise of religion. When the federal government ordered Hobby Lobby and other corporations to provide services to its employees which violate the beliefs of the owners of the store, they ipso facto prohibited the owners from exercising their religious beliefs in the only way that matters — through action. If I oppose abortion on religious grounds, but the government tells me I have to support abortion with my money and my employment policies, then the government is using its power to enslave me as surely as if it had thrown me in the Tower of London.

The Supreme Court could have said that, but it didn't. Instead, its tiny-minded majority opinion only said that Hobby Lobby had the right to refuse to participate in the federal mandate because Congress had passed the Religious Freedom Restoration Act in 1993. That's well and good, but it ultimately says that the government does have the power to restrict my religious freedom as long as it repeals the Religious Freedom Restoration Act.

In other words, religious freedom is granted to Americans by Congress, and is not an inalienable right granted to mankind by God. We enjoy our freedoms only at the pleasure of a tyrannical government.

And that government — or at least the portion of the government controlled by Democrats — is poised to strike. Within days of the court's ruling, legislation was being introduced to overturn it. The government giveth, and the government taketh away.

Montana's liberal Democratic senators put out a press release on July 9 saying that they were introducing the "Protect Women's Health from Corporate Interference Act" to prevent employers "from making healthcare decisions for their employees."

Outrageously, Sen. John Walsh said, "No boss should have a say in the healthcare employees receive," thus confusing health care with employment benefits. They are not the same thing.

Sen. Tester was just as bad. "Thanks to the Supreme Court, a nameless, faceless corporation can stand between a woman and her basic health care needs," he opined. NO THEY CAN'T. Whether or not I have dental insurance, I am free to see the dentist. Whether or not I have vision insurance, I am free to visit the optometrist. And whether or not I have contraceptive coverage, I am free to pop down to the grocery story and pick up whatever kind of "protection" I want to use. It may require a visit to the doctor, but that is my responsibility, not my employer's.

Bottom line: Either we are free or we are not. We are either free to accept employment or we are not. We are either free to offer employment or we are not. And we are either free to reach our own decisions about what we want out of life or we are not.

Employers should be free to offer whatever kind of benefits they wish to offer, and employees or potential employees should be free to make up their own minds whether they want to work for that wage and benefit package. If the workers don't accept the compensation, the company improves it or shuts its doors. Either way, it's none of the government's business, unless the employees in question are government employees.

Is this really too hard to grasp?

One more thing. The demagogues who are trying to take away your freedom have framed the issue as "poor helpless employees" versus "big heartless corporations."

Sen. Walsh wrote that "The five man majority ruled that bosses have a right to tell their employees what type of medical care they deserve."

Well, no they didn't, but any sane person would argue that employers should have the right to tell employees what benefits are available for a certain position in a certain company. And no one but a socialist would argue that government should decide what benefits a private company must offer to its employees.

Of course, one of the main arguments against the Hobby Lobby decision is that it gives corporations rights that only people should have. Huh? So when I as an employer decide to incorporate my business because the government has structured tax laws to make it disadvantageous to remain unincorporated, I have to give up my rights to freedom of religion and conscience? I have to become a tool of the government's agenda and beliefs, not my own?

But take a look back at the First Amendment I quoted above. You will notice that it does not have anything to do with the rights of the individual OR corporations. It doesn't say you as a citizen have the right to freely exercise your religion; it says that "Congress shall make NO law ... prohibiting the free exercise" of religion. It is about restricting government from making oppressive laws, and that restriction is universal and unconditional.

It doesn't matter if the oppressive law takes the form of a regulation of corporations or a provision of a massive health-care law — if it prohibits me from freely following my conscience, it is a violation of the Constitution and an offense against humanity.

Do you care? Or don't you?

RELIGIOUS PERSECUTION NOT JUST
PART OF HISTORY

October 5, 2014

Assuming that they still teach history in school, then students today are learning — just as I did almost 50 years ago — that many of the early settlers of the American colonies were people who were escaping from religious persecution in Europe.

They came to these distant shores to get away from tyrants or oppressive majorities who sought either to impose their beliefs on everyone or to deprive minorities of the ability to freely express their own intrinsic beliefs in their daily lives.

Sadly, many of these persecuted minorities found themselves in colonies which were no better than the countries they had fled. Catholics and Protestants were just as much at war in the New World as in the Old, and non-believers were even worse off. The Maryland Toleration Act of 1649, for instance, protected anyone who "professed to believe in Jesus Christ" but put at risk of death by execution those settlers who denied the divinity of Jesus or even the concept of the Triune God.

Such failed experiments in toleration and diversity led the Founding Fathers in their wisdom to declare matters of conscience and religion to be "off limits." As the First Amendment commanded, "Congress shall make no law respecting an establishment of religion, or prohibiting the free exercise thereof..."

The first part of the amendment has been very successfully implemented down through the decades since 1787. There has been no effort to impose or declare a state religion in the United States that all citizens must follow.

But the second clause "prohibiting the free exercise thereof" has been a much trickier proposition. For years, of course, there was no doubt that freedom to exercise one's religion meant the state had to honor one's religious conscience. Thus, when the state would order young men to join the Army in order to fight and kill an enemy, an exemption would be granted on religious grounds to those who believed it was a sin to kill anyone for any reason.

In recent years, however, the individual's right of conscience has been challenged as a threat to the social order. Thus, the desire of a public official — or even a school valedictorian — to invoke the name or presence of God as a beneficent force in human affairs has been struck down as a harmful intrusion on the mental well-being of non-believers. (Why the failure of non-believers to acknowledge their debt to their Creator is not seen as a harmful intrusion on the mental well-being of believers is never explained, of course!)

And most dangerously, it has now been determined by court after court that Christians or any other believers do not have the right to practice their faith in their daily life if it interferes with secular laws. Thus legislators have required believers to swear allegiance to the state at the cost of their obedience to God.

Examples abound of this perfidy: Pharmacists who are forced to fill prescriptions for abortifacients despite their religious belief that abortion is murder. Bakers who have been forced to close their businesses because they refuse to provide cakes for gay marriages that they believe violate God's law. Business owners who are forced despite their religious and moral objections to offer health insurance that includes coverage for services they consider immoral, again including abortion.

Many of these cases are working their way through the court system now, and it will be up to the Supreme Court to rule whether or not Americans still enjoy freedom of religion or whether that precious liberty has been surrendered to a few loud-mouthed bigots who think they are entitled to live in a world where God is only worshipped behind closed doors.

Think about it. The American experiment in liberty, which crushed those very noxious religious strictures that were so common in the colonies, has now given way to a reverse intolerance that claims that anyone who is offended by a religion has a right to shut it down. Isn't that exactly the condition that existed in Europe in the 17th century from which our ancestors fled in search of freedom?

How could the First Amendment's guarantee that the state can never touch your right to freely exercise your religious beliefs somehow have been twisted today into a cudgel to be used to keep people of faith silent, afraid and in line?

That's both a simple and complicated question, and one beyond the scope of this column, but there may well come a time when people of faith will either have to stand up or be shut down entirely.

The culture we live in no longer esteems the Bible, the Judeo-Christian ethos, nor the traditional values espoused therein — no matter how many people go to church on Sunday. That's fine. Let everyone decide for themselves what they believe or don't believe, but don't try to stamp out belief by force, especially not using the power of the state that represents all of us.

Non-believers, who pride themselves on logic and rational thought, should have no problem with that premise, and believers should recognize the need to take an active role in defending themselves from any attacks that do occur.

Fortunately, there are just such defenders throughout society. People of faith are not timid people, but rather people of power and love and discipline, as Paul notes in his second letter to Timothy. They are urged not to be ashamed of their faith, but to cast out fear and do the right thing.

And although the mainstream media may not report it too often, sometimes the right thing does get done through the efforts of those who labor according to the "purpose and grace" of God. I

Such a one is Pastor Jeanette Golden of Hemphill, Texas, who late last month won her battle to display a Ten Commandments sign on her own property along State Highway 21. The state had first attempted to charge Golden for the right to display the sign, and then tried to remove it altogether.

When I first wrote about Golden last Easter, it was unclear whether she would be one more victim of the increasingly secular state, but with the help of the Liberty Institute, Golden prevailed against the state of Texas, and now private individuals have the right to display non-commercial signs under 96 square feet on their own property. This should have been an obvious principle under that other part of the First Amendment that refers to freedom of speech, but nothing is obvious when a court gets involved. Fortunately, this matter was resolved by the Texas Department of Transportation without a liberal judge having a chance to rewrite the Constitution.

Interestingly, Texas is also taking part in another legal case, but this time whole-heartedly supporting the right of a church to free speech. Indeed, Texas is one of 10 states taking the side of a small Arizona church as it defends its right to display the same size sign as politicians or special-interest groups get to have.

I'm happy to report that Montana's Attorney General Tim Fox joined Texas, West Virginia and other states late last month in filing a "friend of the court" brief with the U.S. Supreme Court in support of the Good News Community Church of Gilbert, Arizona.

The town of Gilbert had passed a sign ordinance that placed restrictive size limits on churches and non-profits, but not on political signs or "ideological" signs, whatever they are. The 9th Circuit Court of Appeals (speaking of liberal judges!) upheld the sign ordinance, but the church appealed to a "higher power" — the U.S. Supreme Court.

As Attorney General Fox said in a press release regarding the appeal, "If the Supreme Court upholds the Ninth Circuit's ruling, it would give governments, including the federal government, the authority to systematically favor speech about certain subjects over speech about other subjects. This would be a dangerous erosion of the rights that all Americans are guaranteed under the First Amendment to the U.S. Constitution."

In other words, it would be one more instance where government is more important than the people, and where certain people are more important than other people. The "dangerous erosion" has already begun, perhaps has already gone so far that there is no going back, but it is heartening to see a few modest efforts at erosion control in a world that more and more seems to be built on shifting sand.

RULE OF LAW OR TYRANNY BY COURTS?

October 12, 2014

Multiple recent court rulings have thrown the concept of self-determination on its head. You remember self-determination, right? That was what we had before we had judicial tyranny.

Thomas Jefferson summed up self-determination in the Declaration of Independence, writing succinctly that "Governments are instituted among Men, deriving their just powers from the consent of the governed..."

Those are two incredibly powerful phrases — "just powers" and "consent of the governed" — but sadly, neither of those can exist when the people are denied the opportunity to shape through legislation the nature of the society they live in, nor to protect the traditions on which that society was founded.

You can easily build a case that the United States no longer has the consent of the governed using as an example the timely but blistering issue of gay marriage. Multiple other issues would illustrate the same principle just as well, but this has been in the news, so let's stick with it, no matter how controversial.

For the sake of this argument, it doesn't matter whether you approve of gay marriage or not — the question for American citizens instead should be whether you approve of self-determination, because clearly the "consent of the governed" has been missing in all these court rulings.

A majority of states — 31 — have state constitutional amendments banning legal recognition of same-sex unions, yet one after another these bans approved by the people or their representatives have been cast aside by federal courts.

These courts, in essence, have ruled that the people no longer have the right to structure their society according to the dictates of their conscience and beliefs, but rather must succumb to the preferences of various judges who individually are prepared to overturn the mandate of the millions. This would have been called tyranny in the day of Thomas Jefferson, but today it is called progress.

Let me stress once again that this argument in favor of self-determination has nothing to do with the propriety of gay marriage. If indeed, the majority of people in a society conclude that gay marriage is an entirely appropriate institution for that society to sanction, then so be it. As a former student of anthropology, I am well aware of the many forms of marriage that exist or have existed on the globe since time immemorial, and I see no reason for one society to impose its beliefs on another society.

But I also see no reason for one judge to impose his or her beliefs on society either. If a people cannot write their own constitution, then where exactly do the "just powers" come from — and where did the "consent of the governed" go? When you take out the emotional froth of achieving victory by any means that clearly stirs the gay marriage proponents, I do not see how anyone could reasonably surmise that cultural revolutions imposed by a minority upon a majority have any chance of long-term success.

Finally, I do not understand how the arguments used by courts to order states to allow gay marriage cannot be applied to every other possible form of marriage. If "equal protection" of law truly makes it illegal for the state to mandate that marriage is between one man and one woman, then it should be illegal for the state to mandate any preference regarding what is appropriate for a marriage covenant.

Having been an avid fan of Robert Heinlein's prophetic science fiction for many years, I am already familiar with the nature of the polyamorous marriage definition that the courts clearly envision for us, but don't acknowledge. Read Heinlein's novel "Time Enough for Love" for more details.

Unlimited marriage is not my cup of tea, but if this is what America wants to become, it should do so through legislation and not through judicial fiat. One of the great things about legislation is that it not only can be passed, but also later repealed if it doesn't work out. How often have you heard of judicial precedent being repealed?

If courts insist on imposing a progressive agenda on a conservative people, then they deserve the result they get. If you need a contemporary example of an effort to shape a society against its will, you need look no further than the great experiment in democratization in Iraq. How's that working out for you?

If that doesn't satisfy you, consult with the Ceausescus, the late Mr. and Mrs., about how the people of Romania felt about living under the communist dictates of the Great Leader. The lesson has always been the same down through history. Don't mess with the people, because the more you oppress them, the messier it gets.

OBAMACARE'S INDECENT AND LONG OVERDUE EXPOSURE

November 16, 2014

A reader wrote last week to ask me whether or not Jonathan Gruber's admissions about the conspiracy to pass Obamacare were being circulated beyond the confines of Fox News.

"Has there been any hint of this in any of the mainstream press," he asked.

At the time there hadn't been, but by now everyone may be familiar with it. Republicans in Congress have seized on Gruber's candid admissions to take renewed aim against the Affordable Care Act, and by Friday the Associated Press could no longer ignore the story, meaning it has now appeared in newspapers across the entire country.

"Lack of transparency is a huge political advantage," Gruber exclaimed in one of the newly uncovered videos that show him telling how the Obama administration tricked the public into supporting the Affordable Care Act. "And basically, call it the stupidity of the American voter or whatever, but basically that was really, really critical to get the thing to pass."

Well, as Mr. Gruber is now finding out, the reverse is true as well. Because when you manipulatively hide the truth from the American public, and then you get pulled out of the shadows to face them, there is hell to pay.

Gruber, an economist at the Massachusetts Institute of Technology, was hired by President Obama's Department of Health and Human Services to provide "technical assistance" on creating the new health-care law sometime around 2009. He did so, and yet he also made public appearances as an apparently independent expert to promote health-care reform as well.

In August 2010, the House Committee on Oversight and Government Reform issued a minority report that pointed out that Gruber was paid nearly $400,000 for his help in shaping the health-care law, but that "Gruber's status as a paid consultant to HHS was not disclosed in interviews with Time, the Washington Post, the New York Times, the New Republic, and elsewhere."

Of course, nowadays, it seems as though Democrats want you to believe they have never heard of Gruber. Former House Speaker Nancy Pelosi actually made that claim, even though she had touted him as an expert in 2009. Indeed, everyone knew he was an expert on the Affordable Care Act until he had the misfortune of chewing on his own foot in public.

A search of the Internet reveals multiple instances over the past several years where he has been referred to as the "chief architect of Obamacare," but now Democrats are trying to minimize his role as much as possible.

To be sure, there are many other pretenders to the throne of "chief architect," ranging from Dr. Ezekiel Emanuel and Elizabeth Fowler to former Rep. Anthony Weiner and former Sen. Max Baucus, and even Republican presidential candidate Mitt Romney, but it doesn't matter what title you give Gruber. The facts are plain that he played a huge role in shaping the Affordable Care Act.

It is also plain — at least in retrospect — that he was comfortable doing so through deception, subterfuge and sleight-of-hand. The video clips of Gruber that have surfaced over the last week are nothing less than stunning in their suggestion of an intentional deception of the American people and perhaps their legislators.

In the first one, Gruber admitted, "This bill was written in a tortured way to make sure the CBO [Congressional Budget Office] did not score the mandate as taxes. If the CBO scores the mandate as taxes, the bill dies. ... Basically, you know, call it the stupidity of the American voter or whatever, that was really really critical to get the thing to pass."

That is highly significant because the question of whether the penalty charged to non-participants in the program was a tax was crucial in the Supreme Court's 5-4 ruling that preserved Obamacare. And by that time, the Obama administration had turned 180 degrees and was now insisting it was indeed a tax.

Perhaps the most important impact of the Gruber videos will be felt in yet another Supreme Court ruling that may come next year.

In particular, one of the videos from January 2012 has Gruber explicitly describing how Obamacare's tax credits were intended only for citizens who used state-established health-insurance exchanges, not for customers of the federal exchange.

Since that very point is the basis of the latest lawsuit against the Affordable Care Act which the Supreme Court has already agreed to hear, that admission is huge.

The Obama administration has been arguing that although the law, as written, clearly states that the subsidy or tax credit is available only to customers of state exchanges, the intention of legislators was just the opposite. Obamacare advocates, in other words, are claiming that the wording was just a big typo — a clerical error that should not stand in the way of the implementation of the law.

But how will they be able to make that case before the Supreme Court with a straight face when one of the architects of Obamacare already told the truth. Judge for yourself. Here is Gruber's analysis:

"I think what's important to remember politically about this is, if you're a state and you don't set up an exchange, that means your citizens don't get their tax credits," Gruber said. "But your citizens still pay the taxes that support this bill. So you're essentially saying to your citizens, you're going to pay all the taxes to help all the other states in the country."

Gruber made it clear that this language was included intentionally in order to encourage the states to set up their own exchanges by depriving a benefit from them if they did not!

"I hope," he said, "that's a blatant enough political reality that states will get their act together and realize there are billions of dollars at stake here in setting up these exchanges, and that they'll do it."

The video on which Gruber confirmed this important information was located and published online by the Competitive Enterprise Institute as long ago as July 2014. It was subsequently noted by a Wall Street Journal blog as well, but its significance remained obscure until Gruber's comments calling the public "stupid" went viral last week.

Well, stupid is as stupid does, and when measuring stupidity one really must acknowledge Gruber's peculiar penchant for undermining the Affordable Care Act which he supposedly helped build as its chief architect.

It is ironic that the great Ayn Rand novel "The Fountainhead" was built around a plot that involved a brilliant young architect blowing up a building of his own design to protect it from being compromised.

But don't get the wrong impression. Gruber is no Howard Roark, the architect hero of Rand's novel. Roark represented the triumph of the individual in what Rand labeled the war of "individualism versus collectivism," whereas Gruber's construct of Obamacare was the enslavement of the individual by the collective.

Now, we must wait to see whether the American public once again embraces freedom, or prefers to remain shackled to a health-care system that has been exposed as a cynical scheme by people who will say or do anything to increase their own power.

We know who's betting the American public is too stupid to pick freedom, but I am putting my money on the same people who just said "enough is enough" to Sen. Harry Reid and his crony in the White House.

WHAT ABOUT GOOD & EVIL?

November 30, 2014

"Woe unto them that call evil good, and good evil; that put darkness for light, and light for darkness; that put bitter for sweet, and sweet for bitter! Woe unto them that are wise in their own eyes, and prudent in their own sight! ... Which justify the wicked for reward, and take away the righteousness of the righteous from him!" —Isaiah 5:20-21, 23

Disconnect.

That is the feeling any sane person must have when watching the rioting in Ferguson, or when listening to the self-proclaimed wise men justify the rioting.

How can anyone blame the policeman who killed Michael Brown for defending himself and the rest of us from violence? How can anyone turn Michael Brown, who first attacked a store owner and stole from him, and then beat a policeman, into a hero? Does attacking a policeman until you are shot dead now qualify you to be a hero?

Like I said... disconnect.

But when you listen to these passionate advocates for locking up the policeman, you know that they are in earnest about protecting the "legacy" of Michael Brown by sending the officer to jail. And while there may be an element of political gamesmanship to it, of mere exploitation and demagoguery to promote an agenda, it seems to me much more than that.

Indeed, it seems like a large percentage of our U.S. population is brainwashed or occluded — as if they cannot discern good and evil. How else can you explain the wish to reward the wicked and take away the righteousness of the righteous?

For another perspective, let us consider the parable of the good Samaritan, as told by Jesus in the Gospel of Luke. This story is well understood as a quiet reminder that good men do not help each other merely because they identify with each other based on religion or other outward criteria such as race, but because they identify with each other as human beings.

That quality has apparently been lost in the national media debate about Ferguson, so it is useful to once again note that it took a Samaritan to treat the beleaguered Jew in the parable as a human being while his fellow Jews passed him by.

That story is told by Jesus in response to a question by a wise man of that day, "a certain lawyer" who no doubt thought he could trip up Jesus by asking him, "Who is my neighbor?"

It is just such a question which the "wise" men of Ferguson, including many lawyers, have asked in regard to the death of Michael Brown. They want to know why Michael Brown does not get treated like a "neighbor" but the parable of the good Samaritan throws light in the dark places of both Ferguson and our national dialogue.

You probably know the outlines of the biblical story.

"A certain man [presumably a Jew] went down from Jerusalem to Jericho, and fell among thieves, which stripped him of his raiment, and wounded him, and departed, leaving him half dead."

Two respected Jews — a priest and a Levite — came down the same road, and when they saw the beaten man, they "passed by on the other side," leaving him to fend for himself.

A short while later, a Samaritan came upon the injured man "and when he saw him, he had compassion on him, and went to him and bound up his wounds, pouring in oil and wine, and set him on his own beast, and brought him to an inn, and took care of him."

Jesus concludes his tale by asking which of the three "was neighbor unto him that fell among the thieves." The lawyer rightfully concludes that the neighbor was the one who showed mercy, the Samaritan, regardless of the fact that Jews and

Samaritans hated each other over sectarian differences that were much more severe than any differences between white America and black America.

Now, let's imagine that the "certain man" who was set upon by thieves was a policeman. Let's say that it was Darren Wilson, the police officer who was traveling down a certain road in Ferguson, Missouri, when he spotted two young men who appeared to match the description of thieves who had just committed a strong-arm robbery a few blocks away.

Who were the highwaymen or thieves in this modern-day parable? Let's imagine it to be Michael Brown, the huge 18-year-old alleged felon, and his traveling companion, Dorian Johnson. It is not hard to cast Brown as a thief in this story because he was grasping a handful of stolen Swisher cigars when officer Wilson, responding to a 911 call, spotted the suspect and tried to talk to him.

Probably Officer Wilson wished he could be anywhere else in the world rather than confronting two potentially violent criminals on a public street that noon hour, but he did not have the choice of "passing by on the other side of the street." Policemen have to walk into the midst of danger everyday, and they have to hope they will walk out of it, but sometimes that doesn't happen.

In this case, Wilson was attacked by Michael Brown through the open window of his SUV patrol vehicle. Brown beat the officer around the face and struggled with him for his gun. Two rounds were fired from the officer's gun during this encounter. At this point, the criminal suspect flees and the policeman has to decide what to do. Being a lawman, and despite injuries to himself, Officer Wilson follows his training and pursues the suspect in order to prevent him from doing harm to anyone else. When Brown turned and approached Officer Wilson, the policeman shot him multiple times, the last shot being a fatal shot to the head.

Eyewitness testimony was no doubt contradictory about exactly how the shooting occurred, but whether Michael Brown had his hands up while he was approaching the policeman has no relevance whatsoever. "Hands up, don't shoot" is the slogan of Brown's supporters, but putting your hands in the air does not give you permission to approach a police officer whom you have just beaten. The correct slogan here is "Hands up, down on the ground." That is the only way to assure you will not be shot in similar circumstances.

The race of either the victim or the defendant is also entirely irrelevant, as there are dangerous people of all races, and police have to react based on threat level, not based on concern about skin color. To remove that opportunity to act decisively from a policeman means that they will increasingly be victims, not protectors.

The Levite and the priest who looked the other way and did nothing to help the man attacked by thieves in Jesus' parable are ultimately not just bad Jews; they are bad people. In a truly colorblind society, we would not talk about a white cop and a black criminal, but rather good and evil.

Those people who walk mockingly around the injured police officer who was set upon by thieves and show him no kindness or respect are just like the Levite and the priest who did not recognize their neighbor. That includes multiple politicians such as President Obama, multiple lawyers such as Attorney General Eric Holder, multiple community organizers such as Al Sharpton, and multiple so-called journalists such as Rachel Maddow.

So finally, who is the good Samaritan? Hopefully, it is you, dear reader, because the hope of the country is in your hands.

'WALKING DEAD,' THE CONSTITUTION, AND THE ROMAN EMPIRE: YOU DO THE MATH

January 4, 2015

Australian historian Paul Ham recently wrote a book called "1914: The Year the World Ended."

He is not the first person to remark upon the cataclysmic changes that transformed the world in 1914, but in fact it was the Old World that ended as the First World War began, whereas the United States found itself atop a new world order.

But now cataclysmic changes are under way again, and it seems not at all unlikely that some future historian will sit down to write a tome entitled "2014: The Year the United States Ended."

Thanks in part to President Barack Obama and his pledge to fundamentally transform the United States, and in even larger measure to the lethargic indifference of the citizens of the country to what is being done to them, the constitutional republic founded in 1787 has more or less ceased to exist.

Call it the political equivalent of "The Walking Dead," those TV zombies who have no brain functions except for the ability to walk around and chew flesh off the bone. We still have a Constitution, but it has been reduced to a mere device by which the resources and traditions of the United States can be chewed off the legal bone and spit in our face.

It's nothing new. This disaster did not happen overnight like the one on the TV series. It's been under way for more than 50 years, maybe ever since 1914 when Woodrow Wilson was president and the progressives started to make "minor" adjustments in how the Constitution was interpreted.

In recent years, it hasn't mattered whether a president was a Republican or Democrat — they all seemed to consider the Constitution more of a hindrance than a help in governing. Same with Congress. Moreover, the Supreme Court by instituting its doctrine of precedent (known as stare decisis) has made a mockery of the Founding Fathers' intentions.

It doesn't matter what the living language of the Constitution says any longer; instead courts are only allowed to apply the zombified Constitution handed down to us by dead judges. Real human beings who are gored by the illegal constructs put in place by presidents and legislators have no "standing" to ask for their rights under the original, the "real" Constitution. They are displaced, disenfranchised and distraught, with no court of appeal.

No wonder really that cynicism is the rule of the day. But yet... but yet... one wishes that the public were more attuned to the theft of their liberty by powerful forces in Washington, D.C.

How can the American citizenry blithely accept the cockiness of a president who makes law without Congress? How can they willingly go along with a Congress that spends trillions of dollars it doesn't have, putting us into hock to China and other countries that bear us enmity? How can they tolerate an attorney general who pits black against white in the guise of protecting civil rights? How could they ignore the terrifying story of how the IRS worked with the Department of Justice to target conservatives for audits and punitive probes? How can they permit the dismantling of the U.S. military at a time when the world is more dangerous than ever?

The answers to those questions are all the same. Bread and circuses. It was how the bad Roman emperors distracted their citizens from the collapse of empire, and it is how our bad presidents and politicians keep the public from asking too many questions as well. There is only so much time in a day, and if you keep Americans focused on football, Facebook and Food Network for enough hours, they won't have time or energy enough left to investigate the case of the missing Constitution.

That 24-hour supply of infotainment — along with an endless string of news stories about Sony hackings, Mideast beheadings, and Malaysian plane crashes — is the equivalent of the Roman Coliseum and its "circuses" of blood and terror. Meanwhile, the most desperate among us, those who have the most to lose by the death of the American Dream, are kept in check by copious portions of largess in the form of food stamps, tax credits for not working, subsidies for this and that, and of course Obamacare.

Too bad a lot of good people will read these words and declare that I am the problem — me and people like me who are crying out against abuses and the corruption of the system by powerful forces that have only their own self-interest in mind. These good Americans are the equivalent of those good Germans who allowed their brilliant society to be destroyed from within because they simply could not fathom the capacity for evil of their own leaders.

Maybe I'm wrong. Maybe 2014 is just one more good year in a series of good years as America traverses an ever-upward trajectory of greatness. Maybe if I drank the Kool-Aid, I could find a silver lining in the cloud of obfuscation coming out of our government, out of our media and out of our own mouths. But I doubt it.

Don't mind me though. Go right ahead and have a happy new year. You've earned it. After all, you're living on borrowed time with borrowed money and a philosophy borrowed from Karl Marx. Eat, drink and be merry, for tomorrow we die (if we haven't already).

IT'S NOT A FUNDING CRISIS; IT'S A CONSTITUTIONAL CRISIS

March 1, 2015

When the history books are written, they won't write about whether or not the Department of Homeland a got funding in February of 2015; they will write about whether or not there was still a homeland at all.

The constitutional republic handed down to us by our Founding Fathers appears to have ceased to exist, and the blustering members of Congress circa 2015, with their sworn duty to support and defend the Constitution of the United States, can't even work up enough outrage to pass a simple bill.

That bill, as originally formulated, would have funded the Department of Homeland Security but would withhold funds from being used to support the president's executive order prescribing benefits, financial and otherwise, for a certain large class of illegal immigrants. The reason this is important is because the Constitution grants to Congress the exclusive authority for making laws; the president has no power to do so — at least not in a nation of laws.

Republicans thought they could force the president to do the right thing by using the congressional power of the purse, but the president used the power of scary words to bend Congress to his will. Those scary words? "Government shutdown!"

Since no one really wants to stop funding the department that defends us against terrorism, it was an inevitable conclusion that a bill would eventually pass sans the restriction on funding for the president's illegal amnesty. The Democrats, as they usually do, had the upper hand politically, and the Republicans shot themselves in the foot again.

Conservatives had warned last fall that the GOP had adopted a strategy of failure when they stumbled upon their idiotic plan to hold the Department of Homeland Security hostage. But Republicans seem not to be capable of grasping the big picture, nor of governing pragmatically. Two vital flaws.

They also have an easy out today, which they are too myopic to see. A federal judge in Texas has already issued a stay preventing the president from proceeding with his executive amnesty. If the Republicans had any political savvy, they would write a bill that fully funds Homeland Security as long as that stay remains in effect. This would merely codify the status quo, and would give both sides something to vote for. Should the stay be overturned, funding for the department would ipso facto cease within 30 days.

But Republicans don't really want a solution; they don't really want to challenge the president. They are as much a part of the problem as the president is, and in many ways they have abrogated their constitutional responsibilities just as much or more than the president has.

Let's make it plain. We the People have a problem. No matter what the mainstream media tells you, this is not a funding crisis; it is not a government shutdown crisis; it is a constitutional crisis. What we have is a president willing to do anything to advance his agenda, and a Congress unable and very possibly unwilling to do anything to stop him. Since they both answer to us — to We the People — then it ultimately falls on us to make them pay a price for their misconduct and arrant disregard for the Constitution.

The issue Congress should be focused on is not immigration reform, nor government spending; the issue is a lawless president who wrested power and authority from the Congress unconstitutionally and got away with it. You don't have to take my word for it; we have it on good authority from President Obama himself.

Here's what he said on March 28, 2011:

"America is a nation of laws, which means I, as the president, am obligated to enforce the law. I don't have a choice about that. That's part of my job... With respect to the notion that I can just suspend deportations through executive order, that's just not the case, because there are laws on the books that Congress has passed .... [W]e've got three branches of government. Congress passes the law. The executive branch's job is to enforce and implement those laws. And then the judiciary has to interpret the laws. There are enough laws on the books by Congress that are very clear in terms of how we have to enforce our immigration system that for me to simply through executive order ignore those congressional mandates would not conform with my appropriate role as president."

This is just one of the many times the president told the American public it would be illegal and unconstitutional for him to unilaterally change the law through executive fiat. That's pretty compelling evidence, yet the gelded Congress can't work up any enthusiasm for defending the Constitution against this blatant usurpation of power.

Time after time, you do hear senators and representatives decry President Obama for taking unconstitutional action, but then they fail to follow through and take the constitutional action they themselves are charged with when a president commits high crimes and misdemeanors, namely impeachment.

There is no argument whatsoever that a president overstepping his or her constitutional restraints is exactly what the Founding Fathers meant when they included the phrase "high crimes and misdemeanors" as grounds for impeachment. They were not concerned with presidents becoming murderers but rather tyrants, and with the near example of King George III in mind, the founders chose language that would provide future generations broad latitude to decide for themselves what abuses of power merited impeachment.

Although inherent to the meaning of the term, it should be pointed out here that impeachment itself does not assume guilt, but rather provides a president the opportunity to defend himself against charges he had overstepped his bounds. The House of Representative may file articles of impeachment against a president with a simple majority of members voting in the affirmative, but to convict a president and remove him from office requires a two-thirds majority of the U.S. Senate.

Impeachment seems like a mighty big word, but it has twice been used for considerably less flagrant offenses than those which are reckoned against this president. President Andrew Johnson was impeached for the offense of firing a member of his Cabinet without consulting the Senate, and President Bill Clinton was impeached for lying to a grand jury (and the nation) about his preference for young brunette interns.

It appears that President Obama is serious about violating the oath he swore that he "will faithfully execute the Office of President of the United States, and will to the best of [his] ability, preserve, protect and defend the Constitution of the United States."

That being the case, when will the Congress get serious about stopping him? Probably never, which raises the question of when will We the People get tired of living in a fake republic and listen to the advice of Thomas Jefferson, who wrote: "But when a long train of abuses and usurpations... evinces a design to reduce them [the people] under absolute Despotism, it is their right, it is their duty, to throw off such Government."

Constitutional convention, anyone?

SENATORS TAKE A STAND FOR THE CONSTITUTION

March 15, 2015

Just look what happens when a senator starts to act like one!

Sen. Tom Cotton, an Arkansas Republican, who has been a U.S. senator for less than three months, rattled the cage of the

White House, the Democratic Party, and Iran's Ayatollah Khamenei , all with a single-spaced, one-page letter on the U.S. Constitution.

Addressed as "An Open Letter to the Leaders of the Islamic Republic of Iran," the missive was signed by Cotton and 47 other Republican senators. The avowed intent of the letter was to educate the Iranians on the nature of the American constitutional system, in particular the role of the U.S. Senate in ratifying treaties negotiated by the president.

The letter is entirely accurate and an appropriate elucidation of the constitutional separation of powers. It does not in any way touch on the substance of the nuclear negotiations underway between the Obama administration and Khamenei 's regime. Yet the letter had the same effect on American liberals that sunlight has on vampires. They screamed, they screeched, and they scrambled. For example:

—The Daily News of New York City went explosive with a WWIII-sized headline that condemned the GOP senators as "TRAITORS."

—Something like 275,000 people signed an online petition at whitehouse.gov declaring that the senators had committed treason and should be prosecuted under the never-before-successfully invoked 1799 law called the Logan Act, which in the words of the petition, "forbids unauthorized citizens from negotiating with foreign governments."

—The Arizona Republic chided Sen. John McCain and the other 46 signatories for their "attempt to wrest foreign policy from the hands of President Barack Obama." The editorial claimed that the senators attempted to "interfere with the negotiations of the elected official with the authority to barter with Iran, the president."

The only problem with all this foaming at the mouth of progressive scribes and petition signers is that it reflects on their own rabid condition, and not on the actual facts of the case.

Anyone who claims that the senators have committed treason does not know what the term means. This crime has the distinction of being defined in the U.S. Constitution, in Article

III, Section 3, where it is noted that "Treason against the United States, shall consist only in levying War against them, or in adhering to their Enemies, giving them Aid and Comfort." If anyone wants to try to make the case that the 47 GOP senators had any intention of "giving aid and comfort" to the enemy (If Iran can even be defined as an enemy by any sort of legal code), good luck to them.

It would not be the first time that Democrats ignored the facts in pursuit of sheer political gain. And as long as we are investigating treasonous activities, maybe we should look into whether freeing five senior Taliban leaders in exchange for the alleged deserter Bowe Bergdahl gave any of our Islamic enemies "aid and comfort."

As for the Logan Act, it is aimed at any citizen who "without authority of the United States, directly or indirectly commences or carries on any correspondence or intercourse with any foreign government or any officer or agent thereof, with intent to influence the measures or conduct of any foreign government or of any officer or agent thereof, in relation to any disputes or controversies within the United States, or to defeat the measure of the United States."

The only time the law has ever been applied was in 1803 when some poor miserable Kentucky farmer wrote an article in the Frankfort Guardian of Freedom proposing a separate nation in the Western territories that would align with France. So much for freedom in Frankfort, and so much for the freedom of speech. Yet this is the ridiculous law that our progressive brethren want to use to punish 47 United States senators.

Moreover, the text of the law itself exonerates the senators from its application. Senators obviously do have the "authority of the United States" to communicate with foreign governments, and have done so for the past 227 years.

Indeed, the U.S. Department of State ruled in 1975 that Sens. John Sparkman, D-Ala., and George McGovern, D-S.D., were entirely in their rights to visit Cuba to hold discussions with officials there. The State Department declared that "Nothing in section 953 [the Logan Act] ... would appear to restrict members of the Congress from engaging in discussions with foreign officials in pursuance of their legislative duties under the Constitution."

That's good for John Kerry, the current secretary of state, who in 1985 as a Democratic senator traveled to Nicaragua along with Sen. Tom Harkin, D-Iowa, to broker a deal with the communist Sandinista government. "If the United States is serious about peace, this is a great opportunity," Kerry declared.

Now, Kerry and the rest of the Democratic Party is saying something entirely different. They think the 47 senators who are trying to prevent a nuclear holocaust in the Middle East are misguided. President Obama said he was "embarrassed for them."

So let's put aside politics and examine this one-page document that led many people to accuse nearly half the Senate of being traitors.

Oddly enough, it does not have anything to say about the substance of the negotiations being carried out by Secretary Kerry and President Obama. It doesn't "attempt to wrest foreign policy" from the hands of the president, and it certainly doesn't "interfere with the negotiations" with Iran, as the Arizona Republic claimed. It's entire argument is about the United States Constitution and the powers assigned to the president and the Congress under it. Just read it. It's almost as exciting as an eighth-grade U.S. history class!

"First, under our Constitution, while the president negotiates international agreements, Congress plays the significant role of ratifying them. In the case of a treaty, the Senate must ratify it by a two-thirds vote."

Does that sound treasonous? How about this:

A so-called congressional-executive agreement requires a majority vote in both the House and the Senate (which, because of procedural rules, effectively means a three-fifths vote in the Senate). Anything not approved by Congress is a mere executive agreement."

You getting a firing squad ready yet? Feeling the love between those 47 senators and Iran yet? Pretty cheeky, if you ask me. Aiding and comforting the enemy indeed!

But wait! It gets better:

"Second, the offices of our Constitution have different characteristics. For example, the president may serve only two 4-year terms, whereas senators may serve an unlimited number of 6-year terms."

No wonder those Democrats and progressives are getting nervous: It appears that Republican senators have read at least part of the Constitution. What if they started following it? Now, that would be revolutionary, but I don't know about treasonous. That just doesn't seem like the right word.

In conclusion, the 47 neophyte students of the Constitution wrote, "What these two constitutional provisions mean is that we will consider any agreement regarding your nuclear-weapons program that is not approved by the Congress as nothing more than an executive agreement between President Obama and Ayatollah Khamenei. The next president could revoke such an executive agreement with the stroke of a pen and future Congresses could modify the terms of the agreement at any time."

This last part, along with a reference earlier to "binding international agreements," is what seems to have gotten both the president and the secretary of state ticked off.

Remarkably, Sen. Kerry told the Senate Foreign Relations Committee that the United States never intended the negotiations with Iran to result in a "quote, legally binding plan." Therefore, it would not have to go to the Senate for ratification. It was, in essence, a "Gentlemen's Agreement" between the former champion of the free world and the largest state sponsor of terrorism in the Middle East.

If you don't know what a "gentleman's agreement" is, then look up the book or movie by that name. Or just read this quote from the movie: "I've come to see lots of nice people who hate [anti-Semitism] and deplore it and protest their own innocence, then help it along and wonder why it grows. People who would never beat up a Jew. People who think anti-Semitism is far away in some dark place with low-class morons. That's the biggest discovery I've made. The good people. The nice people."

If 47 Republican senators are willing to stand up to anti-Semitism, then they have my support. And no, I'm not Jewish, although like the hero of "Gentleman's Agreement," I certainly have taken enough insults from people who think I am.

Don't believe there is any anti-Semitism? Well, the same ayatollah who condemned the U.S. senators' letter as "a sign of the decline in political ethics and the destruction of the American establishment from within," also referred to Israeli Prime Minister Benjamin Netanyahu as a "Zionist clown." And just four months ago, he Tweeted about Israel's government, "This barbaric, wolflike & infanticidal regime of #Israel which spares no crime has no cure but to be annihilated."

As for the idea of a non-binding agreement between the United States and another country, that is certainly an appropriate way to refer to a treaty that was not ratified by two-thirds of the Senate. It is just that — non-binding.

But it is also something else — unconstitutional. The U.S. Constitution is very clear about the powers granted to the president. In Article II, Section 2, it affirms, "He shall have Power, by and with the Advice and Consent of the Senate, to make Treaties, provided two thirds of the Senators present concur..."

There is no treaty without Senate ratification, and there is no other power granted to the president to complete "executive agreements" with foreign countries except with Senate ratification. President Obama may not like it, as he doesn't like so many things in the Constitution, but he's stuck with it.

Now, if we can only get the Republican senators to stick to their principles for a change, things may actually see a turn for the better. It's the Constitution, stupid!

IT'S TIME TO DEFUSE
THE 'NATURAL BORN' TIME BOMB

March 29, 2015

"A foolish consistency," Emerson warns us, "is the hobgoblin of little minds."

I concur, but consistency is also the best defense against being called a hypocrite, which is why I wanted to take this opportunity to explain that the "natural born citizen" qualification for being president of the United States is not just something that was invented to make Barack Obama look bad.

The issue of who is a "natural born citizen," and thus eligible to be president, has been repeatedly raised in campaigns and media reports for at least 135 years, probably longer. Among the most prominent controversies have been those involving the following candidates or potential candidates:

— Republican Chester A. Arthur, the 21st president, was rumored to have been born in Canada. He took office after the assassination of James Garfield, but even while he was president, his claims of being born in Vermont were questioned. In addition, his father was a naturalized citizen who was born in Ireland.

—Republican Charles Hughes, who was defeated by President Woodrow Wilson in the 1916 campaign, was the American-born son of two British subjects.

—Democrat Franklin Delano Roosevelt Jr., the son of the president with the same name, entered Congress in 1949, leading to speculation that he might run for president. Although that never happened, there was considerable discussion about the fact that FDR Jr. was born at the Roosevelt summer home of Campobello Island in New Brunswick, Canada.

—Republican Christian Herter, governor of Massachusetts, whose name was suggested for both president and vice president in the mid-1950s when President Eisenhower's health was questioned, was born in Paris to expatriate parents and spent the first nine years of his life there.

—Republican Barry Goldwater, the 1964 nominee, was born in Arizona before it became a state.

—Republican George Romney (father of Mitt Romney), who ran unsuccessfully for the Republican nomination in 1968, was born in Mexico.

—Republican Lowell Weicker, who like Herter was born in Paris to American parents, made a brief run for the Republican nomination in 1980 but withdrew before any primaries were held.

—And (hold your breath!) Republican Sen. John McCain, who ran against Barack Obama in 2008, was born in the Panama Canal Zone while his father was stationed there as a Naval officer.

By my count, that gives us seven Republicans who have been challenged regarding whether they were natural-born citizens and only two Democrats — FDR Jr. and Barack Obama. It also gives us a count of eight white guys and one black man. Thus, we should be able to retire the charge of racism once and for all, as well as the notion that the "natural born citizen" issue was invented by Republicans simply as a way to hinder Democratic fortunes in the presidential election of 2008.

Indeed, this year, the issue is being raised once again to question the eligibility of Sen. Ted Cruz, the Republican firebrand from Texas, who is the first declared candidate of the 2016 presidential race. Unlike President Obama, who has a birth certificate from Hawaii but is still alleged by some people to have been born outside the United States, Sen. Cruz by his own admission and all the available evidence was indisputably born in Calgary, Alberta.

Does that mean he shouldn't be president? I don't know, and neither does anyone else, because the definition of a "natural born citizen" has never been resolved by the Supreme Court of the United States, nor by the Congress. That is why the issue is important, not because it helps or hurts one particular candidate.

Since natural-born citizenship is one of only three requirements for someone to become president, I have argued consistently that the matter must be settled officially, not for political reasons, but for legal reasons. Yet even though I was one of the few columnists in the country to ever bring up McCain's citizenship status, the fact that I have also insisted that the nation has a right to verify Barack Obama's eligibility to be president means that I have repeatedly been called a birther, a racist, or various other derogatory terms.

So, once and for all, and to anyone who will listen — the debate has nothing to do with Barack Obama; and nothing to do with race. It hinges on the Constitution, and whether or not we are a nation of laws. If the Constitution says that a president must be a natural-born citizen, then we need some kind of mechanism to determine if candidates are indeed eligible under that rule, as well as under the rules that they must be at least 35 years of age and have resided within the country for at least 14 years.

Nor is this just some random academic exercise. It has come up repeatedly throughout the history of the United States, and this year will once again be relevant if either Ted Cruz, Bobby Jindal or Marco Rubio should obtain the Republican nomination for president or vice president.

—Cruz's mother was a U.S. citizen at the time of his birth in Canada, so he is definitely a citizen, but does that qualify him as a "natural born citizen"? We don't know.

—Piyush "Bobby" Jindal was born of two Indian immigrant parents in Baton Rouge, Louisiana, so under the 14th Amendment, he is an undisputed citizen of the United States, but is he "natural born"? No one knows.

—Marco Rubio was born in Miami, Fla., of two parents who were both Cuban citizens. Again, no doubt that he is a native U.S. citizen, but that may not make him a "natural born citizen."

The authors of the Constitution were silent on the meaning of the phrase, which probably means they all knew what it meant and therefore didn't feel the need to define it. That has encouraged amateur historians to research the political climate and common law of the late 18th century and look for clues.

It appears likely the phrase was popularized by philosopher Emerich de Vattel, whose 1758 "The Law of Nations" is considered the pre-eminent text on rules of sovereignty in the 18th century. It is generally presumed that the authors of the Constitution were familiar with the work, and consulted it when drafting the Constitution. George Washington is known to have borrowed a library copy which remains overdue to this day! Samuel Adams, John Adams and Alexander Hamilton all wrote enthusiastically of Vattel's influence on the Constitution. In 1775, Thomas Jefferson even sent his own copy of "The Law of Nations" to Ben Franklin, and received an enthusiastic thank you note.

Here is what Vattel had to say about the matter under discussion:

"Natural born citizens are those born in a country to parents who are also citizens of that country. Particularly, if the father of the person is not a citizen then the child is not a citizen either. Children cannot inherit from parents rights not enjoyed by them."

Of course, Vattel's text does not have the force of law, nor would it be politically correct today because of its inherent sexism, but there is very little else to go on when considering the meaning of the phrase in the Constitution. The point again is not to presume with certainty that someone is or is not eligible to be president, but to assert that the citizenship rule exists and should not be ignored. Up till now, it has only been discussed as a matter of curiosity, and no one seems capable of discovering a sure and sufficient means of enforcement.

But if this year, we have (as it appears we do) at least three potential candidates for the presidency whose eligibility has been questioned, then clearly it is time for the matter to be addressed directly and resolved. And no, it does not matter that the three candidates involved are Republicans, and for the most part Tea Party Republicans, and that I personally would put all three of them in my Top Five candidates for 2016.

It doesn't matter to me whether they would make good or bad presidents; what matters is making sure they are following the law of the land. Hey Americans... It's the Constitution! Love it, or lose it!

Someone needs to challenge one or all three of these candidates if they declare their intention to be president, and one can hope that if these Republicans do indeed love the Constitution, one of them will encourage a court to make a ruling and settle the matter for all of us.

You can call me a RINO (Republican in Name Only) for questioning the eligibility of Cruz, Jindal and Rubio. You can call me a racist for questioning the eligibility of Barack Obama. But one thing you can't call me is a hypocrite. And be sure of this, I will follow the path of principle no matter what foolish names I am called.

JOHN ROBERTS:
WORST CHIEF JUSTICE EVER?

June 28, 2015

I'm giving the chief justice of the United States the benefit of the doubt by including a question mark in my headline. There have certainly been bad chief justices before, and bad decisions rendered by probably all of them, but it is hard to imagine a more self-serving, self-important tool of political correctness than John Roberts.

On Thursday, Roberts released the majority opinion in King v. Burwell, upholding the federal government's assertion that when Congress, or more particularly the Democrats in Congress, wrote that tax credits in the Affordable Care Act were intended only for citizens who used health-insurance exchanges "established by the state," they didn't mean it. In fact, according to Roberts, they meant the opposite.

Actually, Roberts doesn't care what they meant because in his majority opinion he more or less confesses that what is important is not the law, but the outcome.

Thus, at the beginning of his opinion, he writes, "The Patient Protection and Affordable Care Act grew out of a long history of failed health-insurance reform." Clearly, what we have here is an essay written to justify health-insurance reform. The history of health-insurance reform is completely irrelevant to the matter before the court, which was simply, WHAT IS A STATE?

One thing is certain: The federal government is not a state, and more particularly, the secretary of health and human services — who established the federal exchange — is not a state. But the Supreme Court said they are.

As Justice Antonin Scalia wrote in a scathing rebuke of Roberts:

"Under all the usual rules of interpretation... the Government should lose this case. But normal rules of interpretation seem always to yield to the overriding principle of the present Court: The Affordable Care Act must be saved."

In reading the majority opinion, it is obvious that Roberts believes that the Affordable Care Act SHOULD work, so he crafted his opinion in order to guarantee that it COULD work, regardless of the facts. He tips his hand repeatedly, as in the concluding paragraph when he writes, "Congress passed the Affordable Care Act to improve health insurance markets, not to destroy them." It doesn't matter to Roberts that Congress through its own negligence wrote the law poorly. Like President Obama, Justice Roberts has a pen and a phone, and he used his pen to edit the mistakes of Congress and red-line the liberty of American citizens. From this day forward, liberty is whatever Justice Roberts says it is.

If he and his liberal allies did not intend to WRITE a new law in order to RIGHT the error done by Congress, then they could have simply done what was obvious — rule that Congress through incompetence, hastiness, or guile had written the law in such a way that it had certain inevitable consequences — consequences which could only be rectified by Congress in its role as the sole law-making branch of the U.S. government. If Congress meant to say that the tax credits were for everyone enrolled in the program, it should have said so in the first place, but even if it made a mistake it certainly had the ability to correct it today if that were its wish. The Supreme Court should have said so.

But instead Roberts "intuited" that Congress actually meant to give the tax credit to everyone even though it had failed to say so in plain language, and in fact had said the opposite.

Unfortunately for Roberts' legacy, the intent of Congress was made plain not just by the legislation itself but also by its prime architect Jonathan Gruber, who in January 2012 explicitly described how Obamacare's tax credits were intended only for citizens who used state-established health-insurance exchanges, not for customers of the federal exchange.

Here is Gruber's analysis, recorded on video at the time:

"I think what's important to remember politically about this is, if you're a state and you don't set up an exchange, that means your citizens don't get their tax credits," Gruber said. "But your citizens still pay the taxes that support this bill. So you're essentially saying to your citizens, you're going to pay all the taxes to help all the other states in the country."

Gruber made it clear that this language was included intentionally in order to encourage the states to set up their own exchanges by depriving a benefit from them if they did not!

"I hope," he said, "that's a blatant enough political reality that states will get their act together and realize there are billions of dollars at stake here in setting up these exchanges, and that they'll do it."

In other words, the Affordable Care Act was intentionally structured as it was in order to pressure states into creating health-care exchanges. There's no way around that, nor is there any way around acknowledging that the Roberts' ruling now gets states off the hook. Even states that created exchanges originally will now see no need to keep them and their vast bureaucracies, but will likely turn the duty back over to the federal government to expand its death-grip control and authority over every aspect of our lives.

Mind you, I never expected the Supreme Court to rule correctly on the matter of what a state is. If U.S. courts operated on principles of logic and common sense, this case would never even have gotten to the Supreme Court.

According to Chief Justice Roberts, a state is whatever he says it is, which makes him the lead antagonist in the real-life sequel to George Orwell's dystopian nightmare, "1984."

Do you remember O'Brien, the amoral defender of the state in that novel, who holds up four fingers and asks Winston how many he sees? Winston responds truthfully that O'Brien is holding up four fingers.

"And if the Party says that it is not four but five — then how many?"

"Four."

The word ended in a gasp of pain.

That's how it played out in "1984," where Winston is tortured until he accepts the fake reality that the government has constructed, but now it is not the Party that creates reality out of nothing; it is the Supreme Court.

Just imagine this same scene with Roberts playing O'Brien, and the question not about how many fingers he is holding up, but what constitutes a state.

"What is a state, Winston?" Justice Roberts asks.

"A state is one of the 50 sovereign units of the country known as the United States."

"And if the Supreme Court says that a state is not a state?"

"It is still a state."

The word ended in a gasp of pain.

"What if the Supreme Court says that the federal government is a state?

"It is not a state."

More pain. More intense. Eventually you give up and repeat what you are told.

"How many fingers am I holding up, Winston?"

That's easy. As many as the Party says.

Justice Scalia got it right when he said that Obamacare has a new name now — SCOTUS Care, the honorary stepchild of the dishonorable Supreme Court of the United States.

Welcome to "1984."

OBAMA'S PEN STRIKES AGAIN

September 27, 2015

The most important story of the past two weeks was not the visit of Pope Francis to Congress. It was not the visit of Chinese President Xi Jinping to the White House. It was not the resignation of John Boehner as speaker of the House. It was not the debate over whether a Muslim should be president of the United States. It was not the invasion of Europe by Middle Eastern refugees. It was not even the war between Donald Trump and Fox News.

No, the most important story of the past two weeks, perhaps the most important story of the past seven years, is something you almost certainly never heard anything about.

The most important story you never heard anything about in the mainstream media is when President Obama picked up his fabled pen and signed an executive order on Tuesday, Sept. 15, entitled "Using Behavioral Science Insights to Better Serve the American People."

Ladies and gentlemen, you have just been "Nudged."

That is a reference to the title of a book by Obama's former regulatory czar and Harvard Law professor Cass Sunstein. The full title is "Nudge: Improving Decisions about Health, Wealth, and Happiness" and it was co-written with University of Chicago economist Richard H. Thaler. The argument of that 2008 book is summed up by the authors thusly:

"People often make poor choices — and look back at them with bafflement! We do this because as human beings, we all are susceptible to a wide array of routine biases that can lead to an equally wide array of embarrassing blunders in education, personal finance, health care, mortgages and credit cards, happiness, and even the planet itself.... A nudge, as we will use the term, is any aspect of the choice architecture that alters people's behavior in a predictable way without forbidding any options or significantly changing their economic incentives."

Encouraging people to make "the right choices" is called by Sunstein and Thaler "libertarian paternalism" — in other words, you are free to do what we think is best for you!

The executive order (written by Sunstein?) says that "the Federal Government should design its policies and programs to reflect our best understanding of how people engage with, participate in, use and respond to those polices and programs."

It sounds like the government will be changing to respond to what the people want, but in the same paragraph, Obama lets the cat out of the bad — this is really about getting the people to do what the government wants. Listen:

"By improving the effectiveness and efficiency of Government, behavioral science insights can support a range of national priorities, including helping workers to find better jobs, enabling Americans to lead longer, healthier lives; improving access to educational opportunities and support for success in school; and accelerating the transition to a low-carbon economy."

In other words, the government is going to get into your head and try to manipulate you into thinking the government is doing a good job when it tells you what to do with your life: Don't drink soda. Don't drive a truck. Don't buy guns. Don't worry; be happy!

Of course, this is not the first time that government has tried to dominate the rap, Jack, but it has never been so blatant before in its attempt to turn the people into sheeple.

In the old days, there was a certain amount of discretion in the manipulation of public policy. Perhaps the master of this on the public stage was Edward Bernays, the godfather of propaganda who worked for progressive Democratic President Woodrow Wilson. Bernays' daughter Anne described her father's use of propaganda in politics as a form of "enlightened despotism" and said he feared that "they [the American public] could very easily vote for the wrong man or want the wrong thing, so that they had to be guided from above."

In his 1928 book "Propaganda," Bernays wrote:

"The conscious and intelligent manipulation of the organized habits and opinions of the masses is an important element in democratic society. Those who manipulate this unseen mechanism of society constitute an invisible government which is the true ruling power of our country... We are governed, our minds are molded, our tastes formed, our ideas suggested, largely by men we have never heard of..."

That would be even more true under the president's executive order, which commands all executive departments and agencies to "recruit behavioral science experts to join the Federal Government as necessary to achieve the goals of this directive."

The president says this team of experts will be "using behavioral science insights" to manipulate the American people, but a much more accessible term is the old one — behavior modification. Read up on one of the best of the behavioral scientists, B.F. Skinner, to learn for yourself how easy it is to get people to do what you want them to do using positive and negative reinforcement — the old carrot and stick approach taken to extremes.

As citizens, even if you agree with the goals of the prevailing liberal philosophy, you really have to ask yourselves if you can stomach the idea of a public policy that is "of the government, by the government and for the government."

If we are looking for common ground between Republicans and Democrats, between conservatives and liberals, this might be a good place to start.

'FEAR ITSELF': A TALE OF TWO SPEECHES

November 29, 2015

You can count on two things happening whenever America faces danger. First, Republicans will demand action to keep the republic and its citizens safe, and second, Democrats will accuse the Republicans of fear-mongering.

In the current political climate, that fight has taken place over the issue of Syrian refugees, and the Obama administration's plan to resettle thousands of the mostly Muslim refugees in America. ISIS has promised to infiltrate the refugees with terrorists, leading Republican governors to declare their unwillingness to allow the refugee program in their states.

In response, the mantra heard round the land the past two weeks by Democratic talking heads is "the only thing we have to fear is fear itself."

Well, not so quick.

First of all, it is important to recognize that when President Franklin Roosevelt used that phrase in his first inaugural address, he was seeking to reassure the American public that the economic duress they faced in the Great Depression was a problem they could overcome. He was most certainly not saying that people who talked about the severity of the depression were laughable fools or dangerous demagogues. Indeed,

Roosevelt himself catalogued the country's challenges and laid out a comprehensive plan to confront them.

"This is preeminently the time to speak the truth, the whole truth, frankly and boldly. Nor need we shrink from honestly facing conditions in our country today," Roosevelt said, then going on to make his famous pronouncement.

But get this. When he said, "The only thing we have to fear is fear itself," he then described that worrisome fear as "nameless, unreasoning, unjustified terror which paralyzes needed efforts to convert retreat into advance."

I postulate that the fear that Americans feel about Syrian refugees is not "nameless, unreasoning, unjustified terror," but rather its opposite. In fact, it is the entirely rational, entirely justified, easily named terror brought about by being the repeated victim of Islamic radical jihad that has made Americans resist President Obama's insistence that we have a national obligation to welcome Syrian refugees to our homeland.

Democrats contend that people who are afraid of terrorists posing as Syrian refugees (or even of Syrian refugees deciding to become terrorists later) are a greater danger to the country that the Syrian refugee policy itself.

This was summarized by President Obama in a press conference in Manila when he chided Republicans as crass opportunists and cowards.

"Apparently, they're scared of widows and orphans coming into the United States of America as part of our tradition of compassion. First, they were worried about the press being too tough on them during debates. Now they're worried about 3-year-old orphans. That doesn't sound very tough to me. They've been playing on fear in order to try to score political points or to advance their campaigns. And it's irresponsible. And it's contrary to who we are. And it needs to stop, because the world is watching."

We don't have time to properly chastise the president for turning a public policy dispute into a political ambush while he was representing our country overseas, so let's just drill down into this fear factor and consider how reprehensible it is for the president and others to belittle their fellow citizens for their desire to keep Americans safe.

First, a few facts:

• At least two of the Muslims involved in the Paris terror attacks were posing as Syrian refugees, and several others had visited Syria, where ISIS controls a large swatch of the countryside.

• The vast majority of the Syrian "migrants" arriving in Europe and who will appeal to the UN for refugee status are neither widows nor orphans, but rather able-bodied men between the ages of 18 and 30, the same demographic that is associated with suicide bombings and attacks throughout the Muslim world and Europe.

• Five Syrians were apprehended earlier this month in Honduras with fake Greek passports, and other Syrians have been trying to cross the border from Mexico into the U.S. No doubt they have heard that once you are across the border, you stand a pretty good chance of being invited to stay by either a judge, Congress, or a lawless president operating outside the bounds of the Constitution.

Of course, the bottom line is that the United States accepts more refugees than any other country in the world. We do not lack compassion, nor are we afraid of true refugees who seek to start over as part of our American community, but the old adage holds true: "Fool me once, shame on you. Fool me twice, shame on me."

We have been fooled so many times by Muslim immigrants and refugees who turned out to harbor deadly intentions that we can never live down our shame. The screams of the dead should haunt us for all time.

Let's start with the 1993 truck bomb by Ramzi Yousef and other Muslims at the World Trade Center, which killed six people and had the potential to destroy both towers eight years before they were actually destroyed in the Sept. 11 attacks that killed nearly 3,000 people. Did we have more to fear from "fear itself" or from a policy that blindly underestimated the threat to the homeland of those who hate us?

Remember the attack by Nidal Hasan, an American-born Muslim who killed 13 people at Fort Hood. The case of Hasan should repudiate the claims of those who think Americans do not have to fear Muslims who were born in this country. Birthright citizenship is not the same as assimilation, nor does it automatically assure loyalty. Our fear of Hasan should have been magnified, not diminished, before the attack because of his behavior, not his religion.

Let's conclude with the Tsarnaev brothers, who set off two improvised explosive devices in the crowd at the 2013 Boston Marathon, killing three people and injuring 264 more, some severely. Those two brothers had been admitted to the United States with "derivative asylum status" after their father had received asylum as a refugee from Chechnya. Being shown kindness by the American people does not ensure that kindness will be shown in return.

Do we really need to dispute the danger that Muslim immigrants and their families pose to the citizens of the United States? Is there any reason why Americans should be berated by their own president because they are fearful of their safety when Muslims are imported from a dangerous war zone like Syria and plopped down in the middle of American cities, towns and villages with virtually no oversight?

Here is the speech that Democrats should have been proudly quoting in the years following Sept. 11, and which they should take to heart today:

"No matter how long it may take us to overcome this premeditated invasion, the American people in their righteous might will win through to absolute victory... I assert that we will not only defend ourselves to the uttermost, but will make very certain that this form of treachery shall never endanger us again. Hostilities exist. There is no blinking at the fact that our people, our territory and our interests are in grave danger. With confidence in our armed forces — with the unbounding determination of our people — we will gain the inevitable triumph — so help us God."

That is from another speech by President Franklin Roosevelt — the one where he coined the phrase "a date which will live in infamy" to describe Dec. 7, 1941, and to commemorate the sneak attack on Pearl Harbor.

When he said that Americans and the American way of life were in "grave danger," no one accused him of fear-mongering. No one scolded him for forgetting that the only thing we have to fear is "fear itself." We were united as a nation and as a people to protect ourselves from a vicious enemy. If we are going to learn a lesson from Franklin Roosevelt, let's learn that one.

BOEHNER WITH A BEARD: PAUL RYAN'S LEGACY OF SURRENDER

December 20, 2015

On Friday, Dec. 18, 2015, Congress held up a white flag and surrendered its constitutional authority to make laws and to regulate spending on behalf of the United States government.

Instead, Congress has decided to give the president whatever he wants, however much it costs, because they are terrified of being accused of shutting down the government if they insist on responsible spending, representative government, and constitutional separation of powers.

In a span of two days, Congress received a 2,000 page bill that authorizes spending $1.1 trillion on a smorgasbord of hundreds of programs both good and bad, and then passed it with hardly any discussion because... well, um, because they wanted to get home for the Christmas break!

Does anyone really need any further evidence that Congress is doing what is good for Congress and not what is good for the country?

This travesty was set in motion by John Boehner, the former speaker of the House, but new speaker Paul Ryan cannot escape blame. He has shown no inclination to respect the people's will, nor to do the people's business. He is just Boehner with a beard.

In December 2014, Boehner crammed through his own travesty of a spending bill that was infamously called

Cromnibus — defined as the combination of a short-term continuing resolution (or CR) and a long-term omnibus spending bill and thus a CRomnibus bill. But there are several other germane allusions in the name which should not be ignored. It represents the worst of CRony capitalism or just plain CRony establishmentarianism. It also includes a subtle hint of crumminess, which is defined variously as wretched or contemptible, words that certainly apply when describing Congress.

By wrapping funding for hundreds of programs up in one last-minute take-it-or-leave-it bill the week before Christmas, Congress has abrogated its responsibility to make reasoned, measured judgments about what to fund out of the public treasury. Some of the programs are essential and should have been funded weeks or months ago. Unfortunately, all too many of the programs are an insult to the American people and Congress should have been brave enough (wise enough?) to have rejected those funding requests out of hand.

Here are some of the programs that Republicans (the majority party in both houses of Congress) vehemently oppose, but which Republican leadership in Congress acceded to without a fight:

— Funding for sanctuary cities. The murder of 32-year-old Kate Steinle by a repeat-criminal illegal immigrant in San Francisco outraged America, but not Paul Ryan. He allowed funding to continue for law-breaking sanctuary cities

— Funding for the president's illegal executive order to give amnesty to DREAMers, the propaganda name for illegal immigrants who came to the United States as minors.

— Funding for President Obama's highly unpopular refugee-resettlement efforts will continue unabated. So will the outrageous program to resettle illegal immigrants in the heartland of the country when they are captured. Why settle them anywhere when we have so many buses and planes available to send them back where they came?

— Funding an increase in H-2B foreign worker visas is a blatant example of crony capitalism running the show. This is the visa program that Disney and other employers have used to import foreign workers to replace Americans. Adding insult to injury, Disney used the American workers to train their own replacements!

Those are some of the most blatant examples of Congress legislating against the interests of their constituents, but by no means the only ones. A vast majority of Republican voters would never consent to send their representatives to Congress to vote for this mess, but that's just what lots of them did. So what's the explanation?

Call it corruption.

No, the congressmen and women and senators weren't bribed, at least not monetarily, but a CRomnibus bill guarantees votes by larding the bill with programs that are not controversial, but might have a difficult time winning funding were normal order being followed. Senators and representatives have a hard time turning their back on millions of dollars that can be spent in their home district or state.

A prime example is the Land and Water Conservation Fund, a useful program that uses royalties from offshore drilling to pay for conservation projects across the country. That program has funded many park and recreation resources in Montana, but that doesn't mean it qualifies for automatic renewal. In fact, it expired on Oct. 1, and you could easily make the case that when the federal government is running a $19 trillion debt, a better use could be found for nearly a billion dollars in oil and gas royalties every year.

Apparently, that better use is "buying" votes from members of Congress so that they will accept the horrible consequences of a runaway budget process in order to brag back home about what goodies they procured. Sadly, freshman Rep. Ryan Zinke, R-Montana, who has generally been a reliable vote for common sense, got caught up in the game and let himself be played by Speaker Ryan. He sold his conservative credentials for a mess of potage, bragging about how he "made history" by lifting the ban on crude oil exports. Somehow, I think most Montanans would rather see him make history by standing up to a lawless president and a spendthrift Congress.

For the record, both of Montana's senators — one from each party — voted against "CRomnibus 2." Steve Daines, freshman Republican, said the "200-page backroom deal... only takes our nation further down an unsustainable path of more unbridled spending and more debt." Two-term Democrat Jon Tester, like Daines, acknowledged that the massive bill included some programs he supported, but said his biggest concern is that "this bill saddles our kids and grandkids with over $680 billion in additional debt."

Way to go, senators. If we as a nation want to insist on bipartisanship, that's a good place to begin. But until a majority of Congress feels the same way, it is just the beginning of the end. America cannot survive if its leaders are afraid to do the right thing.

Instead, they must be made to suffer the consequences when they don't do the right thing. Hopefully Paul Ryan will go the same way as former Majority Leader Eric Cantor and former Speaker Tom Foley. Vote the bums out.

SHUTTING DOWN FREE SPEECH IN COLLEGE — AND IN POLITICS

March 13, 2016

When I was trudging through my high school years, one thing that kept me going was the vision of "higher" education — the belief that once I got to college, I would be surrounded by intellectuals engaged in lively debate and the exchange of ideas. Think of Plato's "Symposium" except on a grander scale.

Then I got to Tulane University —the Harvard of the South, as they like to call themselves.

Imagine my surprise when I found out that college in 1973 was high school with more sex, drugs and rock 'n' roll. People didn't read Plato; they read Rolling Stone.

Sure, every once in a while I would get into an actual exchange of ideas that didn't involve religious or political dogma, but more often than not my counterparts would stop the conversation at some point with a quizzical look upon their face, hold up their hands in frustration, and query me — "You don't really believe that, do you?"

In other words, the free exchange of ideas on college campuses has always had a somewhat restrictive view of the word "free" — at least since the 1960s. You were free to condemn disgraced President Nixon, for instance, but not free to defend him. You were free to denounce the Vietnam War, but not free to justify it. You were free to praise affirmative action, but not free to question it.

Fast forward 40-plus years and freedom on college campuses has grown even more suffocatingly claustrophobic. Freedom today means the freedom to hear only what you want to hear and to say only what other people want you to say. In other words, freedom is another word for political correctness. The alignment of those two concepts is a perfect example of what George Orwell called "doublethink" — the ability to hold two completely opposite concepts in the brain at the same time without the ability to recognize that they are mutually exclusive.

Thus, college campuses today have become indoctrinators of ideology instead of incubators of ideas. Instead of welcoming debate between those with different ideas, professors and administrators have become protectors of left-wing orthodoxy against any challenge that might invite people to think for themselves. The examples are too numerous to recite, but you are all encouraged to do a Google news search for "free speech in campus" to find numerous examples of the opposite.

You probably heard of Melissa Click, the University of Missouri professor, who was caught on camera calling for "some muscle" to remove reporters from a protest site in 2015. That's no surprise, but what was shocking is that the university later fired her instead of lauding her as a hero. I guess incitement to violence still goes too far.

At lots of college campuses though, it is considered perfectly acceptable to muscle out dissenting viewpoints and to silence speech. A recent example took place at Rutgers University last month when feminists and Black Lives Matter protesters took objection to a speech by that most scary of speakers — a gay Roman Catholic conservative.

Milo Yiannopoulos must have represented a threat to the "safe space" of the college-age adolescents who expect everyone to toe the line of political correctness. Yiannopoulos is a real-life version of Kris Kristofferson's "The Pilgrim": "He's a walkin' contradiction, partly truth and partly fiction."

Yiannopoulos was invited to the New Jersey campus by Young Americans for Liberty to speak on "How the Progressive Left Is Destroying Education." And right on schedule, the progressive left provided a perfect example of it by disrupting the event by smearing blood on their faces and shouting down Yiannopoulos, who was on the first stop of his "Dangerous Faggot Tour." Dangerous indeed!

Not coincidentally, when Donald Trump scheduled a rally on the University of Chicago campus Friday, it was canceled after hundreds of protesters infiltrated the pavilion and raised security concerns because of the potential for violence.

The protesters were jubilant and took to the streets, chanting "We stopped Trump!" No, you stopped free speech.

'1984':
AN EQUAL OPPORTUNITY DISASTER AREA

May 22, 2016

My daughter has been reading George Orwell's "1984" in high school this month. Too bad it's not required reading for all citizens — especially before they vote. If it were, then perhaps Americans would not be so gullible about everything the government tells them.

In the Oceania of "1984," it is standard practice for the so-called Ministry of Truth to manufacture convenient fictions that are tailored to steer public opinion toward acceptance of government-approved propaganda. The depth of the government's ability to manipulate the public is characterized by the illogic of the ruling Party's slogans: War is peace. Freedom is slavery. Ignorance is strength. Boys are girls.

Oh wait, that last one came from Obama's Department of Justice, not Orwell's Ministry of Truth. You probably read about the "guidance" provided by the U.S. Department of Justice and Department of Education that boys should be allowed to enter the girls bathroom, locker room and showers at all the public school districts and colleges in the country. To be fair, girls can also change in the boys locker room in school, although why they would want to is beyond me, remembering as I do just how much boys locker rooms stink.

But what is really bizarre is how silent the country has been over this pronouncement that the physical gender of a human being can be over-ridden by the wish-fulfillment concept of gender identity. Back when I was growing up, they had a different name for boys showering with girls. It was called "indecent exposure."

But let's face it, nothing is indecent anymore, because the very sense of decency requires an acknowledgment of right and wrong, which in turn requires an acknowledgement of good and evil, which in turn requires an acknowledgment of He Who Shall Not Be Named in public schools (the God previously known as YHWH). And that's just not going to happen.

When we kicked God out of the schools, we pretty much started on a glide path toward co-ed showers because without that divinity to provide us real "guidance," we are at the mercy of human nature, and it's not a pretty picture. Not at all.

So where do we go from here?

Does the population of the United States accede to the Ministry of Truth proclamation that boys are girls? Or do we fight back? In "1984," the protagonist Winston Smith tries to hold to the truth that 2+2=4, but he discovers that he is not strong enough to withstand the power of the government to convince him through any means possible including torture that 2+2 equals whatever the government says it is.

We live in that world now. School districts either agree that boys are girls, or they run the risk of losing their millions of dollars of government funding. The government must be believed, even when it doesn't make any sense to do so.

Who will speak up?

"The Emperor's New Clothes" comes to mind. In the fairy tale by Hans Christian Anderson, a cunning pair of con men convince the emperor that they will weave him a set of new clothes made from a fabric invisible to anyone who is unfit for office or incredibly stupid. Actually, the clothes don't exist at all, but no one (including the emperor) wants to admit it because they don't want to look stupid or unfit. The emperor parades down the street in all his glory, until finally one small child shouts out, "But he hasn't got anything on!"

That's where we are now, waiting for a little girl like the child in the fairy tale who will point at the new woman in the locker room and innocently declare, "But she has too many parts!"

The question for us all to ask is will that girl be praised for speaking the truth? Or shamed for pointing out our blindness?

SIT IN, SHUT UP AND DISARM: THE DEMOCRATIC RESPONSE TO TERRORISM

June 26, 2016

If you are old enough, you remember how campus after campus in the 1960s had the president's office "occupied" by students who would rather be making demands" for "social justice" than actually attending class. These ruffians were loud, petulant and self-righteous, and they considered their issues more important than civil behavior, the rights of others or common decency.

Sound familiar? That's because, if you follow the timeline from the late 1960s to now, you will discover that many of those unwashed radicals or their younger siblings are running everything from major corporations to, yep, Congress. And the lesson they learned is that if you are loud enough and obnoxious enough for long enough, you just may be able to get your way after all.

Democratic members of the U.S. House of Representatives showed their true colors Wednesday when they returned to their roots and staged a disruptive "sit-in" to shout down opponents and shut down congressional business because they didn't get their way on gun control.

Now, mind you, gun control is a legitimate topic of debate, and that's why the U.S. Senate held four votes on background checks, terror watch lists and other issues last week. None of the bills managed to garner enough support to be passed, which is why the House of Representatives did not need to follow through with its own votes. Legislation has to be passed by both houses of Congress in order to be sent to the president, and there is no reason to do "show votes" on legislation that won't pass just so various members will have talking points when they return home to stand for re-election.

But this sit-in wasn't about legislation; it was about propaganda. It was about making sure that the crisis brought about by the murder of 49 people in Orlando, Florida, by a Muslim terrorist did not go to waste. It was a prime opportunity for Democrats to push their divisive anti-gun agenda, and so they ignored the obvious lessons of a jihadist massacre and focused not on the killer, but on the weapon. Gun control, after all, is a major plank of the Democratic Party, even in gun-loving Montana.

A statement from Sen. Jon Tester noted that "Jon supports the House members in their efforts to try and hold votes on legislation to keep guns out of the hands of terrorists and those who want to do us harm." A remarkable utterance by a politician who won election in 2008 by declaring that he wanted to make Washington, D.C., more like Montana; apparently, to the contrary, Jon Tester is now more like Washington, D.C., a city which famously once banned all handguns.

Tester now stands firmly with the East Coast and West Coast hypocrites who think the best way to fight crime is penal reform (i.e., putting more criminals back on the street by freeing them from prison), the best way to fight illegal immigration is immigration reform (i.e., rewarding law-breaking border crossers with U.S. citizenship), and the best way to fight greedy health insurance companies is to require all private citizens to buy health insurance (i.e., Obamacare). Most importantly, the best way to fight Muslim terrorism is to invite more Muslims into the United States and cross our fingers that they are not terrorists as well.

But really, what difference does it make anyway if they are radicalized jihadi terrorists as long as they can't get guns? That's the imbecilic argument emanating from the whiny brats in diapers who took over the House of Representatives and thumbed their nose at the rule of law.

Let's face it: If you don't want to offend Muslims, then Muslim terrorism is all about the guns. It's not about the ideology of hate they are taught; it's not about the supremacy mindset that makes Islam consider itself better than all other religions; its just about the guns, stupid.

Well, we will have to see whether this "publicity stunt," as Speaker Paul Ryan called it, will work. The sit-in certainly didn't result in the rape of the Second Amendment that its leaders intended, but the 25-hour protest may just be the first of many. Now that Democrats have gotten a taste for disruption, they may decide it's more conducive to winning elections than doing the hard work that legislators are supposed to do. And they may be right. We will just have to wait and see how perceptive the American voters are these days. I'm not holding my breath.

DEAD VOTERS AND OTHER HORROR STORIES

October 2, 2016

There is nothing more aggravating in the entire liberal canon than the myth of voter suppression.

What exactly is meant by voter suppression? According to most sources, it is the effort to prevent eligible voters from exercising their right to vote.

So what are some examples of that?

Best known is the use of photo ID, requiring voters to demonstrate positively that they are the person they claim to be when they vote. But there are many other allegations of how voting is suppressed, such as requiring proof of citizenship.

Both of these common-sense requirements are widely characterized by liberals as targeting minorities and immigrants, and we are told repeatedly that minorities don't have access to photo ID or to citizenship papers such as a birth certificate.

I don't know about you, but every time I want to get some government service, I have to jump through mandatory hoops to prove my identity and eligibility. That goes for passports, driver licenses, Social Security card replacement — you name it.

It never occurred to me to complain that my rights were being violated. In fact, I was grateful for the government taking every possible precaution. In this age of rampant identity theft, scams and fraud, there is no reason to accept anyone's word for anything.

Except, it seems, the right to vote! For that all-important privilege of citizenship, we are told that it would be cruel and unusual to expect anyone to have to prove they were eligible.

Maybe that's why 20 dead people were allowed to register to vote in Harrisonburg, Virginia, recently. The applications were turned in by a voter registration group called HarrisonburgVOTES, and they probably would have gone unnoticed except for the fact that whoever submitted the phony applications unwittingly included one well-known local resident who had died just two years ago.

Harrisonburg Registrar Debbie Logan said, "applications using a deceased person's real name and address but a false Social Security number would not be flagged in the voter system," according to the Richmond Times-Dispatch.

Apparently, the 20 dead people are going to remain officially registered to vote, but Logan said that if one of them attempts to vote, her office will take "appropriate" measures. Just guessing, but does that mean a stake through the heart?

There was another false alarm about phony voter registration last week that was enlightening. The Burlington, Washington, mall shooting suspect, Arcan Cetin, who immigrated here from Turkey as a child, was originally reported to be a permanent resident who had nonetheless registered to vote.

By week's end we learned that Cetin was indeed a U.S. citizen, and therefore entitled to vote, but during the interim we discovered that Washington state like pretty much every other state operates on the honor system when it comes to citizenship.

"We don't have a provision in state law that allows us — either county elections officials or the secretary of state's office — to verify someone's citizenship," Secretary of State Kim Wyman told KING-5 TV.

Well, isn't that peachy?

But are we surprised? Heck no. Because George-Soros-funded globalist entities and their liberal courtroom allies have been working tirelessly to force states NOT to check citizenship. Arizona had the audacity to pass a law a few years back that required potential voters to establish proof of citizenship. That was called an undue burden on minorities and ruled unconstitutional.

These same groups have suppressed voter ID laws, fought to invalidate bans on felons voting, and generally done anything they could do make it easy for improper voting to take place. States have been ordered to toe the line of U.S. regulations despite the fact that the separate states have always been in charge of their own election laws and have been able to regulate voting as they saw fit.

This is just one of many planks in the liberal platform to undermine American institutions, but because it strikes directly at the integrity of our elections, it is one of the most dangerous.

All you can say is, "It ain't your Founding Fathers' Constitution anymore."

DON'T ASSAULT CONSTITUTION OVER PARTISAN COMPLAINTS

November 27, 2016

Many books will be written about the presidential election of 2016, which was unique in the annals of history, but in some respects it confirms the predictive genius of the Founding Fathers, who planned for every eventuality, even those which we think of as most remarkable.

On the morning of Nov. 8, it appeared to many that the Democratic Party and the liberal faction in America were set to deliver the death blow to the Republican Party and the conservative faction it represents. It is therefore no wonder that progressives and leftists are up in arms over the election of Donald Trump.

After eight years of "fundamental transformation" of the government of the United States by the Obama administration, it would have only taken the election of one more Democratic president to complete the process — both by providing a bulwark against the repeal of countless executive orders initiated in the last eight years and by guaranteeing the appointment of an overwhelming number of liberals to the judiciary who would rubber-stamp laws and policies as constitutional that on their face were not.

Indeed, this potentially crushing blow to American conservatism — which is the prevailing philosophy in the vast majority of states — would have been accomplished handily were the presidential election decided by the popular vote rather than in the Electoral College.

Hillary Clinton, with the help of huge vote leads in places such as California (62-33 percent), New York (59-38 percent) and Massachusetts (61-34 percent), is currently ahead by more than 2 million votes. In California alone, she surpassed Trump by about 3.5 million votes, meaning that if the election were decided by popular vote, that extremely liberal state would wield massive power over much smaller states such as

Montana, Wyoming, Oklahoma and Tennessee, where Trump won by similarly large margins.

This should remind us why the country was established with checks and balances against putting too much power into the hands of any one state, and indeed any one faction.

One of those checks and balances is the Electoral College, to which the Founders gave the responsibility for choosing the winner of the presidency, instead of relying on the popular vote.

The reasons are many, but are primarily understandable, as explained by James Madison in Federalist Paper No. 10, as working to protect the rights of the minority against the "superior force of an interested and overbearing majority."

"Overbearing" is perhaps the best adjective ever invented to describe the liberal mindset of the nanny state that Democrats have imposed on the country over the past 50 years, and without the Electoral College, the popular majority would now be forcing its will upon the substantial minority who wish only to exercise their rights to "life, liberty and the pursuit of happiness" without being forced to toe the line of political correctness.

Madison warned that political parties would tend to work for their own good, not for the good of the people, or as he said, they are "much more disposed to vex and oppress each other than to cooperate for the common good." Thus, allowing a party or faction by simple reason of majority to "carry into effect schemes of oppression" would lead to the destruction of the nation. Instead, as devised by the Founding Fathers, it is important that it is the Union which prevails, not any one party.

Should efforts to obviate the Electoral College prevail, we will be one step closer to that "pure democracy," which Madison warned us has no defense against "the mischiefs of faction."

It may not suit our modern sensibilities, but we tamper with it at our own peril. Consider the words of George Washington in his farewell address that powerful factions will work in their own interests to try to change the system of government to take advantage of you, the people.

"Toward the preservation of your government and the permanency of your happy state, it is requisite not only that you steadily discountenance irregular oppositions to its acknowledged authority but also that you resist with care the spirit of innovation upon its principles, however specious the pretexts. One method of assault may be to effect, in the forms of the Constitution, alterations which will impair the energy of the system and thus to undermine what cannot be directly overthrown."

We have already greatly diminished the "energy of the [constitutional] system" by such changes as the direct election of senators, the effective neutering of the Ninth and 10th Amendments (which protected the rights of the states and the people), and the vast expansion of the powers of the federal government through subsequent interpretations of the 14th Amendment.

Any more "innovation" of the Constitution could very well have the effect of destroying it altogether. The temporary inconvenience of Donald Trump to liberals should not be used as an excuse to undermine the eternal genius of our Founding Fathers.

FILIBUSTER IS SENATE INVENTION TO AID AND ABET SENATORS

September 3, 2017

First of all, let's get it straight. There is no such thing as filibuster in the United States Constitution.

The notion that this was an invention of the Founding Fathers is just wishful thinking by senators who want to give their shameless power grab the imprimatur of legitimacy.

Actually, the Constitution provides that a simple majority in both the House and Senate is sufficient to do business. We know that was the plan because the authors of the Constitution spelled out only a handful of circumstances when a supermajority would be required such as ratifying treaties.

In Federalist Paper No. 58, James Madison spelled out exactly why a super-majority was the wrong idea for a republic:

"In all cases where justice or the general good might require new laws to be passed, or active measures to be pursued, the fundamental principle of free government would be reversed. It would be no longer the majority that would rule: the power would be transferred to the minority."

He goes on to say that creating this new power would allow "an interested minority" to take advantage of it "to screen themselves from equitable sacrifices to the general weal, or, in particular emergencies, to extort unreasonable indulgences."

It should also be noted that until 1970, a filibuster shut down the work of the Senate entirely, and thus could only be sustained in the most dire of circumstances. There was too much work to get done to be able to allow one particular bill to gum up the works. But thanks to Montana Sen. Mike Mansfield and West Virginia Senator Robert Byrd, a two-track system was put in place that allowed other business to be carrie don while the filibuster was taking place. This meant the obstructionists did not have to bear the political heat for their actions any longer.

Moreover, in Federalist No. 22, Alexander Hamilton said the super-majority requirement (which existed in the Article of Confederation) was damaging to the nation as a whole. "The necessity of unanimity in public bodies, or of something approaching towards it, has been founded upon a supposition that it would contribute to security. But its real operation is to embarrass the administration, to destroy the energy of the government, and to substitute the pleasure, caprice, or artifices of an insignificant, turbulent, or corrupt junto, to the regular deliberations and decisions of a respectable majority."

He summed it up that "The public business must, in some way or other, go forward."

Yet today, against the advice of both Madison and Hamilton, we have the super-majority in the Senate, and the public's business is stymied, stifled, and stagnated. Instead of the wisdom of Madison and Hamilton, we are following the folly of Chuck Schumer and Mitch McConnell. The country is at risk, and all our fine senators can do about it is defend their political turf.

There is one voice arguing against the filibuster — President Donald Trump. Using his much condemned Twitter account and political rallies, the president has made his case that the filibuster is preventing reforms the country desperately needs.

When the Senate failed to pass the Obamacare repeal in July, Trump tweeted, "The very outdated filibuster rule must go. Budget reconciliation is killing Rs in the Senate. Mitch M, go to 51 votes NOW and WIN. IT'S TIME!"

Then last week, Trump tweeted, "If Senate Republicans don't get rid of the Filibuster Rule and go to a 51% majority, few bills will be passed. 8 Dems control the Senate!"

Indeed.

The Senate, which was once know as the "greatest deliberative body in the world" is rapidly becoming the greatest obstructionist body in the world. Senate Republican millionaires and Senate Democrat millionaires seem content to sit on their sacred fortunes while their honor and their countrymen's lives are sacrificed to the whims of lobbyists, special interests and campaign donors.

Everyone understands that the Democrats, Never Trump Republicans and the rest of the swamp creatures want to "embarrass the administration," as Hamilton so wisely predicted more than 200 years ago, but if you want to know why Trump got elected in the first place, just look to Congress and its abysmal record for action.

In my research for this column, I found an unexpected ally in the fight to end the filibuster. Former Democratic Congressman Pat Williams, who served nine terms in the U.S. House of Representatives and actually got things done when he was in office, wrote a column in 2009 in which he lamented "the tyranny of the minority" that was caused by the filibuster.

Williams was writing about the ability of 40 senators to stop "health care reform" under President Obama, just the opposite of President Trump's concern about the failure of repeal, but the underlying issue is the same. As Williams put it, "A crucible of our brand of democracy is the will of the majority shall prevail. ... Filibusters have become a perversion of the

American promise of both majority rule and minority protection."

Don't be fooled by Sen. Foghorn Leghorn (er, I mean Sen. McConnell) blathering on about the time-honored traditions of the Senate. Harry Reid dumped the filibuster for lesser court appointments a few years ago, and McConnell ended the filibuster for Supreme Court nominees this year. Face it, senators don't do what's right; they do what gets them re-elected. As for time-honored traditions, the only time our kleptocratic senators honor tradition today is when it pays.

A TRAIL OF CONCESSIONS — AND TEARS

September 24, 2017

When did politics change? Or did it?

Those questions arise in the wake of former Montana Gov. Marc Racicot's address to Flathead Valley Community College last week in which he lamented "a drift" from the principles on which the nation was founded.

Racicot was giving the inaugural Mike Mansfield Lecture at the college, and he drew upon the late Montana senator's lifetime of leadership to make the case that "decency" and "compromise" are the missing elements in today's politics.

As reported in the Inter Lake, Racicot worried that, "The word 'compromise' ... has come to sound like a 'deal with the devil,' and today seemingly represents the sacrifice of the best to suit the worst."

Racicot quoted Mansfield, "I've always felt that the true strength of the Senate lay in the center. Not on the right and not on the left, but with those people who could see both sides. Differences can be abridged. Solutions can be found. Concessions can be made. It is much better to take an inch, than to take nothing at all." The problem with Racicot's argument is that the Senate described by Mike Mansfield doesn't exist any longer. Does anyone believe that the differences between right and left in 2017 can be abridged?

Does anyone believe that solutions can be found? Does anyone believe that concessions are ever made short of a political bribe?

I'm not inclined to think that the politicians in Mike Mansfield's era were better than the ones who serve us now, but I do think the world he lived in was better than the one we find ourselves in today. For one thing, America was a united country — except for a very small minority, we pledged allegiance to the flag of the United States of America instead of protesting against it. We celebrated our superior strength, courage and moral character rather than apologizing for it.

And, most importantly, we were confident that our children's lives and opportunities would be better than our own. That's no longer true for most of us, and rather than closing our eyes to the prospect of a dangerous cliff ahead, or running headlong toward it, many of us have said that the compromises and concessions that previous generations of politicians made on our behalf have led us into mortal peril.

An example on the domestic side of the agenda is health care. When I wrote a cautionary column about the dangers of nationalized health care in 2006, I was only half serious when I said, "old Karl Marx may have the last laugh." I was still optimistic that the innate canniness of the American public would serve us well when the carnival barker was trying to lure us into the tent to see the freak show. Who could possibly fall for the inverted logic of Marx's "From each according to their ability; to each according to their need"?

Well, Jimmy Kimmel, to start with. The millionaire comedian feels guilty because he has enough money to pay for his sick child, while other people go wanting. The problem is that he isn't using his guilt to shell out his own fortune to take care of others; he is asking you and me to do it. Obamacare premiums are going up exponentially for healthy people because they are paying for health care for sick people. The government is shelling out billions of dollars in health expenditures because it feels good to do so, but without acknowledgment of the fact that the national economy is a finite system and that we will bankrupt ourselves long before we eliminate the human pain and suffering that comes from human mortality.

So how did we get here? Compromise. Concessions.

The Republicans didn't support Obamacare initially, of course, but in state after state, they tied their fortunes to the flawed burning chariot called Medicaid expansion. And now they have turned health care into a right and an entitlement so that there is no going back. Though the system is fatally flawed, no one speaks of making concessions to reality and admitting that the Congress cannot play God and order people to be healthy.

On the foreign policy front, we have three issues where concessions and compromise have dug us into deep pits, any one of which could swallow our country whole. The fake hard lines on the Iranian and North Korean nuclear programs both have the potential to cost millions of lives. Concession has led to nuclear blackmail, not global security.

Meanwhile, illegal immigration and legal chain immigration are changing the very fabric of our nation so that the founding principles that Gov. Racicot celebrates today will be forgotten tomorrow. Even now, our Founding Fathers like George Washington, Thomas Jefferson, Ben Franklin are held in contempt by growing numbers of citizens, who don't realize that the good fortune we inherited in the form of a Constitution and Bill of Rights can easily slip away.

Racicot is concerned about preserving "decency," and while that is a noble goal, it pales beside the prospect of surrendering our lives, our liberty, or our ability to pursue our happiness in the false hope of "getting along." When you compromise with people who don't share your fundamental principles, you are either "making a deal with the devil," or you are the devil. Take your choice.

That's why there is a growing divide between the establishment wing of the Republican Party represented by former Gov. Racicot and the conservative wing of the party represented by Steve Bannon and, sometimes, Donald Trump.

If you believe the system we have thrived under for 230 years is being undermined by people who want to "fundamentally transform" the country into something new, you cannot in good conscience compromise. As Winston Churchill urged young Britons when confronted by an implacable foe in Nazism, "Never give in, never give in, never, never, never, never — in nothing, great or small, large or petty — never give in except to convictions of honor and good sense."

The alternative is surrender, and if we give up America, the world is lost.

TRUMP EXPOSES THE FAKE MATH OF OBAMACARE

October 15, 2017

When Congress runs into a problem, it has one solution: Throw money at it.

The Affordable Care Act had one big problem: It was unaffordable. So Congress did what it always does, and threw money at it — other people's money.

You see, everyone always knew that that the Affordable Care Act was a Ponzi scheme, but the Congress of 2010 figured it would be a decade or two before the scheme collapsed and the bills came due. That's because they counted on Democratic presidents playing along with the scheme — first Barack Obama and then, oh I don't know, maybe Hillary Clinton. Congress gave the president the authority to spend as much money as necessary to keep health insurance "affordable" for everyone being forced to buy it. Oh yes, and to make it possible for insurers to do the impossible and offer low-cost health insurance to people who were already sick.

This goes against the very concept of insurance — which is a gamble offered by someone with money to someone with the potential to need money. The insurer is betting that the insured will never need the insurance, and thus the insurer will win his gamble and make a tidy profit. In the case of health care, the insured is betting that they will get sick and recoup the cost of their premiums, and hopefully more, so that they will come out ahead instead of behind when catastrophe strikes.

But Obamacare threw that on its head. By ordering coverage of pre-existing conditions, the government was pretending that math doesn't exist. The only way to fill the gaping actuarial hole in the bottom of Obamacare was for the government to start shoveling money into it — big money — billions of dollars of money. It made everyone feel good except for the taxpayers who were subsidizing the Ponzi scheme, and then — when there wasn't enough money to fill the hole fast enough, it started to aggravate the intended beneficiaries of Obamacare, who were surprised to see their premiums go through the roof.

Oh what a tangled web we weave when at first we do deceive.

But what the Democratic Congress didn't count on in 2010 was that Donald Trump would be president in 2017. Because he is, and because he disagrees with the backwards math of Obamacare, President Trump announced on Thursday that he won't fund the subsidies being paid to insurers that are intended to make up for the artificially low premiums being charged to consumers.

That move by Trump is expected to save the government $10 billion in 2018. It will also leave millions of people in the lurch who have gotten used to the idea that they are entitled to low-cost insurance. Those millions may get mad, and they may hold Trump or the Republican Party responsible for their own financial hardship. That's a gamble that Trump is apparently willing to take in the service of truth.

The fake math of Obamacare has never made sense. Why should the government take money from taxpayers to subsidize other people's health care? Sure, it makes Democrats and liberal Republicans feel good, but sometimes we have to do what's right instead of what feels good.

Congress hasn't written a law that requires the government to help me to pay my life insurance premiums, or to mandate that I carry a minimum amount of insurance — let's say $1 million — even though it would be better for my family if I did.

Nor has the government told my insurance company that it would have to sell me that million-dollar policy at a ridiculously cheap rate — let's say $500 a month — even though I were suffering from a terminal illness and probably wouldn't be alive to make payments for another year.

But that's exactly what Congress has done with health care. The Democrats made up a Peter Pan plan that told everyone the big lie — you can have something for nothing — and then they authorized the president to clap his hands "if he believes."

We watched President Obama clapping his hands furiously for six years, and he convinced a lot of people that Obamacare was the real deal, but the magic has worn off. In Montana, for instance, more than half the individual policy owners in the state are going to see a 22 percent increase in premiums next year. That's just plain unacceptable.

President Trump knows a bad thing when he sees it, so he has stopped clapping, and is instead doing something useful — authorizing executive orders that expose the Affordable Care Act as the sham many of us warned about in the first place. Let the chips fall where they may.

WHAT WOULD G. WASHINGTON MAKE OF D.C. WASHINGTON? (SOME DARE CALL IT A SWAMP)

December 10, 2017

Once again it has become apparent that the partisan divisions within our nation have strained our patriotic foundation to the point of crumbling.

Turn on the TV news any day and you will see competing narratives that seem to have nothing in common. On CNN and MSNBC, the lead story every day is that President Trump or someone close to him did something wrong — horribly wrong — impeachably wrong. On FOX News though, the story is more likely to be that President Trump is the victim of a political conspiracy, and you will learn about a lot of exculpatory evidence that never seems to show up on CNN or MSNBC.

I watch all three news channels, plus Fox Business and C-SPAN, so I get a pretty well-rounded view of what the nation is being told by the opinion-makers. In addition, I read news from the New York Times, the Washington Post, the Wall Street Journal and Breitbart.com every day, in addition to the AP coverage in the Daily Inter Lake.

What I see is frankly terrifying. First of all, the news media no longer make any effort to be unbiased or neutral reporters of fact. You can't even talk about left-leaning media any more; it is now left LEADING. The entire national conversation is being directed by unelected, self-selected arbiters of right and wrong sitting in anchor chairs at "news" channels. Politicians now take their signals from TV talkers, and since they know where the real power lies, they don't dare stray from the party line as defined by those talk-show hosts.

This has been most obvious in the daily onslaught of stories about the Trump candidacy, the Trump transition and the Trump presidency. On one channel, you will hear that Trump colluded with Russians, obstructed justice, broke the law and will probably go to jail. On another channel you will hear that Hillary Clinton and her Democratic allies used the FBI and the corrupt Justice Department as political weapons to first try to disgrace Trump and then to destroy him with manufactured evidence.

Yet it is not only the political future of the country that is in the balance, but the economic future and ultimately the existential future as well.

How exactly can it be, for instance, that a matter of such import to the nation as the tax-reform plan can be decided entirely on a partisan basis? Is there no Democrat who sees the advantage of lowering taxes in order to stimulate the economy? Do Democrats not have any small businesses in the states they represent? Yet when the Senate voted on the tax reform plan recently, it was on a straight party-line vote except for one lone Republican who voted with the Democrats.

Moreover, because of the echo-chamber news outlets, a large majority of Americans reportedly oppose the tax cuts being offered to them because they are being told they are actually tax increases. Huh? How did a tax cut become an increase? That's easy. Because of what Mark Twain called "lies, damned lies and statistics." Most of the statistics being used to show a tax increase for middle-income Americans actually plug in numbers from 2027, the first year after the tax cuts are set to EXPIRE! That is just plain dishonest, but you can't expect the folks in Congress, let alone the folks watching the news on TV, to figure out the truth, can you?

The tax cuts are going to benefit most (not all) Americans, rich and poor, but more importantly, the lower corporate tax rates would stimulate growth in our economy like we have not seen for 30 years. That would result in money flooding back into the country, higher wages and more jobs, and it really doesn't have to be partisan at all. Democrat John Kennedy did the same thing five decades ago.

But this isn't about one vote or one tax plan or even one president. It is about the very nature of our country and our freedom.

George Washington warned, among many other cogent points of advice, in his 1796 "Farewell Address" that partisanship had the capacity to destroy the nation by blinding us to what had brought us together in the first place.

The first president assured us that "the unity of Government, which constitutes you one people" is a "main pillar in the edifice of your real independence, the support of your tranquility at home, your peace abroad; of your safety; of your prosperity; of that very Liberty, which you so highly prize."

In other words, it is our unity of purpose that underlies all our success, yet somehow, miraculously, just eight years into the American experiment, Washington had already foreseen that this "unity of Government" would be under attack for nefarious purpose.

"It is easy to foresee, that, from different causes and from different quarters, much pains will be taken, many artifices employed, to weaken in your minds the conviction of this truth;

as this is the point in your political fortress against which the batteries of internal and external enemies will be most constantly and actively (though often covertly and insidiously) directed, it is of infinite moment, that you should properly estimate the immense value of your national Union to your collective and individual happiness; that you should cherish a cordial, habitual, and immovable attachment to it; accustoming yourselves to think and speak of it as of the Palladium of your political safety and prosperity; watching for its preservation with jealous anxiety; discountenancing whatever may suggest even a suspicion, that it can in any event be abandoned; and indignantly frowning upon the first dawning of every attempt to alienate any portion of our country from the rest, or to enfeeble the sacred ties which now link together the various parts."

I doubt whether Sen. Chuck Schumer, D-New York, or Sen. Mitch McConnell, R-Kentucky, have given much if any thought to these words of George Washington, but surely they are living out the worst nightmare of our first commander in chief. The "immense value of our national Union" is apparent to me and millions of Americans, but sadly I am losing hope that it will withstand the current "attempt to alienate" the red states of Trump Country from the blue states of Clinton Country. God save us.

BABY ON BOARD: PROTECT OUT PRECIOUS U.S. CONSTITUTION

January 21, 2018

You know those signs on the back of cars that say "Baby on Board"? The idea is to reinforce the idea of precious cargo, so anyone tempted to act recklessly will think twice before putting an innocent in danger.

America needs a "Baby on Board" sign at its borders to remind everyone who enters our country that we have precious cargo here, too. Not just our wonderful citizens, whose lives are too often put at risk by disrespectful newcomers, but even more importantly the U.S. Constitution which has guaranteed us our way of life for 228 years. I suppose that seems too old for it to be called a baby, but in the scope of history, it's the blink of an eye, and without proper care and feeding, the Constitution could easily perish.

The question is how do we make sure that the baby is indeed taken care of?

Unfortunately, it is transparently obvious that millions of newcomers to our country come from traditions that have nothing in common with that Constitution. If we assume without evidence that these newcomers, legal or illegal, will value our Constitution, then we should not be surprised when a tragic collision occurs between our shared traditional values and the foreign ideas that prevail in foreign countries.

The obvious — and too often unspoken — truth is that in a democratic republic such as ours, the freedom we enjoy is transitory. It can be voted out of existence any time a majority of people decide to do so. Or as Ronald Reagan said 20 years before he became president:

"Freedom is never more than one generation away from extinction — we didn't pass it on to our children in the bloodstream. It must be fought for, protected, and handed on for them to-do the same, or one day we will spend our sunset years telling our children and our children's children, what it once was like in the United States when men were free."

Does that sound like hyperbole to you? Mere rhetoric? A cheap Republican trick? If it does, then you are part of the problem. The "baby on board" is our shared responsibility, and if you aren't worried about preserving, protecting and defending the Constitution, then you shouldn't be in the driver's seat.

Nor should you have the right to turn the keys over to anyone who walks by, but isn't that what we are doing with our open-door immigration policy? By inviting millions of people into our country who don't share our values, we are putting the Constitution at risk, and with it all the freedoms we hold dear.

Even worse, by turning a blind eye to lawbreakers and rewarding illegal aliens who are already here, we make a mockery of the rule of law. Cities such as Chicago and states such as California that protect illegal aliens by giving them "sanctuary" are not just foolish; they are blatantly violating the Constitution. The Supremacy Clause is unambiguous.

"This Constitution, and the Laws of the United States which shall be made in Pursuance thereof ... shall be the supreme Law of the Land; and the Judges in every State shall be bound thereby, any Thing in the Constitution or Laws of any State to the Contrary notwithstanding."

When California created a law that said the state would stand opposed to U.S. immigration policy, it was not just fighting Attorney General Sessions or President Trump, but the entire U.S. government and the U.S. Constitution that stands behind it. That's no different than what happened prior to the Civil War, when individual Southern states rejected federal supremacy, and faced the wrath of President Lincoln.

I'm not predicting a new civil war this time, but strap the baby in. It's gonna be a bumpy ride.

OUR COUNTRY'S TRAGIC SICKNESS CAN'T BE FIXED WITH A BAND-AID

February 18, 2018

It is natural in the wake of any tragedy to ask questions, to seek answers, to place blame, and particularly to ask how a similar tragedy can be avoided in the future.

Thus, following the school shooting in Broward County, Florida, many people have proposed solutions they think will save lives in the future.

For many people, the answer is to ban guns — if not all of them, then at least the AR-15 style rifles that increase the efficiency of killers. That, however, runs counter to the Second Amendment freedoms that have been guaranteed to us for more than two centuries, nor is there any reason to think mass murderers would not find a way around those restrictions in any case.

For others struggling with school violence and similar episodes, the answer is increased law enforcement — a heightened surveillance and awareness of those most dangerous among us (although that would have little effect if police cannot also lock up people whom they consider dangerous).

Some people point to mental illness, and treatment of people who present a danger to themselves and others, as the key to preventing future shooting tragedies. But, again, our courts have ruled that people who are mentally ill cannot be locked up indefinitely just because of a "potential" threat.

A few think that the answer is arming more people, so that good people will be able to defend themselves and others, but that could result in a Wild West lifestyle that few of us would embrace. It is also unlikely to deter those who are determined to kill the innocent. They will simply take more defensive measures.

Hopefully, we can agree on some things that will make a difference — like working to ensure that mentally ill people will not have easy legal access to guns ... like outlawing bump stocks such as the one used by the Las Vegas massacre killer to mimic an automatic weapon ... like empowering law enforcement to track threats online and to have access to social media accounts when such threats are made.

But none of these solutions — even the ones that are most drastic and restrictive — are going to get to the heart of what ails us. They are more like a cold remedy: They treat the symptoms but are not a cure. Dextromethorphan can suppress a cough, but it can't kill the virus that causes the cough.

By the same token, laws can suppress or diminish violence, but they can't cure the sickness that makes random violence such a virus in our modern society.

And since this is such a modern problem, I think it behooves us to consider what about our modern society is different from earlier societies where slaying innocent children was not so common.

For most of us the modern era of mass shootings began on Aug. 1, 1966, when former Marine sharpshooter Charles Whitman entered the Main Building tower at the University of

Texas and shot more than 40 people, killing 16, after killing his
mother and wife earlier in the day.

What seemed unusual to those of us alive then would now
seem almost commonplace. Columbine, Virginia Tech, Sandy
Hook, Sutherland Springs, along with many others, have taught
us that a sickness in our society can turn fatal at any time —
striking down the good and evil alike, the young and old, the
weak and strong.

But if we are going to do more than treat the symptoms, we
must have the courage to look at the patient and diagnose
honestly just what the sickness in our society is. That means
looking at America before 1963 — before the Kennedy
assassination, before the University of Texas tower shootings,
before Charles Manson — and asking what has changed since
then?

I'll venture my opinion, although it won't be popular among
a generation that believes its own publicity about how brilliant
it is. Rather, I would argue that we have lost our way and are no
longer tethered to what C.S. Lewis called the Tao, the natural
law that used to be nurtured in each of us by our schools, our
churches, our families and our government, until like Satan we
rebelled in order to prove just how smart we were.

Here's what we did in our all-too-finite wisdom:

— Ended school prayer and took the Bible out of schools:
When I started my education in 1960, public schools taught
students that we owed our lives and our sacred honor to the
Creator that is memorialized in the Declaration of
Independence. That was ended by the all-knowing Supreme
Court in 1962 and 1963, so in order to avoid offending atheists,
we offended God.

— Legalized abortion: Thanks to the Supreme Court again,
in the early 1970s, we as a nation declared that life has no value,
not even the most tender, most innocent life. Sixty million dead
babies later, we continue to pretend we are morally superior.

— Celebrated divorce and diluted marriage: The broken
family is the emblem of our sick society. Is it any wonder that
children raised without any moral compass have a hard time
finding true north?

— Legalized street drugs and put legal drugs on the street: At least two and probably three generations have been raised to numb their feelings with marijuana, cocaine, meth, oxycodone. If you play with fire, you are bound to get burned. Many of the most disturbed killers in the last decade have been dosed with dangerous "anti" psychotic drugs whose listed side effects include, delusions, violent fantasies and aggressive behavior.

— Promoted the trivialization of sex and violence in our culture through popular culture: Movies, TV shows and video games have normalized the pornography of both sex and death and have inured children to behavior that previously would have been condemned as decadent.

The common thread in all of these destructive changes is that they are defended as increasing our "freedom." Of course, that was the same excuse that Satan used to tempt Adam and Eve in the Garden of Eden and we all know how that turned out. They were sent out from the innocence of Paradise in order to take their chances in a world full of death and despair.

As Milton's Satan declares after realizing he is to be exiled from God due to his own arrogance, "Farewell happy fields/Where Joy for ever dwells: hail horrors, hail Infernal world."

No, we cannot restore the peaceful era of an earlier America just by banning certain guns or by increasing the police presence. No Band-Aid will set this nation right. As long as we consider ourselves superior to God and natural law, then we will reap the whirlwind.

About the Author

Frank Miele is a conservative columnist at RealClearPolitics.com. He is also the moderator of www.HeartlandDiaryUSA.com. Subscribe for free on the website to get all his posts in your inbox. The author worked as an award-winning community journalist for most of four decades, including 34 years at the Daily Inter Lake in Kalispell, Montana, where he was managing editor from 2000 to 2018. Miele's "Editor's 2 Cents" column was a regular feature in the newspaper from 2004 to 2018 and won him a broad following among conservatives across the nation. He lives with his wife and children in Kalispell.

Made in the USA
Monee, IL
01 August 2020